101 PROBLEMS AND SOLUTIONS IN HISTORICAL LINGUISTICS

101 PROBLEMS AND SOLUTIONS IN HISTORICAL LINGUISTICS

A WORKBOOK

Robert Blust

(With the editorial assistance of Hsiu-chuan Liao)

EDINBURGH
University Press

Edinburgh University Press is one of the leading university presses
in the UK. We publish academic books and journals in our selected
subject areas across the humanities and social sciences, combining
cutting-edge scholarship with high editorial and production values
to produce academic works of lasting importance. For more
information visit our website: edinburghuniversitypress.com

Edinburgh University Press Ltd
The Tun – Holyrood Road, 12(2f) Jackson's Entry, Edinburgh EH8 8PJ

Typeset in Baskerville MT Pro by Biblichor Ltd, Edinburgh,
and printed and bound in Great Britain

A CIP record for this book is available from the British Library

ISBN 978 1 4744 2920 7 (hardback)
ISBN 978 1 4744 2922 1 (webready PDF)
ISBN 978 1 4744 2921 4 (paperback)
ISBN 978 1 4744 2923 8 (epub)

CONTENTS

FOREWORD

I t is probably accurate to say that this book came about through a series of accidents. For many years the graduate programme in the Department of Linguistics at the University of Hawai'i had a Preliminary Examination that was intended to screen students moving on to the Ph.D. from students who would stop at the M.A. This was a four-part, four-day sit-down exam that included: (1) phonology, (2) syntax, (3) historical linguistics, and (4) a 'general' section designed to test creative thinking in often unpredictable ways. Each of the first three examinations was divided into an essay/short answer section that was given for three hours in the morning, and a problem-solving section that was given for another three hours in the afternoon. For about twenty years the writer was the principal architect of problems for the historical linguistics exam. When this method of screening was abandoned in 2009 the materials that had been developed over the years in each of these examinations were shelved, and in most cases forgotten.

Several years after the end of the Preliminary Examinations it occurred to me that the materials for the historical linguistics exam might be useful to graduate students in other linguistics departments, or to faculty who teach historical linguistics and are looking for good problems representing a range of issues. That was the beginning of the present work. I began with some thirty to forty problems in phonological reconstruction and subgrouping, mostly at an intermediate level of difficulty, and I decided that if this was to be a book it should be expanded by the inclusion of more problems representing beginning, intermediate and advanced levels, and a wider range of topics. The result is a workbook that now includes 101 problems in five separate categories: twelve on the establishment of genetic relationship among languages; twenty-four on sound change; thirty-five on phonological reconstruction; ten on internal reconstruction; and twenty on subgrouping.

At least one reviewer referred to the prepublication manuscript as a textbook, but this is a misconception that should be corrected at the outset. Textbooks are intended to lay out a comprehensive overview of a field of study, providing detailed discussion of method and theory, with data used mainly for illustrative purposes rather than hands-on exercises. A workbook has a different focus. Its purpose is to provide ample opportunity for students to analyse data relevant to the concepts they are learning, and to be shown the preferred solutions to the problems they work on, with discussion of various issues that may arise in the course of the analysis. Since there are a number of good textbooks in historical linguistics already, the present workbook should be viewed as a companion volume to be used in *conjunction* with a good textbook, not as a replacement for it. The misconception that this workbook is intended as a text probably arose, first, because a short discursive context is provided before each type of problem, and, second, because I provide a review of textbooks and workbooks at the end to highlight how little hands-on data are currently available for courses in historical linguistics.

I am extremely grateful to the many students over the years – too many to name, or in some cases even recall – who have caught errors or inconsistencies in some problems, and consequently helped to make them better. Lyle Campbell, who joined the University of Hawai'i Linguistics Department late in his career, was generous in sharing resources to fill out my list of past publications that contain problems in historical linguistics, and I thank him sincerely for this contribution. Finally, I have been very fortunate in engaging the services of Hsiu-chuan Liao, a former professional editor, and 2004 Ph.D. from the University of Hawai'i, who has used some of these problems in teaching historical linguistics at Tsing-hua University in Hsin-chu, Taiwan. Entirely on a volunteer basis she dedicated her considerable proofreading skills to catching a surprising number of errors and inconsistencies in an earlier version of the manuscript, and to recommending a number of improvements, most of which have been incorporated in the present version. I am very much indebted to her for the overall quality of the final product, and to her student Andrey Goderich Dmitrievskiy (aka Kuo Yu-hsien) who worked all of the subgrouping problems and drew my attention to several errors and inconsistencies.

It is my hope that both students and faculty with an interest in language history will find the contents of this workbook stimulating and challenging, and that by working through large quantities of carefully constructed data the overall conceptual framework of historical linguistics will be laid bare in a way that cannot easily be done without the integration of theory and data that is the hallmark of all mature sciences.

AUTHOR'S INTRODUCTION

There has long been a pressing need for a good workbook in historical linguistics. On first encountering the subject students often must try to assimilate the conceptual structure of the field in the near absence of a 'hands-on' approach to data. Where problems are given they typically suffer from four shortcomings. First, many lack clear-cut solutions. In the case of reconstruction problems, which are the most common type, this leaves the more enquiring individual wondering about possible undetected conditioning or additional proto-phonemes. Second, few texts which include problems provide solutions for the student to check, and where solutions are provided there is no discussion of the steps that should be followed to reach them, or why one solution is preferable to another. Third, even in the more complete workbooks we have (such as Cowan 1971), the focus is rarely on reconstructing whole forms, even though this is what the practicing historical linguist must do in working with real data. Finally, nearly all problems in published sources deal with sound change or phonological reconstruction, leaving a problem-solving approach to such focal topics as the establishment of genetic relationship or subgrouping untouched. The Appendix following the solutions is annotated to highlight these shortcomings in specific cases.

This workbook is intended to correct these deficiencies in the following ways. First, although natural language data are used in the twenty-four sound change problems and in all but one of the internal reconstruction problems, nearly all other problems use artificial data to ensure that an unambiguous solution is possible within the compass of a manageable set of material – usually no more than twenty-five examples from three or four languages. Second, solutions are provided for all problems in Part II. Third, in many cases the solutions are followed by a discussion of methodological or theroretical issues that arise in working on the problem, as well as an account of why the favoured solution has been chosen.

One feature of the sound change problems which departs from other workbooks is that the data are drawn from languages belonging to only one family. Although some historical linguists are concerned with general linguistic theory, most are specialists. The writer's area of special expertise is Austronesian comparative linguistics, and the material used for problems concerned with sound change draws heavily on Austronesian languages. While some readers may see this as a defect in that it potentially under-represents the diversity of processes of sound change in the world's languages, at least three factors favour the approach adopted here. First, few historical linguists control the comparative data in more than one language family. In workbooks which use data from languages that belong to multiple families the author is thus unable to provide 'insider' analyses, simply citing other sources for the correct solution, with little detail. Providing material from a single language family in which a considerable amount of fairly advanced comparative work has already been done thus has the advantage of affording an insider perspective on the data. Second, although it is a single language family with a time depth of perhaps 5,500 years, the Austronesian family is enormous both in number of languages and in geographical extent. Lewis, Simons and Fennig (2015) report over 1,260 Austronesian languages, or more than 18 per cent of the world total. These extend over 206 degrees of longitude, from Madagascar in the west to Easter Island (Rapanui) in the east, and over 70 degrees of latitude, from northern Taiwan to the south island of New Zealand (Aotearoa). Along with a rich dialect diversity in many languages, Austronesian thus offers a vast natural laboratory for the study of sound change. Moreover, in the millennia of migrations which produced this enormous geographical range Austronesian speakers came into contact with speakers of a variety of unrelated languages, including Mon-Khmer (Austroasiatic) languages in mainland Southeast Asia, Kra-Dai (Tai-Kadai) and Sinitic languages on Hainan island, Bantu languages in Madagascar (or on the Mozambique coast prior to reaching Madagascar), and 'Papuan' languages in New Guinea and other parts of western Melanesia. Contact-induced influences produced additional variety in the types of sound changes observed, with the result that Austronesian languages are not only numerous, but also typologically diverse, and representative of many patterns of historical change.

The overall organisation follows the steps that linguists normally take to solve historical problems: it must be established that two or more languages are genetically related before reconstruction can begin, a familiarity with the general direction of sound change helps to guide reconstruction, which must be done before innovations can be distinguished from retentions in subgrouping languages, and subgrouping is often the key to solving certain problems of culture history, most notably the establishment of centres of linguistic dispersal, or 'homelands' (linguistic approaches to culture-history, which arguably merit a book-length publication in themselves, and would generally attract a different readership than the one served here, are only touched on indirectly in this workbook).

The following conventions have been adopted either to facilitate the presentation of material, or to make artificial data appear more realistic:

- In most problems that contain artificial data languages are cited as 'Language A', 'Language B', etc. However, in a few cases names were invented in the original version of the problem (used for academic screening purposes), and have been retained. Similarly, most problems give forms with glosses, but in problems with five languages this was difficult to do without putting the glosses on a separate line than the forms, and in these few cases the glosses were simply omitted.
- Another issue that involves realism in using artificial data is the balance between sound change and lexical change. The historical record for Austronesian shows that some languages exhibit extensive sound change with relatively little lexical change, others show extensive lexical change with relatively little sound change, and still others show both. In some of the problems using artificial data in this workbook all forms given are cognate; in others some are cognate while others show lexical replacements. For languages with extremely different phonological histories it would be unusual for all words to be cognate, but some problems in the workbook have this form. This may make them less realistic than is desirable, but in the interest of building as much information as possible into the smallest set of data this departure from realism has been tolerated in a number of cases.
- Where natural language data are used, as in the problems devoted to sound change, the orthography follows phonemic conventions common to the region as a whole. Some common IPA symbols are therefore not used, so that for example the palatal nasal is represented by ñ rather than ɲ, *j* represents a voiced palatal affricate, not a palatal glide, etc. In the interest of consistency, similar orthographic conventions are also used in problems that contain artificial data. Where it is felt that the phonetic value of symbols needs to be given, it will be provided *in situ*.
- To avoid unnecessarily tedious bookkeeping the statement of recurrent sound correspondences is limited to phonemes that *differ* in the languages compared (thus /a/ : /a/ : /a/, or /t/ : /t/ : /t/ are not cited, but correspondences such as /h/ : /h/ : /s/ or /t/ : /d/ : /t/ are).

- Genetic relationship problems call for identification of cognate sets as defined by recurrent sound correspondences, but these may be in complementary distribution because of gaps in attestation. In genetic relationship problem 4, for example, the correspondence $h : s : s$ is attested in items 1, 4, 11, 12 and 17. However, only item 4 is represented by cognate forms in all three related languages. By contrast, items 1, 11, 12 and 17 all have non-cognate forms in one language. For 1, 11 and 17 the pattern is $h : s : (\ )$, and for 12 it is $h : (\ ) : s$. To distinguish full from partial exemplifications of correspondence sets the numbers marking sets that are not fully represented are underlined. By contrast, set 9 shows the correspondence $h : \varnothing : s$. However, this is in complementary distribution not because of gaps in the data, but because of distributional complementarity (this is the only example in the problem of word-final *s, hence $h : s : s\ (\underline{1}, 4, \underline{11}, \underline{12}, \underline{17})$, but $h : \varnothing : s\ (9)$.
- The statement of sound correspondences is treated differently in genetic relationship problems than in problems concerned with reconstruction. For the former, correspondences are listed atomistically (thus $a : o / \_\_Cu$ and $a : e / \_\_Ci$), while in listing reflexes of proto-phonemes it is expected that such examples will be seen as divergent realisations of a single change in which *a partly assimilates to the frontness and roundness of a following high vowel. The reason for this differing treatment is that the establishment of genetic relationship must, by its nature, be a conservative procedure that favours detailed, atomistic citation of sound correspondences, while the statement of reflexes for established proto-forms seeks to discern general processes that affected proto-languages in their evolutionary history.
- In the interest of brevity nearly all sound changes are stated in segmental terms, without feature specifications.
- All changes proposed in problems that contain artificial data are constrained by empirical data (see 'Phonological reconstruction, Background'). In the case of *C > $\varnothing$ / __# this might be questioned, since in many of the problems there are no intermediate steps. But this appears to be the case with a number of Austronesian languages, as discussed by Blevins (2004).
- The environment of a conditioned change uses whatever format permits the most compact representation, but may vary between representations of similar length, as with C > $\varnothing$/__# or -C > $\varnothing$. Where a natural class has been affected this usually is represented as a single change, as with *b/d/g > p/t/k/__#. Environments are usually

stated in terms of the phonemes of the proto-language, but may be stated in terms of the phonemes of the daughter language where this is more relevant to understanding conditioning.

- Ordering relations in the statement of reflexes are always stated in the format 'X before Y' (or 'Y before X'), never as 'X after Y' (or 'Y after X'). Changes generally are listed in the order they are found in matching reconstruction to reflex, and so may be at variance with chronological ordering. Exceptions to this practice are made under two sets of circumstances, first for parallel changes that are treated as one, as when *t > ?/__# is found before *p > ?/__# or *k > ?/__#, but the three are represented as *p,t,k > ?/__#, and second when ordering is crucial to understanding the nature and motivation of certain changes, as in sound change problem 18, where the transition from PMP (Proto-Malayo-Polynesian) *bahaR to Bario Kelabit əbhar 'loincloth' resulted from a sequence of changes that did not begin with schwa epenthesis.

- Proto-phonemes are preceded by an asterisk, but many reflexes involve multiple changes, and derived ancestral segments that are intermediate in a derivation are represented without an asterisk. In subgrouping problem 2, for example, *s was lost, but this is most plausibly represented as *s > h followed by loss of h. Since the highest-order proto-language lacks *h, the second step in this change is represented as h > Ø (not *h > Ø). In other words, although the phonemes of an interstage language are also proto-phonemes since they are ancestral to observed reflexes, it is useful to distinguish them in some way from the proto-phonemes being reconstructed or at the highest level of reconstruction, and this is done in the workbook by use of a bare segment.

- Although intermediate steps in sound change are posited where they seem clearly justified, to do this in all cases where a change is saltatory could lead to massive speculation, and is avoided.

- I use 'V' for any proto-vowel, and 'C' for any proto-consonant with no asterisk. Thus, the formula V > ə/__(C)V(C)V(C) indicates that all prepenultimate vowels merged as schwa, and C > Ø/__# indicates that all final consonants were lost.

- Although a clear segregation into discrete categories is difficult, all problems have been divided into 'Beginning', 'Intermediate' and 'Advanced' categories. In some cases there may be disagreements as to whether a problem has been assigned to the proper category, but this probably is unavoidable.

- The treatment of irregularities presents special challenges in a workbook. Real language data almost always show some departures from complete regularity, and the question arises how this should be handled. Since this book uses natural language data almost exclusively in sound change problems, the issue of how to treat irregularity is confined to these examples. One approach in problems that ask the student to list *all* changes that have occurred in a given language is to modify the wording to state 'list all *recurrent* changes that have occurred'. This would leave irregularities as unexplained residues on the side. A different approach would list irregularities after the solution, with at least some discussion of what causal factors might be involved.

  The advantage of the first of these approaches is that it requires a comprehensive investigation, and so is less likely to overlook the influence of one change on another. The advantage of the second approach is that it is more fully explanatory, and is thus likely to have greater appeal for the more advanced student. In this workbook a compromise has been reached. For those problems in which nothing much of explanatory value would be gained by listing exceptions after the solution the student is asked to restrict the statement of changes to those that are recurrent (found in at least two examples), ignoring those that are not. In cases where an explanation of irregularity arguably enhances overall understanding of the problem, on the other hand, irregularities are listed after the solution and some remarks are given on causal factors.

- Solutions are given in Part II. For genetic relationship problems each solution states which languages are related, which forms are cognate (listed by number), and the sound correspondences that justify these claims. For sound change problems changes are listed regularly by segmental transformation, with occasional reference to structural type (shift, split, split-merger, unconditioned merger, etc.). For reconstruction and subgrouping problems each solution consists of the reconstructed forms, a list of the changes in each daughter language, and any ordering requirements. Subgrouping problems further state degrees of genetic relationship based on evidence of exclusively shared innovations. For all types of problems discussions of the preferred solution are generally provided. These include comments on which features of the problem are especially difficult and how they should best be treated, and also in some cases the relevance of the problem to particular issues in historical or theoretical linguistics. A brief survey of published workbooks and textbooks in historical linguistics is given in the Appendix to document the shortage of materials of the kind provided here. A list of general references appears at the end of the volume.

PART I:
PROBLEMS

GENETIC RELATIONSHIP

(12 problems)

Background

When anyone compares two or more languages, no matter how great the differences, it is likely that s/he will notice some similarities. In this respect, languages are like cultures or natural species. The differences are often taken for granted, but the similarities tend to attract attention and to raise questions about cause. These prefatory remarks are intended to provide a concise overview of the causes of similarity between languages.

Linguistic similarity can be attributed to any of four causes: (1) chance, (2) universals, (3) borrowing, or (4) common origin. Causes 1 and 2 are types of convergence, chance similarity arising from limited possibilities (as with word order typology) or sheer randomness (as with isolated lexical resemblances). Similarity due to universals is also a type of convergence, but one that is motivated by properties of the vocal apparatus or cognitive traits shared by all humans, as in the classic case of *mama* and *papa* (Jakobson 1960). Similarity due to borrowing is constrained by certain practical considerations. The first of these is geographical contiguity: language communities must be in physical contact for borrowing between them to occur, so wide geographical separation between language communities decreases the likelihood that shared similarity is due to borrowing. The second is social relationships: language communities may neighbour one another, but if they do not interact because of socially- or culturally-determined attitudes borrowing is not likely to be very extensive, or to take place at all. The third is need. Although it is possible for loanwords to designate referents that were already named, borrowing usually does not affect the most basic elements of the lexicon, since these represent real-world referents that must be named in any language, and so already have native labels. This is the basis for the common distinction between 'basic' vocabulary and 'cultural' vocabulary: both can be borrowed, and sometimes in large amounts, but in all cases known to the writer basic vocabulary is more resistant to borrowing than non-basic vocabulary.

Once chance, universals and borrowing are eliminated as plausible explanations for similarity between languages the only explanation left is genetic relationship: languages are similar because they were once a single community that split into descendants that have diverged over time through the accumulation of innovations. Not all linguists (or geneticists!) are happy with the term 'genetic relationship', and some have suggested alternative expressions for linguistic relationship due to common descent, but the term is well established in the literature, and there seems to be no point in trying to replace it with a terminological neologism at this juncture in time.

The following examples of natural language data illustrate each of these four causes of similarity. The generally accepted genetic affiliations of the languages from which data are cited below are as follows:

Afroasiatic: Hebrew
Arawakan: Chané, Parauhano, Yavitero
Austroasiatic: Vietnamese
Austronesian: Central Cagayan Agta, Cebuano Bisayan, Erai, Gane,
    Hawaiian, Helong, Iban, Kanakanabu, Kayan, Lindrou, Malagasy,
    Malay, Roti, Saaroa, Samoan, Woleaian
Eskaleutian: Yupik
Indo-European: English, German, Irish, Sanskrit, Serbo-Croatian,
    Spanish
Japonic: Japanese
Niger-Kordofanian (Bantu): Swahili
Sino-Tibetan: Mandarin
Tai-Kadai/Kra-Dai: Thai
Utian: Sierra Miwok
Isolates: Ainu, Korean, Zuni

1. Examples of similarity due to chance

1.1.   German *nass*, Zuni *nas* 'wet' (Ruhlen 1987: 11)
1.2.   Sanskrit *dva*, Malay *dua* 'two'
1.3.   English *we*, Parauhano *we*

1.4. Yavitero *axi*, Iban *ari* 'day'

1.5. Yavitero *ani* 'wasp', Erai *ani* 'honeybee'

1.6. Chané *baho*, Helong *baha* 'mouth'

1.7. Swahili *kaka* 'elder brother', Malay *kaka* 'elder sibling'

1.8. Swahili, Lindrou *babu* 'grandfather', Central Cagayan Agta *bábo* 'grandparent', Serbo-Croatian *babu* 'grandmother (acc. sg.)'

1.9. Swahili *bua* 'stalk, stem of larger grasses', Kayan *bua* 'fruit'

1.10. Yupik *tage* 'go up from a body of water', Woleaian *–tage* 'directional suffix: upward'

1.11. Yupik *manik* 'bird's egg', Gane *manik* 'bird'

1.12. Yupik *maani*, Saaroa *naani* 'here'

1.13. Yupik *nani*, Kanakanabu *nanu* 'where?'

1.14. Yupik *tamu* 'chew once', Roti *tamu* 'smack lips while eating'

1.15. Yupik *uya*, Samoan *ua* 'neck'

1.16. Ainu *abe, api*, Malay *api* 'fire'

1.17. Ainu *nunnu* 'suck the breast', Malagasy *nunu* 'breast'

1.18. Ainu *wakka*, English *water*

The great majority of lexical similarities of the type shown here are due to chance convergence. In some cases further comparative data within a language family reveal this even more clearly. For example, the rather striking similarity between Sanskrit *dva*, Malay *dua* 'two' – a comparison which figured prominently in the misguided attempt by the well-known Indo-Europeanist Franz Bopp (1841) to connect Indo-European and Austronesian – loses its initial impact when we see that Malay *dua* reflects Proto-Austronesian *duSa 'two'. Chance resemblances can be identified by their isolated character – unlike genuine cognates they are not embedded in a network of recurrent sound correspondences, but stand essentially alone. In a few cases isolated lexical similarities of this type show up across a broad band of languages, as with Swahili *kaka* 'elder brother', Malay *kaka* 'elder sibling', and similar forms in a number of other genetically and geographically diverse languages (Ruhlen 1994; Bancel and Matthey de l'Etang 2002). Similarly, Swahili, Lindrou *babu* 'grandfather', Agta *bábo* 'grandparent', Serbo-Croatian *babu* 'grandmother' show a striking agreement across three clearly distinct language families (Niger-Congo, Austronesian, Indo-European), yet even the forms in the two Austronesian languages cited here – Lindrou from Manus island in western Melanesia, and Agta from the northern Philippines – appear to be products of historically independent changes, and the -*u* in Slavic forms is an accusative singular ending, not part of the base. The explanation for such comparisons remains to be clarified, but is far more likely to involve still poorly understood types of motivated convergence than common origin or chance.

2. Examples of similarity due to language universals

2.1. Lexical similarities

1) 'mama' and 'papa' (M = mother, F = father, GM/GF = grand-mother/father)

Spanish	*mamá*	'M'	*papá*	'F'
Mandarin	*mama*	'M'	*baba*	'F'
Swahili	*mama*	'M'	*baba*	'F'
Sierra Miwok	*ʔamá.-*	'GM'	*pá.pa-*	'GF'
Samoan	*mama*	'M'	*papa*	'F' (child language)

2.2. Universals of metaphor/semantic universals

1) 'eye of the day' = sun:

   a) Malay *mata hari* (eye day) 'sun'
   b) Irish *suil an la-e* (eye the day-GEN) 'sunrise'
   c) English *daisy* (Middle English *dægesēage* = 'day's eye')

2) 'fish eye', 'chicken eye', etc. = 'callus'

   a) German *Hühnerauge* (chicken eye) 'callus, corn on toe'
   b) Mandarin *jīyǎn* (chicken eye) 'callus'
   c) Malay *mata ikan* (eye fish) 'callus'
   d) Thai *taapla* (eye fish) 'callus'
   e) Korean *thi-nwun* (eye foot) 'callus'

3) 'eye of net' = knot of mesh/hole of mesh

   a) Japanese *ami no me* (net GEN eye) 'mesh of a net (hole)'
   b) Vietnamese *mat luoi* (eye net) 'mesh of a net (knot)'
   c) Thai *taakhàay* (eye net) 'mesh of a net (knot)'
   d) Malay *mata jala* (eye net) 'mesh of a net (knot)'
   e) Hebrew *ayin he refɛt* (eye GEN net) 'mesh of a net (hole?)'

2.3. Word order typology

1) Related languages may have *different* orders of major sentence constituents. Compare the following Indo-European languages:

   a) VSO : Irish
   b) SVO : English, French
   c) SOV : Hindi
   d) SVO (main clauses), SOV (subordinate clauses) : German, Dutch

2) Unrelated languages may have the *same* order of major sentence constituents:

   a) VSO/VOS : Arabic (Afroasiatic/Semitic), Turkana (Nilo-Saharan), Tagalog (Austronesian)
   b) SVO: English (Indo-European/Germanic), Mandarin (Sino-Tibetan), Malay (Austronesian)
   c) SOV: Japanese (Japonic), Tamil (Dravidian), Fore (Trans-New Guinea), Motu (Austronesian)

2.4. Canonical shape. Languages with a preferred canonical shape CVCV (no final consonants) result from natural tendencies to favour open syllables, and this feature of phonological structure provides no reliable information about genetic relationship.

Cross-linguistic similarities due to language universals are products of motivated convergence. Whereas chance convergence produces random similarity as a result of limited possibilities, or as a by-product of the enormous number of lexical items available for comparison in the world's languages, motivated convergence produces similarity due to articulatory or cognitive predispositions that are shared by all humans. For this reason, similarity due to chance convergence typically is confined to single pairs of languages or to sets of closely related languages, while similarity due to motivated convergence is distributed across a wide range of genetically diverse languages. The classic example of *mama* and *papa* is a case in point. For the first few months of their lives human infants have little control over tongue movement, but must be able to control lip movement in order to suckle. As a result the syllables [ma], [pa], [ba] (with varying frontness of the vowel) are produced during the babbling stage before an association of sound and meaning has begun to develop. Because these syllables tend to be repeated, the babbling sequences [mamamama], [papapapa] and [bababa] are commonly heard. Many of the world's languages favour a disyllabic word shape, and so the parents of newborns react in a very similar way wherever they are, assigning the meanings 'mother' and 'father' to words of the form *mama, papa* or *baba* in the belief that their infant child is signalling a recognition of them through vocalisations that are meaningless to the child at this stage in its development.

While the *mama/papa* phenomenon is due to limitations on infant articulation combined with universally similar parental responses, the globally distributed use of the morpheme meaning 'eye' to signal the central, focal or most important part of something evidently reflects a cognitive universal (Deonna 1965). Studies in developmental psychology have shown that infants focus on the eyes more than any other part of the face, and the first features that children typically include in drawing faces are the eyes (Gibson 1969). The eyes thus appear to have a focal meaning in the unfolding human mind. Although other body parts are commonly used cross-linguistically in metaphors (head of a river, foot of a mountain, etc.), only the morpheme for 'eye' seems to have acquired the more abstract sense of central, focal or most important part of something. As a result, an 'eye of water' (= 'spring' in a number of widely distributed and genetically diverse languages) may by chance resemble an eye in shape, but the same can hardly be argued for the mesh of a net, the centre of a storm, or in some languages the blade of a knife, as in Malay *mata pisau* = eye + knife, or the leader of a group in the Papuan language Dedua, where *yiʔ ki-wa* = man eye-poss.

Word order typology presents a mixed bag. While the order of major sentence constituents (subject, verb, object) clearly is subject to massive convergence due to limited possibilities, as first noted by Greenberg (1966) and subsequently by others, features of syntactic structure often come in typological 'packages'. To cite one of many possible examples, SOV languages tend strongly to have postpositions rather than prepositions, modifier-head order, and preposed rather than postposed relative clauses. These correlations are statistically significant, and therefore must be motivated by general principles of information packaging, some of which remain to be fully worked out.

Canonical shape is also subject to universal constraints. One of these is the tendency for open syllables to be preferred to closed syllables. Historically this tendency is realised through the weakening and eventual loss of word-final consonants in many languages. Although this tendency affects both vowels and consonants, the results of final consonant loss have more often led to misguided proposals of genetic relationship, inspired by the canonical similarity of languages that permit few or no final consonants.

3. Examples of similarity due to borrowing

3.1. Japanese *pan*, Spanish *pan*, Portuguese *pão* 'bread'
3.2. English *tea*, Dutch thee, Malay *téh*, Minnan Chinese *te*
3.3. Portuguese *manteiga*, Malay *mentéga* 'butter'
3.4. English *canoe*, Carib *kanoa*
3.5. Cebuano Bisayan *kapáyas*, Spanish *papaya* (ultimately from a South American Indian source)

Probably all languages have some borrowed vocabulary, although the amount and type of borrowing varies dramatically from one language to the next. English has so many French loanwords (many dating from the time of the Norman Conquest, which began in 1066 and remained in force for some 250 years) that some writers have spoken of a 'Romance stratum' in the language. But English has also borrowed liberally from many other languages. By contrast, Mandarin Chinese contains relatively few loans, despite the fact that two of China's major dynasties were under the control of non-Chinese speakers (Mongolian in the case of Yuan, from 1279 to 1368, and Manchu in the case of Qing, from 1644 to 1911).

In general, loanwords are more common with introduced items that were not a part of the traditional culture (plants, animals, manufactured goods). For this reason most loanwords are nouns. However, there are sometimes quite striking exceptions to this generalisation owing to unusual social circumstances (Thomason and Kaufman 1988). The examples given here illustrate the general case. Bread was commonplace in Europe but unknown in Japan (or East Asia generally) at the time of initial European contact. Tea was first domesticated in southern China, and the word for it in nearly all languages today is a borrowing of either the southern Chinese form with *t-*, or a northern Chinese form with a palatal initial. Butter was introduced to the Malay world by the first Portuguese explorers in the sixteenth century, and the word was borrowed with the product. Although the English arrived in the Caribbean aboard ships, they had no watercraft similar to canoes, and so the Carib word *kanoa* was borrowed in an anglicised form for this type of vessel. Finally, the papaya was one of several tropical or subtropical New World cultigens that were introduced to insular Southeast Asia by the Spanish or Portuguese. For reasons that remain unclear Spanish nouns in both Mexican Indian and Philippine languages were often borrowed in their plural forms, and loanwords are commonly subject to mishearing and rephonemicisation. As a result the word for 'papaya' in Philippine languages, although borrowed from Spanish within the past 450 years, often differs in its initial (and sometimes final) consonant: Bontok *papáya*, Pangasinan *apáyas*, Bikol *tapáyas*, Hanunóo *apáya*, Cebuano Bisayan *kapáyas*, Subanon *kopaya*, Tiruray *kafaya?*.

Appeals to borrowing as a cause of similarity are most convincing when (1) the languages in a proposed borrowing relationship are geographically near enough to one another for contact to have plausibly occurred, (2) the forms in question represent referents that are likely to be borrowed, and (3) the proposed donor language has greater prestige than the recipient language. Exceptions to principle (1) are naturally made in those situations where European colonial expansion was of global scope.

4. Examples of similarity due to common origin/genetic relationship (= common origin + divergence over time)

Malay	Hawaiian	English
mata	maka	eye
kutu	?uku	louse
ikan	i?a	fish
laŋit	lani	sky
taŋis	kani	weep, cry
akar	a?a	root
aŋin	ani	wind (Hawaiian: 'blow softly, of wind')

The points to note with this example of just seven words are, first, that there is striking similarity between lexical items of very basic meaning; second, that the languages in question are separated by a distance of over 5,000 miles; and, third, that in words that are similar but show a phonemic difference this difference is recurrent. Malay *mata* and Hawaiian *maka* are the common words for 'eye' in these languages. Taken alone this could be a chance resemblance (compare Modern Greek *mati* 'eye'). The way that chance is eliminated as a plausible explanation for the similarity of Malay *mata* and Hawaiian *maka* is by showing that Malay *t* : Hawaiian *k* is a sound correspondence; that is, a recurrent pattern of resemblance between these languages.

In 'louse' we see a second example of *t* : *k*, if the correspondence of Malay *k* to Hawaiian glottal stop, written ' in the standard orthography (hence *'uku*) can also be shown to be recurrent. In the third example we see a second example of *k* : *?*, if the correspondence of Malay final consonants to zero in Hawaiian can be shown to be recurrent. One of the most basic initial observations about Hawaiian (or other Polynesian languages) is that words must end with a vowel, and so original final consonants evidently were lost. This inference is supported by the word for 'sky', if we can find another example of the correspondence of Malay *ŋ* to Hawaiian *n*. This is provided by the verb 'to weep, cry', which also yields further examples of *t* : *k* and -C : Ø. When we consider all seven words it is apparent that *t* : *k* is found in three examples (eye, louse, weep/cry), *k* : *ʔ* in another three (louse, fish, root), -C : Ø in the last five, and *ŋ* : *n* in the words for 'sky', 'weep/cry' and 'wind'. Experimentation with any two languages chosen at random shows that such recurrent similarity with complete accountability for all segments is impossible to demonstrate unless the languages are assigned to the same family, although in some cases the demonstration of valid genetic relationships may require much more data than are found in this example, and much more extensive discussion of sound change.

Although 'recurrence' may be defined as minimally consisting of two examples, it is advisable to try to find at least three examples of each sound correspondence when proposing a genetic relationship between languages. Other considerations that are important in distinguishing similarity due to common origin from similarity due to chance are the length of the forms compared (e.g. similarity between forms of the shape CVCVC or CVCVCVC is much less likely to be a result of convergence than similarity between forms of the shape CV or just V), and the number of languages, or, more exactly, independent witnesses that exhibit similar forms. For further details and discussion the reader is referred to Greenberg (1957), Campbell (2003) and Campbell and Poser (2008).

Once chance, universals and borrowing have been rejected as likely explanations for linguistic similarity the only alternative left is genetic relationship, or common origin. Genetic relationship is thus the default hypothesis that results from first eliminating other possible explanations of similarity. All things in nature change, and although linguistic change is far more rapid than, for example, geological processes of mountain formation or erosion, it is ordinarily too slow to enter the consciousness of speakers. An awareness of language change is possible only under two types of circumstances. The first is when written records from a much earlier period are available, as with the English of Shakespeare, Chaucer or Beowulf, each of which diverges progressively further from any modern dialect. The second is when a language community has split into two or more descendants, each of which continue to change in somewhat different ways. By comparing the speech of these communities it will then become apparent that they have diverged from a common ancestor, first through the rise of dialect differences, and in time the appearance of distinct, but systematically similar languages. Although some work in historical linguistics can be done by comparing earlier written documents with a contemporary language that is descended from the language of these texts (or a related dialect), most work in historical linguistics is based on use of the comparative method, a set of procedures for systematically determining how attested languages have changed by reconstructing key features of their prehistoric ancestor. Both linguistic typology and historical linguistics thus use comparative data, but the typologist is interested in those commonalities that are best explained by appeal to language universals or diffusion, while the historical linguist is interested in those commonalities that are best explained by appeal to common origin in a single ancestral speech community. Each of the foregoing concepts will be illustrated through a hands-on approach in the problems that follow.

In addition, it is worth emphasising that although genetic relationship between languages can often confidently be established by the comparative method, it is impossible to show that languages are *not* related, since the passage of time will eventually erode all traces of common origin. Most historical linguists somewhat impressionistically accept a span of 6,000 to 7,000 years as the maximum period during which evidence is likely to survive in sufficient quantity to enable shared retentions to be safely distinguished from shared similarity due to chance. Beyond this, all that can be said with certainty is that sufficient evidence has not yet been presented to demonstrate relationship. This naturally leaves open the possibility that some currently unrecognised genetic relationships may be demonstrated in the future. A few historical linguists believe that genetic relationship between languages can be demonstrated at much greater time depths, usually on the basis of retained grammatical features (see Nichols (1992) for a particularly detailed exposition of this position). However, the demonstration of genetic relationship among languages depends on the prior elimination of chance, universals and borrowing as plausible explanations of similarity, no matter how distant the proposed relationship.

Finally, it is worth noting that the common dread of those who construct linguistic problem sets is that some typographical errors or other infelicities may have gone unnoticed despite repeated checking. If that is the case in this workbook I hope the reader will be indulgent, and kindly draw my attention to them.

The following twelve problems are constructed to focus on just one thing, namely the detection of similarities that cannot plausibly be attributed to chance, borrowing or language universals; there is thus no need to propose reconstructions, although the reader is free to do this if it proves helpful (solutions appear in Part II). Although problems are given at beginning and intermediate levels, many of those which appear here are far more difficult than is typical of past workbooks, offering challenges even to experienced historical linguists.

General directions

1. All examples are numbered, and in listing proposed cognates it will be most economical to cite the numbers only.
2. If most words in a given problem are cognate it will be easiest to say 'All but x, y'.
3. To further save labour, restrict your list of sound correspondences to those in which the phonemes *differ* across languages (hence there is no need to cite *a* : *a*, *m* : *m* and the like); it will be assumed that identity need not be explained.

A note on orthography

Some readers have found the use of the symbols *y* and *j* in this workbook confusing. In phonetic transcriptions there has been no occasion to use *y*, while [j] has its normal IPA value of representing a voiced palatal glide. However, in *phonemic* transcriptions /y/ represents the voiced palatal glide, and /j/ is used for a voiced palatal affricate. This is true in all data sets where these segments play a role, and it reflects the practice in the working orthographies of many of the world's languages, where using often cumbersome phonetic symbols is seen as impractical.

LEVEL 1: BEGINNING

GENETIC RELATIONSHIP PROBLEM 1

No.	Lg. A	Lg. B	Lg. C	Lg. D	
01.	sipan	salan	dila	hamu	earth
02.	puray	ikam	fule	savik	water
03.	birut	bilid	birut	taman	grass
04.	usim	pilas	utim	ligat	wood
05.	tajin	sema	tadiŋ	okas	fire
06.	kusir	sotak	hutir	kunil	smoke
07.	itay	unat	ite	tial	cloud
08.	gayar	taram	geal	aras	rain
09.	siraw	akar	hilo	tisar	sky
10.	rukap	tuŋi	luhaf	ilu	sun
11.	nawa	loak	ŋoa	mimil	star
12.	ranus	kua	nulam	sapa	moon
13.	masu	tarip	mahu	pahil	bird
14.	jinap	dulup	diŋaf	balan	egg
15.	narik	osa	narih	saru	feather
16.	sujaw	telak	hudo	huli	wing

INSTRUCTIONS/QUESTIONS:

1. Which of these languages are genetically related?
2. Which words are cognate?
3. List the sound correspondences supporting your answers to questions 1 and 2.

GENETIC RELATIONSHIP PROBLEM 2

No.	Lg. A	Lg. B	Lg. C	
01.	koño	ilo	tok	one
02.	iluh	hilusu	ral	two
03.	pac	pake	mun	three
04.	timol	lama	ŋkel	four
05.	tar	talu	lak	five
06.	iap	polo	ntim	house
07.	hul	fulu	sep	roof
08.	or	odu	guŋ	floor
09.	ciñut	kinutu	ot	wind
10.	cirih	kelese	dur	cloud
11.	hacim	sakimi	mpak	sun
12.	ivak	ebaka	ŋol	rain
13.	mari	madihi	ik	star
14.	toŋ	toŋo	fas	moon
15.	or	holu	lum	day
16.	cariŋ	sadiŋi	vug	night
17.	zivan	zebana	mban	water
18.	hir	sile	ar	river
19.	ivol	ivolo	daŋ	stone
20.	darug	lugana	un	tree
21.	oru	oduhu	vak	branch
22.	sugan	damu	tum	leaf
23.	torih	todisi	pan	fruit
24.	wacil	wakele	mbul	dog
25.	ayan	ayana	lob	pig
26.	hajar	fadala	os	chicken
27.	unic	uneke	tir	hand
28.	iviŋ	ebiŋi	ndap	skin
29.	oar	ohala	das	vein
30.	cirah	kedasa	lub	blood
31.	acir	asili	buk	heart
32.	riza	lezaha	mpoŋ	bone
33.	ucin	ukene	pas	head
34.	rirah	ledafa	bir	ear
35.	juvin	dubene	ŋkut	eye
36.	ruh	lusu	sum	mouth

37.	kara	kadaha	tap	tooth
38.	hicih	fekese	ndul	tongue
39.	ñacil	nakili	ŋgon	chin
40.	caw	sawe	sur	shoulder

Note: c is a voiceless palatal affricate, j a voiced palatal affricate and ñ a palatal nasal.

INSTRUCTIONS/QUESTIONS:

1. Which of the above languages are genetically related?
2. Which words are cognate?
3. List the sound correspondences that justify your answers to questions 1 and 2.

LEVEL 2: INTERMEDIATE

GENETIC RELATIONSHIP PROBLEM 3

1. Lgs. A, B, and C have the following phoneme inventories:

Lg. A (15C, 3V)				**Lg. B (11C, 5V)**				**Lg. C (11C, 5V)**			
<u>consonants</u>				<u>consonants</u>				<u>consonants</u>			
p	t	k	ʔ		t	k	ʔ		t	k	ʔ
b	d	g		m	n			m	n		
m	n	ŋ		f	s			f	s		
	s			v	z		h	v	z		h
	l				r				r		
	r										
w	y										

<u>vowels</u>			<u>vowels</u>			<u>vowels</u>		
i		u	i		u	i		u
			e		o	e		o
	a			a			a	

1. Compare the following vocabulary:

No.	Lg. A	Lg. B	Lg. C	
01.	pasut	fotu	rem	one
02.	ʔabiga	evik	nuh	two
03.	ʔumbari	tes	ozo	three
04.	dalua	zoru	ifu	four
05.	kandu	hor	mah	five
06.	masala	son	unav	six
07.	gayaŋ	kean	reo	seven
08.	dapiʔ	zef	rok	eight
09.	tiŋkam	iham	fus	nine

10.	undawa	uro	hai	ten
11.	naʔir	neir	rehu	earth
12.	sukup	tuhuf	mevi	water
13.	duʔani	ruhak	nem	fire
14.	kiduna	hizun	rori	sun
15.	rudat	ruza	unas	moon
16.	bugaʔ	vuk	orok	star
17.	anduɲu	orun	tohe	storm
18.	nakit	nehi	hazu	rain
19.	alapa	araf	utuf	wind
20.	ŋabila	nevir	azo	sky
21.	kisan	hitan	hito	cloud

INSTRUCTIONS/QUESTIONS:

1. Which, if any, of these languages are genetically related?
2. Which words are cognate?
3. List the sound correspondences that justify your answers to questions 1 and 2.

GENETIC RELATIONSHIP PROBLEM 4

Background. Three of the following languages are genetically related. The fourth shows similarities to the others due to borrowing.

No.	Lg. A	Lg. B	Lg. C	Lg. D	
01.	hafuŋ	sapuŋ	noku	tilak	water
02.	tapin	tabir	tapin	tevil	sorghum
03.	alur	arur	ikup	olug	sand
04.	hahuŋ	hasuŋ	aun	kosuŋ	hoe
05.	ŋarak	nara?	kalan	tami	grass
06.	suna	rugaŋ	laku	lugam	earth
07.	ufaŋ	upaŋ	uta	upaŋ	stone
08.	tiŋan	tinar	sipi	nilak	sky
09.	upuh	ubu	dunu	uvus	cloud
10.	paŋun	banur	panun	voŋul	pot
11.	lihiŋ	risiŋ	lanik	tola	knife
12.	ahif	luna?	kiban	esip	arrow
13.	magan	magar	suku	pikat	spear
14.	ranur	danur	lanul	donug	drum
15.	laham	rahaŋ	puli	lakam	eye
16.	lutuŋ	rutuŋ	keda	lutuŋ	nose
17.	haŋuk	sanu?	apo	amuk	ear
18.	uhan	uhar	ipot	ukal	hair
19.	puhut	maku	tilan	vukut	hand/arm
20.	rara	rada	mulo	gada	shoulder

INSTRUCTIONS/QUESTIONS:

1. Which language cannot be shown to be related to the others?
2. List the recurrent sound correspondences that justify your answer to question 1.
3. Which words are loans?
4. What is the source language for the loanwords?
5. In general, what type of word has been borrowed?

GENETIC RELATIONSHIP PROBLEM 5

No.	Lg. A	Lg. B	Lg. C	Lg. D	
01.	kanɔk	timu	hoya	klarnɔʔ	grass
02.	dubus	bunik	raliŋa	ladraŋ	mountain
03.	matam	sabuy	akino	matraŋ	house
04.	pɛta	rigo	tambino	plɛktə	floor
05.	selu	sapaku	kurilo	hrelə	rain
06.	nocɛr	ile	masawa	rindaʔ	wind
07.	abem	hačin	ulona	ableŋ	cloud
08.	gatup	nola	sampoyo	gahtuʔ	snow
09.	tarita	uŋini	tulapa	hoklaŋ	ice
10.	sukIt	tipuŋ	baletu	hulkIʔ	fire
11.	ikun	čuno	arere	ikluŋ	stone
12.	tatu	hoto	lanuya	todrit	water
13.	ranɛp	lusan	puloku	radnɛʔ	bird
14.	ubaki	sulet	dari	ubrakə	snake
15.	ɔpiŋ	namak	umato	ɔpriŋ	dog
16.	akit	tumap	royi	arkiʔ	fish

INSTRUCTIONS/QUESTIONS:

1. Which of these languages are genetically related?
2. Which forms are cognate?
3. List all recurrent sound correspondences that support your analysis.

GENETIC RELATIONSHIP PROBLEM 6

Background information. Lgs. A and C are geographically contiguous, whereas Lg. B is geographically separated from them. A is a language of local importance, while C is not.

No.	Lg. A	Lg. B	Lg. C	
01.	dah	ole	ramnu	one
02.	landap	rara	korli	two
03.	reŋ	nera	tiɲan	three
04.	tarp	tappu	tarpu	four
05.	mant	maro	manti	five
06.	ugut	marole	ugut	six
07.	laŋk	marorara	laŋku	seven
08.	halpiŋ	maronera	alpiŋ	eight
09.	tamb	marotappu	tambu	nine
10.	kalg	raramaro	kalgu	ten
11.	hamp	kasavu	ragay	head
12.	kornut	karulla	tanom	hair
13.	kanur	kaʔalu	pave	blood
14.	lamp	karavi	lugnat	bone
15.	duman	kazali	rital	skin
16.	haŋo	sonoa	morak	earth
17.	luh	rusu	gulan	stone
18.	ant	hara	darup	water
19.	kamb	ʔavu	sugi	grass
20.	rand	luzo	randi	sweet potato
21.	hiloŋ	sirona	dili	feather
22.	ŋundul	nuru	larnu	bird
23.	laŋk	duri	laŋku	horse
24.	naŋk	laxi	salon	fish
25.	koh	ʔosu	nuliŋ	cockroach
26.	iŋkoh	hixo	rutik	ant
27.	hurp	suppusuppu	hipihi	butterfly
28.	dorum	humu	roroŋ	bee
29.	ambak	ava	ruɲi	house
30.	kompal	ʔova	tanik	roof
31.	hunil	suli	raki	floor
32.	utah	lona	suman	door

33.	ambaŋ	ahava	tamaŋ	eat
34.	aŋul	aroni	ilom	drink
35.	lontak	arora	sagut	chew
36.	hurt	asuttu	takun	sleep
37.	liŋkiŋ	arixi	daviŋ	walk
38.	taluŋ	litaruna	nusi	black
39.	arkil	lihakki	galis	white
40.	hundan	lisura	kumak	red
41.	rampi	liravia	sukot	green
42.	morum	linila	tavil	yellow

INSTRUCTIONS/QUESTIONS:

1. Which of the above languages are genetically related?
2. Which words are cognate? (List numbers only.)
3. In the order in which they are encountered, list the sound correspondences that justify your answers to questions 1 and 2, along with the numbers of all supporting examples.
4. What is the best explanation for the similarities shared by Lgs. A and C?

LEVEL 3: ADVANCED

GENETIC RELATIONSHIP PROBLEM 7

No.	Lg. A	Lg. B	Lg. C	
01.	bugis	arat	laya	head
02.	falak	rani	dɛ	hair
03.	ali	nene	mesi	ear
04.	sumu	əmbar	əba	nose
05.	orat	moray	uki	eye
06.	markal	tinduk	tidu	cheek
07.	ani	ia	ɛ	arm
08.	duma	sita	kəba	shoulder
09.	silak	sau	salu	house
10.	nukur	manu	mɔ	roof
11.	alira	uasa	ulasa	door
12.	pasat	kiɲot	kiɲo	grass
13.	utul	banik	bɛ	tree
14.	kori	peas	pela	stone
15.	dupa	inam	ɛ	water
16.	rora	ambaw	apalu	rat
17.	akasu	radaŋ	mira	dog
18.	limak	urap	uya	bird
19.	tufu	ubus	luku	sky
20.	irtas	mandik	mati	cloud
21.	kanup	aram	lada	star
22.	barti	riaka	dɛka	wind
23.	sisa	sanu	sɔ	rain
24.	fita	rorak	yoya	sun
25.	iu	aip	lɛ	moon

INSTRUCTIONS/QUESTIONS:

1. Which of the above languages are genetically related?
2. List the numbers of all forms that you regard as cognate.
3. List all recurrent sound correspondences holding between the languages which you consider to be genetically related.

GENETIC RELATIONSHIP PROBLEM 8

No.	Lg. A	Lg. B	Lg. C	
01.	kopi	mɛːtɛ	kuli?	skin
02.	taia	hʌgu	taliŋa	ear
03.	ae	hei	lette?	leg
04.	ima	wabi	lima	arm
05.	rata	au	susu	breast
06.	ase	gʌma	ate	liver
07.	turia	usulu	buku	bone
08.	sina	mau	indo?	mother
09.	tama	babu	ambe?	father
10.	hui	weinim	bulu	feather
11.	hani	banɛm	pani?	wing
12.	gatoi	rokum	tallo?	egg
13.	ai huahua	sɛrɛ-num	bua	fruit
14.	utu	inɛ	kutu	louse
15.	lai	youpi	aŋin	wind
16.	medu	sa dipi	uran	rain
17.	lahi	hɛgɛni	api	fire
18.	hua	geilɛ	bulan	moon
19.	kiri	tɛig	taa	laugh
20.	tai	fili	taŋi?	cry
21.	kamonai	is	raŋi	hear
22.	mase	hum	mate	die
23.	guri	tɛn	tanaŋ	bury
24.	lau	iyɛ	aku	1sg., I
25.	toi	sulsɛg	tallu	three

INSTRUCTIONS/QUESTIONS:

1. Two of the above three languages are genetically related. Which two are they?
2. List the numbers of words that are cognate.
3. List all recurrent sound correspondences that support your analysis.

GENETIC RELATIONSHIP PROBLEM 9

No.	Lg. A	Lg. B	Lg. C	Lg. D	
01.	yegi	pason	damot	oruŋ	dog
02.	waku	sapult	nukas	wou	rat
03.	ɔsom	rand	rambi	ooŋ	bat
04.	sarɔt	kempas	ulia	alo?	hand
05.	kulak	ukus	sakun	ula	finger
06.	tɛkia	gent	apa	alutu	fingernail
07.	ŋasim	sokum	uluku	ŋeiŋ	person
08.	lindaŋ	asipm	mania	lilaŋ	house
09.	mosot	lakomp	lamput	moo?	tree
10.	rogus	rasuot	sukum	loku	branch
11.	ulif	limp	ritas	ulih	leaf
12.	sombu	kumubm	intai	sita	earth
13.	fɔgan	sump	walu	hokaŋ	water
14.	gɛmɛs	oroŋg	kunik	keme	bird
15.	iliili	lambig	kamkam	nemineŋ	butterfly
16.	mulɛm	kusunt	silap	puo?	caterpillar
17.	palun	dumak	ritan	foluŋ	mosquito
18.	makuri	ralitn	buda	ulila	white
19.	masimak	nupilt	urik	imala	black
20.	mapurum	osokŋ	timal	fuluŋula	red
21.	matepi	lirat	sisik	tefila	hot
22.	maluŋiŋ	pasudn	panus	luɲiŋila	cold
23.	maitur	tilakŋ	lapan	itulula	heavy
24.	maisɔt	kisip	siki	iotola	small
25.	manusuk	gulugŋ	tulap	nuula	big
26.	marani	sorupm	kunti	lenila	beautiful

INSTRUCTIONS/QUESTIONS:

1. Which of the above languages are genetically related?
2. Which forms are cognate?
3. List the recurrent sound correspondences that justify your analysis.
4. If this appears too difficult, try to reconstruct proto-forms as a way to anchor your statement of correspondences.

PROBLEMS: LEVEL 3

GENETIC RELATIONSHIP PROBLEM 10

No.	Lg. A	Lg. B	Lg. C	Lg. D	
01.	lasi	rotu	tensik	ramba	water
02.	uutu	uku	pani	tuku	river
03.	fauru	woku	hamas	taipi	stone
04.	aaha	kaka	riltak	suliŋ	grass
05.	hafina	sewia	delbar	vila	vine
06.	aini	keki	kimbus	ilu?	tree
07.	turaa	tulaka	sarpit	lundu	fruit
08.	ahufu	kosu	kinda	laŋgu	fire
09.	utuu	utu	impor	kinta?	wind
10.	hana	sua	muni	sapu?	sky
11.	musihi	muti	kapul	falua	sun
12.	nunuu	nu	hukup	tinaŋ	cloud
13.	fanisi	weiti	lutas	manu	moon
14.	rufana	rua	alu	simpa	star
15.	tanimi	tei	kutom	rasu	person
16.	mau	moku	harpit	umpaŋ	head
17.	raisi	reki	silduk	anusu?	hair
18.	rafii	lewi	nokon	sula	eye
19.	sihutu	tisu	puli	tuva?	ear
20.	hafu	sowu	simpu	lusi?	nose
21.	ururu	ulu	iara	ranti	mouth
22.	ahaa	asa	ultik	afa	tooth
23.	nasini	neti	osun	rindiŋ	tongue
24.	fafi	wewi	yoan	ili?	cook
25.	raata	laka	waki	urua	burn
26.	ranuu	rou	olak	tuni	sit
27.	nifunu	niwu	sanlin	pilu?	stand
28.	anisi	kei	lusi	saya	walk
29.	irau	iloku	serit	uliŋ	sleep
30.	tawaa	tawa	mano	inti?	dream
31.	huufu	suku	ahua	lufu?	breathe
32.	manau	moku	rindo	tisa	laugh
33.	uruu	ulu	anut	uku	cry
34.	asii	keti	luka	lumpi	small
35.	mana	anu	ilsak	rusa	big
36.	huraa	sula	onu	pavi?	heavy

37.	huara	suka	rompu	tawaŋ	light
38.	sifai	tiweki	sinas	ruku	black
39.	wairi	weki	punas	faraŋ	white

INSTRUCTIONS/QUESTIONS:

1. Two of the above languages are genetically related. Which languages are they?
2. Which forms are cognate?
3. A mechanical listing of sound correspondences will not work in a problem of this complexity, as several correspondences are misaligned due to divergent patterns of innovation. As a result, the only effective way to identify synchronic correspondences is to reconstruct proto-forms and present the evidence for genetic relationship entirely in diachronic terms. Propose reconstructions for the ancestor of the languages you consider related, and state reflexes of all proto-phonemes in each of its descendants.

Note that the language you reconstruct should not have long vowels/vowel clusters.

GENETIC RELATIONSHIP PROBLEM 11

No.	Lg. A	Lg. B	Lg. C	Lg. D	
01.	fəduh	paruk	pasim	ər	hand
02.	enahi	enaki	musok	ila	head
03.	bohaŋ	bokaŋ	vugu	limak	eye
04.	hanəl	kanar	liner	al	nose
05.	adih	arik	inu	ar	ear
06.	nulon	nuron	silum	luy	mouth
07.	lefa	repa	tayas	yi	earth
08.	fune	pune	kuvan	ul	sky
09.	ədam	aram	lumiŋ	ər	rain
10.	hiben	biki	fuli	ih	eat
11.	baŋo	baŋo	abar	han	drink
12.	abəh	abak	ruram	yima	sleep
13.	hohe	koke	golek	u	speak
14.	lanoh	ranok	nafo	luyu	walk
15.	dudəl	rurar	uvin	rur	laugh
16.	nefon	nepon	mumak	li	cry
17.	obuli	oburi	lurar	uhuy	dream
18.	ŋifit	ŋipit	sukal	ni	wake

INSTRUCTIONS/QUESTIONS:

1. Which of the above languages are genetically related?
2. Which forms are cognate?
3. List the recurrent sound correspondences that justify your analysis.

GENETIC RELATIONSHIP PROBLEM 12

No.	Lg. A	Lg. B	Lg. C	
01.	su	sufat	it	man
02.	ləni	tumaŋk	nuŋ	woman
03.	ras	porxə	alah	child
04.	ppit	sapna	parfa	village
05.	spol	raknip	tufaŋ	house
06.	psek	lurp	fita	fire
07.	klum	surfə	hinuŋ	to cook
08.	snur	kuspe	tunul	to eat
09.	kur	tapma	lakus	to drink
10.	ksu	sular	hut	to sleep
11.	pul	kusant	afuŋ	to talk
12.	lim	famb	iniŋ	to walk
13.	blut	tusim	vunut	big
14.	tmis	riŋ	tumih	small
15.	slon	sump	tunaŋ	long
16.	pru	rimpa	makat	short
17.	ləmip	antək	numif	hot
18.	rəkas	polŋə	lahah	cold
19.	sis	karp	utih	strong
20.	rrek	namp	lila	weak
21.	skun	salna	tuhuŋ	black
22.	dənu	korfa	riŋ	white
23.	kus	sipte	ahuh	red
24.	mmu	tarkan	maŋ	one
25.	psi	bonle	fah	two
26.	ben	kamta	ivaŋ	three

INSTRUCTIONS/QUESTIONS:

1. Which of the above languages are genetically related?
2. Which forms are cognate?
3. List the recurrent sound correspondences that justify your analysis.

SOUND CHANGE

(25 problems)

Background

Sound change problems are commonly included in texts that provide practice exercises. These are often given as as a prelude to doing reconstruction, since by first working through them the student can gain a better understanding of natural directions of sound change, a type of knowledge that is critically important in doing reconstruction. The exercises that follow are based on real language data, all of it taken from members of the enormous and widespread Austronesian family, with some 1,257 languages (Lewis, Simons and Fennig 2015) spread over 206 degrees of longitude and about 72 degrees of latitude. The selection of languages has been guided to a large extent by the relevance of certain types of change to various issues in linguistic theory, ranging from whether we must assume that all sound change is phonetically motivated, to whether alpha-switching rules or claims of rule reordering in early Generative phonology are justified by real language data that may initially appear to support them.

Sources of data for the sound change problems are as follows:

1. Hawaiian (Pukui and Elbert 1971)
2. Arosi (Fox 1970)
3. Rejang (Blust 1980a)
4. Kayan (Blust 1971b)
5. Muna (van den Berg 1991, 1996)
6. Leipon (Blust 1975)

7. Rotuman (Churchward 1940)
8. Mukah Melanau (Blust 1988)
9. Tangoa (Tryon 1976)
10. Seimat (Blust 1975)
11. Iban (Richards 1981)
12. Javanese (Pigeaud 1938; Horne 1974)
13. Chamorro (Topping, Ogo and Dungca 1975)
14. Palauan (McManus and Josephs 1977)
15. Taba, Buli, Numfor, Munggui (van Hasselt and van Hasselt 1947; Maan 1951; Anceaux 1961)
16. Thao (Blust 2003)
17. Levei (Blust 1975)
18. Bario Kelabit (Blust 1971b)
19. Long Terawan Berawan (Blust 1971b)
20. Miri (Blust 1971b)
21. Chuukese (Goodenough and Sugita 1980)
22. Sa'ban (Blust 1971b)
23. Hawu (Wijngaarden 1896)
24. Sundanese (Coolsma 1930)

Proto-languages from which the data are derived are:

1. PAN: Proto-Austronesian.
2. PMP: Proto-Malayo-Polynesian, ancestral to all Austronesian languages outside the island of Taiwan.
3. PNS: Proto-North Sarawak, ancestral to about a dozen languages in northern Sarawak.
4. PKLD: Proto-Kelabit-Lun Dayeh, ancestral to two or three languages and many dialects in northern Sarawak and adjoining areas of Borneo.
5. POC: Proto-Oceanic, ancestral to about 460 Austronesian languages in the Pacific regions of Melanesia, Micronesia and Polynesia.
6. PADM: Proto-Admiralty, ancestral to twenty-five to thirty languages in the Admiralty Islands of Papua New Guinea.
7. PMAN: Proto-Manus, ancestral to about twenty languages on the island of Manus in the Admiralty group.
8. PC: Proto-Chamic, ancestral to about ten languages in Vietnam, Cambodia, Laos and on Hainan island, China.

In a few cases an attested language, A, is derived from a slightly earlier historical stage, 'pre-A'.

LEVEL 1: BEGINNING

SOUND CHANGE PROBLEM 1

Proto-Malayo-Polynesian (PMP) to Hawaiian

No.	PMP	Hawaiian	
01.	*balay	hale	house
02.	*taləs	kalo	taro
03.	*susu	ū	female breast
04.	*tiRəm 'oyster'	kio	shellfish sp.
05.	*zalan	ala	path, road
06.	*uRat 'vein, tendon'	uaua	sinewy
07.	*tasik	kai	sea, saltwater
08.	*paŋədan (> pandan)	hala	pandanus
09.	*ənəm	ono	six
10.	*pitu	hiku	seven
11.	*walu	walu	eight
12.	*batu	(po)haku	stone
13.	*daqan kahiw (> raʔan kayu)	lāʔau	tree
14.	*quzan	ua	rain
15.	*ba-b<in>ahi (> babinay)	wahine	woman
16.	*wahiR	wai	freshwater
17.	*qudaŋ	ula	lobster
18.	*baqəRu	hou	new
19.	*hapuy	ahi	fire
20.	*ma-sakit	maʔi	sick
21.	*pija	hia	how many?
22.	*salaq	hala	wrong; error
23.	*hikan	iʔa	fish
24.	*taqun 'year'	kau	season
25.	*qalejaw (> ʔajaw)	ao	day
26.	*daləm 'inside'	lalo	below, under
27.	*babaw 'above'	waho	outside
28.	*kasaw	ʔaho	rafter
29.	*daŋdaŋ (> randaŋ)	lala	warm by a fire
30.	*lisəhaq (> lisaʔ)	lia ~ liha	nit, louse egg
31.	*taŋis	kani	weep, cry

32.	*bəRsay	hoe	canoe paddle
33.	*ijuŋ	ihu	nose
34.	*baqbaq (> baba?)	waha	mouth
35.	*dahun	lau	leaf
36.	*layaR	lā	sail
37.	*laŋaw	nalo	housefly
38.	*pəñu	honu	green turtle
39.	*haŋin 'wind'	ani	blow, of wind
40.	*ma-qudip	mauli	living, alive
41.	*zaRum 'needle'	hou	inject
42.	*qatay	ake	liver
43.	*niuR	niu	coconut tree
44.	*baba	waha	carry on back
45.	*tumbuq	kupu	sprout, growth

Note: PMP is the ancestor of all Austronesian languages outside the island of Taiwan. Some intermediate steps have been provided, and where this is done statements of sound change should begin with them. PMP *q, a uvular stop, had already become *ʔ in Proto-Polynesian. Finally, it is not clear why the first vowel of *maʔi* is short.

INSTRUCTIONS/QUESTIONS:

1. State all mergers in the data, and list the numbers of illustrative examples.
2. There is one split-merger: what is it?
3. What was the order of the changes affecting *t, *k and *q? Illustrate with specific examples, showing why a different order would not work.

SOUND CHANGE PROBLEM 2

Proto-Oceanic (POC) to Arosi (Southeast Solomon Islands)

No.	POC	Arosi	
01.	*qate	sae-	liver
02.	*raun	rau-	leaf
03.	*masuR	masu	satiated, full
04.	*au	sau	1sg.
05.	*tolu	oru	three
06.	*onom	ono	six
07.	*kaso	ʔato	rafter
08.	*Rumaq	ruma	house
09.	*puqaya	huasa	crocodile
10.	*ñamuk	namu	mosquito
11.	*patu	hau	stone
12.	*salan	tara	path, road
13.	*matakut	maaʔu	fear, be afraid
14.	*quraŋ	ura	shrimp
15.	*suRuq	suru	juice, sap; soup
16.	*-ña	-na	3sg.
17.	*walu	waru	eight
18.	*qupi	uhi	yam
19.	*mata	maa	eye
20.	*ikan	iʔa	fish
21.	*mayaq	masa	shy, ashamed
22.	*lima	rima	five
23.	*masawa	matawa	open sea
24.	*oliq	ori	to return
25.	*aRu	saru	shore tree: *Casuarina*
26.	*Rusan	ruta	cargo
27.	*tasik	asi	sea, saltwater
28.	*ira	ira	3pl.
29.	*kulit	ʔuri	skin
30.	*solo	toro	mountain, hill
31.	*tawan	awa	tree: *Pometia pinnata*
32.	*sinaR	sina	sun
33.	*qatun	sau	bonito, skipjack tuna

34.	*kua	ʔua	how?
35.	*poñu	honu	green turtle
36.	*sei	tei	who?
37.	*qawa	sawa	milkfish; mullet
38.	*qume	ume	unicorn fish
39.	*tina	ina	mother
40.	*qusan	uta	rain
41.	*maqati	mai	low tide, exposed reef
42.	*mañawa	manawa	breath, fontanelle
43.	*raqan	raa	branch of a tree

Note: the hyphens in *sae-* and *rau-* indicate obligatorily possessed nouns; the hyphen in *-na* marks this morpheme as a suffix.

INSTRUCTIONS/QUESTIONS:

1. What are the reflexes of Proto-Oceanic *s? State specific conditions if there is more than one reflex.
2. What are the sources of Arosi /s/? Are any of these surprising? Why or why not?
3. State one prominent shift and one prominent merger in Arosi.

LEVEL 2: INTERMEDIATE

SOUND CHANGE PROBLEM 3

PMP to the Musi dialect of Rejang (southern Sumatra, Indonesia)

Background. Assumed phonetic values for proto-phonemes are: *q = voiceless uvular stop, *R = alveolar trill, *z = voiced palatal affricate, ñ = palatal nasal. The PMP schwa, which has traditionally been represented as *e is here written with the appropriate phonetic symbol to avoid possible confusion. For a closer approximation to a language immediately preceding the modern forms of Rejang cf. McGinn (2005).

No.	PMP	Rejang	
01.	*qabu	abəw	ash
02.	*aluR	aloa	to flow
03.	*anak	ana?	child
04.	*anay	anie anie	termite
05.	*tali	tiləy	rope
06.	*zalan	dalən	path, road
07.	*hikət	eket	to tie
08.	*dilaq	diləa?	tongue
09.	*laɲit	leɲet	sky
10.	*ipən	epen	tooth
11.	*qatay	atie	liver
12.	*Ratus	otos	hundred
13.	*bulat	bulət	round
14.	*kawil	kewea	fish-hook
15.	*manuk	mono?	chicken
16.	*bulu	buləw	body hair, feather
17.	*pənuq	pənoa?	full
18.	*Rakit	eket	raft
19.	*ñawa	ñabəy	to breathe
20.	*laRiw (> laRi)	liləy	to run
21.	*batu	butəw	stone
22.	*apuR	opoa	betel lime
23.	*matay	matie	to die; dead
24.	*zaRum	dolom	needle
25.	*baRani (> bani)	binəy	courageous

26.	*punay	ponoy	dove
27.	*danaw	danuəw	lake
28.	*duha	duəy	two
29.	*təlu	tələw	three
30.	*sapu	supəw	broom
31.	*qasiRa (> siRa)	siləy	salt
32.	*hutək	oto?	brain
33.	*kasaw	kasuəw	rafter
34.	*waRi	biləy	day
35.	*mata	matəy	eye
36.	*daRaq	daləa?	blood
37.	*gənəp	gənəp	complete
38.	*panas	panəs	hot
39.	*pəRəs	pə?əs	to squeeze
40.	*bunuq	bonoa?	to kill
41.	*iliR	elea	downstream
42.	*hisaŋ	isaŋ	gills
43.	*tumpul	topoa	dull, blunt
44.	*niuR	nioa	coconut palm
45.	*hapuy	opoy	fire
46.	*laŋaw	laŋuəw	horsefly
47.	*aku	akəw	acknowledge
48.	*qudaŋ	udaŋ	shrimp, lobster
49.	*putiq	putea?	white
50.	*ma-iRaq	miləa?	red
51.	*balik	bele?	return

INSTRUCTIONS/QUESTIONS:

1. Describe the conditions under which the sequences -*e*C*e*- and -*o*C*o*- developed, and list all examples of this change by number. Are there any exceptions to this development? Which forms are exceptional and what would the expected forms be?
2. Describe the conditions under which *a was raised to a high vowel, and list all examples of this change by number.
3. PMP *q and *k merged word-finally in Rejang. How can we still tell which of these proto-phonemes a given final glottal stop reflects? Illustrate with examples.

PROBLEMS: LEVEL 2

SOUND CHANGE PROBLEM 4

Pre-Kayan to Uma Juman Kayan (Sarawak, Malaysian Borneo)

Background. Although the focus in this problem is on Uma Juman Kayan, data from the Uma Bawang dialect are also given for the light they shed on the Uma Juman changes. The orthography used here is partly phonetic. In particular, even though high and mid vowels are contrastive in Uma Juman, high vowels automatically lower before certain final consonants, the most important of which is glottal stop. They are given their phonetic values here in order to provide a clue to what is perhaps the most puzzling feature of the historical phonology of this dialect (and some other Kayan dialects and closely related languages). Other automatic phonetic processes, such as lengthening of word-final vowels, are not indicated.

No.	Pre-Kayan	UJ Kayan	UB Kayan	
01.	*mata	mata?	mata?	eye
02.	*təluR	təloh	təloh	egg
03.	*bulu?	bulu	bulu?	bamboo sp.
04.	*daRa?	daha	dahaa?	blood
05.	*dua	dua?	dua?	two
06.	*təlu	təlo?	təlo?	three
07.	*lima	lima?	lima?	five
08.	*ənəm	nəm	nəm	six
09.	*tana?	tana	tanaa?	earth
10.	*laki	lake?	lake?	male
11.	*bulu	bulo?	bulo?	feather
12.	*bəRas	baha	baha	husked rice
13.	*dəduR	doh	doh	female; woman
14.	*bua?	bua	buaa?	fruit
15.	*ədaw	do	do	day, daylight
16.	*alu	alo?	alo?	rice pestle
17	*punti	pute?	pute?	banana
18.	*buaya	baya?	baya?	crocodile
19.	*uay	ue	ue	rattan
20.	*uli?	uli	uli?	return home
21.	*salaR	halah	halah	nest
22.	*ta?i	ta?e?	ta?e?	faeces

23.	*tudu?	turu	turu?	leak, as a roof
24.	*batu	bato?	bato?	stone
25.	*suŋay	huŋe	huŋe	river
26.	*puti?	puti	puti?	white
27.	*atay	ate	ate	liver
28.	*kudən	kurən	kurən	cooking pot
29.	*pusu?	pusu	pusu?	heart
30.	*sia	hia?	hia?	3sg.
31.	*suRu?	suhu	suhu?	order, request
32.	*Ruma?	uma	umaa?	house
33.	*diRi	jihe?	jihe?	housepost
34.	*qabu	avo?	avo?	ashes/hearth
35.	*Ratus	atu	atuh	hundred
36.	*babuy	bavuy	bavuy	wild boar

QUESTIONS:

1. What is the Uma Juman reflex of Pre-Kayan final glottal stop? Of Pre-Kayan final vowel? Do these constitute a single change, and if so how might it be explained?
2. Do the predictable differences of vowel height (high vowels automatically lowered before final glottal stop) suggest another explanation for the switch of final glottal stop and zero? If so, how would they do this, and where might you search for additional supporting evidence?

SOUND CHANGE PROBLEM 5

PMP to Muna (southeast Sulawesi, Indonesia)

No.	PMP	Muna	
01.	*qatəp	ghato	roof
02.	*mata	mata	eye
03.	*buhək	wuu	head hair; body hair
04.	*babuy	wewi	pig
05.	*kasaw	saho	rafter
06.	*qətut	ghotu	fart
07.	*dahun	roo	leaf
08.	*ŋajan	nea	name
09.	*qitəm	ghito	black
10.	*binəhiq	wine	seed rice; seed
11.	*ka-wanan	suana	right side
12.	*qalipan	gholifa	centipede
13.	*baRah	wea	ember
14.	*daləm	lalo	inside; heart, feelings
15.	*buŋa	wuna	flower
16.	*quləj	ghule	maggot; worm
17.	*zalan	sala	road
18.	*bəsuR	wehi	satiated
19.	*pahuq	foo	mango
20.	*qapuR	ghefi	lime (for betel)
21.	*laŋuy	leni	swim
22.	*paniki	ponisi	flying fox; small bat
23.	*kahiw (> kayu)	sau	tree, wood
24.	*quzan	ghuse	rain
25.	*pajay	pae	riceplant
26.	*babaw	wawo	on, over
27.	*qabaRa	ghowea	shoulder
28.	*dəpa	rofa	fathom
29.	*tasik	tehi	sea
30.	*laŋit	lani	sky
31.	*sakit	saki	sick
32.	*qatəluR	ghunteli	egg
33.	*bibiR	wiwi	lip

34.	*pusəj	puhe	navel
35.	*dəmdəm	rondo	dark
36.	*qasiRa	ghohia	salt
37.	*paqit	paghi	bitter
38.	*daRaq	rea	blood
39.	*aləm	alo	night
40.	*qapəju	ghufei	gall, gall bladder
41.	*qaləjaw	gholeo	day
42.	*baqəRu	bughou	new
43.	*pəRəs	feo	squeeze out
44.	*dakəp	rako	catch, capture
45.	*duha	dua	two
46.	*qatay	ghate	liver
47.	*taqun	taghu	year
48.	*panij	pani	wing
49.	*putiq	pute	white
50.	*tuhud	tuu	knee
51.	*zaRum	deu	needle
52.	*tuzuq	tusu	point to, indicate
53.	*tuduq	turu	leak, drip
54.	*təŋtəŋ	tonto	stare, look fixedly
55.	*wahiR	oe	freshwater
56.	*hapuy	ifi	fire
57.	*kaRat	sia	to bite
58.	*kali	seli	to dig

Note: PAN *R probably was an alveolar trill that became uvular in many daughter languages. Muna *gh* is a voiced dorso-uvular fricative (van den Berg 1989: 16).

INSTRUCTIONS/QUESTIONS:

1. What are the reflexes of last-syllable *u in Muna? If there is more than one reflex what are the conditions for this split?
2. PMP final consonants disappeared in Muna. Is there any evidence that they left traces of their former presence before disappearing? Be specific, and cite the number of each supporting example.
3. Is there any consonant reflex that seems unusual to you? Which one

PROBLEMS: LEVEL 2

is it and what are the examples illustrating this change? Are there any exceptions to this change, and is there reason to suspect that at least one of these is a loan? Finally, does this change have to be ordered with respect to any other, and if so which one?

4. PMP *a > Muna *o* in the antepenult almost certainly was through *a > ə > *o*. What conditioned *a > *u* in the antepenult? Do you find this surprising? Why or why not?

SOUND CHANGE PROBLEM 6

Proto-Admiralty (PADM) to Leipon (Admiralty Islands, Papua New Guinea)

Background. Proto-Admiralty *na is the common noun article. *br* and *dr* = bilabial and alveolar trills respectively (represented phonetically as [b̃] and [d̃]). All voiced obstruents are automatically prenasalised in both languages, and hyphenated nouns are obligatorily possessed.

No.	PADM	Leipon	
01.	*rua-pu	ma-rwe-h	two
02.	*lima-pu	ma-lme-h	five
03.	*ono-pu	ma-wno-h	six
04.	*sa-ŋaRatus	ma-sŋet	100
05.	*na raRaq	dray	blood
06.	*na taliŋa	delŋa-	ear
07.	*na mata	minde-	eye
08.	*na puki	bri-	vulva, vagina
09.	*na pulan	brul	moon
10.	*na natu	netu-	child
11.	*na pudi	brudr	banana
12.	*na padran	padr	pandanus
13.	*na kuluR	kul	breadfruit
14.	*na puaq	brua-	fruit
15.	*na talise	delis	a tree: *Terminalia catappa*
16.	*na taqi	de-	faeces
17.	*na putun	brut	a tree: *Barringtonia asiatica*
18.	*na kutu	kut	head louse
19.	*na pataŋ	pite-	tree trunk
20.	*na salan	cal	path, road
21.	*na Rabia	epi	sago palm
22.	*na saku layaR	colay	swordfish
23.	*na kanase	kines	mullet
24.	*na panapa	pinah	needlefish
25.	*na pakiwak	pew	shark
26.	*na kuRita	kit	octopus
27.	*na puqaya ·	bruey	crocodile

28.	*na toRas	drow	a tree: *Intsia bijuga*
29.	*na purit	brur	tail end
30.	*na tasik	das	saltwater, sea
31.	*na ranum	dran	freshwater
32.	*na tapuRi	dah	conch shell
33.	*na kamali	kimel	man, male
34.	*na tokalaur	tolaw	north wind
35.	*na paRa	pay	firewood shelf
36.	*na tama	time-	father
37.	*na baluc	pal	pigeon
38.	*na katapa	kitah	frigate bird
39.	*na kanawe	kinew	seagull
40.	*na pupu	bruh	basket trap for fish
41.	*na kuron	kur	clay cooking pot
42.	*na qalimaŋo	elmaŋ	mangrove crab
43.	*mate	met	die, dead
44.	*matiruR	mender	to sleep
45.	*taŋis	teŋ	to cry
46.	*nipinipi	ninih	to dream
47.	*mawap	hol-maw	to yawn
48.	*sapa	cah	what?

INSTRUCTIONS/QUESTIONS:

1. What is the source of the typologically rare bilabial trills?
2. POC *a is raised to both *e* and *i* under different conditions. List all examples of *a > *e*, and then of *a > *i*. What conditions each of these changes?
3. Have any of the vowels that conditioned *a > *e* disappeared? If so are there irregularities in the form of this conditiong? List exceptions to the process.

SOUND CHANGE PROBLEM 7

POC to Rotuman (central Pacific)

No.	POC	Rotuman	
01.	*patu	hɔfu	stone
02.	*tolu	folu	three
03.	*lima	lima	five
04.	*lako	laʔo	go
05.	*pula	hula	moon
06.	*ʔuta	ufa	inland
07.	*ʔipi	ifi	Tahitian chestnut
08.	*tuki	tuki	hammer, pound
09.	*ika	iʔa	fish
10.	*pili	hili	choose, select
11.	*waka	vaʔa	root
12.	*paka-	faka-	causative prefix
13.	*kutu	ʔufu	louse
14.	*tuna	funa	eel
15.	*pata	hata	shelf
16.	*koti	ʔofi	clip, cut
17.	*pose	hose	canoe paddle
18.	*puti	futi	pluck
19.	*limu	rimu	seaweed/lichen
20.	*toko	toko	punting pole
21.	*kuli	ʔuli	skin
22.	*tanipa	tanifa	fish sp.
23.	*pitu	hifu	seven
24.	*pulu	furu	body hair, feathers
25.	*sika	siʔa	net needle
26.	*sulu	sulu	torch
27.	*tapi	tɔfi	sweep
28.	*toka	toka	settle down
29.	*sala	sara	err, be wrong
30.	*ʔusa	usa	rain
31.	*sala	sala	path, road
32.	*tawake	tævæke	tropic bird
33.	*sapu	sɔfu	falling water

34.	*paRi-	hɔi-	reciprocal prefix
35.	*sele	sere	cut
36.	*ma-tuʔa	mafua	old (of people)
37.	*tusi	tusi	write, make marks
38.	*walu	vɔlu	eight
39.	*kaRati	ʔɔfi	bite
40.	*siwa	siva	nine
41.	*kai	ʔɔi	tree, wood
42.	*ʔate	æfe	liver

INSTRUCTIONS/QUESTIONS:

1. Rotuman shows double reflexes of many proto-phonemes, including the voiceless stops *p, *t, and *k and the liquid *l. List the reflexes for each of these proto-phonemes by number.
2. Based on co-occurrences in the data given here identify two strata in the vocabulary, and show the reflex of *p, *t, *k and *l in each stratum.
3. Which stratum do you think is native, and why?
4. Rotuman has also expanded the POC five-vowel system (*i, *u, *e, *o, *a) to one with at least ten contrasts. What are the two novel vowels reflected in the above data, and how did they develop? (Cite the numbers of all examples illustrating each development.)

SOUND CHANGE PROBLEM 8

PMP to Mukah Melanau (coastal Sarawak, Malaysian Borneo)

Background. 'Melanau' is a dialect chain that stretches about 180 miles along the coast of Sarawak in Malaysian Borneo, from Balingian in the north to the mouth of the Rejang River in the south, and from there upriver to Kanowit, about 100 miles inland. There is a considerable phonological variation in Melanau speech communities, much of it shared with Mukah, but some of it fairly different. In all of these communities for which field data are available stress follows a pattern similar to that of Malay, falling on the penultimate vowel unless that vowel is schwa followed by a single consonant, in which case it shifts rightward to the last syllable. Malay influence is strong in the vocabulary, and some words cited here probably are Malay loans. These are marked (L). Note that *r* is uvular, sequences of like vowels are distinct syllable peaks and the orthography shows more phonetic detail than may be required in a strictly phonemic orthography. PMP *j probably was [gʲ], and *z almost certainly was [ɹ].

No.	PMP	Mukah Melanau	
01.	*anak	aneə?	child
02.	*bəli	bələy	buy
03.	*silu	siləw	claw
04.	*layaR	layeəh	sail
05.	*daRaq	daa?	blood
06.	*duRi	duəy	thorn
07.	*gətgət	gəgət	gnaw
08.	*iluR	iloh	channel
09.	*itik	itiə?	duck
10.	*buŋbuŋ	bubuəŋ	ridge of roof
11.	*buluq	bulo?	large bamboo sp.
12.	*biRbiR	bibeəh	lip
13.	*diŋdiŋ	didiəŋ	wall of house
14.	*kulit	kulit	skin
15.	*bataŋ	bateəŋ	tree trunk
16.	*piliq	pile?	choose
17.	*titik	titiə?	spot, dot
18.	*qaRəm	aam	pangolin

19.	*sandaR	sadeəh	lean on
20.	*bəjbəj	bəbəd	tie up
21.	*padaŋ	padeəŋ	uncultivated field
22.	*bəduk	bəduə?	large monkey sp.
23.	*panas	panaih	hot; flash of anger
24.	*kasaw	kasaw	rafter
25.	*qatay	atay	liver
26.	*sali-matək	sələmatək	jungle leech
27.	*nipaq	ñipa?	nipah palm
28.	*manuk	manuə?	bird
29.	*əpat	pat	four
30.	*bəRat	baat	heavy
31.	*qapəju	pədəw	gall
32.	*nanaq	nana?	pus
33.	*Ratus	ratuih (L)	hundred
34.	*ŋajan	ŋadan	name
35.	*qasawa	sawa	spouse
36.	*qatəluR	tələh	egg
37.	*labuq	labo?	fall
38.	*tuktuk	tutuə?	knock, pound
39.	*tali	taləy	rope
40.	*ənəm	nəm	six
41.	*zuRuq	juu?	juice
42.	*qudaŋ	udeəŋ	lobster
43.	*taŋis	taŋeh	weep, cry
44.	*buhək	buə?	head hair
45.	*laluŋ	laluəŋ	cock, rooster
46.	*isak	iseə?	ripe, cooked
47.	*təRas	taaih	ironwood tree
48.	*quzan	ujan	rain
49.	*asaŋ	aseəŋ	gills
50.	*bituka	bətuka	intestines
51.	*matuqa	mətua (L)	parent-in-law
52.	*quləj	uləd	maggot
53.	*taqu	ta?əw	know
54.	*qaRus 'current'	auih	current of air
55.	*nipən	ñipən	tooth
56.	*zalan	jalan	path, road
57.	*buaq niuR	bəñoh	coconut
58.	*buqaya	baya	crocodile

59.	*Rusuk	usuə?	ribs; chest
60.	*puqun	puʔun	base of tree; origin
61.	*dutdut	dudut	pluck, pull out
62.	*ma-qudip	m-udip	to live, be alive
63.	*təktək	tətək	cut, hack
64.	*təbək	təbək	stab
65.	*taqi	taʔəy	faeces
66.	*Rakit	akit	raft
67.	*taqun	taʔun	year
68.	*hasaq	asaʔ	whet, sharpen
69.	*pa-uliq	puleʔ	to return
70.	*saliR 'to flow'	baʔay saleəh	ebb-tide

Note: *j* is a voiced palatal affricate, and ñ a palatal nasal.

INSTRUCTIONS/QUESTIONS:

1. List the reflexes of PMP *i, *u, and *a in the final syllable of Mukah words.
2. What are the conditions for splitting of high vowels?
3. What are the conditions for splitting of *a?
4. PMP *k and *q merged as Mukah -ʔ. Is it still possible to determine the source of any given -ʔ in native Mukah words? How does this compare with the similar issue in Rejang (sound change problem 3)?
5. Do you find any of these conditions unexpected? Why or why not?

SOUND CHANGE PROBLEM 9

POC to Tangoa (Vanuatu, Melanesia)

Background. Proto-Oceanic *b^w and *m^w were labiovelars, and all POC voiced obstruents were automatically prenasalised. Tangoa p̬, ṽ and m̬ are apico-labial stop, fricative and nasal phonemes (tongue tip touching upper lip). These are written with a bracket under the *p*, *v* (or rather β), and *m* in Maddieson (1989b), but I have encountered fewer typographical problems when they are used as superscripts. In other languages of the region these have evolved into alveolars or interdentals (*t*, ð, *n*, etc.). Hyphens mark obligatory possession, and some historically intermediate stages are given in parentheses.

No.	POC	Tangoa	
01.	*b^watu	patu-	head
02.	*pulu	vulu-	body hair
03.	*meme	m̃em̃e-	tongue
04.	*mata	m̃ata-	eye
05.	*lima	lim̃a-	hand
06.	*susu	susu-	breast
07.	*tinaqi	tine-	guts
08.	*buto	puto-	navel
09.	*taqi	te-	faeces
10.	*suRi	sui-	bone
11.	*kulit	huri-	skin
12.	*tama	tam̃a-	father
13.	*tina	tina-	mother
14.	*Rumaq (> im^{w}a)	ima	house
15.	*kamali	ham̃ali	men's house
16.	*boe	poi	pig
17.	*laŋo	laŋo	housefly
18.	*m^wata	mata	snake
19.	*kuRita	huita	octopus/squid
20.	*pakiwak	p̃aheu	shark
21.	*bebe	p̃ep̃e	butterfly
22.	*kani	xanixani	eat; food
23.	*topu	tovu	sugar cane

24.	*niuR	niu	coconut
25.	*puaq	vua	fruit
26.	*pituqon (> pituqun)	vitu	star/moon
27.	*waiR	wai	freshwater
28.	*qusan	usa	rain
29.	*qone	oneone	sand
30.	*patu	ṽatu	stone
31.	*tasik	tasi	sea
32.	*mate	m̃ate	dead, die
33.	*masa	m̃am̃asa	evaporate/dry
34.	*pati	mo-ṽati	four
35.	*lima	mo-lim̃a	five
36.	*pisa	mo-visa	how many?
37.	*boŋi	poŋi	night
38.	*raqani	rani	day
39.	*kamami	kam̃am	we (pl., excl.)
40.	*kite	xite	see
41.	*kaRati	xati-a	bite
42.	*roŋoR	roŋo-a	hear
43.	*taŋis	taŋis	weep, cry
44.	*pano	ṽano	go, walk
45.	*mai	m̃ai	come
46.	*turu	turu	stand
47.	*inum	inu	drink
48.	*matakut	m̃ataxu	fear

INSTRUCTIONS/QUESTIONS:

1. What are the Tangoa reflexes of POC *p, *b, *bʷ, *m, and *mʷ?
2. Under what conditions did the typologically rare apico-labial or linguo-labial consonants develop? Are there any apparent exceptions to this pattern?
3. Is there an apparent unconditioned phonemic split in this language that is unconnected with the development of the apico-labials? Which phoneme shows a split, and what are the examples of its reflexes? (List numbers of each reflex.)

SOUND CHANGE PROBLEM 10

PADM to Seimat (Admiralty Islands, Papua New Guinea)

Background. To maximise the amount of material needed to illustrate the points highlighted in this problem Seimat is derived from Proto-Admiralty (PADM) rather than the temporally more remote Proto-Oceanic. PADM *dr was a prenasalised alveolar trill, and *mʷ a labiovelar nasal. Nasal vowels are marked with a superscript tilde; a hyphen marks a noun that is optionally or obligatorily possessed, or part of a whole, or it marks a verb that normally appears with a suffix; V marks an indeterminate final vowel. Vowels (and in some cases -CV sequences) that appear only under suffixation are in parentheses.

No.	PADM	Seimat	
01.	*api	ah	fire
02.	*qalu	al	barracuda
03.	*kalia	ali	grouper
04.	*kami	ami-te	1pl excl.
05.	*kani	an(i)-	eat
06.	*yabia	api	sago palm
07.	*qate	at(e)-	liver; heart
08.	*qatolu	atol(u)-	egg
09.	*qawa	aw(a)-	mouth
10.	*asa	ax(a)-	gills
11.	*qase	ax(e)-	chin, jaw
12.	*qasu	ax(u)-	gall (bladder)
13.	*pane	han	to climb
14.	*patu	hat	stone
15.	*poñu	hon	green turtle
16.	*pose	hox(e)-	canoe paddle
17.	*pua	hua	fruit
18.	*roŋo	hõŋ(o)	to hear
19.	*puqaya	hua	crocodile
20.	*rua-pua	hũõ-hu	two (serial counting)
21.	*dramʷa	kaw(ã)-	forehead
22.	*matiru	mati(hũ)	to sleep
23.	*qura	uh	lobster

24.	*wara	wah(ã)-	root
25.	*waka	wa	boat
26.	*mʷalutV	wãlut	dove sp.
27.	*wao	wao-	vine; vein, tendon
28.	*mʷata	wãt	snake; earthworm
29.	*mʷaqane	wã-wãn	man, male
30.	*balu	pal	dove
31.	*kuli	uli-	skin, bark
32.	*qura	uh	lobster
33.	*dranu	kan	freshwater
34.	*dru	ku-ku	housepost
35.	*ñamu	nam	mosquito

INSTRUCTIONS/QUESTIONS:

1. What are the historical sources of Seimat *h*? (List all examples by number.) Are there clues in the following vowel that tell us which source a given *h* reflects?
2. What are the historical sources of Seimat *w*? Are there also clues in the following vowel that tell us which source a given *w* reflects?
3. Is there any reflex that is phonetically surprising? Which one? (List examples.)

SOUND CHANGE PROBLEM 11

Pre-Iban to Iban (Sarawak, Malaysian Borneo)

Background. Pre-Iban *j, *c and Iban *j, c* are palatal affricates (voiced and voiceless respectively). Changes made to the standard orthography include writing ə rather than e, ñ rather than ny, and -ai and –au as –ay and –aw respectively. Iban is closely related to Malay, and almost certainly has been subject to significant Malay contact influence as well.

No.	Pre-Iban	Iban	
01.	*jalan	jalay	path, road
02.	*tətawak	tətawak ~ ttawak	signal gong
03.	*kətəm	kətam ~ kətaw	to cut, harvest
04.	*susu	tusu	breast
05.	*datəŋ	datay	come
06.	*buruŋ	buruŋ	bird
07.	*tərbaŋ	tərəbay	to fly
08.	*cacat	tacat	defect, blemish
09.	*ragəŋ	ragaŋ ~ ragaw	crawl
10.	*bukan	bukay	no, not
11.	*ləlayaŋ	ləlayaŋ ~ llayaŋ	swallows, swifts
12.	*sasak	tasak	plaitwork
13.	*cicak	ticak	gecko
14.	*diəm	diaw	quiet
15.	*undaŋ	unday	shrimp
16.	*kanan	kanan	right side
17.	*pantay	pantay	beach; earth, soil
18.	*ləlaki	ləlaki ~ llaki	male, man
19.	*pəgaŋ	pəgay	to hold
20.	*daun	daun	leaf
21.	*səsupit	səsupit ~ ssupit	matwork sack
22.	*tulaŋ	tulaŋ	bone
23.	*pəsən	pəsaw	to order
24.	*ulun	ulun	slave, serf
25.	*səsəl	təsal	to regret
26.	*təlanjaŋ	təlanjay	naked
27.	*kasaw	kasaw	rafter

28.	*urəm	uraw	cloudy
29.	*jəjal	dəjal	stopper, cork
30.	*bulan	bulan	moon
31.	*panjaŋ	panjay	long
32.	*paraw	paraw	hoarse
33.	*injəm	injaw	to borrow
34.	*makan	makay	to eat
35.	*jaja	daja?	to hawk, peddle
36.	*ikan	ikan	fish
37.	*ñaman	ñaman ~ ñamay	pleasant, comfortable
38.	*itəm	itam	black
39.	*suman	sumay	to cook
40.	*tajəm	tajam	sharp
41.	*pulaŋ	pulay	go home
42.	*jarum	jarum	needle
43.	*bubun	bubun	fontanelle
44.	*iriŋ	iriŋ	walk single file
45.	*cincin	tincin	finger ring
46.	*maləm	malam	night
47.	*jujuh	dujoh	pour out; diarrhoea

INSTRUCTIONS/QUESTIONS:

1. What are the reflexes of final nasals in Iban?
2. Is it possible to state conditions for these multiple splits? If so, state them and list examples supporting each condition.
3. List the reflexes of the fricatives and affricates in Iban. Is there any process that gives rise to multiple reflexes of these proto-phonemes?

SOUND CHANGE PROBLEM 12

PMP to Javanese (Java, Republic of Indonesia)

Background. Javanese is notable for several reasons. First, with nearly 100 million first language speakers it is the largest member of the Austronesian family (CIA – The world factbook, February 2016). Second, it has the longest continuous or near-continuous tradition of written documentation for any Austronesian language, starting with Old Javanese, written between the ninth and fifteenth centuries in an Indic script on palm-leaf manuscripts that were preserved in Bali after the Islamisation of Java itself, and continuing with later written documents into the modern era (Uhlenbeck 1964). Third, Javanese is noteworthy for its socially determined 'speech levels'. Unless marked with 'kr' (*kromo*), all material used here is from the *ngoko*, or unmarked register.

Despite its current numerical dominance Javanese has throughout much of its history been subjected to strong contact influence from Malay, a language that had begun to achieve significant status as a lingua franca by the seventh century in connection with sea routes for the India-China trade. Old Javanese texts provide glimpses into an earlier form of the language, and some Old Javanese forms are given in parentheses after PMP to provide interstage comparisons. Note that *a-* in 1, 24, 28 and 36 is a stative verb prefix that is fossilised in some forms, and that *ḍ* is traditionally called a 'retroflex' stop, but is actually alveolar to post-alveolar, as opposed to *d*, which – like *t* – is postdental.

No.	PMP	Javanese	
01.	*bəRəqat (> a-bwat)	abot	heavy
02.	*bulu	bulu	feather headdress
03.	*duha (> ro)	loro	two
04.	*baRa (> wa ~ wā)	wawa	ember
05.	*taqun	taun	year
06.	*buta	wuta (kr)	blind
07.	*pəRəs	pərəs	squeeze
08.	*dapuR	ḍapur	hearth; kitchen
09.	*bulu	wulu	fur, feathers, body hair
10.	*taRuq	toh	wager, bet
11.	*Rakit	rakit	raft
12.	*uRat (> ot-wat)	otot	vein, vessel
13.	*qabu	awu	ash

14.	*n-ia	-ne	3sg. possessor
15.	*paRih (> pe)	pe, pepe	stingray
16.	*habaRat	barat	west wind; west
17.	*dahun (rwan ~ ron)	ron ~ roŋɖon (kr)	leaf
18.	*tuqah	tua	old, mature
19.	*Ratus	atus	hundred
20.	*dəkəp	dəkəp	seize, grasp
21.	*tuduŋ	tuɖuŋ	head cloth
22.	*pahuq	poh	mango
23.	*qudaŋ	uraŋ	shrimp
24.	*təRas (> twas)	atos	hard
25.	*daRa (> rara)	lara	virgin
26.	*zuRuq (> duh)	duduh	syrup, gravy
27.	*bisik	bisik	whisper
28.	*laun	alon	slow
29.	*tuduR	turu	sleep
30.	*binəhiq	winih	seed rice
31.	*paqit	pait	bitter
32.	*m-uda	muɖa	young
33.	*buka	buka	open(ing)
34.	*daRaq (rah ~ rãh)	rah (kr)	blood
35.	*buaq	woh	fruit
36.	*zauq	adoh	far, distant
37.	*buqaya	baya	crocodile
38.	*bəRas (> wəas)	wos (kr)	husked rice
39.	*zalan	dalan	road
40.	*sual	sol	to uproot
41.	*quzan	udan	rain
42.	*waRi 'day'	udan wewe	sunshower
43.	*taqi	tai	faeces
44.	*qatimun	timun	cucumber
45.	*lahud	lor	seaward; north
46.	*taRum	tom	indigo

INSTRUCTIONS/QUESTIONS:

1. The four PMP vowels *i, *u, *ə and *a developed into Modern Javanese *i, *u, *e, *ə, *o, *ɛ, and *a (in addition [ɔ] occurs as an

allophone of /a/). Based on the data given here, how did Javanese develop /o/ and /e/? (List numbers of all relevant examples.)

2. What consonants had to disappear before /o/ and /e/ could develop in all the forms in which they occur today? What consonant that has since disappeared prevented the crasis of adjacent vowels? (List numbers of supporting data for each statement.)

3. PMP strongly favoured a disyllabic canonical shape, but sound change yielded a number of monosyllabic content morphemes in Javanese. There were two ways this problem was addressed in many cases. What were they? (Cite specific examples.)

4. Which PMP phonemes show multiple reflexes with no apparent conditions in Javanese? List numbers of examples for each. How might this have come about?

SOUND CHANGE PROBLEM 13

PMP to Chamorro (western Micronesia)

Background. PMP *q = a voiceless uvular stop, *z = a voiced palatal affricate, *R = an alveolar trill that became uvular in many languages, and *j probably = a palatalised voiced velar stop [gʲ]. In the standard Chamorro orthography the voiceless palatal affricate (IPA [ʧ]) is written *ch*, *gw* (a voiced labiovelar stop) is written *gu* and the voiced alveolar affricate (IPA [ʤ]) is written *y*. In the interrest of phonetic transparency the latter is written *dz* here, and word-final postvocalic *i* and *o* are written *y* and *w*, as in 1 or 10. Pre-Chamorro stress was penultimate except when the penult contained schwa, in which case it shifted to the final syllable. On the advice of Sandra Chung I have changed unstressed (last-syllable) *e* and *o* in my source (Topping, Ogo and Dungca 1975) to -*i* and -*u* respectively, since these are phonetically high vowels that are written as mid vowels in the orthography of my primary source for reasons that need not be discussed here. In addition, Chamorro has an /a/ : /æ/ contrast that is not reflected in the traditional orthography, but is now marked (as /å/ : /a/ respectively) in the official orthographies of Guam and the Commonwealth of the Northern Mariana Islands. Its origin is puzzling, and it is not noted further in this problem.

No.	PMP	Chamorro	
01.	*qazay	achay	chin
02.	*qapuR	åfuk	lime
03.	*qawa	ågʷa	milkfish
04.	*qadiq	åhiʔ	no
05.	*qali-maŋaw	atmaŋaw/akmaŋaw	mangrove crab
06.	*qaləp	aluf	to beckon
07.	*qabaRa	apåga	(carry on) shoulder
08.	*qasawa	asagʷa	spouse
09.	*qasiRa	asiga	salt
10.	*qaləjaw	åtdaw	day, sun
11.	*duha	hugʷa	two
12.	*zauq (> zawuʔ)	chåguʔ	far
13.	*zalan	chålan	path, road
14.	*zəbzəb	chopchup	to suck
15.	*paqit	faʔit	bitter
16.	*paniki	fanihi	flying fox

17.	*pija	fiʔa	how much/many?
18.	*pəRəq	fuguʔ	to press, squeeze
19.	*ənəm	gunum	six
20.	*hapuy	gʷåfi	fire
21.	*aku	gʷåhu	1sg., I
22.	*hasaŋ	gʷasaŋ	gills
23.	*uRat	gugat	vein, vessel
24.	*hikan	gʷihan	fish
25.	*ini	gʷini	here
26.	*ia	gʷidza	3sg., he/she/it
27.	*daRaq	hagaʔ	blood
28.	*dahun (> dawun)	hågun	leaf
29.	*kawil	hagʷit	fish-hook
30.	*dalij	håliʔ	buttress root
31.	*daya	hådza	upriver, landward
32.	*təRab	tugap	belch
33.	*dəŋəR	huŋuk	hear
34.	*laləj	låluʔ	housefly
35.	*ñamuk	ñåmu	mosquito
36.	*baqəRu	påʔgu	new; now, today
37.	*baRiuh (> bagyu)	påkdzu	typhoon
38.	*kamiu	(> kamyu)	hamdzu 2pl., you
39.	*qatəp	åtuf	roof
	*qatəp-i	åft-i	to roof, put on a roof
40.	*ma-qasin	ma-ʔasin	salty
	*qasin-i	åsn-i	to pickle, apply salt
41.	*buaq	pugʷaʔ	betel nut
42.	*quzan	uchan	rain
43.	*qənay	unay	sand
44.	*tuqəlaŋ	toʔlaŋ	bone
45.	*ma-qəti	måʔti	low, of tide
46.	*bukbuk	poppu	powder from decay
47.	*layaR	lådzak	sail
48.	*dəmdəm	homhum	dark
49.	*nabək	nåpu	surf, breakers
50.	*bakbak	påppa	strip off bark
51.	*lahud (> lawud)	lågu	seaward; north, west
52.	*kita	hita	we (incl.)
53.	*qipil	ifit	a tree: *Intsia bijuga*
54.	*niuR	nidzuk	coconut tree

INSTRUCTIONS/QUESTIONS:

1. Does Chamorro show final devoicing? If so, what is the evidence for this change? (List examples.)
2. What is the source of Chamorro /g^w/? List numbers of examples. Is it necessary to assume ordering relations to find a unitary source for this phoneme? Is there a parallel source for *dz*? Be specific.
3. Is the contrast of /g/ and /g^w/ neutralised in any environment? If so, where? (List examples.)
4. What are the reflexes of PMP *l as syllable onset and syllable coda in Chamorro?
5. Is there a phonetically surprising merger in Chamorro? What is it? (Cite examples.)

LEVEL 3: ADVANCED

SOUND CHANGE PROBLEM 14

PMP to Palauan (Republic of Palau, western Micronesia)

Background. PMP *j probably was a palatalised voiced velar stop ([gʲ]). Pre-Palauan stress was penultimate. The standard orthography has been altered to better represent the phonemic changes that have occurred.

No.	PMP	Palauan	
01.	*nunuk	lulk	banyan
02.	*batu	bað	stone
03.	*susu	tut	breast
04.	*daRaq	rásə?	blood
05.	*uRat	ŋurð	vein, artery
06.	*lumut	yumð	moss; algae
07.	*qatay	?að	liver
08.	*ba-b<in>ahi (> babinay)	babíl	female
09.	*laləj	yays	housefly
10.	*duha	e-rú-ŋ	two
11.	*kanasay	kəlát	mullet
12.	*lima	e-yím	five
13.	*hikan (> ikan)	ŋíkəl	fish
14.	*pitu	e-wíð	seven
15.	*qajəŋ	?as	charcoal; soot
16.	*sawaq	tao?	channel
17.	*layaR	yars	sail
18.	*titay	ðið	bridge
19.	*ibəR	ŋíbəs	drooling saliva
20.	*zalan	rayl	path, road
21.	*qaləjaw	?yos	sun
22.	*kutu	kuð	louse
23.	*tian	ðiyl	abdomen
24.	*hapuy (> api)	ŋaw	fire
25.	*təRas	ðort	ironwood tree
26.	*puki	wuk	vagina
27.	*anay	ŋal	termite

28.	*ia	ŋiy	3sg.
29.	*manuk	malk	chicken
30.	*buaq	buwʔ	betel nut
31.	*laŋit	yaŋð	sky
32.	*habaRat (> abaRat)	ŋəbárð	west (wind)
33.	*paniki	olík	flying fox
34.	*dapdap	róro	Indian coral tree
35.	*anak	ŋálək	child
36.	*balabaw	byab	rat
37.	*ləñəb	yéləb	submerge; flood
38.	*qapuR	ʔaws	betel lime
39.	*ijuŋ	íis	nose
40.	*aku	ŋak	I, me
41.	*zaRum	rasm	needle
42.	*ləbaq	yóbəʔ	ravine, valley
43.	*kaRakap	kəsáko	land crab
44.	*aRuhu (> aRu)	ŋas	casuarina
45.	*dalij	rays	buttress root; root
46.	*Ratus	ðart	hundred
47.	*quzan	ʔull	rain
48.	*qatəp	ʔáðo	roof
49.	*pəñu	wel	green turtle
50.	*qayam	ʔarm	animal
51.	*ŋipən	wíŋəl	tooth
52.	*dəpa	réo	fathom
53.	*banua	bəlúw	village
54.	*kahiw (> kayu kayu)	kərrəkár	tree, wood
55.	*ŋajan	ŋakl	name
56.	*ənəm (> ənə ənəm)	-lóləm	six

INSTRUCTIONS/QUESTIONS:

1. What is the Palauan reflex of PMP *R?
2. There are two sources for Palauan ŋ-. One is PMP *ŋ-. What is the other?
3. What is the relative order of changes affecting *n, *l, and *y? Those affecting *R, *s, and *t? State explicitly how you know this.
4. Two forms show consonant metathesis. Which ones are they, and what are the transposing segments in each case?

PROBLEMS: LEVEL 3

SOUND CHANGE PROBLEM 15

PMP to Taba, Buli, Numfor and Munggui (northeast Indonesia)

Background. Taba, Buli, Numfor and Munggui belong to the South Halmahera-West New Guinea (SHWNG) branch of Austronesian languages, spread over a roughly 700-mile stretch of land and sea in northeast Indonesia. These languages are distributed geographically from west to east in the order stated, with Taba and Buli being western neighbours that are more closely related to one another than they are to any of the eastern languages, and Numfor and Munggui being eastern neighbours that are more closely related to one another than they are to any of the western languages.

No.	PMP	Taba	Buli	Numfor	Munggui	
01.	*kutu	kut	ut	uk	utu	louse
02.	*təlu	p-tol	tol	kor	bo-toru	three
03.	*manuk	manik	mani	man	n/a	bird
04.	*hikan	ian	ian	ian	ty-ian	fish
05.	*Rəbək	opak	opa	rob	yoba	to fly
06.	*kasaw	kas	as	as	aso	rafter
07.	*lima	p-lim	lim	rim	bo-rim	five
08.	*hajək	asok	aso	yas	yaso	smell
09.	*pitu	p-hit	fit	fik	bo-itu	seven
10.	*paniki	pnik	fni	fni	nii	fruit bat

INSTRUCTIONS/QUESTIONS:

1. Consider only reflexes of *k and vowels word-finally (*k that remained intervocalic after the loss of final vowels disappeared in all languages, seen here in 'fish'; this can be ignored for purposes of this problem). Is there any evidence that the order of these two changes differs across languages? Which languages are affected, and what is the order of changes in each?

2. How might this ordering difference be accounted for in a theory of language change?

3. Are there other ways to explain the facts? Describe explicitly how you might account for the data without an appeal to rule reordering.

4. Can you show that one alternative is superior to the other? In what ways?

SOUND CHANGE PROBLEM 16

Proto-Austronesian (PAN) to Thao (central Taiwan)

Background. Thao is down to a handful of speakers living in what the government of Taiwan has promoted as the Thao Cultural Village at the popular tourist location of Sun Moon Lake in the mountains of central Taiwan. It is the last surviving member of the Western Plains subgroup, which appears to be a primary branch of the Austronesian language family. The IPA values of the orthographic symbols used here are:

PAN *s probably = [ʃ]   Thao sh = [ʃ]
PAN *S probably = [s]   Thao c = [θ]
PAN *C probably = [ts]   Thao z = [ð]
PAN *N probably = [ʎ]   Thao q = [q]
PAN *z probably = [ɟ]   Thao lh = [ɬ]

No.	PAN	Thao	
01.	*lima	rima	five
02.	*susu	tutu	breast
03.	*kumiS	kumish	beard
04.	*batu	fatu	stone
05.	*Cakaw	cakaw	steal
06.	*aNak (> aNa-aNak)	azazak	child
07.	*CaqiS	shaqish	sew
08.	*Sinaw	shinaw	wash (dishes)
09.	*dapaN	sapaz	sole of the foot
10.	*kuCu	kucu	head louse
11.	*baRuj	falhuz	dove sp.
12.	*kudkud	kuskus	hoof; foot, leg
13.	*zaRum	lhalhum	needle
14.	*Sidi	sisi	serow, wild goat
15.	*bəRuS	flhush	a plant: *Rhus semialata*
16.	*daNum	sazum	water
17.	*zalan	saran	road, path
18.	*RaSuŋ	lhashun	ambush
19.	*RaməC	lhamic	root
20.	*diRi	lhilhi	stand
21.	*daqiS	shaqish	face

22.	*Səpat	shpat	four
23.	*daya	saya	upriver
24.	*Cau	cau	person, human being
25.	*SəRəC (> əRəC)	lhic	tight, constricted
26.	*quzaN	qusaz	rain
27.	*taRa	talha	wait
28.	*dakəS	shakish	camphor laurel
29.	*kuRu	kulhu	scabies
30.	*duma	suma	other people
31.	*saləŋ	tarin	pine tree
32.	*daRa	lhalha	Formosan maple
33.	*Sajək	shazik	smell, odour
34.	*RiNaS	lhizash	tail feathers
35.	*bukəS	fukish	head hair
36.	*qəlud	qrus	housepost
37.	*qaRəm	qalhum	pangolin, anteater
38.	*pija	piza	how much/how many?
39.	*qaləb	qaruf	knee
40.	*qətut	qtut	fart
41.	*piRaS	pilhash	roe, fish or crab eggs
42.	*ma-ləmləm	ma-rumrum	dim, unlit
43.	*dakəp	sakup	catch, seize
44.	*Cali	lhari	taro
45.	*Cəməl	lhmir	grass, herbs
46.	*luCuŋ	rucun	Formosan rock monkey
47.	*Caliŋa	lharina	ear
48.	*Cukud	sukus	punting pole
49.	*CəkəS	shkish	slender bamboo sp.
50.	*tuzuq	tusuq	to point
51.	*asu	atu	dog
52.	*huRaC	ulhac	vein, tendon
53.	*aCay	acay	to die
54.	*Cumay	cumay	Formosan black bear
55.	*zamuq	samuq	dew

INSTRUCTIONS/QUESTIONS:

1. List each reflex of PAN *C, *d, *z and *S in Thao.

2. If there is more than one reflex of each of these proto-phonemes what is the reflex that occurs in the 'elsewhere' environment, and what are the conditions for splitting?
3. Is there a global property shared by all of these conditions, and if so what is it?
4. How might this data be used to raise questions about accepted natural classes in phonological theory?
5. What are the conditions for the split of last-syllable schwa, and which examples support your statement?

SOUND CHANGE PROBLEM 17

Proto-Manus (PMAN) to Levei (Manus, Admiralty Islands, Papua New Guinea)

Background. Levei is a small language spoken in the western part of the island of Manus in the Bismarck Archipelago, Papua New Guinea. The symbol 'V' represents a vowel of indeterminate quality, a hyphen indicates an obligatorily possessed noun, and -ŋ is a possessive suffix.

No.	PMAN	Levei	
01.	*kuro	kʷiŋ	cooking pot
02.	*pose	poh	canoe paddle
03.	*pakiwa	peʔep	shark
04.	*poe	pup	pig
05.	*koro	koŋ	village
06.	*yapaya	yaha	NW monsoon
07.	*sama	saŋ	outrigger float
08.	*alu	aŋ	barracuda sp.
09.	*balu	pʷaŋ	pigeon
10.	*putu	puk	a tree: *Barringtonia* sp.
11.	*sala	soŋ	path, road
12.	*alia	lip	ginger
13.	*puaya	puep	crocodile
14.	*one	oŋ	sand
15.	*ia	ip	3sg.
16.	*ñamu	nuŋ	mosquito
17.	*kulu	kuŋ	breadfruit
18.	*kayu	kep	tree, wood
19.	*sa-ŋapulu	ronoh	ten
20.	*sa-ŋatu	ranak	hundred
21.	*dra-	ca-	blood
22.	*ŋoʔo-	noʔo-	nose
23.	*pula	pʷiŋ	moon
24.	*kalia	kalip	grouper
25.	*drui-	cui-	bone
26.	*pudri	puŋ	banana
27.	*buleV	pʷilip	rat

28.	*mwata	mʷok	snake
29.	*kanawe	kanap	seagull
30.	*lipo-	lihi-	tooth
31.	*dranu	ceŋ	freshwater
32.	*kutu	kuh	louse
33.	*payi	pep	stingray
34.	*muta	muh	to vomit
35.	*laya	pe-lep	sail
36.	*katapa	katah	frigate bird
37.	*mati	mak	dry reef
38.	*kuita	kuih	octopus
39.	*puki	pʷiʔi-	vulva, vagina
40.	*tokalau	tolau	east wind
41.	*patu	pok	stone
42.	*-ña	-ŋ	3sg.
43.	*ipi	ih	a tree: *Intsia bijuga*
44.	*matiru	mesiŋ	sleep
45.	*sulu	suŋ	coconut leaf torch
46.	*taŋi	e-tæŋ	weep, cry
47.	*kawasV	kawah	friend
48.	*yapi	jih	fire
49.	*ñalato	nolok	stinging nettle
50.	*tama-gu	tomo	my father
51.	*tina-gu	sine-ŋ	your mother
52.	*tikV	si	to plait, weave
53.	*kayalV	kayaŋ	pandanus with edible fruit
54.	*watiV	wasi	monitor lizard

INSTRUCTIONS/QUESTIONS:

1. What are the sources of Levei -ŋ? List the numbers of examples for each source.

     What generalisation can you reach based on this collection of examples?

2. List the reflexes of Proto-Manus *t in Levei. What are the conditioning factors for each development?

3. What are the sources of Levei -ɸ? Do you have any suggestions about how this surprising change may have come about?

SOUND CHANGE PROBLEM 18

PMP to Bario Kelabit (northern Sarawak, Malaysian Borneo)

Background. The Bario dialect of Kelabit has three stop series: voiceless *p*, *t*, *k*, *ʔ*, voiced *b*, *d*, *j* (rare), *g*, and voiced aspirated *bh*, *dh*, *gh*. The voiced aspirates begin voiced and end voiceless. For some speakers they sound like clusters [bp], [dt], [gk], but structural information shows that they are unit phonemes. For other speakers there is some aspiration in the release, a feature that is especially prominent for [dt], which may vary between [dtʰ] and [dʤʰ]. Surface voiced aspirates occur only intervocalically. These alternate under suffixation with their plain voiced counterparts, both in deaspirating underlying voiced aspirates, as in [tə́bpʰəŋ] 'felling of trees' : [təbə́ŋ:ən] 'fell it!' (imper.), and in creating surface voiced aspirates from underlying plain voiced stops, as in [ŋárəg] (/ŋ-arəg/) 'break into crumbs' : [rə́gkʰən] (/arəg-ən/) 'be broken into crumbs'. Stress is penultimate in the word, and so shifts rightward under suffixation.

The voiced aspirates are approximately twice the length of the plain voiced stops, and most consonants are automatically geminated after a stressed schwa, hence /əpat/ = [ə́p:at] 'four' (cp. /apad/ = [apad] 'mountain range'), /pətuk/ = [pə́t:ʊk] 'bump the head' (cp. /patuk/ = [pátʊk] 'arrowhead'), /təkən/ = [tə́k:ən] 'punting pole' (cp. /takuŋ/ = [tákʊŋ] 'pond'), /təlu/ = [tə́l:uh] 'three' (cp. /aluh/ = [áluh] 'eight'), etc. Compare the absence of gemination in /kəlabət/ = [kəlábət] 'gibbon' or /kəlio/ = [kəlíjo] 'wild bovid', where the consonant follows an unstressed schwa, or the phonetic alternation in forms such as /gətəp/ = [gə́t:əp] 'bite' vs. /gətəp-ən/ = [gətə́p:ən] 'be bitten', where stress shift correlates with allophonic gemination (Blust 2006). Finally, note that in Kelabit and many other Austronesian languages the schwa is treated as a 'like vowel' in processes of crasis, or vowel coalescence.

No.	PMP	Bario Kelabit	
01.	*bahaR (> baR > əbbaR >)	əbʰar	loincloth
02.	*qali-matək	ləmatək	jungle leech
03.	*qaləjaw (> əldaw > əddo >)	ədʰo	day
04.	*təlu	təluh	three
05.	*qatimun	simun	cucumber
06.	*bahaq (> baʔ > əbbaʔ >)	əbʰaʔ	floodwater; water
07.	*qatay	ate	liver
08.	*dəmdəm (> dəddəm >)	dədʰəm	dark
09.	*təbu	təbʰuh	sugar cane
10.	*dakdak (> dəddak >)	dədʰak	tamp down earth

11.	*qapəju	pədʰuh	gall (bladder)
12.	*bakbak (> bəbbak >)	bəbʰak	peel off; torn
13.	*dadaŋ	dadaŋ	warm by a fire
14.	*batu	batuh	stone
15.	*tuktuk	tutuk	pound; pestle
16.	*bubu	bubuh	bamboo fish trap
17.	*tina-q	sina?	mother
18.	*butbut	bubʰut	pluck, pull out
19.	*Ratus	ratu	hundred
20.	*bədiq	bədʰi?	vulva, vagina
21.	*qatəluR	tərur	egg
22.	*basəq	baa?	wet
23.	*paqa	pa?əh	thigh
24.	*buhək (> buk > əbbuk>)	əbʰuk	head hair
25.	*salaR	arar	nest
26.	*bəkbək (> bəbbək >)	bəbʰək	crush by pounding
27.	*pagpag	pəpag	slap
28.	*ini	inih	this
29.	*huluR	urur	fall; to lower
30.	*baRa	barəh	ember
31.	*baqəRu	bəruh	new
32.	*kaRaw	karo	scratch an itch
33.	*bunbun (> bubbun >)	bubʰun	heap, pile
34.	*qaləsəm	laam	sour
35.	*quləj	uləd	maggot
36.	*timəRaq	səməra?	tin; lead
37.	*buqaya	bayəh	crocodile
38.	*taqi	ta?ih	faeces
39.	*tuqa	tu?əh	hard, strong
40.	*kudkud	kukud	hoof

QUESTIONS:

1. What is the source of the typologically rare voiced aspirates of Bario Kelabit?

2. What are the reflexes of PMP *l in Bario Kelabit? What type of conditioning plays a role in the split of this proto-phoneme?

3. What are the reflexes of PMP *t in Bario Kelabit? What type of conditioning factor plays a role in the split of this proto-phoneme?

SOUND CHANGE PROBLEM 19

Proto-North Sarawak (PNS) to Long Terawan Berawan (Sarawak, Malaysian Borneo)

Background. Of the four Berawan dialects (Long Terawan, Long Teru, Batu Belah, Long Jegan) Long Terawan is the most divergent, and may form a separate but closely related language. These language communities have an unusually complex phonological history, some aspects of which may be difficult to resolve without more data. A few changes, as *d > *l* in example (1), are unique or nearly so and can be ignored in stating generalisations. In the data given here *j* and *c* represent voiced and voiceless palatal affricates. Note also that stress is penultimate, and while consonants are regularly geminated after penultimate schwa gemination is not written in this environment, since it can be stated by rule.

No.	PNS	Long Terawan Berawan	
01.	*dua	ləbih	two
02.	*təlu	təloh	three
03.	*lima	dimməh	five
04.	*pulu?	pulo	ten
05.	*bəRuaŋ	kəbiŋ	sun bear
06.	*dəRian	kəjin	durian
07.	*bəRas	bəkəh	husked rice
08.	*mə-buat	kəbəi?	long
09.	*mə-bəsuR	kəco	satiated
10.	*mə-Raya	kijjih	big, large
11.	*Ratus	gitoh	hundred
12.	*Ribu	gikkuh	thousand
13.	*paRa	pakkih	storage rack
14.	*lakaw	lakaw	walk
15.	*aku	akkuh	1sg., I
16.	*batuk	bito?	neck
17.	*mata	mattəh	eye
18.	*bulu	bulluh	body hair, feathers
19.	*ikuR	iko	tail
20.	*kutu	kuttoh	head louse
21.	*təmədʰuR	təməcu	rhinoceros
22.	*duRi	dukkih	thorn

23.	*kayu	kajjuh	wood, tree
24.	*daʔun	dion	leaf
25.	*bawaŋ	biwaŋ	open expanse; lake
26.	*ujan	usin	rain
27.	*təbʰu	təpuh	sugar cane
28.	*abu	akkuh	ashes
29.	*batu	bittoh	stone
30.	*bulan	bulin	moon
31.	*tali	talleh	rope
32.	*tuba	tukkih	fish poison
33.	*pusəd	pusən	navel
34.	*buluʔ	bulu	large bamboo sp.
35.	*ubi	ukkih	yam
36.	*aləb	ləm	knee
37.	*diRi	dəkih	housepost
38.	*daʔan	diʔən	branch
39.	*lulud	lulon	shin
40.	*tadi	tarreh	younger sibling
41.	*atay	atay	liver
42.	*kuyad	kuyan	grey langur
43.	*tanaʔ	tana	earth, soil
44.	*baRa	bikkih	shoulder
45.	*bataŋ	bitaŋ	tree trunk, log
46.	*likud	likon	back (of body)
47.	*tuduR	turo	sleep
48.	*pusuʔ	atay puso	heart
49.	*asu	accoh	dog
50.	*ukab	ukam	hatch (egg)
51.	*bəRat	bəkaiʔ	heavy
52.	*lia	ləjəh	ginger
53.	*bubu	bukkuh	bamboo fish trap
54.	*paʔa	paʔəh	thigh
55.	*siku	sikkoh	elbow
56.	*Rusuk	gusoʔ	chest
57.	*udu	urroh	grass
58.	*Rataʔ	gita	coconut milk
59.	*əbʰaʔ	pi	water
60.	*anak	anaʔ	child
61.	*udaŋ	uraŋ	shrimp
62.	*laləd	dilən	housefly

63.	*ŋadan	ŋaran	name
64.	*tawa	tabbəh	laugh
65.	*uləd	ulən	maggot, caterpillar
66.	*baya	bijjih	crocodile
67.	*puki	pukkeh	vagina
68.	*bədʰuk	bəcuk	coconut macaque
69.	*paday	paray	riceplant
70.	*təRəp	təki?	k.o. breadfruit tree
71.	*balu	billoh	widow
72.	*k<um>an	kuman	eat
73.	*tumid	tumin	heel
74.	*laki	lakkeh	man, male
75.	*Rəjʰan	acin	ladder
76.	*kapaj	kapan	thick, as a board
77.	*uta?	uta	vomit
78.	*dədʰuR	dicu	woman, female
79.	*ia	jəh	3sg.
80.	*puan	pəban	squirrel
81.	*tu?u	tu?oh	true, real

INSTRUCTIONS/QUESTIONS:

1. How did the PNS vowel sequences *-ua- and *-ia- develop in Long Terawan Berawan? (Cite examples by number.)
2. Under what conditions did phonemic geminates develop in this language? Be specific, and cite numbered examples. Does this change need to be ordered in relation to any other? Which ones and how? Note that consonants automatically geminate after penultimate schwa, and gemination is not written in this position.
3. Are there any phonemes that did not geminate under the usual conditions? Which ones?
4. What are the reflexes of PNS *a in Long Terawan Berawan, and what conditioned this split?
5. List the reflexes of PNS *b, *d and *R in all positions, citing examples by number. Is there anything unusual in this pattern? If so, what is it?

SOUND CHANGE PROBLEM 20

PNS to Miri (Sarawak, Malaysian Borneo)

Background. Assumed phonetic values for Proto-North Sarawak phonemes are: *j : voiced palatal affricate; *R : alveolar or uvular trill; bʰ, dʰ : voiced aspirates (voiced stops with terminal devoicing that probably carried into the onset of a following vowel). PMP *R contrasted with *r (an alveolar tap); there is some evidence that the *r/R contrast persisted in PNS, but it is limited. Miri *r* is an alveolar tap.

No.	PNS	Miri	
01.	*mata	matah	eye
02.	*tali	talayh	rope
03.	*ujan	ujen	rain
04.	*tama	tamah	father
05.	*baya	bajeh	crocodile
06.	*dua	dəbeh	two
07.	*danaw 'lake'	danaw	pond
08.	*adan	aden	name
09.	*bəRat	baret	heavy
10.	*dəpa	dəpah	fathom
11.	*daRaʔ	dareʔ	blood
12.	*buaʔ	beʔ	fruit
13.	*baRa 'shoulder'	bareh	arm
14.	*butan	butan	coconut
15.	*lia	ləjeh	ginger
16.	*uban	uben	gray hair
17.	*anak	anak	child
18.	*tian	təjen	belly
19.	*bana	banah	husband
20.	*ədʰan	asen	notched log ladder
21.	*bəRas	bəre	husked rice
22.	*baŋaw	baŋaw	heron
23.	*tuba	tubeh	fish poison
24.	*əbʰaʔ	feʔ	water
25.	*jalan	jalen	path, road
26.	*bakaw	bakaw	mangrove

27.	*ədʰa	seh	one
28.	*ma-kapal	mafal	thick
29.	*pagər	fager	fence
30.	*anak	anak	child
31.	*diaʔ	jeʔ	good
32.	*daʔan	daʔen	branch
33.	*bəbʰər 'fan'	fer	blow on
34.	*buat	bet	long
35.	*baŋaR	baŋar	stench
36.	*bituka	batukah	intestines
37.	*busak	buek	flower
38.	*pusəd	fuat	navel
39.	*paʔa	faʔah	thigh; leg
40.	*kulit	ulayt	skin, bark of tree
41.	*təlu	təlawh	three
42.	*gatəl	gatal	itchy
43.	*daləm	(d)alem	in, inside
44.	*Ratus	ma-rataw	100
45.	*əsi	sayh	meat, flesh
46.	*batu	batawh	stone
47.	*lipis	lifay	thin, of materials
48.	*laŋit	laŋayt	sky
49.	*masin	masayn	salty; sweet
50.	*taŋis	taŋay	weep, cry
51.	*upan	ufan	bait
52.	*alat	alat	k.o. basket

INSTRUCTIONS/QUESTIONS:

1. What are the Miri reflexes of PNS last-syllable high vowels?
2. What were the conditions for fronting of last-syllable *a or *ə in Miri?
3. Do blocking consonants play a role in apparent exceptions to low vowel fronting? What are the blocking consonants, and which examples illustrate their operation?
4. How do the conditions for low vowel fronting in Miri differ from those in Long Terawan Berawan (Problem 19)? Be specific.

PROBLEMS: LEVEL 3

SOUND CHANGE PROBLEM 21

POC to Chuukese (Caroline islands, Micronesia)

Background. The historical phonoloogy of Chuukese (Trukese) has been studied in some detail, beginning with Dyen (1949), and continuing with the broader work of Jackson (1983). The digraph *ch* is described by Goodenough and Sugita (1980: xvi) as 'a voiceless, usually retroflex, affricate, voiced (unless double) between vowels. For some speakers it is an alveo-palatal affricate (like English *ch* and *j*), and for some it is an alveolar affricate'. The /y/ is a palatal glide, and vowels have their IPA values. Final hyphen marks bound forms.

No.	POC	Chuukese	
1a.	*tina	iin	mother
1b.	*tina-ña	ina-n	his/her mother
2a.	*tama	saam	father
2b.	*tama-ña	sama-n ~ sema-n	his/her father
3a.	*natu	naaw	child
3b.	*natu-ña	nəwi-n	his/her child
4a.	*Rumaq	iimʷ	house
4b.	*Rumaq-ña	imʷa-n	his/her house
05.	*qatop	ɔɔs	roof
6a.	*kulit	siin	skin
6b.	*kulit-ña	sini-n	his/her skin
7a.	*qate	æææyæ	liver
7b.	*qate-ña	æææyææ-n	his/her liver
8a.	*mata	maas	eye, face
8b.	*mata-ña	masa-n ~ mesa-n	his/her face
9a.	*tasik	sæææt	sea, saltwater
9b.	*tasik-i	seti	sea (in compounds)
10.	*kutu	kɨɨ	louse
11a.	*laŋit	næææŋ	sky, heaven
11b.	*laŋit-i	neŋi	sky (in compounds)
12.	*kami	æææm	we (excl.)
13.	*qusan	wɨɨt	rain
14.	*rua	riwa-	two
15.	*tolu	wɨnɨ-	three

16.	*pati	fææ-	four
17.	*lima	niim, nima-	five
18.	*onom	woon, wono-	six
19.	*pitu	fiis, fisu-	seven
20.	*walu	waan, wani-	eight
21.	*siwa (> sisiwa)	ttiiw	nine
22a.	*api	ææf	fire
22b.	*api-ña	efi-n	his fire
23.	*qumun	wuumʷ	earth oven
24.	*quraŋ	wiir	lobster
25.	*pa-Rapi (> papi)	fææf	dinner, evening meal
26.	*qanitu	ani, əni	spirit of the dead
27.	*kuRita (> kʷita)	kiis	octopus
28.	*salan	aan	path, road
29.	*susu	tti	breast
30.	*taliŋa	seniŋ	ear
31.	*lumut	nuumʷ	seaweed, moss
32a.	*tali	sææn	rope
32b.	*tali-ni	senin	rope of
33.	*masakit	metek	painful
34.	*roŋoR	roŋ, roŋo-roŋ	hear
35.	*pudi	wuuch	banana
36.	*nopu	noow	scorpion fish
37.	*laŋo	nɔɔŋ	housefly
38.	*kima	siim	giant clam
39a.	*patu	faaw	stone
39b.	*patu-ni	fəwi-n	stone of
40.	*tutuk-i	ssuk	knock, rap, beat
41.	*muri	mʷiri-	afterwards
42.	*pukot	wuuk	dragnet
43.	*puliq	pʷiin	cowrie shell
44.	*kilala (> kila)	siin	know
45.	*mate	mææ-	die, dead
46.	*topu	woow	sugar cane
47.	*motus	mʷii-	break off
48.	*qumaŋ	wumʷowumʷ	hermit crab

INSTRUCTIONS/QUESTIONS:

1. List the Chuukese reflexes of Proto-Oceanic *t, stating the conditions under which each is found. Are there any exceptions to this pattern? If so, state them, with examples. Note that all final consonants were lost in Proto-Micronesian, and therefore do not figure in later changes, and that rounded vowels (*o, *u) that came to be initial developed a labiovelar glide onset.
2. List the Chuukese reflexes of Proto-Oceanic *s. How do you think POC *t and *s avoided merger?
3. Consider pairs of words like (1) and (2), which consist of nominal stems and their suffixed counterparts. The length of the vowel in unsuffixed monosyllables has been viewed traditionally as due to a process of 'compensatory lengthening'; when the final vowel was lost the remaining stem vowel lengthened to maintain a bimoraic word, as an expression of the so-called 'minimal word constraint'. Which examples raise problems for this analysis, and why? Be specific.
4. How did the Chuukese labiovelars *mw* and *pw* develop? (List examples and full details.)

SOUND CHANGE PROBLEM 22

Proto-Kelabit-Lun Dayeh (PKLD) to Sa'ban (northern Sarawak, Malaysian Borneo)

Background. Sa'ban is a small language, surrounded by larger and more influential ethnic groups in interior Borneo. It's phoneme inventory is typologically very aberrant for the region, with perhaps nine vowels, geminated stops, nasals, fricatives and liquids only word-initially, and voiceless sonorants. The symbols *c* and *j* represent palatal affricates, doubled consonants are geminates, *hm*, *hn* and *hŋ* are voiceless nasals, and *hl* and *hr* are voiceless liquids. Sa'ban stress is final.

No.	PKLD	Sa'ban	
01.	*aban	abin	because
02.	*agag	ajiəp	rice sieve
03.	*bada	bidi	sand
04.	*baka	aka	wild pig
05.	*bakul	bakol	basket
06.	*bariw	biriəw	wind
07.	*bataʔ	ataʔ	green
08.	*batuh	ataw	stone
09.	*bəbʰən	pən	cover, lid
10.	*bədʰək	sək	nasal mucus
11.	*bədʰuk	ssuək	coconut monkey
12.	*bəli	bləy	purchases
13.	*bibir	ibiəl	lip
14.	*buaʔ	wəiʔ	fruit
15.	*bulan	blin	moon
16.	*buruk	bruək	rotten
17.	*dadan	adin	old, long time
18.	*dadaŋ	ladeəŋ	heat of a fire
19.	*dalan	alin	path, road
20.	*daʔan	laʔin	branch
21.	*daraʔ	areəʔ	blood
22.	*duəh	wəh	two
23.	*gatəl	jatəl	itch, itchy
24.	*gənuluh	jənləw	empty rice head

25.	*giləg	peləp	skittish
26.	*gətiməl	hməl	bedbug
27.	*tina-n	hna-n	his/her mother
28.	*inih	nay	this, these
29.	*k-inih	hnay	this way; now
30.	*ikuh	cəw	elbow
31.	*kapal	apal	thick
32.	*kayuh	ayəw	wood, tree
33.	*kəmuʔ	hmuʔ	short
34.	*kukud	kkuət	foot, leg
35.	*kulat	loət	mushroom
36.	*lawid	awit	fish
37.	*layuh	layəw	wither
38.	*liməh	emah	five
39.	*matəh	atah	eye
40.	*məri	mray	dried up (stream)
41.	*muka	ŋkoə	early
42.	*pədʰuh	ssəw	gall (bladder)
43.	*pənuʔ	hnoʔ	full (container)
44.	*pəpag	ppap	a slap
45.	*pudut	dduət	way, manner; shape
46.	*puluʔ	pluʔ	ten
47.	*raʔit	laʔet	raft
48.	*mə-ratu	p-lataw	hundred
49.	*rəbʰun	ləpun	smoke
50.	*riər	liəl	turn the head
51.	*rinuh	enaw	winnowing basket
52.	*rumaʔ	maʔ	house
53.	*rurug	hrop	fall; pour out
54.	*rurut	rruət	bring down
55.	*sinuŋ	hnoəŋ	happy
56.	*siri	hray	straight
57.	*tanaʔ	tanaʔ	earth
58.	*təbʰuh	ppəw	sugar cane
59.	*təŋəb	hŋəp	riverbank
60.	*tərur	hrol	egg
61.	*tubaŋ	bbeəŋ	wild cat
62.	*tuduʔ	ddəuʔ	seven
63.	*adaʔ	adəiʔ	shadow; ghost
64.	*gərawat	pəlawət	tangled; complicated

65.	*tulaŋ	hloəŋ	bone
66.	*tulud	hlut	to fly
67.	*tutud	ttuət	burning
68.	*uab	wap	to yawn
69.	*ubi	bəy	yam; tapioca
70.	*udan	din	rain
71.	*uluh	ləw	head
72.	*uta?	toə?	vomit
73.	*uyut	yuət	carrying basket
74.	*ənəm	nəm	six
75.	*iban	ibin	in-law
76.	*iləg	eləp	separate, divorce
77.	*ilək	elək	armpit
78.	*irup	erop	drink

QUESTIONS/INSTRUCTIONS:

1. In most languages phonological erosion at word margins takes place at the 'right edge', or end of words. Is this true of Sa'ban? What general conditions can you state for consonant loss in this language? For vowel loss?

2. List the reflexes of the plain voiced obstruents *b, *d and *g. Which of these reflexes can be characterised as products of natural, phonetically motivated change? Which are hard to characterise in these terms?

3. What is the source of the Sa'ban geminates? Of the voiceless sonorants? (List the numbers for examples of each.)

4. How does low vowel fronting appear to work in Sa'ban? Is it more like the related phenomenon in Miri, or in Long Terawan Berawan?

SOUND CHANGE PROBLEM 23

PMP to Hawu (Lesser Sunda Islands, eastern Indonesia)

Background. Intermediate forms are given in some cases to make it easier to relate Proto-Malayo-Polynesian to Hawu. Note that item 14 shows consonant metathesis, and item 15 may reflect a fossilised verb-forming process of homorganic nasal substitution that is still active in most languages of the Philippines and western Indonesia, as well as in Malagasy, Chamorro and Palauan.

No.	PMP	Hawu	
01.	*b-in-ahi (> binay > bine)	bəni	woman
02.	*buta	ɓədu	blind
03.	*tuna	dəno	freshwater eel
04.	*isa	əhi	one
05.	*pusəj (> uha)	əhu	navel
06.	*hikət (> ika)	əki	tie, bind
07.	*kudən (> ura)	əru	cooking pot
08.	*Rumaq (> uma)	əmu	house
09.	*sukat	həku	measure
10.	*lima	ləmi	five
11.	*ma-qitəm (> mitəm > mita)	mədi	black
12.	*um-utaq (> muta)	mədu	vomit
13.	*miñak	məñi	fat, oil
14.	*qulun-an (> luna)	nəlu	headrest
15.	*kita	ŋədi	to see
16.	*ŋuda	ŋəru	young
17.	*pija	pəri	how much/many?
18.	*p-ijan	pəri	when?
19.	*bulan	wəru	moon/month
20.	*baRani (> mbani)	ɓani	brave
21.	*manuk	manu	chicken
22.	*batu	wadu	stone
23.	*qate	ade	liver
24.	*pajay (> pare)	are	riceplant
25.	*laləj	lara	housefly
26.	*anak	ana	child
27.	*mata	mada	eye

28.	*bəli	wəli	buy; price
29.	*əpu	əpu	grandmother
30.	*ənəm	əna	six
31.	*bəkaq	bəka	split
32.	*kulit	kuri	skin
33.	*ma-putiq (> mputi)	pudi	white
34.	*nabək	nawa	wave, surf
35.	*ma-qudip (> murip)	muri	alive
36.	*qanitu (> nitu)	nidu	ghost
37.	*susu	huhu	female breast

INSTRUCTIONS/QUESTIONS:

1. List the vowel changes between PMP and Hawu, giving the numbers of supporting examples.
2. Is there anything in any of these changes that seems unusual? What is it?
3. What alternative explanations might be entertained to account for these changes?

SOUND CHANGE PROBLEM 24

Pre-Sundanese to Sundanese (western Java, Republic of Indonesia)

Background. Sundanese is spoken by nearly 40 million people in both coastal and montane portions of western Java. It is surrounded by speakers of Javanese, a larger and historically more prominent language. The symbol *c* represents a voiceless palatal affricate, and *y* a palatal glide.

No.	Pre-Sundanese	Sundanese	
01.	*wahiR	cai	freshwater; stream
02.	*lawaʔ	lancah	spider
03.	*sawa	sanca	python
04.	*karawaŋ	karancaŋ	openwork
05.	*dəpa	dipa	fathom
06.	*kiwa	kenca	left side
07.	*kawaʔ	kancah	vat, cauldron
08.	*rawa	ranca	swamp
09.	*bahaʔ	caʔah	flood
10.	*dahun	daun	leaf
11.	*badas	cadas	gravel
12.	*bayaR	caya	to pay
13.	*baŋkudu	caŋkudu	*Morinda* sp.
14.	*bataŋ	cataŋ	tree trunk
15.	*buaʔ	buah	fruit
16.	*laban	lancan	oppose; opponent
17.	*banir	canir	buttress root
18.	*bariŋin	cariŋin	banyan, fig tree
19.	*bauŋ	cauŋ	catfish
20.	*baluluk	caruluk	fruit of the sugar palm
21.	*bisul	bisul	pimple
22.	*bayur	cayur	*Pterospermum javanicum*
23.	*katumbar	katuncar	coriander seed
24.	*ləmbaŋ	lincaŋ	swollen with water
25.	*buhək	buʔuk	hair
26.	*luhəʔ	luʔuh	tears; come crying
27.	*baliŋbiŋ	caliŋciŋ	starfruit: *Averroha carambola*

INSTRUCTIONS/QUESTIONS:

1. List all consonant changes between Pre-Sundanese and Sundanese.
2. Are any of these changes surprising? Which ones, and why are they surprising?

PHONOLOGICAL RECONSTRUCTION

(35 problems)

Background

Problems in phonological reconstruction are central to historical linguistics, and this section is consequently longer than others. The format adopted for reconstruction problems includes five steps: (1) reconstruct proto-forms, (2) list sound changes, (3) indicate any necessary ordering relations, (4) list examples of each change by number, (5) discuss issues that may arise in connection with the problem.

In reality some steps precede reconstruction, since it is usually the case that sound correspondences must first be identified, and it must be determined whether they are in complementary distribution or contrast before reconstructions can be proposed. To avoid tedious extensions of the description these will be omitted. However, one type of information which must be collected before doing phonological reconstruction will be given prior to presenting the problems. When confronting a sound correspondence that involves different phonemes in two or more languages, say x : y, the first problem that many students encounter is how to determine directionality: did *x become y, did *y become x, or did both sounds develop from some third proto-phoneme *z?

There are basically two ways to determine the directionality of sound change. The first is through what might be called the 'many-to-one vs. one-to-many' problem. This holds that if Lg. A has two phonemes that correspond in cognate forms to a single phoneme in Lg. B in the same environment the optimal solution is to treat Lg. A as conservative and Lg. B as innovative, since the opposite choice would force the analyst to accept an unconditioned phonemic split:

	*r	*l
Lg. A	r	l
Lg. B	r	r

Despite the famous claims of the Neogrammarians, unconditioned phonemic splits do occur in natural language data, but they are the exception rather than the rule, and it is always good method to try to avoid the recognition of unconditioned phonemic splits if this can be done while remaining faithful to the data.

The second way the directionality of sound change can be determined is based more on experience than on method, and is thus empirical rather than theoretical. Over the course of the past two centuries historical linguists working at first mainly with Indo-European languages, but later in many different language families, have found recurrent patterns of change that can sometimes be confirmed by written records of earlier periods. There are exceptions to these patterns, but the patterns hold in the great majority of cases and so can serve as useful guidelines in deciding directionality. The following remarks are based on information that is readily available to the writer. It is thus biased in favour of data from the Austronesian language family. However, an effort has been made to collect examples of representative changes from languages that belong to other families. The statements on common directions of sound change which appear below represent an ongoing process of information collection, and will no doubt be modified in some ways as more data on sound change from a wide range of language families become available.

Class changes

The following changes affect entire *classes* of segments.

1. **Voicing of stops**. Voiceless stops are commonly voiced intervocalically, or when following a nasal (hence: in voiced environments).

2. **Final devoicing**. Voiced stops tend to devoice word-finally. Examples are seen in German, and in such Austronesian languages as Malay, Kenyah and Chamorro.

3. **Merger as final glottal stop**. If voiceless stops merge in final
   position they are likely to merge as glottal stop. Examples include
   several Austronesian languages (Berawan of northern Sarawak,
   Buginese and Makasarese of southern Sulawesi).

4. **Intervocalic spirantisation**. Voiced stops may become fricatives in intervocalic position. Usually, *b becomes a voiced bilabial
   fricative [ß] or a labiodental fricative [v], and *g becomes a voiced
   velar fricative [ɣ], but *d becomes [r] at least as often as it becomes
   [ð] or [z]. Spanish changed Latin intervocalic voiceless stops to
   voiced bilabial, interdental and velar fricatives. Western Bukidnon
   Manobo of the southern Philippines, reflects *-b-, *-d- and *-g- as
   -v-, -r/-z- and [ɣ] respectively.

5. **Nasal place assimilation**. Nasals tend to assimilate in place of
   articulation to a following obstruent (stop, affricate, fricative).
   However, clusters of velar nasal + /s/ may occur even when no
   other heterorganic nasal + obstruent cluster is found. A further
   development in some languages is for the preconsonantal nasal to
   assimilate *fully* to a following obstruent, producing geminates. This
   is more likely to happen with nasal + voiceless obstruent than with
   nasal + voiced obstruent. The geminate consonant may then
   reduce, yielding a simple stop.

6. **Merger as final velar nasal**. Over time nasals tend to merge
   word-finally as -/ŋ/. This generally seems to proceed in two steps:
   (1) *m and *n merge as -/n/, (2) *n (from both sources) and *ŋ
   merge as –ŋ. Examples include Mandarin Chinese, and such
   Austronesian languages as Buginese or Makasarese of south
   Sulawesi in Indonesia.

7. **Loss of final consonants**. Word-final consonants tend to be
   lost. This can be seen as a move toward the optimal syllable type:
   CV. This has happened in many Austronesian languages, including
   Nias (aka Niha), spoken in the Barrier islands west of Sumatra,
   many of the languages of Sulawesi in central Indonesia, Bimanese,
   spoken in the Lesser Sunda Islands of Indonesia, and in most of
   the Austronesian languages of the Pacific region, including Fijian
   and the Polynesian languages, among many others. In other Austronesian languages, as Malagasy, spoken in Madagascar, or Mussau

or Dobuan, spoken in western Melanesia, supporting vowels have been added to create open syllables (e.g. Proto-Malayo-Polynesian *laŋit > Malagasy *lanitra* 'sky', *bulan > Mussau *ulana* 'moon').

8. **Weakening of unstressed vowels**. Unstressed vowels tend to be weakened to schwa, or lost. This sometimes happens to word-final vowels, as in the history of the Germanic languages (Anglo-Saxon *mūs-i* > modern English *mice*), but may also happen to initial vowels, especially in longer words: *qasawa > Western Bukid-non Manobo (southern Philippines) *əsawa*, but Bintulu (Borneo) *saba* 'spouse'. Syncope (loss of a medial vowel) may produce consonant clusters, which are then subject to further changes.

9. **Monophthongisation**. Word-final diphthongs (or vowel-glide sequences) have been monophthongised independently in many Austronesian languages. The usual changes are *-ay > -e, *-aw > -o, and *-uy, *-iw > -i.

10. **Consonant clusters**. General rules governing the development of consonant clusters are difficult to state, since so many types of clusters may occur. In some languages heterorganic consonant clusters yield geminate consonants, as with Latin *factu* ([faktu]) 'done' > Italian *fatto* 'fact, feat'. In other languages the cluster may reduce through loss of either consonant, without further change. In still others the qualities of the consonants may fuse to produce an articulation distinct from either member of the original cluster, as with Latin *nocte* ([nokte]) > Spanish *noche* ([notʃe]) 'night'.

Segmental changes

The following changes affect individual segments. The list is not exhaustive, and is meant only to familiarise the reader with sound changes that are known to occur in more than one language, and whenever possible in more than one language family. Note that most reconstructed languages do not use IPA symbols, nor are IPA symbols commonly used in practical orthographies of modern languages. In the following discussion I use *c* for a voiceless palatal affricate, *j* for a voiced palatal affricate, *y* for a voiced palatal glide, and *š* for a voiceless palatal fricative.

Examples

1. *p. The 'erosion sequence' *p > *f* > *h* > zero, or parts of it, is well attested in many languages and in several language families, including Indo-European, Austronesian and Japonic. A derived *f may further develop into /v/, and then /w/, and a derived *h may further develop into /ʔ/.

*p > f: Proto-Indo-European (PIE) to Germanic (part of Grimm's law); Proto-Finno-Ugric to Hungarian; Proto-Austronesian (PAN) to Tiruray (Philippines), Malagasy (Madagascar), Chamorro (Micronesia) or Proto-Polynesian (PPN); Proto-Arawakan to Arauá.

*p > h Old Japanese to modern Japanese (through intermediate *ɸ); PAN to Atoni (Timor), Motu (New Guinea), Hawaiian (through intermediate *f); Proto-Arawakan to Yavitero, Mandawaca; Proto-Tupian to Kamayura (before *u).

*p > zero PAN to Helong (Timor), Manam (New Guinea); Proto-Tupian to Sirionó.

*f > h: Latin to written Spanish; PPN to Hawaiian.

*f > zero: Latin to spoken Spanish.

*p > /ʔ/: PAN to Nuaulu, Asilulu (Moluccas) intervocalically; PAN to Rarotongan (Polynesia) unconditionally (through intermediate *f and *h).

*p > v: Latin to Spanish intervocalically; PAN to Lakalai, Nggela unconditionally.

*p > w: PAN to Palauan (Micronesia), Selau (Solomon Islands).

2. *t. In general *t remains coronal (alveolar, palatal), even when it changes. In some Indo-European and Austronesian languages it has disappeared, probably through intermediate steps, but these are unknown.

*t > s: PAN to Chuukese and other languages of Micronesia.

*t > s/__i: Proto-Finnic to Finnish; PAN to Isnag (Philippines), Kelabit (Borneo), Numfor (New Guinea), Motu (New Guinea), Tongan (Polynesia).

*t > r/V__V: PAN to Nali and other languages of eastern Manus; the flapping of /t/ in American English is similar.

*t > c/__i: Old Japanese to modern Japanese; Proto-Tupian to Asurini.

*t > c/__i#: PAN to Long Jegan Berawan (Borneo), Tontemboan (Sulawesi).

3. *c. Since many reconstructed languages lack a palatal series (while very few lack labial, alveolar and velar consonants), attempts to generalise about the evolution of palatal consonants are at an empirical disadvantage. In Austronesian languages the palatal series tends to merge with the alveolars, and a similar outcome is known from languages in at least one other language family (Tupian).

*c > s: PAN to Ilokano, Tagalog (Philippines), Kayan (Borneo), Proto-Oceanic; Proto-Tupian to Tupinambá, Sirionó.

4. *k. The 'erosion sequence' *k > *x* > *h* > zero is well attested in many languages and several language families, and roughly parallels the similar set of changes for *p. In some Austronesian languages *k appears to have changed directly to a glottal stop.

*k > x: PIE to Germanic (part of Grimm's law).

*k > h: Proto-Finno-Ugric to Hungarian (before back vowels); PAN to Miri (Borneo), Toba Batak (Sumatra), Malagasy, Chamorro (Micronesia), all unconditionally.

*k > zero: PAN to Kalamian Tagbanwa (Philippines), Buli (Moluccas), Numfor (New Guinea).

*k > /ʔ/: PAN to Arosi (Solomon Islands), Samoan, Hawaiian.

*k > c: PIE to Sanskrit, English, French (before front vowels); PAN to Long Jegan Berawan (word-finally after *i).

5. *ʔ. Glottal stop and *h have few possible change paths, since they are articulated without the use of the tongue. Earlier *ʔ has become /h/ in some Austronesian languages. In others it has disappeared.

*ʔ > h: PAN to Malay, Javanese, Lakalai (New Britain).

*ʔ > zero: PAN to Samoan, Hawaiian, etc.; Proto-Tupian to Siriono.

6. *b. In non-final position a simple (non-prenasalised) *b generally weakens to a fricative or glide. However, unconditioned devoicing is attested in both Indo-European and Austronesian languages.

*b > v: PAN to Paiwan (Taiwan), Kadazan (Borneo).

*b > w: PAN to Javanese (sporadic), Bimanese, Ngadha (eastern Indonesia); Proto-Tupian to Asurini.

*b > f: PAN to Thao, Amis (Taiwan), Rotinese (eastern Indonesia).

*b > h: PAN to Mambai (Timor), Kamarian (Moluccas).

*b > p: PIE to Germanic (part of Grimm's law); PAN to Chamorro.

*b > m: PAN to Rhade; Proto-Tai to Po-ai.

*b > m/__#: PAN to Karo Batak (Sumatra), Long Terawan Berawan (Borneo).

7. *d: When it changes *d generally weakens to a liquid if non-final and non-prenasalised.

*d > r: PAN to Javanese (sporadic), Bikol (Philippines), Proto-Oceanic.

*d > l: PAN to Tagalog (probably through intermediate *r).

*d > t: PIE to Proto-Germanic (part of Grimm's law).

*d > n/__#: PAN to Karo Batak (Sumatra), Long Terawan Berawan (Borneo).

8. *j. In Austronesian languages, the voiced palatal affricate [ɟ] (conventionally written *z) has tended to merge with the corresponding alveolar. In some languages this has meant merger with *d; in others it has meant merger with *s. This change thus parallels *c > *s*.

> ***j > d:** PAN to Tagalog (Philippines), Kelabit (Borneo), Rotinese, Tetun (Timor).

> ***j > s:** PAN to Galoli (Timor), Talise (Solomon Islands), Proto-Oceanic.

9. *g. The voiced velar stop is generally stable in Indo-European and Austronesian languages that maintain a voicing distinction in the stops. Otherwise it tends to merge with *k, either regularly or sporadically. Sporadic voicing crossover is particularly common for velar stops for aerodynamic reasons.

> ***g > k:** PIE to Proto-Germanic (part of Grimm's law); PAN to Tagalog, Maranao (Philippines), Ngaju Dayak (Borneo), all three cases sporadic, and Proto-Oceanic, where it is regular.

10. *m. The bilabial nasal is among the most stable phonemes in all languages. However, some Austronesian languages in the Oceanic subgroup have developed labiovelar reflexes under certain conditions (generally next to a rounded vowel). Others have merged all final nasals as -ŋ, a development that was discussed under 'class changes'.

> ***m > mw:** PAN to Bipi, Nali (Admiralty Islands), Mota (Vanuatu), Chuukese, Pohnpeian (Micronesia). Changes in all of these languages are partly conditioned, partly sporadic.

11. *n. The alveolar nasal is generally stable, but may be palatalised when adjacent to a high front vowel. When it does change unconditionally it generally becomes *l* in Austronesian languages.

> ***n > l:** PAN to Langalanga (Solomon Islands), Woleaian, Palauan (Micronesia).

> ***n > ñ/__i:** PAN to Kayan (Borneo), Malay.

12. *ñ. In Austronesian languages the palatal nasal generally merges with *n, but in Oceanic languages it sometimes becomes *y*, either unconditionally or word-finally.

> ***ñ > n:** PAN to Ilokano, Tagalog (Philippines), Kelabit (Borneo), Standard Fijian, Proto-Polynesian.

> ***ñ > y:** PAN to Western Fijian.

> ***ñ > y/__#:** PAN to Bipi, Sori (Admiralty Islands).

13. *ŋ. The velar nasal tends to be fairly stable cross-linguistically. When it changes it generally merges with *n, but shows other, less common developments in some languages.

> ***ŋ > n:** PAN to Babuza, Thao (Taiwan), Malagasy (Madagascar), Hawaiian.

> ***ŋ > k:** PAN to South Island Maori, Northwest Marquesan (Polynesia).

> ***ŋ > ?:** PAN to Tahitian (Polynesia; probably through earlier *k).

> ***ŋ > h:** Proto-Tai to various Southern Thai dialects.

14. *s. Sibilants written with this symbol have various phonetic realisations in the world's languages, sometimes even among different speakers of the same language (as English). In many languages *s tends to weaken to *h*. In some Austronesian languages it has been strengthened to *t*.

> ***s > h:** PIE to Greek; PAN to Atayal (Taiwan), Uma (Sulawesi), Kambera (eastern Indonesia), Tongan.

> ***s > t:** PAN to Thao, Paiwan (Taiwan), Arosi (Solomon Islands), Chuukese (Micronesia).

> ***s > š/__i:** Old Japanese to modern Japanese.

15. *h. In most language families laryngeals such as glottal stop or *h are inherently unstable, and likely to be lost. In Austronesian languages *h has become glottal stop in some languages, and has disappeared in many others.

16. *l. Liquids tend to influence one another in successive syllables, so that many languages show historical changes which involve either assimilation or dissimilation of *l or *r (*lVr > lVl or rVr, *lVl > lVr or rVl, etc.). The unconditioned shift of *l to *r*, or *r to *l* is also common. Apart from this *l sometimes changes to a glide, or in final position merges with *n.

*l > r: PAN to Bimanese (eastern Indonesia), Numfor (New Guinea), Arosi (Solomon Islands), Tahitian (Polynesia).

*l > y: PAN to Nali (Admiralty Islands), Palauan (Micronesia).

*l > n: PAN to Chuukese, Pulo Anna (Micronesia).

*l > d/__i: PAN to Long Terawan Berawan (Borneo), Malagasy (Madagascar), Tonsea (Sulawesi).

*l > n/__#: Proto-Tai to Standard Thai; PAN to Bintulu (Borneo), Loniu, Likum (Admiralty Islands).

17. *r. This is a cover term for many articulation types. Alveolar *r often becomes *l*, particularly if it is a flap rather than a trill. Trilled *r, whether alveolar or uvular, appears to have more radical tendencies to change. PAN had both *r (presumably an alveolar flap) and *R (usually assumed to be an alveolar or uvular trill).

*r > l: PAN to Tagalog, Samoan, Hawaiian.

*R > l: PAN to Pangasinan (Philippines), Asilulu (Moluccas).

*R > g: PAN to Atayal (Taiwan), Tagalog (Philippines), Berawan (Borneo), Chamorro (Micronesia).

*R > r: PAN to Malay, Numfor, Palauan (before dentals).

*R > s: PAN to Bonfia (Moluccas), Palauan (not before dentals).

*R > y: PAN to Ivatan, Kapampangan (Philippines), many languages in the Admiralty Islands.

*R > h: PAN to Ngaju Dayak (Borneo), Gorontalo (Sulawesi).

*R > zero: PAN to Javanese (Java), Wuvulu (Admiralty Islands), Fijian, Proto-Polynesian.

18. *w. Both weakening (lenition) and strengthening (fortition) of glides are well attested in the world's languages. *w and *y tend to undergo parallel developments.

*w > zero: PAN to Malay, Toba Batak (Sumatra).

*w > v: PAN to Bunun (Taiwan), Samoan (Polynesia).

*w > f: PAN to Rotinese (eastern Indonesia).

*w > gw: PIE to Icelandic; PAN to Chamorro (Micronesia); Spanish accent in English.

*w > g: Germanic loans in French; PAN to Tunjung (Borneo).

*w > b: PAN to Bintulu, Miri, Berawan (Borneo). There is documentary evidence that this change, at least in Bintulu, passed through a stage in which *w > *gw*.

19. *y > zero. PAN to Proto-Polynesian.

*y > r: PAN to Palauan (Micronesia).

*y > s: PAN to Sa'a, Arosi (Solomon Islands).

*y > z: PAN to Tsou (Taiwan), Bintulu (Borneo), Malagasy (Madagascar).

*y > j: PAN to Miri (Borneo); Spanish accent in English.

*y > dz: PAN to Chamorro (Micronesia).

20. Vowels. Apart from the weakening of unstressed vowels ('class changes') it is difficult to find cross-linguistic tendencies in the evolution of vowels. One clear exception to this, however, is low vowel assimilation, in which *a is partly assimilated to the height and frontness of *i, and to the height and backness + roundness of *u in a following syllable, hence *a > *e*/__C*i*, and *a > *o*/__C*u*.

Some generalisations

1. *Lenition and fortition.* Most consonant changes appear to be lenitions. The major exception is with glides, in which changes may be either lenitive or fortitive, both developments being fairly common.
2. *Assimilation.* Conditioned changes tend to be assimilations.
3. *Suprasegmentals.* Stress commonly plays a role in vocalic changes, and much less commonly in consonantal changes (as in Verner's law).
4. *Glottalic consonants.* This is a cover term for implosives and ejectives. These tend to reflect consonant clusters, although unconditioned shifts of voiced stops to voiced implosives are known.
5. *Labiovelars.* Labiovelar stops or nasals can become simple labials or simple velars with the same manner of articulation. In Welsh and other members of 'P-Celtic' PIE *kʷ became *p*, maintaining the stop quality of *k and the place of *w. Likewise, PTG *pʷ became Guarani, Sirionó *kw*, the velar quality of *w evidently backing the *p, and Proto-Oceanic *mʷ became Proto-Polynesian *ŋ. In other Oceanic languages, however, *m and *mʷ merged as *m*, and less commonly *mʷ became *w*.

Keep in mind

1. Most innovations are stated as plausible changes, not as reflexes. So, if both *s and *h have disappeared, rather than stating these as *s > Ø (which is phonetically unnatural), and *h > Ø (which is phonetically natural), I state them as *s > *h*, then *h > Ø. Because changes are stated in the order in which they are encountered in the data, *s > *h* may be listed as change (1), and *h > Ø as change (5) or (6), with various other changes intervening. In all such cases ordering relationships are explicitly marked, thus (1) *s > *h* (before change (2)), (2) *h > Ø.
2. Not all forms will necessarily be cognate. If more than one sound correspondence in the same form is irregular it is generally best to assume that the similarity with other forms is due to chance.
3. For all sound changes list the numbers of supporting examples after the change.

LEVEL 1: BEGINNING

RECONSTRUCTION PROBLEM 1

No.	Proto-AB	Lg. A	Lg. B	
01.		tanhi	tamti	earth
02.		tomfat	tumfa	stone
03.		ehenhi	isimti	water
04.		corak	cura	river
05.		fentara	fintara	tree
06.		garhil	garsi	leaf
07.		hihin	tisi	house
08.		donte	dunti	path
09.		lintam	linta	forest
10.		arondar	arunda	fruit
11.		humbi	sunbi	flower
12.		ilamu	ilamu	seed
13.		kohihi	husiti	person
14.		hembor	simbu	man
15.		haŋkek	samki	woman
16.		ohif	uti	child
17.		kahi	hasi	son
18.		iŋkil	inki	daughter

INSTRUCTIONS:

1. Reconstruct Proto-AB 1–18.
2. List all changes in Lgs. A and B, noting any necessary ordering relationships.

RECONSTRUCTION PROBLEM 2

No.	Proto-ABC	Lg. A	Lg. B	Lg. C	
01.		tizaw	diho	tisu	one
02.		rumo	lumo	lumu	two
03.		pajan	paja	padan	three
04.		saroti	halodi	saluti	head
05.		ñenu	nenu	ninu	hair
06.		huber	kube	kubir	ear
07.		konay	gone	guni	eye
08.		ucewa	usewa	usiwa	nose
09.		eriray	elire	iliri	mouth
10.		rawraw	roro	ruru	tooth
11.		torozi	dorohi	turusi	earth
12.		deden	dede	didiŋ	water
13.		botbot	bobo	butbut	stone
14.		sine	hiŋe	siŋi	tree
15.		dunat	duŋa	duŋat	sky
16.		iraya	ilea	ilia	rain
17.		dayday	dede	didi	star
18.		tatir	dadi	tatir	moon
19.		cahcah	sasa	saksak	lightning
20.		kuron	guro	guruŋ	thunder
21.		razan	raha	rasaŋ	storm
22.		tukan	duga	tugan	flood
23.		june	june	duni	sand
24.		tañah	dana	tanak	mud

Note: c = voiceless palatal affricate, j = voiced palatal affricate, ñ = palatal nasal.

INSTRUCTIONS:

1. Reconstruct Proto-ABC 1–24.
2. State all changes in each language, indicating any ordering requirements.
3. List the consonants and vowels of Proto-ABC in chart form.

RECONSTRUCTION PROBLEM 3

No.	Proto-AB	Lg. A	Lg. B	
01.		fofok	pupuk	stone
02.		hunar	sunal	earth
03.		katay	hante	tree
04.		ule	uli	branch
05.		ləmat	lomot	leaf
06.		natal	natal	root
07.		tihaf	tisop	grass
08.		kino	hinu	water
09.		ipat	impot	rain
10.		aŋaw	aŋo	cloud
11.		təfak	topok	sky
12.		əlaŋ	olaŋ	sun
13.		wakor	wahul	moon
14.		lifay	lipe	star
15.		ekul	ihul	house
16.		lukoŋ	luhuŋ	roof
17.		kuhaf	husop	floor
18.		ofar	upol	door
19.		luke	luŋki	person
20.		ulaf	ulap	man
21.		mərah	molos	woman
22.		tunaw	tuno	child
23.		lapih	lampis	fish
24.		rokuf	luŋkup	dog

INSTRUCTIONS:

1. Reconstruct Proto-AB 1–24.
2. List all changes in each language, noting any necessary ordering relationships.

RECONSTRUCTION PROBLEM 4

No.	Proto-Tarawan	Taraw	Ikung	Sawe	
01.		daya	taya	taraʔ	one
02.		omel	homey	omel	two
03.		iram	idam	idam	three
04.		sivuŋ	hibuŋ	sibuŋ	sun
05.		kima	kima	kima	star
06.		yumo	yumo	rumo	wind
07.		yus	hiuh	ius	water
08.		ŋivi	ŋiwi	ŋiwi	grass
09.		ukuv	ukub	ʔukup	stone
10.		ŋurut	ŋurut	ŋulut	earth
11.		rasis	ratih	latis	tree
12.		ur	uud	uʔut	bark
13.		virol	biroy	bilol	leaf
14.		ayag	ayag	arak	flower
15.		reŋu	deŋu	deŋu	fruit
16.		davas	tawah	tawas	rotten
17.		mulat	muyat	mulat	angry
18.		lisuk	yihuk	lisuk	painful
19.		vui	bui	buiʔ	swollen
20.		asom	ahom	ʔasom	eat
21.		vat	waat	waʔat	drink
22.		ravaw	dabaw	dabo	walk
23.		levak	yewak	lewak	sleep
24.		sisav	tihab	tisap	think
25.		way	uhay	ue	no/not
26.		radus	ratuh	latus	because
27.		ake	ake	ake	perhaps
28.		imas	himah	imas	when

INSTRUCTIONS/QUESTIONS:

1. Reconstruct Proto-Tarawan 1–28.
2. List all changes in each language, noting any necessary ordering relationships.

3. Draw up a phoneme inventory for this language.
4. Do you notice anything typologically peculiar about the inventory? Should this cause you to question the reconstruction? Can you justify changing the reconstruction in any way to make it typologically more believable?

RECONSTRUCTION PROBLEM 5

No.	Proto-ABC	Lg. A	Lg. B	Lg. C	
01.		liliput	rilliput	rilliput	mythical country
02.		lilaranu	rinaraŋu	rirayanu	hailstone
03.		rilolo	riroro	yiroro	butterfly
04.		ayaro	ayato	azayo	ghost
05.		irurup	irrutup	irruyup	shadow
06.		riroro	ritoro	yiyoyo	whirlwind
07.		nalu	ŋallu	nallu	centipede
08.		liliput	ririput	ririput	mushroom species
09.		litolo	rittoro	rittoro	elf
10.		rololo	rorollo	yorollo	echo
11.		ranu	raŋu	yanu	stone
12.		liroro	riroro	riyoyo	firefly
13.		ritolo	rittoro	yittoro	earthworm
14.		liriput	ririput	riyiput	rainbow
15.		lila	rina	rira	rain
16.		zilayak	rinayak	zirazak	cannibal
17.		rina	rinna	yinna	ant
18.		rozorozo	rorororo	yozoyozo	bumblebee

INSTRUCTIONS:

1. Reconstruct Proto-ABC 1–18.
2. State all sound changes in each daughter language, together with any ordering requirements.

RECONSTRUCTION PROBLEM 6

No.	Proto-ABC	Lg. A	Lg. B	Lg. C	
01.		hiŋod	finot	piŋo	head
02.		sagay	salay	saɣe	eye
03.		amuŋ	amun	amu	nose
04.		busik	putih	buti	ear
05.		duli	tuli	ɾuɾi	tooth
06.		kənah	hənaf	kona	hand
07.		ŋulu	nulu	ŋulu	elbow
08.		tokaw	tohaw	toko	belly
09.		nesig	nesil	nesi	leg
10.		wala	wala	waɾa	water
11.		udag	utak	uɾa	stone
12.		lilih	lilif	lili	grass
13.		gulat	lulat	ɣula	hill
14.		hayas	fayas	paya	rain
15.		alab	alap	aɾa	wood
16.		sagel	sakel	sage	fire
17.		ləhay	ləfay	ɾofe	smoke
18.		ugisi	uliti	uɣiti	ashes
19.		tuhək	tufəh	tupo	hole
20.		guan	kuan	gua	snake
21.		siug	tiul	tiu	bird
22.		gabuŋ	kapun	gabu	wing
23.		ukol	uhol	uko	feather
24.		hikan	fihan	fika	egg

Note: /ɾ/ = an alveolar flap, /r/ = an alveolar trill.

INSTRUCTIONS/QUESTIONS:

1. Reconstruct Proto-ABC 1–24.
2. Describe all changes in each language, noting any ordering requirements.
3. Are any proto-phonemes difficult to characterise phonetically? Which ones, and what are the options that you can imagine?
4. Are any reconstructions ambiguous? Which ones, and for what segments?

RECONSTRUCTION PROBLEM 7

No.	Proto-ABC	Lg. A	Lg. B	Lg. C	
01.		sipak	sifah	hibak	hand
02.		biraŋ	biraŋ	bilaŋ	foot
03.		unus	unus	unuh	knee
04.		pusut	fusut	puhud	elbow
05.		uvi	ubi	ubi	head
06.		tukal	tuhal	tugal	hair
07.		rasam	rasam	laham	eye
08.		kalup	halup	kalub	nose
09.		duŋu	duŋu	duŋu	ear
10.		iruk	iduh	iduk	mouth
11.		surup	suruf	hulup	tooth
12.		baŋit	baŋit	baŋit	tongue
13.		dilap	dilaf	dilap	skin
14.		puri	fudi	pudi	breast
15.		atap	ataf	adap	liver
16.		lavu	labu	labu	blood
17.		bukas	buhas	bugah	water
18.		barak	badak	badag	earth
19.		damar	damar	damal	stone
20.		arat	arat	alat	river
21.		lipit	lifit	libid	mountain
22.		nalip	nalip	nalib	sky
23.		davak	dabak	dabag	sun

INSTRUCTIONS/QUESTIONS:

1. Reconstruct Proto-ABC 1–23.
2. List all sound changes in each daughter language, noting any ordering requirements.
3. Certain changes produced phonemic merger in some enviroments. Which changes were these, and what were the environments in which merger occurred?

LEVEL 2: INTERMEDIATE

RECONSTRUCTION PROBLEM 8

No.	Proto-AB	Lg. A	Lg. B	
01.		darak	rākit	head
02.		ilar	ilau	hair
03.		tar	taip	eye
04.		dur	ruis	ear
05.		munis	munisa	nose
06.		akar	akaun	mouth
07.		satil	satilik	tooth
08.		kurud	kūru	tongue
09.		kulud	kuluru	hand/arm
10.		kudur	kurū	body
11.		pasit	pasiti	foot/leg
12.		tam	tamus	cloud
13.		ratal	atali	water
14.		rurut	ūtus	sky
15.		rut	utis	rain
16.		ukuk	ukuka	earth
17.		tarir	taia	tree
18.		ilar	ilā	grass
19.		timan	timanu	fish
20.		kur	kū	bird
21.		irad	iarat	feather
22.		duruk	rūku	dog

INSTRUCTIONS:

1. Reconstruct Proto-AB 1–22 (note that this limited set of data is not representative of the entire phoneme inventory).
2. List all changes in each language, stating ordering relations where necessary.

RECONSTRUCTION PROBLEM 9

No.	Proto-Abaic	Abai	Soxun	Otile	
01.		təlapa	siráha	tilafa	water
02.		səpat	suhát	huvaʔ	sky
03.		mokay	móxay	moke	earth
04.		supat	súhat	hufaʔ	tree
05.		kufan	xúhan	kufaŋ	root
06.		ətak	itáx	idaʔ	stone
07.		təfin	tahín	taviŋ	dust
08.		atola	átora	atola	river
09.		itar	ítar	itar	boat
10.		rəkaw	ruxáw	rugo	oar
11.		təpu	atuhú	atuvu	rapids
12.		ətar	itár	idar	waterfall
13.		kəpu	xehú	kevu	rainbow
14.		səte	isuté	ihude	morning
15.		lutip	rúsih	lutiʔ	evening
16.		otum	ótum	otuŋ	night

Note: stress, which is phonemic in Soxun, is penultimate in Abai and initial in Otile.

INSTRUCTIONS:

1. Reconstruct Proto-Abaic 1–16.
2. State the sound changes in each daughter language together with any ordering requirements, paying particular attention to vowel correspondences.

RECONSTRUCTION PROBLEM 10

No.	Proto-ABC	Lg. A	Lg. B	Lg. C	
01.		pratum	praktum	prattũ	bread
02.		sodino	surtiru	sottĩlo	wheat
03.		unanino	urariru	ũlãlĩlo	oats
04.		kloru	krutru	klottu	cow
05.		grumbe	grumbi	grũbe	milk
06.		rimanaŋ	rimaran	rĩmãlã	sky
07.		orazu	utrasu	ottasu	rain
08.		nutini	ruptiri	luttĩli	water
09.		blarazo	brarasu	blaraso	flood
10.		mutoni	mukturi	sogoku	ditch
11.		salagon	sarakur	salakõ	hill
12.		razande	razarti	razãtte	grass
13.		dumaru	urasi	dũmaru	tree
14.		enonam	iruram	ẽlõlã	bark
15.		sodine	surtiri	sottĩle	head
16.		amanudu	amarutu	ãmãlutu	eye
17.		tambuŋi	tampuni	tãppũni	ear
18.		ogunama	ugurama	ogũlãma	nose
19.		serinom	sirirum	serĩlõ	skin
20.		aradomu	aradumu	aradõmu	hand
21.		lundine	rurdiri	lũdĩle	liver
22.		koraŋa	kuprana	koppãna	lungs
23.		lambesa	rambisa	lãbesa	blood

INSTRUCTIONS/QUESTIONS:

1. Reconstruct Proto-ABC 1–23.
2. State the sound changes that have occurred in each daughter language, citing any ordering requirements. How would you describe the origin of the geminate consonants in Lg. C?

RECONSTRUCTION PROBLEM 11

No.	Proto-ABC	Lg. A	Lg. B	Lg. C	
01.		pusu	fuhuʔ	puuku	earth
02.		mane	mane	mane	grass
03.		kuti	ʔutir	kutili	root
04.		rara	rarah	raraa	worm
05.		waya	wayar	wayara	beetle
06.		tapi	tafin	tapini	water
07.		lulu	ruruʔ	luluku	river
08.		sasa	hahaf	aapa	rain
09.		sapa	hafa	apa	flood
10.		tia	tiaf	tiapa	sky
11.		ulu	uruh	uluu	sun
12.		susu	huhu	uu	egg
13.		nunu	nunuʔ	nunuku	chicken
14.		asa	ahaf	aapa	feather
15.		lipa	rifah	lipaa	bird
16.		kori	ʔorih	korii	fish
17.		sami	hamir	amiri	snake
18.		nasi	nahiŋ	naiŋi	house
19.		leka	reʔa	leka	roof
20.		piŋi	fiŋi	piŋi	door
21.		misa	mihah	miaa	floor
22.		pusa	fuhar	puala	hearth

INSTRUCTIONS:

1. Reconstruct Proto-ABC 1–22.
2. List all changes in each language, including any ordering requirements.

RECONSTRUCTION PROBLEM 12

No.	Proto-ABC	Lg. A	Lg. B	Lg. C	
01.		ʔulaʔ	hula	kurak	grass
02.		hanupa	honufa	anufa	earth
03.		luru	ruru	ruru	water
04.		tiʔapu	tihofu	tikafu	rat
05.		tomuru	tomuru	tomuru	owl
06.		tapis	tefis	tafis	feather
07.		arun	orun	arun	fish
08.		liheʔ	lihe	riek	frog
09.		hupaʔ	hufa	ufak	snake
10.		pahiri	fehiri	fairi	eagle
11.		leraʔi	rerehi	reraki	hawk
12.		ʔanup	honuf	kanuf	pig
13.		laruʔ	loru	raruk	dog
14.		ʔilala	hilala	kirara	tree
15.		imiri	imiri	imiri	forest
16.		lehiʔi	lehihi	reiki	village
17.		malurus	morurus	marurus	river
18.		ʔanih	heni	kani	bridge
19.		pasimi	fesimi	fasimi	mountain
20.		luruh	luru	ruru	cloud

INSTRUCTIONS:

1. Reconstruct Proto-ABC 1–20.
2. Indicate changes in all three languages, together with any necessary ordering relations.

RECONSTRUCTION PROBLEM 13

No.	Proto-ABC	Lg. A	Lg. B	Lg. C	
01.		xafata	kavata	ʔabata	earth
02.		rasiŋ	rahiŋ	rasiŋ	clay
03.		filax	pilak	hilaʔ	mud
04.		urani	urani	urani	stone
05.		tutaf	turap	tudah	hill
06.		lanisa	laniha	lanisa	tree
07.		xufit	ɣupit	gupit	trunk
08.		nadᶻasa	nayaha	naaha	branch
09.		siruxi	hiruki	siruʔi	leaf
10.		lefixa	lepika	lehiʔa	fruit
11.		tagʷaf	rawap	daah	bird
12.		maxulu	maɣulu	magulu	snake
13.		fiʔat	piat	hiʔat	fish
14.		fisan	vihan	bisan	dog
15.		tinas	tinah	tinas	sky
16.		siafa	hiapa	siaha	cloud
17.		ixaxa	iɣaka	igaʔa	sun
18.		uxuf	ukuv	uʔup	moon
19.		dᶻulux	yuluɣ	uluk	star
20.		haxulin	akulin	haʔulin	rain
21.		tihafa	tiapa	tihaha	house
22.		orosim	orohim	orosim	person
23.		ʔuxal	ukal	ʔuʔal	man
24.		finit	pinir	hinit	woman
25.		gʷatoʔ	wato	atoʔ	child
26.		faxix	pakiɣ	haʔik	old
27.		rusut	ruhur	rusut	strong
28.		sarif	hariv	sarip	weak

INSTRUCTIONS:

1. Reconstruct Proto-ABC 1–28.
2. List all changes in each language, including any ordering requirements.

RECONSTRUCTION PROBLEM 14

No. Proto-ABC	Lg. A	Lg. B	Lg. C	
01.	təbe	tavi	tapeh	earth
02.	io	iku	ixoh	water
03.	fərat	pora?	palat	wind
04.	ilih	ilis	ilih	rain
05.	ləfo	lapo	lapoh	cloud
06.	omaŋ	homaŋ	homaŋ	storm
07.	dəwə	rawo	tawah	mountain
08.	iho	kiso	xiso	river
09.	munti	muti	mudi	stone
10.	biləh	vilos	pilah	tree
11.	ŋura	ŋure	ŋuleh	forest
12.	rue	ruki	luxeh	house
13.	əŋko	aku?	aguh	village
14.	tuləf	tulo?	tulap	person
15.	hompu	sopu	sobu	man
16.	əuh	kahus	xahuh	woman
17.	lide	liri?	litih	child
18.	ənah	kones	xaneh	dog
19.	afe	hepi?	hepix	bird
20.	tano	tenu	tenoh	eat
21.	uam	ukaŋ	uxam	drink
22.	fərin	pariŋ	palin	sleep
23.	rəntə	roto?	ladax	dream
24.	fue	pu?i?	puhih	wake up
25.	uho	usu?	uhux	stand
26.	ota	kota	xota	walk

INSTRUCTIONS:

1. Reconstruct Proto-ABC 1–26.
2. Indicate changes in all three languages, together with any necessary ordering relations.

RECONSTRUCTION PROBLEM 15

No.	Proto-ABCD	Lg. A	Lg. B	Lg. C	Lg. D	
01.		riman	liman	liman	limaŋ	hand
02.		tunuʔ	tono	tunu	tonoʔ	finger
03.		hiray	kele	kilay	kele	nail
04.		ihur	eko	ikuh	ekoh	joint
05.		fasik	patik	ranut	patiʔ	duck
06.		hunir	hone	sunih	soneh	goose
07.		ruhi	huki	huki	huki	mouth
08.		urif	ulip	tamal	uliʔ	lip
09.		pinuk	uhuk	uhuk	uhuʔ	tooth
10.		riaw	leo	liaw	pisih	tongue
11.		irih	ihih	ihis	eheh	lip
12.		sihiʔ	tehe	tisi	teseʔ	saliva
13.		nuhaʔ	nuka	nuka	nukaʔ	head
14.		fəhir	pohe	pəsih	poseh	hair
15.		sirit	arak	tilit	poloʔ	ear
16.		hutun	kutun	kutun	kutuŋ	nose
17.		huhur	hoho	susuh	sosoh	neck
18.		rimət	lemot	limət	lemoʔ	arm
19.		tafay	tape	tapay	tape	back
20.		arut	ahut	ahut	ahuʔ	boat
21.		əray	ohe	əhay	ohe	paddle
22.		miruʔ	meho	mihu	mehoʔ	swim
23.		hifah	hipah	sipas	sipah	float
24.		rifaw	hepo	hipaw	kala	drift
25.		haruh	kaluh	kalus	kaloh	sink
26.		hafiʔ	hape	sapi	sapeʔ	drown
27.		uram	ulam	ulam	ulaŋ	die
28.		ruhəf	hokop	hukəp	hokoʔ	bury

INSTRUCTIONS/QUESTIONS:

1. Reconstruct Proto-ABCD forms 1–28.
2. List all changes in each language, including any ordering requirements.
3. Which forms are *not* reflexes of the reconstructions?

RECONSTRUCTION PROBLEM 16

No.	Proto-ABC	Lg. A	Lg. B	Lg. C	
01.		tepin	tapiŋ	tápin	head
02.		irak	ila?	ilák	hair
03.		uti	uti	úri	eye
04.		ifas	ipa	ipáh	ear
05.		ulup	ulu?	úlup	nose
06.		oxum	akuŋ	akúm	mouth
07.		sipis	sipi	hípih	tooth
08.		aran	alaŋ	alán	tongue
09.		uxu	uku	ukú	neck
10.		rapan	lapal	lápal	shoulder
11.		salat	sala?	hálat	hand
12.		hakap	aka?	ákap	foot
13.		itip	iti?	írip	man
14.		etin	atil	áril	woman
15.		rokut	laku?	lákut	child
16.		suxi	suki	hukí	father
17.		hili	ili	íli	mother
18.		lufin	lupiŋ	lupín	house
19.		fekis	paki	pákih	door
20.		turam	tulaŋ	tulám	floor
21.		xuas	kua	kúah	hearth
22.		titak	tita?	tirák	window

Note: stress is penultimate in Lgs. A and B, but phonemic in Lg. C.

INSTRUCTIONS:

1. Reconstruct Proto-ABC 1–22.
2. List all changes in each language, paying particular attention to phonological conditioning.

LEVEL 3: ADVANCED

RECONSTRUCTION PROBLEM 17

No.	Proto-ABC	Lg. A	Lg. B	Lg. C	
01.		kirru	cilar	kilalu	road
02.		pekka	penak	penaga	hill
03.		kuhit	kušit	kuhi?	meadow
04.		leppo	lenap	lenabo	grass
05.		tolon	tolon	toloŋ	tree
06.		akki	ampac	appagi	branch
07.		sitta	cirit	silida	root
08.		takki	tamic	tamigi	leaf
09.		hitteŋ	šimiteŋ	himideŋ	water
10.		musso	mucis	mugiho	wind
11.		urro	ulur	ululo	sky
12.		runnu	rucin	lusinu	sun
13.		hoika	soik	hoiga	cloud
14.		irah	iras	ilah	river
15.		atti	hacit	agidi	rain
16.		ulla	umal	umala	man
17.		sokki	cotac	sodagi	woman
18.		loak	lohak	loa?	child
19.		pullu	puncil	puttilu	give
20.		kiasep	ciacep	kiase?	think
21.		hakka	sambuk	hambuga	eat
22.		ippa	iŋgap	iŋgaba	sleep
23.		hiliu	šilihu	hiliu	dream
24.		totto	toŋkat	tokkado	wake up
25.		himan	šiman	himaŋ	yawn

Note: Proto-ABC stress was initial; in Lg. B *c* is a voiceless palatal affricate and š a voiceless palatal fricative.

INSTRUCTIONS:

1. Reconstruct Proto-ABC 1–25.
2. List all changes in each language, together with ordering requirements. Note that in stating changes geminate consonants should be treated as distinct from their singleton counterparts.

RECONSTRUCTION PROBLEM 18

No.	Proto-Makuan	Mok	Kuma	Ilaka	
01.		pahik	fahik	kepede	man
02.		hunbi	sumbi	kiubbi	woman
03.		hita	tiha	ketede	child
04.		ramhi	hanti	keledde	house
05.		uhia	uhia	keodee	chicken
06.		alu	aru	keolo	dog
07.		tara	taha	ketele	bird
08.		hatuŋ	sahuŋ	keodo	water
09.		bari	bahi	kebele	tree
10.		idap	ihaf	keere	root
11.		kahap	kasaf	kekee	stone
12.		tapi	tafi	tebe	drink
13.		huru	suhu	ulu	eat
14.		taŋtaŋ	tantaŋ	tadda	walk
15.		hari	hasi	lee	speak
16.		lihua	risua	leoo	sit
17.		hiba	siba	ebe	stand
18.		unda	unda	oddo	black
19.		hinhi	tinti	tiddi	white
20.		rapu	hafu	lobo	red
21.		dumpat	dumfat	dobbo	yellow
22.		padih	fahis	pere	green/blue

INSTRUCTIONS/QUESTIONS:

1. Reconstruct Proto-Makuan 1–22 (note that this limited set of data is not representative of the entire phoneme inventory).
2. List all changes in each language, stating ordering relations where this is necessary.
3. One form in one language shows metathesis. Which form is it, and which segments have metathesised?

RECONSTRUCTION PROBLEM 19

No.	Proto-ABCD	Lg. A	Lg. B	Lg. C	Lg. D	
01.		beřen	biřin	belin	biri	sun
02.		fukul	pugul	pukun	pugu	rain
03.		fanak	pannak	panhak	parna	cloud
04.		řiuk	řiuk	liuk	riu	sky
05.		safo	sappu	xanpo	salbu	wind
06.		kutiŋ	huttiŋ	kuthiŋ	kurdi	earth
07.		etoř	idur	etuh	idu	water
08.		kafit	happit	kanpit	kalbi	grass
09.		řoto	ruttu	hontu	rundu	flower
10.		sifal	sibal	xipan	siba	stone
11.		mutun	mudun	muton	mudu	bird
12.		fogos	pugus	pogox	pugu	feather
13.		ibuř	ibuř	ibol	ibu	snake
14.		lefem	lippim	nenpem	lilbi	house
15.		ifat	ippat	impat	imba	person
16.		umul	ummul	umhon	urmu	man
17.		oden	udin	odin	udi	woman
18.		řamete	ramidi	hameti	ramidi	child
19.		sete	sitti	xethi	sirdi	hand
20.		siti	sitti	xilte	sirdi	root
21.		sořof	surup	xohup	suru	tree
22.		iluř	ilur	inuh	ilu	leaf

Note: /ř/ = an alveolar flap, /r/ = an alveolar trill.

INSTRUCTIONS:

1. Reconstruct Proto-ABCD 1–22, paying particular attention to conditioned changes in the vowels.
2. List all changes in each language, including ordering relationships when needed.

RECONSTRUCTION PROBLEM 20

No.	Proto-ABC	Lg. A	Lg. B	Lg. C	
01.		piraʔ	pitak	fidaʔ	many
02.		raŋih	lanis	laŋis	few
03.		adiʔ	andip	andif	alone
04.		iraŋ	hilan	hilaŋ	how many?
05.		hagu	saku	saʔu	when?
06.		agʷaʔ	oat	aat	how?
07.		mutu	mundu	muttu	where?
08.		hihilan	sisilan	sisinaŋ	what?
09.		bureʔ	bulit	bulet	alive
10.		tipo	timbu	dippo	dead
11.		usal	udal	uzan	road
12.		kalira	kalita	ʔanida	dust
13.		buzuʔ	buyut	buut	weeds
14.		raragu	lalaku	lalaʔu	locust
15.		ŋeri	nili	ŋeli	cricket
16.		luŋihi	lunisi	nuŋisi	honeybee
17.		luvuh	lubus	nubus	ant
18.		moran	muran	modaŋ	dog
19.		kulun	kulum	ʔunuŋ	forest
20.		sivor	divul	zifon	tree
21.		huuʔ	suhuk	suhuʔ	branch
22.		piih	pihis	fihis	leaf
23.		ihin	isim	isiŋ	fruit
24.		gʷazan	wean	aaŋ	eat
25.		ubaŋ	humban	humbaŋ	drink
26.		kous	kuhud	ʔohuz	sleep
27.		ivah	ibas	ibas	wake up
28.		duzal	ruyal	duan	sit
29.		arih	atis	adis	stand
30.		hakuʔ	saŋgup	sakkuf	talk
31.		iruh	irus	idus	walk
32.		tunaza	tunea	dunaa	fall

INSTRUCTIONS:

1. Reconstruct Proto-ABC forms 1–32.
2. List all changes in each language, including any ordering requirements.

RECONSTRUCTION PROBLEM 21

Background. Wuvulu, Loniu and Lou are among the twenty-five to thirty languages of the Admiralty Islands in Papua New Guinea. These languages form a well-defined subgroup within the Oceanic branch of Austronesian. Within this subgroup Loniu and Lou form a unit as opposed to Wuvulu which, together with its sister dialect Aua, is spoken some 250 miles further to the west. Note that Loniu *c* is a voiceless palatal affricate, and a hyphen following a word indicates that it is an obligatorily possessed noun.

No.	Proto-Loniu-Lou	Wuvulu	Loniu	Lou	
01.		palu	pan	pol	dove sp.
02.		lita	lis	lis	nit, louse egg
03.		ʔalia	taliŋa-	teliŋa-	ear
04.		tala	can	sal	path
05.		naʔu	ñat	not	tree sp.
06.		nofu	noh	noh	stonefish
07.		lao	laŋ	laŋ	housefly
08.		tae	sak	sak	climb
09.		loʔo	lot	lot	abscess
10.		ʔai	taŋ	teŋ	cry, weep
11.		uʔu	kut	kut	louse
12.		afi	ah	eh	fire
13.		bea	pek	pek	fruit bat
14.		naʔu	natu-	notu-	child
15.		ani	kan	ken	eat
16.		manu	man	monmon	bird
17.		ʔaki	tas	tes	saltwater
18.		maʔi	mat	met	low tide
19.		maʔe	mat	mat	die, dead

INSTRUCTIONS/QUESTIONS:

1. Reconstruct items 1–19 for the immediate common ancestor of Loniu and Lou (Proto-Loniu-Lou), but using data from *all three* languages.

2. List all changes that have taken place in Loniu and Lou, together with any necessary ordering relations.

3. Write a paragraph or two explaining how this problem differs from others that you have done so far. In your explanation be sure to describe the specific ways in which you need to modify the comparative method in order to reconstruct all details of Proto-Loniu-Lou. Are there any precedents for this approach to reconstruction in the literature of Indo-European historical linguistics?

RECONSTRUCTION PROBLEM 22

No.	Proto-ABCD	Lg. A	Lg. B	Lg. C	Lg. D	
01.		hʷɛtəs	hʷɛtəs	xʷɛtəs	wetis	snow
02.		itnɔh	ʔitnɔh	hitnɔh	ʔitnoʔ	ice
03.		qtil	qtin	ʔcil	qtil	freeze
04.		nɛhʷa	snɛhʷa	snɛhʷa	snewa	storm
05.		wahɔ	wahɔ	wahɔ	aʔo	wind
06.		nhul	nhun	nxul	nxul	fog
07.		kʷakʷə	sxʷaxʷə	skʷakʷə	sgʷagʷɨ	rain
08.		fahʷəl	hahʷən	faxʷəl	fawɨl	fire
09.		ihʷə	ihʷə	ihʷə	iwɨ	bird
10.		ayuq	ayuq	ayuʔ	auq	fish
11.		suqoh	suqoh	suʔox	suqox	seal
12.		wuuf	wuʔuh	wuhuf	uʔuf	whale
13.		yumə	yumʔə	yumhə	umʔɨ	bear
14.		əmɛs	ʔəmɛs	həmɛs	ʔimes	dog
15.		hlohʷ	hlohʷ	hloxʷ	ʔlow	ivory
16.		hɛkʷ	shɛxʷ	skɛkʷ	sxɛgʷ	stone
17.		hose	hose	xose	xose	bone
18.		uhqan	uhqan	uhʔan	uʔqan	skin
19.		fuhi	huhiʔ	fuhih	fuʔiʔ	fat
20.		mehtɔ	mehtɔ	mextɔ	mexto	blood
21.		lɛhəm	lɛhəm	lɛhəm	leʔim	hair/fur
22.		naws	snaws	snaws	snaws	water
23.		nuqma	nuqma	nuʔma	nuqma	land
24.		ɛwɛhʷ	ɛwɛhʷ	ɛwɛhʷ	ɛwɛh	house
25.		afkʷah	ahxʷax	afkʷax	afgʷax	village
26.		thal	than	tkal	txal	person
27.		kʷəɔh	xʷəʔɔh	kʷəhɔh	gʷɨʔɔʔ	man
28.		hʷin	hʷin	hʷin	win	woman
29.		foyɛq	hoyɛq	foyɛʔ	foeq	child
30.		laqəm	laqəm	laʔəm	laqim	food
31.		tikʷə	tixʷə	cikʷə	tigʷɨ	eat
32.		nilqəs	nilqəs	nilʔəs	nilqis	drink

INSTRUCTIONS:

1. Reconstruct Proto-ABCD 1–32.
2. List all sound changes in each daughter language, noting any ordering requirements.

RECONSTRUCTION PROBLEM 23

No.	Proto-ABCD	Lg. A	Lg. B	Lg. C	Lg. D	
01.		honus	faʔuh	vuɲus	paɲuʔu	fish
02.		tutuh	turuʔ	tutuk	tuluku	frog
03.		ilat	inat	inat	inala	snail
04.		suraga	hulago	suraka	ʔulaga	worm
05.		tiyih	tilif	silif	tilipi	snake
06.		hisum	fihup	visuŋ	piʔumu	spider
07.		runu	luʔu	ruɲu	luɲu	rain
08.		sago	hago	saku	ʔago	water
09.		wehi	waʔi	viki	aki	river
10.		mehul	meʔut	mikuŋ	mekunu	grsass
11.		besir	wahil	pisir	vaʔili	tree
12.		ahat	aʔat	hakat	ʔakala	branch
13.		oyuh	aluʔ	uluk	aluku	leaf
14.		hula	ʔuno	kuna	kuna	root
15.		subiy	huil	supil	ʔuvili	bark
16.		oliti	oniri	unisi	onili	eat
17.		guyal	gulat	kulaŋ	gulana	drink
18.		yidas	lirah	litas	liraʔa	walk
19.		hial	fiat	vihaŋ	piʔana	sit
20.		edih	ariʔ	itik	ariki	stand
21.		huin	fuiʔ	vuhiŋ	puʔiɲi	sleep
22.		eah	ayaf	ayaf	apa	dream
23.		mohu	maʔu	muku	maku	talk
24.		suha	hufo	suva	ʔupa	breathe
25.		bitis	wirih	pisis	viliʔi	white
26.		iol	iwat	ivaŋ	iana	black
27.		ayam	alap	alaŋ	alama	red
28.		netil	ʔarit	ɲisiŋ	ŋalini	yellow
29.		wiat	wiat	viat	iala	green
30.		hewil	ʔawit	kiviŋ	kaini	blue
31.		saye	halay	salay	ʔala	tall
32.		roru	lalu	riru	lalu	short
33.		guseh	guhef	kusif	guʔepe	when?
34.		oat	awat	avat	ala	where?

INSTRUCTIONS:

1. Reconstruct Proto-ABCD 1–34.
2. List all changes in each language, including any ordering requirements.

RECONSTRUCTION PROBLEM 24

No.	Proto-ABC	Lg. A	Lg. B	Lg. C	
01.		lodu	luddu	rond	garden
02.		upat	uppat	urufət	weeds
03.		uap	huap	uəf	grass
04.		kandih	kassil	kantər	flower
05.		salai	salehi	sar	fruit
06.		sak	sahak	saək	seed
07.		ana	anna	aran	tree
08.		utile	usili	utir	wood
09.		hibus	libbus	rimbəs	vine
10.		kohop	kulup	korəf	forest
11.		une	unnay	urun	lake
12.		hambi	lappi	ramp	river
13.		akiŋ	akkiŋ	arakəŋ	water
14.		terin	tidin	tedən	shore
15.		luruh	ludul	rudər	fish
16.		alim	helim	arəm	stone
17.		maŋgit	makkit	maŋkət	boulder
18.		simo	simaw	sim	sand
19.		ruan	duahan	duən	earth
20.		pahuh	polul	farər	house
21.		tibas	sibbas	tiribəs	village
22.		ahuna	oluna	arun	man
23.		somil	summil	soromər	woman
24.		igu	iggu	iŋg	child
25.		petik	pissik	feretək	sun
26.		rarap	dadap	dadəf	moon
27.		lehute	lilutay	rerut	star
28.		kahinu	kelinu	karin	meteor
29.		amau	amohu	ama	lunar halo
30.		mateŋ	matiŋ	matəŋ	fog

INSTRUCTIONS/QUESTIONS:

1. Reconstruct Proto-ABC 1–30.
2. List all sound changes in each daughter language, noting any ordering requirements.
3. Certain reconstructions are ambiguous. Which ones are they, and what are the ambiguous segments?

RECONSTRUCTION PROBLEM 25

No.	Proto-ABC	Lg. A	Lg. B	Lg. C	
01.		kutuʔ	hudu	kuptu	eat
02.		taniŋ	dali	tamni	drink
03.		uhuih	uru	ulsu	talk
04.		saŋaʔ	sana	saŋta	sleep
05.		akaŋ	aha	akna	dream
06.		ŋulo	nuro	ŋuro	wake up
07.		lisoʔ	risə	riskə	stand up
08.		usel	use	usre	sit down
09.		putiŋ	fudi	putŋi	walk
10.		wakihi	vahiri	wakli	give
11.		sipaŋ	sifa	sipŋa	pick up
12.		uhuŋ	uru	ulnu	wait
13.		sadaŋ	sara	sadŋa	village
14.		kihil	hiri	kilri	house
15.		toloʔ	doro	torko	door
16.		koniʔ	həli	kənti	window
17.		pehu	feru	pelu	roof
18.		natah	lada	natla	floor
19.		duhiŋ	ruri	dulni	road
20.		puduta	furuda	putta	dust
21.		siwiʔ	sivi	siwti	fire
22.		utaʔ	uda	ukta	smoke
23.		bakuŋ	wahu	bakŋu	ashes
24.		inaŋ	ila	iŋna	sparks
25.		tiboih	diwə	tipsə	hearth
26.		sodoʔ	sərə	səptə	cooking pot
27.		amaih	ama	ansa	water
28.		ukuŋ	uhu	ukŋu	steam
29.		pahila	farira	palra	burn

INSTRUCTIONS/QUESTIONS:

1) Reconstruct Proto-ABC forms 1–29.
2) List all changes in each language, including any ordering requirements.
3) Four reconstructions show metathesis. Which ones are they, and what is the condition for metathesis?

RECONSTRUCTION PROBLEM 26

No.	Proto-ABC	Akman	Birina	Coshon	
01.		luhaʔ	hugʷat	rupat	sun
02.		hino	inaw	pinaw	hot
03.		hanaʔ	anar	panat	moon
04.		muluʔ	muhut	murut	cold
05.		ayaʔ	ajav	ap	star
06.		siluʔ	sirur	sirut	wind
07.		balaŋ	vaham	baram	fire
08.		huha	ugʷa	pupaʔ	tree
09.		tiaŋ	tijan	tian	water
10.		luniʔ	runi	runip	fish
11.		lawe	hagʷay	ray	sand
12.		tuliʔ	turiv	turip	earth
13.		tauʔ	tau	taʔup	mud
14.		wali	gʷahi	ari	man
15.		siha	sija	sipa	woman
16.		winu	gʷinu	inuʔ	child
17.		kuaʔ	kugʷa	kuap	dog
18.		nihuʔ	nijuk	nipuk	bird
19.		tahu	tau	tapu	eat
20.		liaŋ	hijaŋ	riaŋ	sleep
21.		dali	rari	dariʔ	wake up
22.		hiaʔ	iat	piʔat	cold
23.		uiʔ	ugʷig	uik	itchy
24.		ahali	ari	apari	tired
25.		wuyaʔ	gujak	uak	bored
26.		dugaʔ	rugag	dugak	dark
27.		liwuŋ	riguŋ	riuŋ	light
28.		bui	vui	buʔi	fear
29.		liaŋ	hiaŋ	riʔaŋ	fight
30.		kubo	kuvaw	kubaw	kill
31.		luhuʔ	huk	rupuk	die

Note: in Birina /j/ is a voiced palatal affricate, and /gʷ/ a labiovelar stop.

INSTRUCTIONS/QUESTIONS:

1. Reconstruct Proto-ABC 1–31.
2. List all sound changes in each daughter language, noting ordering relationships where needed.
3. Do you consider any of the sound correspondences 'unnatural'? Why, or why not?

RECONSTRUCTION PROBLEM 27

No.	Proto-KST	Kulak	Saru	Toto	
01.		kap	kawi	kapi	man
02.		sɔrüc	haruki	sarki	woman
03.		röcin	rutina	rutna	child
04.		mɛni	manie	manii	person
05.		jimɔl	dimalu	dimaru	chief
06.		arop	arup	arup	village
07.		atet	atitu	attu	field
08.		leŋɔs	liŋahu	riŋasu	earth
09.		tonel	tunil	tunir	stone
10.		lɛmiš	lamihi	ramsi	water
11.		pokɔl	wukalu	pukaru	river
12.		sɔröj	horudi	surdi	grass
13.		usɛc	uhati	usati	tree
14.		wɔk	waku	oku	animal
15.		tɛji	tegia	tigia	fat, grease
16.		kɔrüj	karudi	kardi	meat
17.		nɛnut	nenuti	ninti	blood
18.		lɛwik	lawik	roik	eat
19.		lɔsu	lahuo	rasuu	drink
20.		asɔ̈c	ahoki	aski	walk
21.		latas	latahi	ratasi	sleep
22.		kaseŋ	kahiŋ	kasiŋ	sit
23.		picin	wikinu	piknu	stand
24.		akep	akiwu	akpu	dark
25.		taw	tawa	toa	night
26.		cilis	tiliha	tirsa	star
27.		ket	kiti	kiti	moon
28.		takɛc	taketi	takti	sun
29.		šipɛj	hiwadi	sipadi	comet
30.		lelɛp	lilep	ririp	eclipse
31.		wal	walu	oru	rain

Note: stress in Proto-KST was word-initial. *c* is a voiceless palatal affricate, *j* a voiced palatal affricate, š a voiceless palatal fricative, ü a high front rounded vowel, ö a mid-front rounded vowel, and ɔ̈ a lower mid-front rounded vowel. Sequences of like vowels are separate syllable peaks.

INSTRUCTIONS/QUESTIONS:

1. Reconstruct Proto-KST 1–31.
2. List all sound changes in each language, noting any ordering requirements.
3. Are any reconstructions ambiguous? If so, which ones, and what are the ambiguous segments?

RECONSTRUCTION PROBLEM 28

No.	Proto-ABC	Lg. A	Lg. B	Lg. C	
01.		haak	feaxa	payah	chicken
02.		kuyu	xulu	hul	duck
03.		abaw	ampo	apaw	pig
04.		lalah	larafa	rarap	dog
05.		sukabi	uxampi	huhap	flea
06.		talom	tarumu	ʔaron	cricket
07.		yulut	lurudu	lurud	man
08.		suyaki	ulaxi	hulah	woman
09.		tulana	turana	ʔuran	child
10.		kigit	xiŋkiti	hikiʔ	house
11.		laluŋ	larunu	raruŋ	roof
12.		hedas	fintaa	petah	door
13.		kaas	xoaa	hawah	floor
14.		yeray	lide	leday	fire
15.		sidap	intaba	hitab	cook
16.		yiyin	lilini	lilin	pot
17.		liduk	rintuxu	rituh	ladle
18.		hugin	fuŋkili	pukil	soup
19.		ŋoli	nuri	ŋor	meat
20.		unari	unadi	unad	grass
21.		yiis	liwii	liwih	tree
22.		rabak	dampaga	dapag	leaf
23.		huut	fuyudu	puyud	branch
24.		taan	toala	ʔawal	flower
25.		ludum	runtumu	rutun	fruit
26.		bagaal	baŋkeara	bakayar	sun
27.		hulaɲi	furani	puraŋ	moon
28.		utol	uturu	uʔor	star
29.		hitun	fitunu	piʔun	storm
30.		biluli	biluri	birur	hail

Note: sequences of identical vowels are separate syllable peaks.

INSTRUCTIONS/QUESTIONS:

1. Reconstruct Proto-ABC 1–30.
2. Describe all changes in each language, noting any ordering requirements.
3. There are four correspondences that involve /l/ in at least one language. How many phonemes need to be reconstructed to account for these?

RECONSTRUCTION PROBLEM 29

No.	Proto-ABC	Lg. A	Lg. B	Lg. C
01.	fà	ua	uba	water
02.	tùk	raruk	lalku	eye
03.	túf	atup	aptu	snake
04.	tùf	tirup	telpu	belly
05.	kíx	pikis	peksi	die
06.	tíŋ	wisiŋ	bitŋi	arrow
07.	fǎt	mapat	mapata	cloud
08.	nim	anim	amni	spirit
09.	téf	atip	atepe	sleep
10.	kèn	wagin	bagene	pig
11.	kíx	pakis	paksi	rice field
12.	fǎl	rupal	lopala	waterfall
13.	tèn	kurin	kulene	village
14.	kí	puki	poki	navel
15.	nom	tanum	tanomo	headhunting
16.	ták	watak	bataka	axe
17.	kóf	akup	okopo	earthquake
18.	tík	wasik	bakti	night
19.	kàx	gugas	gugasa	star
20.	fìk	suwik	supki	lunar halo
21.	té	titi	tete	comet
22.	ruŋ	kuruŋ	kulŋu	chief
23.	xí	masi	masi	noble
24.	ŋaf	suŋap	suŋapa	slave
25.	rix	piris	pilsi	enemy
26.	lut	rulut	loltu	captive
27.	tìf	ririp	lilpi	war
28.	kùx	gagus	gaksa	peace
29.	fùt	nawut	naptu	corpse
30.	xúŋ	rusuŋ	lusŋu	ghost
31.	num	inum	emnu	dream

Note: in Lg. A an acute accent marks high tone and a grave accent low tone. Following sonorants vowels have a predictable level tone, which is unmarked.

INSTRUCTIONS/QUESTIONS:

1. Reconstruct Proto-ABC 1–31.
2. List all changes in each language, noting any ordering relationships where necessary.
3. Five reconstructions contain an ambiguous segment. Which reconstructions are they, and what are the two possibilities for the ambiguous proto-phoneme?
4. Is there contradictory evidence for stress placement in the changes that have affected these languages? How might this be reconciled by changes in the history of particular languages?

RECONSTRUCTION PROBLEM 30

Proto-Nsam-Kuni-Palu

No.	Proto-NKP	Nsam	Kuni	Palu	
01.		nsek	saxi	matehi	red
02.		mapm	afnu	mawonu	strong
03.		mop	afu	mowu	rotten
04.		lant	lantu	renitu	to smell
05.		kil	xila	hira	to eat
06.		mpil	filu	mewiru	long
07.		unt	utu	undu	to drink
08.		aŋk	aka	aŋga	dog
09.		matk	atxa	motuha	big
10.		ŋkol	xalu	mahoru	heavy
11.		mask	asxi	motuhi	angry
12.		kaŋk	xaŋxi	hemihi	to run
13.		nsul	sula	motura	sick
14.		samp	sapu	tombu	water
15.		ulp	ulfi	urewi	snake
16.		lask	lasxu	ratohu	to sleep
17.		mul	uli	muri	deep
18.		miŋk	ika	miŋga	dark
19.		ans	ansi	onuti	person
20.		tamp	tapa	tamba	man
21.		iŋk	iŋxa	iniha	woman
22.		et	ati	eti	child
23.		sump	sumfa	tunua	house

INSTRUCTIONS/QUESTIONS:

1. Reconstruct Proto-NKP 1–23, indicating morpheme boundaries in the reconstructions where appropriate.
2. List all changes in each language, indicating chronological order where appropriate.

3. What was the stress pattern in Proto-NKP?
4. What was the shape of the stative prefix, and what conditioned its allomorphy?

RECONSTRUCTION PROBLEM 31

No.	Proto-ABC	Lg. A	Lg. B	Lg. C	
01.		sihaz	hizas	kɛz	head
02.		ayak	razak	rɛak	hair
03.		lul	nunu	nunu	brain
04.		ursil	ukkin	ulkin	eye
05.		suad	uvat	sɔd	ear
06.		kawah	habau	kapɔ	mouth
07.		niuz	ŋizus	ŋüz	nose
08.		rohuk	louk	lʊk	chin
09.		isah	rizai	risɛ	neck
10.		sivuz	hivvus	kirvuz	shoulder
11.		zieg	zirek	zireg	back
12.		unua	uŋuva	uŋɔ	arm
13.		wolot	ponodi	ponoti	bone
14.		sinia	iŋiza	siŋɛ	blood
15.		aiv	raif	rɛv	earth
16.		sirab	ilap	silab	water
17.		waltot	pattot	pantot	mountain
18.		savin	avinu	savinu	tree
19.		tomoka	tomoha	tomoka	forest
20.		eiaw	erizap	erɛp	grass
21.		uad	uruvat	urɔd	vine
22.		lat	nadu	natu	stone
23.		tua	tuba	tupa	river
24.		uhos	uvohi	ʊki	wind
25.		zahag	zak	zag	storm
26.		wuir	puvil	pül	flood
27.		sihil	in	sin	to swim
28.		wak	varak	warak	to drown
29.		wais	paizu	pɛsu	to rescue

Note: in Lg. C /ü/ is a front rounded vowel and /ʊ/ a lower-high back vowel.

INSTRUCTIONS:

1. Reconstruct Proto-ABC 1–29.
2. List all sound changes in each daughter language together with any ordering requirements.

RECONSTRUCTION PROBLEM 32

No.	Proto-ABCD	Lg. A	Lg. B	Lg. C	Lg. D	
01.		labu	lambut	labuʔ	lamutu	grass
02.		igã	igam	igaŋ	iɣama	sky
03.		əfanu	tilap	kifonu	hifanu	cloud
04.		hətua	sattuk	satuka	sanduha	rain
05.		milã	milaŋ	bakuŋ	milaa	water
06.		torũ	torum	toruŋ	torumu	earth
07.		napu	noap	noopu	noafu	fire
08.		au	ekah	ekohu	ehahu	sand
09.		pila	uppil	upila	umbila	river
10.		puda	pundak	pudaʔ	funaha	man
11.		haku	sakkup	sakuʔ	saŋgufu	woman
12.		tapĩ	tapin	tepiŋ	tafini	child
13.		dudũ	dundun	duduŋ	rununu	head
14.		eti	kettil	keti	hendili	hair
15.		faũ	fakuŋ	fokuŋ	fahuu	eye
16.		poo	ippoh	ipoho	imboho	nose
17.		naga	naŋgat	nagaʔ	naɲata	ear
18.		bibĩ	biŋbiŋ	bibiŋ	vimii	mouth
19.		lapar	alapar	alapa	alafara	tooth
20.		lamũ	lamuŋ	lomuŋ	lamuu	hand
21.		abĩ	hambin	habiŋ	hamini	elbow
22.		halu	sual	suolu	amuhu	back
23.		əbaka	kumbak	kubaka	humaŋga	belly
24.		rudu	rudup	ruduʔ	rurufu	leg
25.		bara	ibarak	ibaraʔ	ivaraha	heart
26.		hali	sial	sieli	siali	liver
27.		gagã	gangan	gagaŋ	ɣaŋana	lungs
28.		ləmari	lamar	lameri	lamari	blood
29.		birã	ratul	ubiraŋ	uviraa	vein
30.		gorã	goran	goraŋ	ɣorana	brain
31.		tutũ	tuttum	tutuŋ	tundumu	gall
32.		iŋa	hiŋat	hiŋaʔ	hiata	bone

INSTRUCTIONS:

1. Reconstruct Proto-ABCD 1–32.
2. State all changes in each daughter language, noting any ordering requirements.

RECONSTRUCTION PROBLEM 33

No.	Proto-ABC	Lg. A	Lg. B	Lg. C	
01.		cumu	tisuŋ	titumə	bird
02.		mala	mana	marə	feather
03.		ula	ua	urə	rain
04.		ahapa	āf	akapə	clothing
05.		mala	mā	maharə	horse
06.		himi	īŋ	kihimə	dog
07.		bata	vasaʔ	batatə	pig
08.		mala	masaŋ	matarə	rope
09.		ulili	uiŋ	urirə	land
10.		puhu	fū	puhukə	house
11.		jala	diaŋ	diarə	door
12.		uru	suru	turə	roof
13.		jala	dia	diharə	road
14.		ca	tiā	tiahə	dust
15.		imutu	imuʔ	imutə	to eat
16.		alu	auh	harutə	to sleep
17.		da	dasa	datə	to dream
18.		rita	ritah	ritatə	afraid
19.		pai	fasi	patə	worried
20.		tulaha	tuna	turakə	desperate
21.		titi	titi	titə	panicky
22.		hi	ī	kihə	dead
23.		hubaŋa	uvaŋ	kubaŋə	ghost

Note: c, j = voiceless and voiced palatal affricates respectively.

INSTRUCTIONS:

1. Reconstruct Proto-ABC 1–23.
2. State all changes in each daughter language, noting ordering requirements where necessary.

RECONSTRUCTION PROBLEM 34

No.	Proto-ABCD	Lg. A	Lg. B	Lg. C	Lg. D	
01.		lauk	hahu	hou?	auh	fish
02.		latah	rata	latah	yatos	water
03.		ayut	aru	oyuŋ	aun	wave
04.		ehap	heha	ehaŋ	esom	sky
05.		ilup	iru	iluf	iuf	wind
06.		tula	tuha	tuha	tuo	earth
07.		uhik	uhi	uhiŋ	usiŋ	grass
08.		pool	foho	foh	fo	stone
09.		malu	maru	molu	mayu	wake
10.		uyah-a	mu-ura	m-uyah	uos-o	wash
11.		inul-a	mu-ilu	mu-lahaf	inuy-o	drink
12.		hapel-a	mu-hafe	mu-hafeh	safe-o	eat
13.		aŋati	hanasi	aŋesi	limu	walk
14.		panim	fali	feniŋ	fanim	fire
15.		hulat	huha	huha?	suot	smoke
16.		laup	rahu	louŋ	yaum	ash
17.		tiap	sia	siaf	tiof	hearth
18.		kayali-a	mu-harahi	mu-mutuk	hai-o	burn
19.		anuŋ	alu	onuŋ	anuŋ	rubbish
20.		nitak	lita	nitaŋ	nitoŋ	house
21.		pukap	oraha	oyaha	oao	roof
22.		tikuk-a	sihu	sihuŋ	tihuŋ-o	work
23.		ŋatik	nasi	ŋesi?	sihif	sleep
24.		uŋan	una	uŋaŋ	etom	dream
25.		lamak	rama	lama?	yamoh	shadow

INSTRUCTIONS/QUESTIONS:

1. Reconstruct Proto-ABCD 1–25, assuming that Lgs. B and C form a subgroup.
2. Note all changes in each language, together with any ordering requirements.
3. Do any of the sound changes strike you as odd? Why?
4. What affix or affixes can be reconstructed for Proto-ABCD?

PROBLEMS: LEVEL 3

RECONSTRUCTION PROBLEM 35

No.	Proto-ABCD	Lg. A	Lg. B	Lg. C	Lg. D	
01.		talãp	talã	talab	talaŋ	grass
02.		kefã	kipã	kepa	kepa	tree
03.		nuyuh	nuyu	nuzuʔ	nujuh	earth
04.		alõp	alũ	alob	aloŋ	stone
05.		hiul	hiu	izul	hiju	water
06.		kũĩk	kũĩ	kuvig	kugʷiŋ	sky
07.		hanit	sani	ʔanid	haniʔ	rain
08.		ãhar	ãha	aar	aha	storm
09.		mitãt	mitã	mitad	mitaŋ	cloud
10.		liaf	lia	lizap	lijaʔ	hand
11.		wato	watu	vato	gʷato	arm
12.		hua	hua	uva	hugʷa	elbow
13.		avũt	abũ	abud	abuŋ	knee
14.		harah	sara	ʔaraʔ	harah	house
15.		rawik	rawi	ravik	ragʷiʔ	wall
16.		lufĩh	lupĩ	lupi	lupih	roof
17.		utap	uta	utab	utaʔ	dog
18.		vihek	bisi	biʔek	biheʔ	ant
19.		faluk	palu	palug	paluʔ	fly
20.		gulũh	gulũ	guluʔ	guluh	see
21.		orat	uda	odat	odaʔ	hear
22.		rahũk	dasũ	daʔug	dahuŋ	eat
23.		iŋuh	iŋu	iŋu	iŋuh	drink
24.		yavet	yabi	zabet	jabeʔ	sleep
25.		fafah	papa	papa	papah	dream

Note: Proto-ABCD did not have a glottal stop.

INSTRUCTIONS:

1. Reconstruct Proto-ABCD 1–25.
2. List all changes in each daughter language and their relative chronology.
3. In addition, list the inventory of Proto-ABCD phonemes. Pay particular attention to sound correspondences which are in complementary distribution, as these should be assigned to a single proto-phoneme.

INTERNAL RECONSTRUCTION

(10 problems)

Background

Internal reconstruction is the use of distributional patterns and phonological atlernations within a single language to reach inferences about the earlier condition of that language. Internal reconstruction is often applied to language isolates, since these give no scope for application of the comparative method, but it can be applied to any language, including reconstructed languages.

Most treatments of internal reconstruction begin with phonological alternations, but the unification of allophones into phonemes based on complementation can be seen as another form of the same procedure. In Wuvulu, spoken in the Admiralty Islands of western Melanesia, for example, [ʧ] varies freely with [s], and this pair of segments is in complementary distribution with [t], the former two allophones occuring before high vowels and the latter before non-high vowels, as with [ʧuʧu] ~ [susu] 'breast' or [muʧilau] ~ [musilau] 'honeybee' next to [oto] 'digging stick', [late] 'betel nut', or [talija] 'flying fish'. A consideration of other phones in the language and their distribution favours the interpretation that [ʧ], [s] and [t] should all be represented by /t/, so in terms of reconciling distributional properties this can be seen as a first step in internal reconstruction. Note that an internal reconstruction may not always correspond to the results obtained by the comparative method. The Proto-Oceanic word for 'breast', for example, was *susu, but what the Wuvulu facts reflect is that *s first became /t/ at an earlier stage in the history of Wuvulu, and this /t/ then developed allophones conditioned by the height of a following vowel. This is a common shortcoming – internal reconstruction can provide insights into earlier stages of a language, but they usually are short-term insights by comparsion to the longer-term insights provided by cognate sets.

A second area in which single-language data can shed light on earlier historical stages, and one that is commonly overlooked in textbook discussions of internal reconstruction, is neutralisation. To cite one of many possible examples, Malay has both voiceless and voiced stops, *p, t, k, b, d, g*, but only the former occur word-finally. Unlike German, which has undergone final devoicing but still preserves the contrast of voiced and voiceless stops in suffixed forms, Malay shows no voicing alternations under suffixation. The contrast of *p, *t, *k and *b, *d, *g has thus been neutralised in synchronic terms (as a result of merger in diachronic terms). While this state of affairs could in principle reflect the distributional properties of a remote proto-language, this is unlikely, and comparative data support the inference that can be reached purely through neutralisation that Malay underwent final devoicing at some point in its history.

The most common type of data used in internal reconstruction are provided by phonological alternations. In many Austronesian languages of the large (460-member) Oceanic subgroup original final consonants have been lost, but reappear (sometimes altered by analogy or other processes) under suffixation. In languages with even greater phonological erosion 'from the right' original CVCVC forms have been reduced to CVC by loss of the last -VC, and under suffixation in some forms the 'lost' vowel-consonant sequence reappears. A good example is Mota of the Banks Islands in northern Vanuatu, which has lost original final high vowels, but not non-high vowels, and shows pairs such as the intransitive *matag-tag* 'to fear', next to the transitive *matagut* < POC *ma-takut 'to fear, be afraid of'.

Finally, internal reconstruction can be applied to a proto-language that has already been reconstructed through application of the comparative method. The most famous example of this is undoubtedly that of the pivotal Swiss linguist Ferdinand de Saussure, who sought to explain the origin of the pattern of verbal ablaut in many Indo-European languages typified by examples like English *sing : sang : sung*, a pattern that was attributed in his day to a Proto-Indo-European system of 'vowel grades' or apophony. Saussure proposed to derive this system of variable values by positing a set of previously unrecognised consonants that he characterised as purely abstract entities called 'sonantic coefficients': these coloured the adjacent vowels, and before disappearing produced the attested pattern of vowel variation seen in various daughter languages. Since none of these abstract elements (which soon came to be interpreted as laryngeal consonants) was actually present in any of the modern languages, Saussure's interpretation was essentially ignored until after his death in 1913. Then, dramatically, the discovery of ancient Hittite manuscripts provided a new window on the Indo-European past, and the most startling feature of this material was the presence of written symbols corresponding closely to the positions of Saussure's 'sonantic coefficients'. Needless to say, this discovery has been memorialised as one of the great empirical confirmations of a theoretical prediction in the history of the field.

Because they are relatively few in number, and vary only slightly in level of difficulty, the internal reconstruction problems are not ordered by level.

INTERNAL RECONSTRUCTION PROBLEM 1

Toba Batak (northern Sumatra, Indonesia)

Background. The following is a rather simple problem in the use of internal reconstruction for Toba Batak, one of a group of six fairly closely-related languages spoken in northern Sumatra, Indonesia (the others are Alas, Karo Batak, Dairi-Pakpak Batak, Angkola-Mandailing Batak and Simalungun Batak). Toba Batak has a traditional Indic-based syllabary used for writing the language, and in this orthographic system the geminate consonants *pp, tt, kk* and the affricate *ts* are written as prenasalised obstruents *mp, nt, ŋk,* and *ns* (thus, e.g., *maŋ-haŋkaŋ-i* is written *maŋ-haŋkaŋ-i*). Like most other languages in the Philippines and western Indonesia, Toba Batak makes use of homorganic nasal substitution with active verb prefixes, as in *pansur* 'a stream of water', *ma-mansur* 'to spray water'.

The data in (A) show all environments in which [h] is found in this language, and the data in (B) do the same for [k]. A small number of loanwords violate these patterns, but are ignored here in the interest of understanding the phonology of the native forms. The special interest of this problem is in the issue it raises for the traditional terminology used to describe phonological alternations, and the relationship of morpheme boundaries to the description of phonological processes:

(A)
1. haha 'elder sibling of the same sex'   (initially before /a/)
2. heas 'maggot'   (initially before /e/)
3. hita '1pl. incl.'   (initially before /i/)
4. hobol 'invulnerable'   (initially before /o/)
5. humala 'quartz talisman'   (initially before /u/)
6. maŋ-hilala 'to feel, sense'   (following a nasal + morpheme boundary)
7. hurhur-an 'coconut grater'   (postconsonantally in a historically reduplicated monosyllable)

(B)
1. ma-bakbak 'to flow, of tears'   (preconsonantally in a historically reduplicated monosyllable)
2. akkut-akkut 'k.o. wasp'   (in geminates)
3. apporik 'rice bird'   (word-finally)

INSTRUCTIONS/QUESTIONS:

1. Given this information posit underlying forms for the reduplicated or affixed words in the following sets:

   (a) andoh-andok 'rice sack'
   (b) otoh-otok 'shrub with yellow blossoms'
   (c) maŋ-hakkaŋ-i 'hold s.t. tightly between the legs'
   (d) anak 'child' : par-anah-on 'relation between father and child'
   (e) lapuk 'mold, fungus' : lapuh-on 'moldy, mildewed'
   (f) m-urak 'be ashamed' : ha-urah-on 'disgrace, scandal'
   (g) m-oltuh-oltuk 'tasty (of fruits, sweet potatoes)'
   (h) tar-tuktuk 'stumble, knock against' : ma-nuktuh-i 'knock on, pound on'

2. What is the phonological relationship of [h] and [k] in Toba Batak?
3. Why is the traditional (American Structuralist) term 'morphophonemic alternation' inappropriate for describing the relationships of these phones?

INTERNAL RECONSTRUCTION PROBLEM 2

Western Bukidnon Manobo (southern Philippines)

Background. The following problem is also a relatively simple one for Western Bukidnon Manobo, one of perhaps a dozen Manobo languages spoken on the island of Mindanao in the southern Philippines. Consider the data in (A):

(A)

amur 'to gather together' : kə-ʔəmur-an 'a celebration of any kind'

amut 'to contribute' : əmut-aʔ 'a contribution'

apuʔ 'grandparent/grandchild' : əpuʔ-an 'line of descent'

balak 'come together' : bəlak-an 'crossroads'

bəl-vəlay-an 'a toy' : baləy-valəy 'to play'

baras 'to serve assiduously' : baras-baras 'do something thoroughly'

bantug 'fame' : mə-vantug 'famous'

barək 'colour' : bə-vərək-aʔ 'many-coloured'

basuk 'to till the soil' : mə-vasuk 'industrious in farming'

bavaʔ 'shortness' : mə-vavaʔ 'short'

bəɣat 'weight' : mə-vəɣat 'heavy'

bulawan 'gold' : kə-vuləwan-an 'wealth; splendour'

bunsud 'set a long object on end' : bunsuz-an 'area at foot of ladder'

buwad 'to reproduce' : kə-vuwaz-an 'one's posterity'

mə-zakəl 'many' : dəkəl-aʔ 'big'

dəŋdəŋ 'lie motionless (fish)' : pəzə-zəŋdəŋ 'motionless, unresponsive (person)'

dəsən 'strength' : mə-zəsən 'strong'

duwa 'two' : ikə-zuwa 'second' : tig-duwa 'by twos'

gəvuʔ 'weakness' : mə-ɣəvuʔ 'weak, fragile'

giŋəy 'to make pregnant' : iŋkə-ɣiŋəy 'illegitimate child'

guyɣuy 'trampled sword grass'

hiləw 'unripe' : kə-hilaw-an 'humanity'

lalag 'to speak' : kə-ləlaɣ-an 'a helpful, considerate person'

lambəg 'to meet someone' : ləmbaɣ-an 'crossroad'

paʔid-paʔid 'have an abundance of the best of everything'

mə-rayag-rayag 'light-skinned (person)'

sanap-sanap 'reduced to a trickle (stream)'

sandig-sandig 'lean back on something'

savuŋ-savuŋ 'bangs in the hair'

surud 'fine-toothed comb' : suruz-an 'comb-like part of loom'
takəw 'to steal' : təkaw-ən 'a thief'
tulis 'to rob by force' : tulis-an 'a bandit'

QUESTIONS:

1. What are the underlying forms of [əmutaʔ] 'a contribution', [əpuʔan] 'line of descent', and [bəlakan] 'crossroads'?
2. What are the underlying forms of [məvantug] 'famous', [bəvərəkaʔ] 'many-coloured', and [məvavaʔ] 'short'?
3. What are the underlying forms of [bunsuzan] 'area at foot of ladder', [məzakəl] 'many', and [məzəsən] 'strong'?
4. What are the underlying forms of [məɣəvuʔ] 'weak, fragile', [guyɣuy] 'trampled sword grass', and [ləmbaɣan] 'crossroad'?
5. What are the underlying forms of [bəlvəlayan] 'a toy', [kəhilawan] 'humanity' and [təkawən] 'a thief'?
6. What explanation can you give for the retention of the prepenultimate low vowel in [barasbaras] 'do something thoroughly', [sandigsandig] 'lean back on something' or [savuŋsavuŋ] 'bangs in the hair'?

INTERNAL RECONSTRUCTION PROBLEM 3

Samoan (western Polynesia)

Consider the following simple bases and one type of suffixed form:

No	Base	Suffixed form	
01.	inu	inumia	drink; be drunk by s.o.
02.	utu	utufia	fill a container; be filled by s.o.
03.	afã	afãtia	storm; be affected by a storm
04.	sala	sasalaina	cut; be cut by s.o.
05.	ua	uaina	rain; be rained on
06.	fana	fana?ia	shoot; be shot by s.o.
07.	taŋi	taŋisia	weep; be mourned by s.o.
08.	alofa	alofaŋia	love; be loved by s.o.
09.	pulu	pulutia	caulk; be caulked by s.o.
10.	ulu	ulufia	enter; be entered by s.o.
11.	manatu	manatulia	think; be thought by s.o.
12.	tū	tūlia	stand; be erected by s.o.
13.	tā	tāia	beat; be beaten by s.o.
14.	tautala	tautalaŋia	speak; be discussed by s.o.
15.	fuli	fulisia	turn over; be turned over by s.o.
16.	?eli	?elia	dig; be dug up by s.o.
17.	tanu	tanumia	bury; be buried by s.o.
18.	tunu	tunua	broil; be broiled by s.o.
19.	ato	atoina	thatch; be thatched by s.o.
20.	tau	tauia	reach; be reached by s.o.

QUESTIONS:

1. What are the underlying forms of items 1–20?
2. Is it possible that native speakers of Samoan and linguists might have different interpretations of what the underlying forms are? Why might this be?

INTERNAL RECONSTRUCTION PROBLEM 4

Seimat (Admiralty Islands, Papua New Guinea)

(A)

No.	Base	3sg. possessed form	
01.	min	minan	hand
02.	sus	susun	breast
03.	put	puton	navel
04.	ut	utin	penis
05.	pat	patun	head
06.	kaw	kawãn	forehead
07.	pul	pulan	eye
08.	aw	awan	mouth
09.	nis	nisun	tooth
10.	xoh	xohen	gums
11.	leh	lehon	tongue
12.	kinaw	kinawen	neck
13.	taxiŋ	taxiŋan	ear
14.	uk	ukun	head hair
15.	kaka	kakaun	blood
16.	atol	atolun	brain
17.	mapu	mapuan	sweat
18.	loh	lohun	friend

(B)

No.	Base	Continuative form	
01.	ikoik		mussel
02.	suhusuh		conch shell
03.	pakapak		shrimp
04.	solisol		tidal wave
05.	ponapon		swamp
06.	hatuhat		four-cornered fish
07.	uliul		side board of canoe
08.	paŋapaŋ		moon
09.	konokon		prow of canoe
10.	taŋ 'to cry'	taŋitaŋ	be crying
11.	aŋ 'to eat'	aŋiaŋ	be eating

12.	mut 'vomitus'	mutumut	be vomiting; to vomit
13.	tasutas		nasal mucus
14.	utuut		corner
15.	axaax		fire plough
16.	hatahat		storage shelf
17.	kuhukuh		*Alocasia* taro
18.	silisil		tuna sp.
19.	tioti		large barbelled fish
20.	kawakaw		bamboo
21.	paxapax		sandfly
22.	kioki		kingfisher
23.	un 'to drink'	unuun	be drinking
24.	hoŋ 'to hear'	hoŋohoŋ	be hearing
25.	siwisiw		black hummingbird
26.	laŋalaŋ		sailing
27.	pak 'song; to sing'	pakupak	be singing
28.	leŋeleŋ		to fight, of animals
29.	hilehil		to fight in war
30.	telei 'to kill'	teletel	be killing
31.	ha-puta 'to drop'	putaput	to fall; be falling
32.	manuman		drift on a current

INSTRUCTIONS/QUESTIONS:

1. Compare the eighteen Seimat nouns and their 3sg. possessive forms in section (A); then consider forms 1–32 in section (B). Note that some verbs in the first column of section (B) may not be base forms.
2. What are the underlying forms of bases 1–18 in section (A)?
3. What synchronic rule relates these to the suffixed possessives?
4. What are the underlying shapes of the continuative forms in section (B)?
5. Finally, should the nouns in section (B) be attributed an underlying shape different from the surface form? Why or why not?

PROBLEMS

INTERNAL RECONSTRUCTION PROBLEM 5

Kapampangan (Central Luzon, Philippines)

No.	Base	Verb
01.	abú 'ash'	man-abú 'become ash'
02.	águs 'current'	mam-águs 'to flow'
03.	ámbun 'dew'	mam-ámbun 'be about to rain'
04.	ágiʔ 'spiderweb'	man-ágiʔ 'remove cobwebs'
05.	ínaʔ 'weakness'	mim-ínaʔ 'grow weak'
06.	íkab 'belch'	man-íkab 'to belch'
07.	áŋin 'wind'	mam-áŋin 'to blow, of the wind'
08.	ampíl 'a stack'	man-ampíl 'to stack (dishes)'
09.	urúd 'haircut'	man-urúd 'get a haircut'
10.	úna 'first'	mum-úna 'go first, be first'
11.	atád 'escort'	mam-atád 'to escort'
12.	apán 'bait'	man-apán 'put out bait'
13.	igpit 'tight'	man-igpit 'to tighten'
14.	íkat 'a braid'	mim-íkat 'to braid'
15.	ulíʔ 'go home'	man-ulíʔ 'to go home'
16.	iʔ 'urine'	mim-íʔ 'to urinate'
17.	úkyat 'climbing'	mum-úkyat 'to climb'
18.	ípus 'servant'	man-ípus 'to serve'
19.	úlu 'medicine'	man-úlu 'curer'
20.	urán 'rain'	mum-urán 'to rain, be raining'
21.	úpa 'rent'	man-úpa 'to rent'
22.	útak 'brain'	mum-útak 'to use one's brain'
23.	ísip 'think'	man-ísip 'to think'
24.	íŋat 'caution'	mim-íŋat 'to beware'

INSTRUCTIONS/QUESTIONS:

1. Consider the preceding twenty-four verbs in Kapampangan. How many prefixes do you identify in the data?
2. What prefixal allomorphs do you see, and how are they conditioned?
3. Is there anything surprising about this conditioning, and if so what?
4. Is it possible to state a single underlying shape for these prefixes? Why or why not?

INTERNAL RECONSTRUCTION PROBLEM 6

Thao (central Taiwan)

Consider the following word bases in column A, and the corresponding Actor Voice verbs in column B from Thao, spoken at Sun Moon Lake in central Taiwan. Note that *c* is a voiceless interdental fricative, *z* its voiced counterpart, *lh* a voiceless alveolar lateral, *sh* a voiceless palatal fricative, and stress is penultimate.

No.	(A)	(B)
01.	apa 'carry on the back'	mapa 'to carry on the back'
02.	ishur 'prying up'	mishur 'to pry something up'
03.	utaq 'vomit'	mutaq 'to vomit'
04.	liliz 'following'	mliliz 'to follow someone, to tail'
05.	rinuz 'earthquake'	mrinuz 'to shake, of an earthquake'
06.	zai 'advice'	mzai 'to advise'
07.	ca-capu 'broom'	cmapu 'to sweep'
08.	hurhur 'barking'	hmurhur 'to bark'
09.	kawar 'wall hook'	kmawar 'to hang on a hook'
10.	lhipir 'a fold'	lhmipir 'to fold, as paper or cloth'
11.	qucquc 'binding'	qmucquc 'to tie, bind'
12.	siraq 'a kiss'	smiraq 'to kiss, to lick'
13.	shuruz 'pull'	shmuruz 'to pull'
14.	tiktik 'hacking, chopping'	tmiktik 'to hack, to chop'
15.	patash 'tattoo; writing'	matash 'to write'
16.	pushizi 'separation'	mushizi 'to separate'
17.	fariw 'buying'	fariw 'to buy'
18.	fuilh 'inform'	fuilh 'to inform'
19.	qpit 'pinching'	qumpit 'to pinch'
20.	qtut 'a fart'	q<um>tut 'to fart'
21.	shkash 'fear'	sh<um>kash 'to fear'
22.	shqa 'bequeath'	sh<um>-qa [ʃúNqa] 'to bequeath'
23.	shnara 'burn'	sh<um>nara 'to burn'
24.	cnit 'wring out'	c<um>nit 'to wring out'
25.	shrak 'untying'	sh<um>rak [ʃúndrak] 'to untie'
26.	kriu? 'stealing, theft'	k<um>riu? [kúndreu?] 'to steal'

INSTRUCTIONS/QUESTIONS:

1. What is the underlying form of the Actor Voice affix in Thao, and where is it inserted? Write the underlying forms of all words in column B.
2. What phonetic factors condition the observed allomorphy? Be specific, by listing each allomorph separately and stating under what conditions it occurs.

INTERNAL RECONSTRUCTION PROBLEM 7

Sangir (northern Sulawesi, Indonesia)

Consider the following active verbs in column A, and the morphologically related instrumental nouns in column B from Sangir, spoken in the Sangihe Islands between Sulawesi and Mindanao. Note that *gh* is a voiced fricative.

No.	Active verb (A)	Instrumental noun (B)
01.	maɲaki 'extend a fishline'	laaki 'extension piece on fishline'
02.	mamaŋgo 'to beat'	bawaŋgo 'a cudgel'
03.	mamuaŋ 'fasten with transverse pin'	bawuaŋ 'transverse pin'
04.	dumǝkaʔ 'to stick, adhere'	darǝkaʔ 'plaster, paste'
05.	mǝndupa 'to hammer'	darupa 'a hammer'
06.	maɲǝkiŋ 'give a brideprice'	laǝkiŋ 'a brideprice'
07.	maɲǝmmuʔ 'wipe off'	laǝmmuʔ 'dustcloth, washcloth'
08.	mǝŋgataʔ 'carry under the arm'	gaghataʔ 'bamboo tongs'
09.	mǝhimadǝʔ 'use a gouging tool'	lahimadǝʔ 'gouging tool'
10.	maɲikiʔ 'to tie'	laikiʔ 'anything used for tying'
11.	maɲǝtuŋ 'seize with pincers'	kakǝtuŋ 'pincers'
12.	mǝlauʔ 'to mix'	dalauʔ 'tool used for mixing'
13.	mǝlǝdaŋ 'to file the teeth'	dalǝdaŋ 'a tooth file'
14.	mamaŋkulǝʔ 'hit with stick'	papaŋkulǝʔ 'stick used for hitting'
15.	mamǝgoŋ 'tie round the middle'	papǝgoŋ 'belt'
16.	manapu 'to sweep'	sasapu 'broom'
17.	sumindaʔ 'to breathe'	sasindaʔ 'anything that assists breathing'
18.	manapisǝʔ 'to sift'	tatapisǝʔ 'a sieve'
19.	manubuŋ 'knock down fruit'	tatubuŋ 'fruiting pole'
20.	maɲuhasǝʔ 'to wash'	lauhasǝʔ 'water used for washing'

INSTRUCTIONS/QUESTIONS:

1. List the underlying forms of the instrumental nouns.
2. Which of these do you consider to be straightforward? Which do you consider to be obscure?
3. How do you suppose such a system might have developed?

INTERNAL RECONSTRUCTION PROBLEM 8

Bario Kelabit (Sarawak, Malaysian Borneo)

Consider the following simple bases and their affixed forms.

No.	A	B	
01.	atur	ŋatur	an order; to order
02.	pudut	mudut	a shape; to shape
03.	bilaʔ	milaʔ	to split
04.	tərəm	nərəm	to sink; force under water
05.	dalan	nalan	path; to walk
06.	kiluʔ	ŋiluʔ	a bend; to bend
07.	laak	ŋəlaak	cooked; to cook
08.	raʔit	ŋəraʔit	raft; travel by raft
09.	taban	təbanən	elopement; to elope
10.	badil	bədilən	gun; be shot
11.	irup	rupan	drink; watering hole
12.	arəg	rəgʰən	fragment; broken to bits
13.	taʔut	pətaʔut	fear; to frighten
		pintaʔut	was frightened
14.	piŋur	təpiŋur	echo; echoing back and forth
		simpiŋur	was used to make echoes
15.	təbʰək	sibʰək	pierce mark; was pierced by
16.	təl:ən	silən	swallow; was swallowed by
17.	təbʰar	nəbʰar	wages; to pay
		təbaran	Pay him! (imper.)
18.	təbʰəŋ	nəbʰəŋ	felling of trees; to fell
		təbəŋ:ən	Fell it! (imper.)
19.	ulud	ludən	words; will tell (near future)
20.	əbʰaʔ	ŋəbʰaʔ	water; to add/remove water
		baʔən	Add/remove water! (imper.)
21.	kədʰa	ŋədʰa	able to take pain; to suffer
		kədaan	suffering
22.	turuʔ	sinuruʔ	an order; was ordered by s.o.
23.	kək:əb	kəkəbʰən	lid; be covered by s.o.
24.	agag	gagən	rice sieve; to sift
25.	uit	muit	way of bringing; to bring

26.	turun	təmurun	descent; to descend
27.	əl:əg	məl:əg	cessation; to stop
		ləgʰən	be stopped by s.o.
28.	bəbʰəd	bəbədʰən	bundle; tie by winding round
		bibʰəd	was tied by winding round
29.	gət:əp	gətəp:ən	bite mark; be bitten by
30.	bəl:ih	məl:ih	buying; to buy
		bəliən	Buy it! (imper.)

Note: *bh, dh, gh* represent true voiced aspirates (unit phonemes that begin voiced and end voiceless, with voiceless onset to a following vowel for some speakers; these have about twice the length of their simple voiced counterparts). Stress is penultimate in all words, both monomorphemic and polymorphemic, and allophonic gemination (which is relevant to understanding the phonology) is marked by a colon.

QUESTIONS:

1. What are the underlying forms of the affixed words in column B?
2. What are the synchronic phonological processes that produce these results?

INTERNAL RECONSTRUCTION PROBLEM 9

Mukah Melanau (Sarawak, Malaysian Borneo)

Background. Consider the following data from Mukah Melanau, an Austronesian language spoken in coastal Sarawak, Malaysian Borneo. Glosses correspond roughly to the meaning of the base form, while verbal forms are active, passive, or in some cases causative (*biləm* 'black' : *mə-biləm* 'blacken, make s.t. black', *nə-biləm* 'was blackened by s.o.', but *ulin* 'rudder of a boat' : *m-ulin* 'steer a boat using the rudder' : *n-ulin* 'was steered by s.o., of a boat', *asəw* 'dog' : *məŋ-asəw* 'to hunt using dogs', etc.).

Base	Active verb	Passive verb	
(1)			
baat	mə-baat	nə-baat	heavy
balas	mə-balas	nə-balas	revenge
biləm	mə-biləm	nə-biləm	black
bin	mə-bin	nə-bin	carrying on back
bukut	mə-bukut	nə-bukut	punching
dipih	mə-dipih	nə-dipih	hiding (s.t.)
duga	mə-duga	nə-duga	estimate
gaday	mə-gaday	nə-gaday	pawning
gaduŋ	mə-gaduŋ	nə-gaduŋ	green
gahut	mə-gahut	nə-gahut	scratching
galaŋ	mə-galaŋ	nə-galaŋ	throwing
gatuŋ	mə-gatuŋ	nə-gatuŋ	hanging
gaul	mə-gaul	nə-gaul	mixing
gaup	mə-gaup	nə-gaup	blowing
gutiŋ	mə-gutiŋ	nə-gutiŋ	scissors
jaja	mə-jaja	mə-jaja	selling
jaʔit	mə-jaʔit	nə-jaʔit	sewing
(2)			
aat	m-aat	n-aat	squeezing
agəm	m-agəm	n-agəm	gripping
añam	m-añam	n-añam	plaiting
aŋit	m-aŋit	n-aŋit	angry
asaʔ	m-asaʔ	n-asaʔ	whetting

asiʔ	m-asiʔ	n-asiʔ	pity
iap	m-iap	n-iap	counting
ibay	m-ibay	n-ibay	buying
isak	m-isak	n-isak	cooking
ituŋ	m-ituŋ	n-ituŋ	counting
ulin	m-ulin	n-ulin	rudder
upuk	m-upuk	n-upuk	washing
uʔəm	m-uʔəm	n-uʔəm	soaking
uug	m-uug	n-uug	scrubbing

(3)

gəga	guga	giga	chase away
gəgət	gugət	gigət	gnaw
kəkay	kukay	kikay	rake
kəkut	kukut	kikut	digging
ləpək	lupək	lipək	fold(ing)
ləpəw	lupəw	lipəw	picking
ñəñaʔ	ñuñaʔ	ñiñaʔ	chewing
ŋəŋət	ŋuŋət	ŋiŋət	gnaw
səbət	subət	sibət	making
səkəl	sukəl	sikəl	strangling
səpət	supət	sipət	blowpipe
səsəp	susəp	sisəp	sucking
təbək	tubək	tibək	stabbing
tətək	tutək	titək	cutting
tətəŋ	tutəŋ	titəŋ	drinking

(4)

katay	mə-ŋatay	k<ən>atay	stop working
kiap	mə-ŋiap	k<ən>iap	hand fan
kulit	mə-ŋulit	k<ən>ulit	skin
padaʔ	mə-madaʔ	p<ən>adaʔ	request
pajəm	mə-majəm	p<ən>ajəm	extinguish a fire
paləy	mə-maləy	p<ən>aləy	taboo
paliʔ	mə-maliʔ	p<ən>aliʔ	wound, cut
paʔid	mə-maʔid	p<ən>aʔid	wipe
piliʔ	mə-miliʔ	p<ən>iliʔ	choice, choosing
pisit	mə-misit	p<ən>isit	wringing out
sadar	mə-ñadar	s<ən>adar	lean on
sapəw	mə-ñapəw	s<ən>apəw	broom

siŋuəh	mə-ñiŋuəh	s<ən>iŋuəh	cool
suʔun	mə-ñuʔun	s<ən>uʔun	shouldering
tabik	mə-nabik	t<ən>abik	reaching for
tabun	mə-nabun	t<ən>abun	cover, lid
taŋih	mə-naŋih	t<ən>aŋih	weeping, crying
tikaw	mə-nikaw	t<ən>ikaw	theft
timan	mə-niman	t<ən>iman	praise
tuduy	mə-nuduy	t<ən>uduy	sleep
tulak	mə-nulak	t<ən>ulak	pushing

(5)

adək	məŋ-adək	n-adək	sniffing, smelling
añit	məŋ-añit	n-añit	sharp
asəw	məŋ-asəw	n-asəw	dog
ukur	məŋ-ukur	n-ukur	measuring

Notes: (1) passive verbs are obligatorily perfective regardless of how they are formed, (2) the prefixes *mə-* and *nə-* as used by speakers born around 1955 were infixes *-əm-* and *-ən-* in the speech of persons born around 1915, (3) schwa is not allowed before another vowel, or in the environment VC__CV, (4) all vocalic oppositions are neutralised as schwa in prepenultimate syllables, (5) consonant clusters do not occur.

QUESTIONS:

1. How many active verb affixes can be reconstructed, and what are their shapes?
2. How many passive verb affixes can be reconstructed, and what are their shapes?

INTERNAL RECONSTRUCTION PROBLEM 10

(Artificial data)

No.	Proto-ABC	Lg. A	Lg. B	Lg. C	Gloss
01.		viki	vihi	wiʔi	moon
02.		ronok	galu	ganuʔ	sun
03.		teme	sima	tema	day
04.		rovot	ruvat	ruat	sleep
		rovot-a	ruvat-a	ruat-a	put to sleep
05.		rarba	ragba	rabba	bird
06.		sordop	hugduf	hodduh	dog
07.		ulup	urup	urup	cry
		uluv-a	uruv-a	uru-a	make s.o. cry
08.		osop	uhuf	ohuh	happy
		osop-a	uhuf-a	ohuh-a	make s.o. happy
09.		lerte	ragsi	rakti	wing
10.		polot	farut	harut	fall
		polor-a	farur-a	harur-a	drop
11.		turi	turi	turi	tree
12.		kunis	hulih	ʔunih	slide
		kunis-a	huli-a	ʔunih-a	push
13.		orpok	ugfa	okkaʔ	feather
14.		rilit	ririt	ririt	hot
		rilit-a	ririt-a	ririt-a	to heat
15.		vuris	vugih	wugih	fish
16.		etet	isit	itet	fear
		eter-a	isir-a	iter-a	frighten
17.		rutup	gutup	gutup	sky
18.		senet	hinat	henat	cloud
19.		lekep	rahif	raʔih	healthy
		lekep-a	rahif-a	raʔih-a	to heal
20.		enep	ilap	inap	angry
		enev-a	ilav-a	inaw-a	to anger
21.		nertep	ligsif	nektih	die
		nertep-a	ligsif-a	nektih-a	kill
22.		kusut	huhut	ʔuhut	water
23.		tirbu	sigbu	tibbu	lake

Note: assume that the relationship of Lgs. A, B, and C is equally distant – that is, each one is a primary branch of the language family.

INSTRUCTIONS/QUESTIONS:

1. Reconstruct the base forms for items 4, 10, 14 and 16. How do the final consonants of 4 and 14 differ from those of 10 and 16? How would the reconstructions you have proposed differ if the suffixed forms did not exist?
2. Reconstruct the base forms for items 7, 8, 19, 20 and 21. How do the finals of 7 and 20 differ from those of 8, 19 and 21? How would the reconstructions you have proposed differ if the suffixed forms did not exist?
3. Are any of the proto-phonemes you have reconstructed in complementary distribution? If so, how might you modify your reconstruction to account for this?
4. Does internal reconstruction suggest that any of the reconstructions based on non-alternating forms are ambiguous? Which one(s), and what is the ambiguity?

SUBGROUPING

(20 problems)

Background

Subgrouping is one of the major tasks of historical linguistics, and one with few connections to other branches of the field. The task of subgrouping languages is in many ways conceptually more akin to problems in biological taxonomy than it is to other problems in linguistics, a fact that has become increasingly clear with the rising interest in linguistic classification among scholars trained in evolutionary biology who have begun to import the cladistic methods of modern biological phylogenetics to other fields (Atkinson and Gray 2005; Greenhill, Blust and Gray 2008; Gray, Drummond and Greenhill 2009).

The basic issues that are involved in constructing family trees are presented in an admirably succinct and readable form in Greenberg (1957), a discussion that in my view has not been superseded in the more than half a century since it was written. In its simplest form the problem of linguistic subgrouping can be stated as follows: given three related languages, is there any evidence that two of these languages are more closely related to one another than either is to the third? If the answer is negative, then the tree will have three primary branches, one for each language, and will consequently lack internal structure. If it is positive there are three possible trees: (1) AB : C, (2) AC : B, and (3) A : BC. As many writers have noted, the number of possible trees rises rapidly with the number of languages compared, and soon becomes so astronomical that the task of subgrouping would become impossible without a well-established method.

The key to subgrouping is the distinction between innovation and retention, a distinction that was first clearly recognised in linguistics in the nineteenth century (Brugmann 1884). Surprisingly, the comparable distinction in biological classification was not recognised explicitly until the establishment of cladistics in the middle of the twentieth century (Hennig 1950), although biologists have now advanced beyond the comfort level for many historical linguists in developing statistical tools for phylogenetic classification. It should be added that it is often very hard to evaluate linguistic classifications based on Bayesian inference or other now popular forms of computational phylogeny, since the actual cognate decisions in which they are rooted are rarely made explicit.

Languages are subgrouped on the basis of exclusively shared innovations – that is, changes that are shared only by certain members of a language family. The fundamental idea is that a change which happens in a given speech community will be inherited in languages that descend from it, pointing to an innovation in a common ancestor that is not ancestral to the entire collection of related languages. However, this statement must be qualified in certain ways. First, some sound changes are so common that they are likely to happen independently. Needless to say, innovations such as *h > Ø will be weak evidence for subgrouping even if they are exclusively shared, simply because they are extremely common in the world's languages. Second, there are certain structural pressures at work in any language at a given period of its history, and if speakers separate into descendant communities these daughter languages will share the same tendencies to change, increasing the likelihood that some changes will happen in parallel among related languages after they are no longer in contact. Sapir (1921), who provided the classic description of such parallel changes with the example of pluralising umlaut in the history of English and High German (but not Low German), proposed the term 'drift' to describe the tendency for related languages to change in similar ways because of the continued operation of inherited structural pressures. Although it met with some initial scepticism, drift is now widely recognised as a factor that complicates the use of exclusively shared innovations to subgroup languages.

Finally, most work in linguistic subgrouping tacitly assumes a family tree model of linguistic relationships – that is a model in which language splits happen abruptly and without further contact. It has been known since at least Schmidt (1872) proposed the wave model as an alternative to the family tree model of subgrouping, that changes can spread from centres of political or cultural influence to outlying areas through the diffusion of prestige features, and few historical linguists today believe that language split is either abrupt or free from subsequent diffusion. It is important to recognise, however, that integration of the wave model into the paradigm of historical linguistics has not led to outright rejection of the family tree model. Rather, it is recognised that both models are valid under given conditions, the wave model providing a better description of language split at a period when communities speaking dialects of the same language are still in contact, and the family tree model providing a better description of independent linguistic change after related languages have separated widely both in space and in time.

LEVEL 1: BEGINNING

SUBGROUPING PROBLEM 1

No.	Proto-ABCD	Lg. A	Lg.B	Lg. C	Lg. D	
01.		ʔutil	util	kuril	kulil	fish
02.		ihara	iara	isara	isala	water
03.		naʔ	na	nak	nak	earth
04.		popat	fofaʔ	popat	popat	rain
05.		uruʔ	uru	uru	ulu	cloud
06.		hitu	itu	siru	silu	wind
07.		lami	lami	lami	lami	man
08.		narit	nariʔ	narit	nalit	woman
09.		helu	elu	helu	helu	child
10.		mumaŋ	mumaŋ	mumaŋ	mumaŋ	house
11.		alah	ala	alas	alas	forest
12.		hutup	utuʔ	surup	sulup	walk
13.		rumun	rumuŋ	rumun	lumun	speak
14.		ʔurom	uroŋ	kurom	kulom	sleep
15.		atar	atar	arar	alal	bathe
16.		ʔaʔu	au	aku	aku	black
17.		tiʔan	tiaŋ	tian	tian	white
18.		tetu	tetu	teru	telu	red
19.		lahiʔ	lai	lahik	lahik	green
20.		hapiʔ	afi	sapi	sapi	grass

INSTRUCTIONS:

1. Reconstruct Proto-ABCD 1–20.
2. List all changes in each language, noting any ordering requirements.
3. Propose a family tree based on exclusively shared innovations.

SUBGROUPING PROBLEM 2

No.	Proto-ABC	Lg. A	Lg. B	Lg. C	
01.		anaŋ	anaŋ	anaŋ	frog
02.		kitup	ketuf	keruh	willow tree
03.		rampid	rampit	rapit	swamp
04.		nunum	nunun	nunuŋ	cattail
05.		lalag	lalak	lalak	fish
06.		futul	futol	hurol	bird
07.		upuŋ	hofuŋ	hohuŋ	eagle
08.		apat	safat	sahat	hawk
09.		untik	untik	utik	snake
10.		amar	samar	samar	lizard
11.		ulub	ulup	ulup	earthworm
12.		lirat	lerat	lerat	maggot
13.		pani	fani	hani	tree
14.		kaid	kasit	kasit	root
15.		ulan	olan	olaŋ	branch
16.		kuam	kuhan	kuhaŋ	leaf
17.		uluk	uluk	uluk	sun
18.		intab	sintap	sitap	star
19.		kunip	kunif	kunih	moon
20.		mapug	mafuk	mahuk	wind
21.		tama	tamas	tamas	rain
22.		fitun	fitun	hiruŋ	stone

INSTRUCTIONS:

1. Reconstruct Proto-ABC 1–22.
2. List all sound changes in each language, stating any ordering requirements needed.
3. Based on exclusively shared innovations propose a subgrouping of these languages.

SUBGROUPING PROBLEM 3

No.	Proto-Jalish	Aki	Jali	Suya	Rian	Elis
01.		halin	halit	sarin	aliŋ	halin
02.		fahi	fati	paʔi	hai	pati
03.		fataŋ	fatak	paʔaŋ	hataŋ	pataŋ
04.		fuhak	buhak	busak	huak	buhak
05.		ahan	ahap	asam	aaŋ	aham
06.		hihif	hitif	siʔip	iih	hitip
07.		umahi	umati	umaʔi	umai	umati
08.		kulan	kurat	kuhan	kulaŋ	kuran
09.		hafat	habat	sabaʔ	ahat	habat
10.		ufuŋ	ufuk	upuŋ	uhuŋ	upuŋ
11.		talih	talih	ʔaris	tali	talih
12.		hilan	tirap	ʔiham	ilaŋ	tiram

INSTRUCTIONS:

1. Reconstruct Proto-Jalish 1–12.
2. State the changes that have taken place in each daughter language, noting any necessary ordering requirements.
3. On the basis of exclusively shared innovations propose a subgrouping for these five languages. In looking for exclusively shared innovations pay particular attention to phonemic mergers and splits.

SUBGROUPING PROBLEM 4

No.	Proto-ABCD	Lg. A	Lg. B	Lg. C	Lg. D	
01.		natuŋ	nadum	nadum	narum	star
02.		mair	mahir	maʔil	maʔir	moon
03.		timaŋ	siman	siman	siman	night
04.		pasaŋ	pahan	paʔan	paʔan	dark
05.		pai	paʔi	paʔi	paʔi	wind
06.		piiŋ	pihin	piʔin	piʔin	rain
07.		simas	hemah	ʔemaʔ	ʔemaʔ	storm
08.		ulaʔ	ulap	ulap	urap	hail
09.		ratal	radal	ladal	rarar	stone
10.		luku	lugo	lugo	rugo	water
11.		pusiʔ	puhik	puʔik	puʔik	house
12.		lapur	labur	labul	ravur	roof
13.		isiŋ	ʔihim	ʔiʔim	ʔiʔim	door
14.		kura	kura	kula	kura	floor
15.		mulas	mulah	mulaʔ	muraʔ	tree
16.		akuŋ	agon	agon	agon	leaf
17.		ritiŋ	rideŋ	lideŋ	rireŋ	branch
18.		siŋaʔ	hiŋap	ʔiŋap	ʔiŋap	bird
19.		lariʔ	larek	lalek	rarek	nest
20.		tuuʔ	tuʔuk	tuʔuk	tuʔuk	laugh
21.		taniʔ	tanip	tanip	tanip	cry
22.		puaʔ	puhat	puʔat	puʔat	speak
23.		titiŋa	sisiŋa	sisiŋa	sisiŋa	wash
24.		upu	hobu	ʔobu	ʔovu	clean

INSTRUCTIONS:

1. Reconstruct Proto-ABCD 1–24.
2. List all changes in each language, including ordering relationships.
3. Based on exclusively shared innovations, propose a subgrouping of the languages.

SUBGROUPING PROBLEM 5

No.	Proto-ABCD	Lg. A	Lg. B	Lg. C	Lg. D	
01.		basi	pati	fet	vat	rat
02.		koŋas	koŋah	koŋ	koŋas	snake
03.		tanor	tanol	tan	tanor	dog
04.		pusaŋ	puhaŋ	fu	fusaŋ	pig
05.		lehip	lehip	he	lehif	liver
06		rupe	lupe	huf	ruf	blood
07.		haluki	haluki	ohuk	haluk	skin
08.		pahani	pahani	faen	fahan	hair
09.		abutun	aputun	ofut	avutun	eat
10.		sahil	hahil	e	sahil	sleep
11.		siapu	tiapu	tiof	tiaf	drink
12.		kuhama	kuhama	kuam	kuham	walk
13.		apit	apit	ef	afit	hit
14.		orudu	oludu	ohud	orud	fall

INSTRUCTIONS:

1. Reconstruct Proto-ABCD 1–14.
2. List changes in each language, noting any necessary ordering requirements.
3. Based on step 2 determine what innovations, if any, are exclusively shared, and propose a family tree for Lgs. A, B, C and D.

LEVEL 2: INTERMEDIATE

SUBGROUPING PROBLEM 6

No.	Proto-Kwosi	Ayon	Dunas	Kwosi	Fafak	
01.		suu	cuy	cuyu	cuyu	water
02.		ʔusa	ʔus	usa	uha	rain
03.		mʷapa	ŋin	mʷafa	mafa	wind
04.		kuti	kud	xuti	huti	earth
05.		yisa	top	lisa	liha	stone
06.		panua	panu	sano	hano	grass
07.		soka	sok	soxa	hoha	mud
08.		paa	pay	faya	faya	lake
09.		xuma	xum	xuma	huma	island
10.		ʔuyo	ʔul	ulo	ulo	river
11.		yaha	kian	xiana	hala	fish
12.		muta	mud	lua	lua	bird
13.		patu	pad	fatu	fatu	tree
14.		ua	uy	uya	uya	leaf
15.		pixi	pix	fixi	fihi	branch
16.		kouyu	koul	suli	houlu	fruit
17.		pasi	pac	faci	faci	seed
18.		hoya	kum	xumʷi	humi	field
19.		mano	man	mano	nafi	rock
20.		xayu	xal	xalu	halu	cliff

Note: c = voiceless palatal affricate.

INSTRUCTIONS/QUESTIONS:

1. Reconstruct Proto-Kwosi 1–20.
2. List all changes in each daughter language, together with any ordering requirements.
3. State any subgrouping relationships that exist among these languages.
4. What exclusively shared phonological innovations support your subgrouping?
5. What exclusively shared lexical innovations support your subgrouping?

SUBGROUPING PROBLEM 7

No.	Proto-ABCD	Lg. A	Lg.B	Lg. C	Lg. D	
01.		pomu	fomu	fomu	fomu	stone
02.		lahuk	hau	hou?	auk	fish
03.		litas	rita	ritah	litas	water
04.		ayut	au	ouŋ	ayun	wave
05.		hesap	eha	ehaŋ	esam	sky
06.		ilup	iru	iruf	iluf	wind
07.		tula	tuha	tuha	tua	earth
08.		wasik	vahi	vehiŋ	vasiŋ	grass
09.		malu	maru	moru	malu	wake
10.		uyas	ua	uah	uyas	wash
11.		haŋati	anahi	aŋehi	muli	walk
12.		solet	hohe	hohe?	soet	speak
13.		lahip	rai	reiŋ	laim	fire
14.		tiap	hia	hiaf	tiaf	smoke
15.		kayili	haihi	mutuh	kayii	burn
16.		nitak	lita	nitaŋ	nitaŋ	house
17.		pukap	oaha	oaha	oyaka	roof
18.		tikuk	hihu	hihuŋ	tikuŋ	work
19.		ŋatik	nahi	ŋehi?	sihaf	sleep
20.		unat	ula	unaŋ	unan	dream
21.		sapep	hafe	hafef	safef	eat
22.		lilahu	hirau	hirou	ilau	drink
23.		kiwis	hivi	hivih	kivis	run

Note: not all forms are cognate.

INSTRUCTIONS:

1. Reconstruct Proto-ABCD 1–23.
2. List all changes in each language, including ordering relationships.
3. Based on exclusively shared innovations propose a subgrouping of these four languages.

SUBGROUPING PROBLEM 8

No.	Proto-Hamuan	Hamu	Fiak	Tolno	Luk	Gloss
01.		hottis	furdis	fortis	foltis	bear
02.		alli	azuri	azli	azuw	fish
03.		ruhod	rugut	ruod	lukot	fox
04.		suneh	sunik	sune	sunek	storm
05.		dikku	dimagu	dimo	rimak	sky
06.		hanna	padina	fatna	patin	wind
07.		mayaw	mayaw	mayo	mazaf	cloud
08.		luha	ruga	lua	wuk	rain
09.		tomay	tumay	tome	tomas	earth
10.		biwa	bia	viva	bif	stone
11.		valla	vazura	vasla	vasow	grass
12.		bazu	bazu	vazu	bas	eat
13.		heloh	kirup	elof	kewop	drink
14.		wimma	irma	virma	vilm	walk
15.		uyah	uyak	uya	uzak	talk
16.		tiffani	tirbani	tilfani	tiwpan	sleep
17.		hanni	karni	arni	kaln	black
18.		halay	faray	fale	fawas	white
19.		halub	karup	aluv	kawup	red
20.		dayah	dayap	dayaf	razap	yellow
21.		rinno	rirnu	rilno	liwn	green
22.		hukkan	purgan	fulan	puwkan	not yet
23.		zurri	zuvuri	zufri	zuful	still
24.		lenis	rinis	lenis	wenis	worm
25.		hulug	puruk	fulug	puwuk	snake
26.		tahi	tagi	te	tak	lizard
27.		ahhih	arbik	arfi	alpik	hill
28.		laggo	razigu	lasgo	wasik	river

INSTRUCTIONS:

1. Reconstruct Proto-Hamuan 1–28.
2. List all changes in each language, including ordering relationships.
3. Based on exclusively shared innovations, propose a subgrouping of the languages.

SUBGROUPING PROBLEM 9

No.	Proto-ABC	Lg. A	Lg. B	Lg. C	
01.		fasul	pahun	pau	fence
02.		tiraf	tenap	tera	garden
03.		dambut	dambot	davo	water
04.		silam	tinam	tira	rain
05.		kumar	kuman	kuma	cloud
06.		fuŋga	poŋga	poɣa	flood
07.		lampak	nambak	rava	drown
08.		sifi	hipe	ipe	mud
09.		araŋ	anaŋ	ara	swim
10.		hura	hona	ora	fish
11.		sundu	hondu	oru	frog
12.		cimus	kimoh	kimo	hill
13.		unsin	undin	uri	grass
14.		ranci	naŋgi	raɣi	sun
15.		fanuf	panop	pano	day
16.		luhik	nohik	roi	wind

Note: c is a voiceless palatal affricate.

INSTRUCTIONS:

1. Reconstruct Proto-ABC 1–16.
2. State the changes in all languages, together with any necessary ordering relationships.
3. On the basis of exclusively shared innovations propose a subgrouping for these languages. In searching for exclusively shared innovations pay particular attention to phonemic mergers and splits.

SUBGROUPING PROBLEM 10

No.	Proto-ABCD	Lg. A	Lg. B	Lg. C	Lg. D	
01.		fəko	hoka	hiha	paxa	fire
02.		hiho	hiso	hiho	hiso	ashes
03.		kufih	kuhis	huhih	xupis	hearth
04.		tanidi	tanili	təniri	tanini	pot
05.		dilaf	dirap	rirah	rirap	stone
06.		utuli	uturi	duri	ururi	ember
07.		henubo	šenuba	hənuba	senuva	smoke
08.		huhin	sušin	huhin	susin	burn
09.		batən	baton	badin	varan	cook
10.		didik	lidik	ririh	nirix	boil
11.		lato	rata	rada	rara	roast
12.		mohio	mošio	məhio	mosio	fry
13.		lihe	rihe	rihe	rihe	stand
14.		foluh	holus	holuh	fonus	sit
15.		əfət	ohot	ihit	apat	walk
16.		datəf	datof	radih	raraf	bird
17.		matih	masis	madih	maris	wing
18.		hulaf	hulaf	hulah	hunap	feather
19.		tidin	silin	tirin	tinin	beak
20.		ikado	ikada	hara	ixara	claw
21.		luti	lusi	ludi	nuri	stick
22.		dinu	linu	rinu	ninu	stone

INSTRUCTIONS:

1. Reconstruct Proto-ABCD 1–22.
2. State the changes in all languages, together with any necessary ordering relationships.
3. On the basis of exclusively shared innovations propose a subgrouping of these languages.

SUBGROUPING PROBLEM 11

No.	Proto-ABC	Lg. A	Lg. B	Lg. C	
01.		hifɛŋ	tihen	tihe	pine tree
02.		ɔhup	osup	osu	canyon
03.		alah	alati	alati	suspension bridge
04.		okal	ukin	hokə	cliff
05.		ŋuf	nuha	nuha	eagle
06.		iŋ	ini	hine	rattlesnake
07.		fɔh	hosi	hosi	squirrel
08.		nehim	litim	neti	fish
09.		hafon	sihun	səho	bird
10.		fɛhiŋ	hetini	hetini	river
11.		kɔah	koiti	kohəti	riverbank
12.		peŋi	pinia	penia	canoe
13.		hɔnah	solis	sonə	person
14.		oŋ	uni	one	man
15.		fuha	husie	husəhe	woman
16.		nuɛf	lueh	nueh	child
17.		tahɔ	taso	taso	eat
18.		motuf	mutuha	motuha	drink
19.		amal	aman	ama	talk

Note: assume that all words in each row are cognate and that none are borrowed.

INSTRUCTIONS:

1. Reconstruct Proto-ABC 1–19.
2. State the changes in each daughter language in the order in which they occur.
3. Choose one of the following statements and justify it by reference to instruction 2:

    (a) AB form a subgroup apart from C

    (b) AC form a subgroup apart from B

    (c) BC form a subgroup apart from A

    (d) The evidence is insufficient to support a subgrouping.

SUBGROUPING PROBLEM 12

No.	Proto-Arucan	Aruca	Atoyot	Tassap	Urabus	
01.		sara	al	saha	caa	man
02.		turu	tot	totu	tuu	woman
03.		mara	mat	mata	maa	child
04.		pahu	pa	pahu	fasu	house
05.		sila	il	kila	cila	stone
06.		hura	ulap	kuhap	kua?	village
07.		miri	meti	metik	mii?	water
08.		hani	anip	kanip	kani?	black
09.		sani	inap	kinap	cani?	white
10.		usi	uin	usin	uciŋ	tree
11.		aŋi	aŋit	aŋit	aŋi?	cloud
12.		taha	taal	takah	taka	rain
13.		hari	ati	katik	kai?	storm
14.		hira	elaŋ	hehaŋ	siaŋ	earth
15.		asi	a	aki	aci	sun
16.		raŋa	laŋal	haŋal	aŋaŋ	moon
17.		pusi	puin	pukin	fuciŋ	day
18.		suha	oat	sokat	cuka?	night
19.		luhu	loum	lohum	lusuŋ	wind
20.		paraha	pala	pahaka	faaka	spirit
21.		huri	util	kutil	kuiŋ	ghost

Note: c is a voiceless palatal affricate.

INSTRUCTIONS:

1. Reconstruct Proto-Arucan 1–21.
2. List all changes in each language, noting ordering relationships where relevant.
3. Draw a family tree for these four languages, noting evidence of exclusively shared innovations where a subgroup is recognised.
4. Are there any exclusively shared innovations supporting your subgroup that do not derive from regular sound change?

SUBGROUPING PROBLEM 13

No.	Proto-ABC	Lg. A	Lg. B	Lg. C	
01.		lubaw	rubo	lubaw	water
02.		ilik	ərəg	ili?	grass
03.		udut	ulur	udu?	stone
04.		lisit	arisət	əlisi?	butterfly
05.		lirak	lərak	lira?	bird
06.		rilap	lirap	rila?	wing
07.		tasil	tasir	tasi	feather
08.		karur	kalur	karu	river
09.		turap	turab	tura?	fish
10.		watiŋ	watiŋ	watiŋ	mountain
11.		lilit	ulirit	əlili?	wind
12.		adul	alur	adu	sky
13.		ilik	irik	ili?	sun
14.		rərana	larana	rərana	moon
15.		diti	riti	diti	star
16.		pasay	pase	pasay	house
17.		siti	siti	siti	woman
18.		tisut	tisur	tisu?	man
19.		ipun	əpun	ipuŋ	child
20.		putir	putər	puti	grandmother
21.		lulup	lurub	lulu?	grandfather
22.		duri	luri	duri	fire
23.		dimam	rimam	dimaŋ	hearth
24.		tənulit	tinulir	tənuli?	charcoal

INSTRUCTIONS/QUESTIONS:

1. Reconstruct Proto-ABC 1–24, paying particular attention to correspondences that contain the liquids /l/ and /r/.
2. List the correspondences that include at least one liquid.
3. List all changes in each language, noting any ordering requirements.
4. Based on exclusively shared innovations, which two languages appear to form a subgroup?

SUBGROUPING PROBLEM 14

No.	Proto-ABCD	Lg. A	Lg. B	Lg. C	Lg. D	
01.		weŋi	wani	wani	waɲi	wind
02.		hana	hana	ana	ana	rain
03.		ʔume	kume	hume	kumi	cloud
04.		feu	pehi	pei	piu	star
05.		bulat	vula	bulat	bulat	moon
06.		sohuf	dahi	taip	haup	sun
07.		delim	lali	ralim	dalim	earth
08.		ʔoruʔ	koli	horik	kuruk	water
09.		telifa	dalipa	talipa	talipa	stone
10.		lubun	luvi	lubin	lubun	grass
11.		fosu	padi	pasi	pahu	person
12.		neŋif	nani	nanip	naɲip	man
13.		tilaʔ	dila	silak	tilak	woman
14.		idu	ili	iri	idu	child
15.		simumu	dimumi	simumi	himumu	dog
16.		ʔiruŋ	kili	hirin	kiruŋ	house
17.		sineti	dinadi	sinasi	hinati	village
18.		futim	pudi	pusim	putim	eat
19.		mesiŋ	medi	mesin	mihiŋ	sleep
20.		saŋo	dano	tano	haɲu	go
21.		riŋus	lini	rinit	riŋuh	stand

INSTRUCTIONS:

1. Reconstruct Proto-ABCD 1–21.
2. State all changes in each language, including ordering requirements.
3. Based on exclusively shared innovations, propose a family tree for these four languages.

LEVEL 3: ADVANCED

SUBGROUPING PROBLEM 15

No.	Proto-ABCD	Lg. A	Lg. B	Lg. C	Lg. D	
01.		lihata	riat	likaʔ	likat	wind
02.		sahu	hou	safuʔ	hafuʔ	cloud
03.		mawana	mawan	magʷaŋ	maan	sky
04.		tulapa	turap	tulaʔ	turap	rain
05.		habi	appi	kampi	kapi	earth
06.		lisuhu	rihu	lisuʔ	rihuk	water
07.		sulipa	huripa	sulipa	huripa	stone
08.		nuhala	nuar	nuhan	nuhar	grass
09.		hiana	ian	fijaŋ	fiaŋ	tree
10.		tahunu	tounu	takuŋu	takuŋu	wood
11.		amala	amara	amala	amala	fire
12.		hihasi	iehi	hikasi	hikati	hearth
13.		uyu	uyu	ujuʔ	uuʔ	smoke
14.		agunu	akkun	aŋkuŋ	akuŋ	cook
15.		maulu	mour	maʔun	maʔul	eat
16.		sisuma	hihuma	sisuma	tihuma	walk
17.		lahisi	reih	lakis	rakih	sit
18.		uhasihi	uehi	uhasiʔ	uhatik	stand
19.		lidanu	rittonu	lintanu	ritanu	reach
20.		suhumu	suum	sukuŋ	hukun	push
21.		wawasa	wawah	gʷagʷas	aah	carry

INSTRUCTIONS:

1. Reconstruct Proto-ABCD 1–21.
2. List all changes in each language together with any necessary ordering requirements.
3. Construct a family tree based on exclusively shared innovations.

SUBGROUPING PROBLEM 16

No.	Proto-ABCD	Lg. A	Lg. B	Lg. C	Lg. D	
01.		piteta	fireh	pite	pitit	head
02.		tati	tahi	tasi	tasi	hair
03.		urina	urin	uriə	uriŋ	eye
04.		kaduna	karun	kadu	karun	nose
05.		ope	ofay	opa	upi	mouth
06.		pohaka	foak	poha	puhak	tooth
07.		tutina	hurin	sutiə	tusiŋ	ear
08.		nomina	nomin	ŋomi	ŋumin	neck
09.		tedoka	terok	tedo	tiruk	hand
10.		nanu	lanu	nanu	nanu	blood
11.		tikuka	hikuk	sikuə	sikuk	liver
12.		tibo	hibo	sibo	sibu	skin
13.		atipa	arip	ati	asip	sky
14.		tite	tiray	tita	siti	rain
15.		numita	numit	numi	numit	wind
16.		huna	una	huŋa	huŋa	water
17.		ine	ile	ine	ini	tree
18.		duyuna	duyun	duyuə	ruyuŋ	climb
19.		bato	baraw	bata	batu	stone
20.		tahika	haik	sahiə	tahik	fish
21.		tano	hanaw	saŋa	taŋu	bird
22.		dabana	daban	daba	raban	eat
23.		tatuna	harun	satuə	tatuŋ	sleep
24.		nerana	leran	nera	niraŋ	walk
25.		kanima	kalim	kani	kanim	speak

INSTRUCTIONS:

1. Reconstruct Proto-ABCD 1–25.
2. List all changes in each language, indicating any necessary ordering requirements.
3. Based on evidence of exclusively shared innovations provide a subgrouping of these languages, stating in full the evidence for your decision.

SUBGROUPING PROBLEM 17

No.	Proto-ABCD	Lg. A	Lg. B	Lg. C	Lg. D	
01.		haha	utap	haha	aaʔ	wind
02.		puhka	pusak	puha	pukka	dust
03.		puha	pusak	puha	puaʔ	forest
04.		ulna	kasi	uluna	unna	trail
05.		utu	utuk	utu	utuʔ	pond
06.		paki	pakit	pait	pekiʔ	eagle
07.		tiku	sehap	siup	tikuʔ	hawk
08.		kuka	kukã	wan	kukaŋ	crow
09.		hoka	okat	wat	temiŋ	day
10.		katne	katin	asini	kanne	night
11.		hema	semak	hima	emaʔ	moon
12.		lupka	lupuk	lupua	lukka	black
13.		akti	akit	aisi	atti	white
14.		opo	opor	upur	opo	red
15.		hapna	sapun	hapuna	anna	yellow
16.		tohka	tosak	tuha	tokka	big
17.		rakmi	rakam	rami	rammi	long
18.		teti	tetĩ	tisim	tetiŋ	small
19.		hatka	atik	asia	akka	short
20.		aku	akũ	aun	okuŋ	heavy
21.		mosi	motis	musi	moi	round
22.		tahi	tasik	tahi	teiʔ	hand
23.		pahu	paul	paul	pou	foot
24.		ote	otẽ	utin	pasu	walk

INSTRUCTIONS:

1. Reconstruct Proto-ABCD 1–24.
2. List the changes that have occurred in each language.
3. Based on exclusively shared innovations draw a tree showing the subgrouping relationships of these languages.
4. One exclusively shared innovation involves a sporadic change. Identify this and state the type of change involved.

SUBGROUPING PROBLEM 18

No.	Proto-ABCD	Lg. A	Lg. B	Lg. C	Lg. D	
01.		bayat	bayata	wat	baya?	river
02.		in	hiŋu	hit	hinu	water
03.		usan	usana	usat	uhal	rain
04.		tafa	tawahi	tahah	tafahi	cloud
05.		nus	ŋusu	nus	nuhu	earth
06.		afa	awala	ahal	afal	sand
07.		kumin	kumini	kumit	kumil	grass
08.		faan	walaŋa	halat	falaŋ	tree
09.		nia	nera	nial	liar	leaf
10.		imot	limoto	limut	limo?	root
11.		moan	moraŋa	mulat	morana	house
12.		sib	siba	siw	hiba	roof
13.		fun	wuŋu	hut	funu	person
14.		duef	durepa	rulip	durepa	woman
15.		itam	itama	itap	itaŋ	man
16.		yufit	yupiti	upit	yupiti	child
17.		fek	weka	hik	feka	dog
18.		ab	habe	haw	habe	bird
19.		duaf	dopa	ruap	dua?	snake
20.		aus	rosu	laus	rauh	fish
21.		koam	kolama	kulap	kolaŋ	black
22.		uak	uraka	ulak	ura?	white

INSTRUCTIONS:

1. Reconstruct Proto-ABCD 1–22.
2. State all changes in each daughter language, together with any ordering requirements.
3. Based on exclusively shared innovations in phonology propose a subgrouping of the four languages.

SUBGROUPING PROBLEM 19

No.	Proto-ABCD	Lg. A	Lg. B	Lg. C	Lg. D	
01.		were	waro	ahi	gʷel	water
02.		dafi	tewi	tapi	tafi	lake
03.		efe	kekiwo	kaɣi	ef	river
04.		yəva	ikopo	iɣi	iəb	forest
05.		anudu	onuto	anu	anut	snake
06.		ehe	aso	ahi	es	fish
07.		fahimi	wesimo	pasi	fasim	lizard
08.		ho	suako	sua	so	bird
09.		romu	domu	domu	lomu	bee
10.		uvara	kupalo	kuba	ubal	wasp
11.		foro	wokuro	paɣu	fol	cricket
12.		rawi	dewi	dai	lagʷi	ant
13.		wara	ukaro	uɣa	ol	cook
14.		nofo	nawo	nahu	nof	eat
15.		hema	sekima	saɣima	sema	drink
16.		vərana	porano	bira	bəlan	walk
17.		oro	oro	oho	ol	run
18.		fəda	wokoto	piɣi	fət	fall
19.		awafa	kawawo	kaa	agʷaf	give
20.		rada	rato	raha	lat	heavy
21.		rufu	lukuo	luɣu	luf	light
22.		mida	mitoko	miti	mitə	big
23.		iri	ikido	iɣi	il	small
24.		vehe	pekiso	baɣi	bes	wet
25.		ofo	okuo	aɣu	of	dry
26.		yuhu	yuso	ihu	üs	hot
27.		dəro	toruka	tiruɣa	təlo	sun
28.		hufidi	suito	supi	sufit	moon
29.		ururu	udulo	udu	ulul	star
30.		fe	piako	piha	fe	meteor
31.		wini	ukino	uɣi	ün	rain

INSTRUCTIONS:

1. Reconstruct Proto-ABCD 1–31.
2. State all changes in each daughter language, together with any ordering requirements.
3. Based on exclusively shared innovations in phonology propose a subgrouping of the four languages.

SUBGROUPING PROBLEM 20

No.	Proto-ABCD	Lg. A	Lg. B	Lg. C	Lg. D	
01.		lehil	ʔarit	aŋele	nasina	ant
02.		xuha	ʔuza	ko	kuso	bee
03.		rufex	rupiʔ	lupeke	hupeka	worm
04.		izaf	iap	epe	yapa	fly
05.		hizul	tiluʔ	tihuŋu	siluna	wasp
06.		hili	siʔi	iŋi	sini	dog
07.		vehir	wazir	wele	wasiha	bird
08.		fuvax	puhaʔ	poko	puaka	pig
09.		uvaza	uala	oha	walo	one
10.		falat	paʔat	paŋata	panata	two
11.		zutum	lurup	hutumu	lutuma	three
12.		hizaz	lira	ehe	siala	eye
13.		lohu	nazu	no	nasu	nose
14.		toluh	taʔus	taŋuu	tanusa	ear
15.		ihal	hizat	ene	isana	mouth
16.		xehiz	ʔazil	kehe	kasila	tooth
17.		tolar	tunar	tonala	tonaha	sky
18.		ela	hiʔa	eŋa	eno	sun
19.		rexit	riʔit	lekiti	hekita	star
20.		izah	ilas	ihaa	ilasa	moon
21.		miaxa	manur	manolo	manoha	walk
22.		hilal	tiʔat	tiŋana	sinana	eat
23.		xevil	ʔawit	kawini	kawina	drink

INSTRUCTIONS/QUESTIONS:

1. Reconstruct Proto-ABCD 1–23.
2. List all changes in each language, including any ordering requirements.
3. Are any forms non-cognate? Which ones?
4. Propose a subgrouping based on exclusively shared innovations.

PART II: SOLUTIONS

SOLUTIONS TO GENETIC RELATIONSHIP PROBLEMS

LEVEL 1: BEGINNING

SOLUTION TO GENETIC RELATIONSHIP PROBLEM 1

1. Lgs. A and C are genetically related.
2. All forms in these two languages are cognate except 1 and 12.
3. The recurrent sound correspondences (only where the phonemes *differ*) are:

Lg. A		Lg. C	Examples
p	:	f	2, 10, 14
r	:	l	2, 8–10
ay	:	e	2, 7, 8
s	:	t/__i	4, 6
j	:	d	5, 14, 16
n	:	ŋ	5, 11, 14
k	:	h	6, 10, 15
s	:	h	9, 13, 16
aw	:	o	9, 11, 16

Discussion. This is an elementary problem. The chief difficulty is scarcity of data. In general, it is advisable to find at least three examples of every sound correspondence in order to rule out chance as a plausible alternative to common origin. All but one of the (non-identical) phoneme correspondences cited here meet this requirement, and the one that does not (s : t/__i) appears to be in complementary distribution with a better-attested correspondence (s : h). Even with such a small data set the probability that Lgs. A and C are descendants of a common proto-language is high, since there is clear evidence of recurrence in sound correspondences, and the basic meanings of the proposed cognates makes borrowing an unlikely alternative.

SOLUTION TO GENETIC RELATIONSHIP PROBLEM 2

1. Lgs. A and B are genetically related.
2. All forms are cognate except 1, 4, 6, 20 and 22.
3. The recurrent sound correspondences are:

Lg. A		Lg. B	Examples
Ø	:	h	2, 13, 15, 21, 29, 32, 37
h	:	s	2, 10, 11, 18, 23, 30, 36, 38
Ø	:	-V	2, 3, 5, 7–19, 21, 23–40
c	:	k	3, 9–11, 24, 27, 30, 33, 38, 39
r	:	l	5, 10, 15, 18, 26, 29, 31, 32, 34, 36
h	:	f	7, 26, 34, 38
r	:	d	8, 13, 16, 21, 23, 30, 34, 37
ñ	:	n	9, 39
i	:	e	10, 12, 17, 24, 27, 28, 30, 32–35, 38
v	:	b	12, 17, 28, 35
c	:	s	16, 31, 40
j	:	d	26, 35

Discussion. This is a fairly straightforward problem. Perhaps the only surprise is that if reconstruction were attempted there would be no proto-forms with final consonants, matching the situation in Lg. B. But the loss of all final consonants is a change that has occurred in many languages, and there is no reason why a language which starts from this stage could not give rise to daughter languages that lose final vowels. Precisely this series of steps has occurred in a number of languages that belong to the Oceanic branch of Austronesian: Proto-Oceanic had *CVCVC forms, perhaps 90 per cent of its descendants lost final consonants (many of these independently), and then most languages in Micronesia, and the Admiralty Islands, and many in Vanuatu lost the vowel that originally preceded the final consonant, produc-ing a new 'generation' of word-final consonants. One other peculiarity of this problem, which would appear more clearly if reconstruction were required, is that earlier mid-front vowels evidently raised in Lg. A, but the correspond-ing back vowels remained in place. While one would normally expect all mid vowels to raise, rather than a subset defined by frontness, similar conditions are known in empirical cases, as where the lax front vowels of New Zealand

English have raised (and centralised in the case of [ɪ]) in a manner reminiscent of the Great Vowel Shift of Middle English, while the back vowels have remained unaffected (unlike the case in the Great Vowel Shift).

LEVEL 2: INTERMEDIATE

SOLUTION TO GENETIC RELATIONSHIP PROBLEM 3

1. Lgs. A and B are genetically related.
2. All forms in these two languages are cognate except 3, 6 and 13.
3. The recurrent sound correspondences are:

Lg. A		Lg. B	
p	:	f	1, 8, 12, 19
a	:	o/___(C)Cu	1, 4, 5, 17
s	:	t	1, 12, 21
t	:	Ø	1, 9, 15, 18
ʔ	:	Ø	2, 8, 11, 16
a	:	e/___Ci	2, 8, 11, 18, 20
b	:	v	2, 16, 20
g	:	k	2, 7, 16
-V	:	Ø	2, 4, 5, 10, 14, 17, 19, 20
d	:	z	4, 8, 14, 15
l	:	r	4, 19, 20
k	:	h	5, 12, 14, 18, 21
nd	:	r	5, 10, 17
ay	:	e	7
ŋ	:	n	7, 17, 20
ŋk	:	h	9
aw	:	o	10

Discussion. This problem presents complications that are not present in the earlier two problems. A major methodological issue that is raised here is the independence of typology and genetic relationship. Languages B and C are given with identical phoneme inventories as a temptation for the unwary to jump to conclusions about common origin based only on shared features of structure. However, once sound correspondences are known it becomes clear that Lgs. A and B must derive from a common proto-language, while

SOLUTIONS

there is no evidence that Lg. C is a sister of these two. It must be concluded, then, that the identical phoneme inventories for Lgs. B and C are a product of convergence, and have no historical significance.

The vocabularies of Lgs. A and B share many recurrent sound correspondences that allow us to rule out chance, universals or borrowing as plausible explanations of the similarity observed. This is true even without reconstructed forms, although in most cases these would be easy to supply. It is also clear even without reconstruction that some ordering of changes would be necessary to accommodate the correspondences as regular reflexes of proto-forms. Thus, the correspondence -V? : Ø, seen only in forms 8 and 16, can be seen as equivalent to ? : Ø and –V : Ø by assuming that the glottal stop disappeared before the loss of final vowels.

Other correspondences that may raise questions are *ay* : *e* and *aw* : *o*. Although each of these is unique, they are mutually supportive, and hence together they show a recurrent contraction of a low vowel and a following glide. It might also be asked whether these sound correspondences are distinct from *a* : *e*/__Ci and *a* : *o*/__Cu, since the conditioning segments (*i*/*y* and *u*/*w*) are syllabic and non-syllabic equivalents of one another. In either case the recurrence is evident, and supportive of common origin. Likewise, although ŋ*k* : *h* is unique, it is equivalent to the well-supported *k* : *h* on the assumption that consonant clusters were reduced to single segments before the lenition of *k. Finally, the word for 'cloud' in Lg. C shows some similarity with the word in Lg. B, but this is best considered a chance resemblance.

SOLUTION TO GENETIC RELATIONSHIP PROBLEM 4

1. Lg. C cannot be shown to be related to the others.
2. The recurrent sound correspondences are as follows. Underlined numbers indicate correspondences that are incompletely represented in the relevant cognate sets:

Lg. A		Lg. B		Lg. D	
h	:	s	:	s	1, 4, 11, 12, 17
f	:	p	:	p	1, 7, 12
a	:	a	:	e/__Ci	2, 12
p	:	b	:	v	2, 9, 10, 19
n	:	r	:	l	2, 8, 10, 13, 18
a	:	a	:	o/__Cu	3, 4, 10, 14
l	:	r	:	l	3, 6, 11, 15, 16
r	:	r	:	g	3, 5, 14, 20
h	:	h	:	k	4, 15, 18, 19
ŋ	:	n	:	ŋ/__V	5, 8, 10, 17
k	:	ʔ	:	(no data)	5, 17
m	:	ŋ	:	m	6, 15
h	:	Ø	:	s	9
r	:	d	:	d	14, 20

3. The loanwords in this set of data are (02) 'sorghum', (04) 'hoe', (10) 'pot', and (14) 'drum'.
4. Lg. C appears to have borrowed from Lg. A. Because it has no /h/, /ŋ/ or /r/ it has dropped /h/ and replaced /ŋ/ by /n/ and /r/ by /l/ in loanwords.
5. The borrowed vocabulary is confined to terms for agriculture and manufactured products, that is, to 'cultural' vocabulary.

Discussion. The type of borrowing seen here is typical for many parts of the pre-industrial world, and implies that speakers of Lg. C probably were hunter-gatherers when they came into contact with speakers of Lg. A. Two of the loanwords relate specifically to agriculture, and pottery is part of the neolithic cultural complex that includes plant and animal domestication in many regions. It might seem surprising that a word for 'drum' would be borrowed, but in language families such as Austronesian the earliest musical instruments that can be inferred from comparative linguistic data or distributional evidence based on the artefacts themselves are the nose flute and the Jew's harp, and the earliest drums appear to have been slit-gongs (hollowed logs with a slit at the top, that are beaten with sticks). Note that despite its general phonetic similarity, *amuk* 'ear' in Lg. D cannot be related to the forms in Lgs. A and B through recurrent sound correspondences.

SOLUTION TO GENETIC RELATIONSHIP PROBLEM 5

1. Lgs. A and D are genetically related.
2. All forms are cognate except 2, 6, 9 and 12.
3. Recurrent sound correspondence are:

No.	Lg. A	:	Lg. B	
1.	Ø	:	l/C_	1, 4, 7, 11
2.	Ø	:	r/_C	1, 16
3.	k	:	ʔ/__#	1
4.	Ø	:	r/C_	3, 5, 14, 15
5.	m	:	ŋ/__#	3, 7
6.	Ø	:	k/_C[-cont]	4
7.	-V	:	ə	4, 5, 14
8.	s	:	h	5, 10
9.	Ø	:	h/_C	8
10.	p	:	ʔ/__#	8, 13
11.	Ø	:	l/_C	10
12.	t	:	ʔ/__#	10, 16
13.	n	:	ŋ/__#	11
14.	Ø	:	d/_C	13

Discussion. The establishment of genetic relationship in this problem depends upon just twelve forms. Nonetheless, these are sufficiently long and the correspondences sufficiently regular to confidently establish a genetic connection. Perhaps the most prominent feature of the sound correspondences between these languages is the presence of numerous consonant clusters in Lg. D that are not permitted in Lg. A. Although this problem can be solved without reference to sound change, it appears that in clusters with a liquid the liquid dropped, regardless of its position, while other clusters were simplified by loss of the first member. Other correspondences, such as -p/t/k in Lg. A corresponding to -ʔ in Lg. B, or –m/n in Lg. A corresponding to -ŋ in Lg. B are commonly found types.

SOLUTION TO GENETIC RELATIONSHIP PROBLEM 6

1. Lgs. A and B are genetically related.
2. All forms in these two languages are cognate except 1, 6–10, 12, 15, 20, 23, 28, 32, 34 and 42.
3. In the order that they are encountered, the recurrent sound correspondences demonstrating genetic relationship are:

No.	Lg. A		Lg. B	
1.	l	:	r	2, 14, 17, 21, 35, 37, 38
2.	nd	:	r	2, 22, 40
3.	-C	:	Ø	2, 13, 22, 26, 29–31, 33, 35, 37, 39, 40
4.	ŋ	:	n	3, 16, 21, 22, 38
5.	r	:	r	3
6.	rC	:	C_iC_i	4, 27, 36, 39
7.	Ø	:	-V	4, 5, 11, 14, 16–19, 21, 24, 25, 27, 36, 38, 41
8.	nt	:	r	5, 18, 35
9.	h	:	s	11, 16, 17, 21, 25, 27, 31, 36, 40
10.	mp	:	v	11, 14, 30, 41
11.	k	:	ʔ	13, 19, 25, 30
12.	n	:	l	13, 24, 31
13.	Ø	:	h	18, 26, 33, 39
14.	mb	:	v	19, 29, 33
15	ŋk	:	x	24, 26, 37

4. Languages A and C share similarities due to borrowing from A by speakers of C. Borrowed terms include words for both domesticated animals and domesticated plants, suggesting that speakers of Lg. C may have been pre-agricultural at the time of contact. Borrowed numerals for 4–10 suggest that commercial relations existed between these language communities, with speakers of Lg. A being in a dominant position. It is noteworthy that loanwords in Lg. C often contain a final vowel that is not present in Lg. A. The most plausible explanation for this discrepancy is that these words still contained a final vowel at the time they were borrowed, and that Lg. A lost final vowels at a subsequent period.

Discussion. This is a relatively difficult problem in several respects. First, it requires a prior morphological analysis of Lg. B, which shows that words for body parts contain a prefix *ka-*, verbs contain a prefix *a-* and colour words contain a prefix *li-*. If these elements are not first separated from the base the cognation of most of these forms with those in Lg. A may be overlooked.

Second, the interaction of the sound correspondences -C : Ø and Ø : -V can lead to some initial confusion about regularity. Third, although Lgs. A and B show clear evidence of genetic relationship Lg. A has a decimal counting system while Lg. B has a quinary system, and Lg. C has borrowed all numerals higher than three from Lg. A. As already noted, to account for the shape of these loanwords it must be assumed that borrowing took place before Lg. A lost final vowels. Fourth, it must be assumed that the word for 'butterfly' in Lg. B is reduplicated.

None of these assumptions is empirically unreasonable. Affixes or clitics that mark particular word classes occur in many languages, and although these usually signal categories broader than say, colour words, some languages mark some or all colour terms specifically by reduplication (Blust 1999: 170, 2001a). With regard to the use of different principles for numeration, Proto-Austronesian had a base ten system, but many of its daughters have imperfect decimal systems (1, 2, 3, 4, 5, 5+1, 5+2, 5+3, 5+4, 10), quinary systems (1, 2, 3, 4, 5, 5+1, 5+2, 5+3, 5+4, 5+5) or other systems that appear more cumbersome than one founded on base ten. Retentions in loanwords of features that have been lost from the lending language are well known from East Asia, where Chinese loans in Japanese or Korean sometimes preserve features that have been lost in the northern varieties of Chinese itself. Similar cases can be cited from insular Southeast Asia, where Sanskrit loanwords that passed through Malay to Tagalog and other Philippine languages sometimes retain features in languages at the end of this borrowing chain that have been lost in Malay (e.g. Sanskrit *mukha* > Malay *muka* > Tagalog *mukhá?* 'face').

Finally, words for 'butterfly' are reduplicated in many languages, evidently through a type of iconicity that attempts to capture the restless flight of this insect via a process often used to mark plural, iterative and the like. Examples in Austronesian languages include Ilokano *paroparo*, Mamanwa *kaba?kaba?*, Malay *kupukupu*, Delang *ramoramo*, Kokota *tatala* and Sikaiana *pepepe*.

LEVEL 3: ADVANCED

SOLUTION TO GENETIC RELATIONSHIP PROBLEM 7

1. Languages B and C are genetically related.
2. All BC comparisons are cognate except 3, 5, 8, 17 and 19.
3. Sound correspondences are as follows:

No.	Lg. B		Lg. C	Examples
1.	Ø	:	l	1, 9, 11, 14, 16, 21, 25
2.	r	:	y	1, 18, 24
3.	-C	:	Ø	1, 4, 6, 12–15, 18, 20, 21, 24, 25
4.	r	:	d	2, 21, 22
5.	ani,ia,ina,ai	:	ɛ	2, 7, 13, 15, 22, 25
6.	mb	:	b	4
7.	nd	:	d	6
8.	anu	:	ɔ	10, 23
9.	mb	:	p	16
10.	w	:	u/V__#	16
11.	nd	:	t	20

Discussion. This is a relatively difficult problem, due in part to the brevity of many forms in Lg. C, and in part to the absence of common segments in comparisons such as *rani* : *dɛ* 'hair', *inam* : *ɛ* 'water', or *aip* : *lɛ* 'moon'. Despite these difficulties it is clear that the similarities between these languages cannot plausibly be attributed to chance, since correspondences 1 through 5 are attested in multiple forms. Although a number of other sound correspondences appear to be unique, 6, 7, 9 and 11 can be attributed to parallel changes, namely loss of a preconsonantal nasal after voicing assimilation had first affected the stop in Lg. B, and correspondence 10 can be seen as a natural desyllabification of a postvocalic high vocoid that resulted from prior loss of a consonant between vowels. The most opaque relationships are those in which the sequences *ani* or *anu* in Lg. B correspond to a single vowel *ɛ* or *ɔ* in Lg. C, presumably the result of *n > Ø/V__V, with subsequent coalescence of the resulting vowel sequence. While the loss of *n between a low vowel and a following non-low vowel may seem to be phonetically unmotivated, a change of this type that is recurrent, but not fully regular, is found in Proto-Polynesian, as with Proto-Oceanic *qanitu > Proto-Polynesian *ʔaitu 'spirit, ghost', or *kani > *kai 'eat; food'.

SOLUTION TO GENETIC RELATIONSHIP PROBLEM 8

1. Lgs. A and C are genetically related.
2. Cognate sets in this data include 2, 4, 6, 10–15, 17, 18, 20, 22, 24 and 25.
3. Evidence of recurrent sound correspondences is as follows:

No.	Lg. A	:	Lg. C	
1.	Ø	:	l	2, 4, 10, 18
2.	Ø	:	ŋ	2, 15, 20
3.	s	:	t/__e	6, 22
4.	h	:	b	10, 13, 18
5.	i	:	u	10, 25
6.	h	:	p	11, 17
7.	Ø	:	-C	11, 12, 15, 18, 20
8.	o	:	a	12, 25
9.	Ø	:	ll	12, 25
10.	i	:	o	12
11.	Ø	:	k	14, 24
12.	l	:	Ø	15, 17, 24

Discussion. This is the only genetic relationship problem in this workbook that uses natural language data (A = Motu of Southeast New Guinea, and C = Tae' of central Sulawesi, both Austronesian, but only distantly related; Lg. B is an invention). Of the proposed sound correspondences linking Lgs. A and C, five (1, 2, 4, 7, 12) are supported by at least three examples. Among those that are less well attested in this data sample, correspondence 3 (s : t/__e) is clearly conditioned and so is the equivalent of t : t in comparisons 2, 12, 14 and 20, where t in both languages precedes a non-front vowel, correspondence 4 (h : b) is very similar to correspondence 6 (h : p), correspondence 9 (Ø : ll) may be considered the equivalent of correspondence 1 (Ø : l), and correspondence 10 (i : o) may be considered the equivalent of correspondence 5 (i : u). In short, there is far more recurrence among the correspondences linking Lgs. A and C (Motu and Tae' respectively) than can plausibly be explained by chance, and the basic character of many of the meanings essentially rules out borrowing as a likely explanation for the observed similarities. Perhaps the only questionable feature of this solution is the treatment of *gatoi* and *tallo?* as cognates, since the initial CV- of the Motu form is left unaccounted for, and forces us to make an otherwise unsupported morpheme division into *ga-toi*. However, the striking parallelism of 12 and 25 lends support to this analysis.

SOLUTION TO GENETIC RELATIONSHIP PROBLEM 9

1. Lgs. A and D are genetically related.
2. All forms are cognate except 1, 6, 12, 15 and 16.
3. The sound correspondences that show this relationship are as follows:

No.	Lg. A	:	Lg. D	
1.	a	:	o/__(C)u	2, 17
2.	k	:	Ø	2, 5, 18, 19, 25
3.	ɔ	:	o	3, 4, 13, 24
4.	s	:	Ø	3, 4, 7, 9, 10, 14, 19, 24, 25
5.	m	:	ŋ/__#	3, 7, 20
6.	r	:	l	4, 10, 18, 20, 23, 26
7.	t	:	?/__#	4, 9
8.	a	:	e/__(C)i	7, 26
9.	nd	:	l	8
10.	g	:	k	10, 13, 14
11.	f	:	h	11, 13
12.	n	:	ŋ/__#	13, 17
13.	ɛ	:	e	14
14.	p	:	f	17, 20, 21

4. Proto-AD reconstructions are:

No.	Proto-AD	Lg. A	Lg. D	
1.	(none)	yegi	oruŋ	dog
2.	*waku	waku	wou	rat
3.	*ɔsom	ɔsom	ooŋ	bat
4.	*sarɔt	sarɔt	alo?	hand
5.	*kulak	kulak	ula	finger
6.	(none)	tɛkia	alutu	fingernail
7.	*ŋasim	ŋasim	ŋeiŋ	person
8.	*lindaŋ	lindaŋ	lilaŋ	house
9.	*mosot	mosot	moo?	tree
10.	*rogus	rogus	loku	branch
11.	*ulif	ulif	ulih	leaf

12. (none)	sombu	sita	earth
13. *fɔgan	fɔgan	hokaŋ	water
14. *gɛmɛs	gɛmɛs	keme	bird
15. (none)	iliili	nemineŋ	butterfly
16. (none)	mulɛm	puo?	caterpillar
17. *palun	palun	foluŋ	mosquito
18. *kuri	makuri	ulila	white
19. *simak	masimak	imala	black
20. *purum	mapurum	fuluŋula	red
21. *tepi	matepi	tefila	hot
22. *luŋiŋ	maluŋiŋ	luŋiŋila	cold
23. *itur	maitur	itulula	heavy
24. *isɔt	maisɔt	iotola	small
25. *nusuk	manusuk	nuula	big
26. *rani	marani	lenila	beautiful

Discussion. This problem is sufficiently difficult that reconstructions are proposed to clarify the nature of the sound correspondences. The chief elements causing difficulty are limited data and varying patterns of morphology for adjectives or stative verbs. The limited data lead to some sound correspondences being represented by single forms, as with *nd* : *l*, and *ε* : *e*, and *asi* : *ei*. However, this limitation is overcome either by parallel examples or by ordering. Next to *nd* : *l*, for example, there are six examples of *r* : *l*, supporting a general inference that *nd > r > l*. Similarly, next to the unique example of *ε* : *e* there are four examples of *ɔ* : *o*, supporting the general inference that an original distinction of tense and lax mid vowels has been lost through merger in Lg. D.

The second feature of this problem that introduces some difficulty is the divergent patterns of affixation for adjectives or stative verbs. Not only does this involve prefixation in Lg. A vs. suffixation in Lg. D, but the latter language shows a pattern in which *-la* is suffixed directly to vowel-final stems, while consonant-final stems take *-Vla*, where V is a copy of the last stem vowel. The point of these examples is to underscore the lesson that before recurrent sound correspondences can be identified it is necessary to ensure that the data have first been subjected to a full morphological analysis.

SOLUTION TO GENETIC RELATIONSHIP PROBLEM 10

1. Lgs. A and B are genetically related.
2. All words are cognate except 1, 10 and 35.
3. The sound correspondences that justify these statements cannot easily be listed mechanically, and are best expressed as divergent reflexes of proto-phonemes, leading to phonological reconstruction as a tool for establishing genetic relationship where this cannot be shown in other ways. Proto-AB can be reconstructed as follows:

No.	Proto-AB	Lg. A	Lg. B	
01.	(none)	lasi	rotu	water
02.	*ukut	uutu	uku	river
03.	*pakul	fauru	woku	stone
04.	*kakas	aaha	kaka	grass
05.	*sapina	hafina	sewia	vine
06.	*kakin	aini	keki	tree
07.	*tulaka	turaa	tulaka	fruit
08.	*kasup	ahufu	kosu	fire
09.	*utuk	utuu	utu	wind
10.	(none)	hana	sua	sky
11.	*mutis	musihi	muti	sun
12.	*nunuk	nunuu	nu	cloud
13.	*paniti	fanisi	weiti	moon
14.	*rupan	rufana	rua	star
15.	*tanim	tanimi	tei	person
16.	*maku	mau	moku	head
17.	*rakit	raisi	reki	hair
18.	*lapik	rafii	lewi	eye
19.	*tisut	sihutu	tisu	ear
20.	*sapu	hafu	sowu	nose
21.	*ulur	ururu	ulu	mouth
22.	*asak	ahaa	asa	tooth
23.	*natin	nasini	neti	tongue
24.	*papi	fafi	wewi	cook
25.	*lakat	raata	laka	burn
26.	*ranuk	ranuu	rou	sit
27.	*nipun	nifunu	niwu	stand

28.	*kanit	anisi	kei	walk
29.	*ilaku	irau	iloku	sleep
30.	*tawak	tawaa	tawa	dream
31.	*sukup	huufu	suku	breathe
32.	*manaku	manau	moku	laugh
33.	*uluk	uruu	ulu	cry
34.	*katik	asii	keti	small
35.	(none)	mana	anu	big
36.	*sulak	huraa	sula	heavy
37.	*sukal	huara	suka	light
38.	*tipaki	sifai	tiweki	black
39.	*wakil	wairi	weki	white

4. Reflexes in Lgs. A and B in the order they are encountered are:

Change		**Examples**
Lg. A		
1. *k > Ø	:	2–4, 6–9, 12, 16, 18, 22, 25, 26, 28, 34, 36–39
2. $V_iC > V_iCV_i$ (before 1, 6)	:	2–4, 6, 8, 9, 11, 12, 14, 15, 17–19, 21–23, 25–28, 30, 31, 33, 34, 36, 37, 39
3. *p > f	:	3, 5, 8, 13, 14, 18, 20, 24, 27, 31, 38
4. *l > r	:	3, 7, 18, 21, 25, 29, 33, 36, 37, 39
5. *s > h (before 6)	:	4, 5, 8, 11, 19, 20, 22, 31, 36, 37
6. *t > s/__i	:	11, 13, 17, 19, 23, 34, 38
Lg. B		
1. C > Ø/__#	:	2–4, 6, 8, 9, 11, 12, 14, 15, 17–19, 21–23, 25–28, 30, 31, 33, 34, 36, 37, 39
2. *p > w (before 7)	:	3, 5, 8, 13, 14, 18, 20, 24, 27, 31, 38
3. *a > o/__Cu	:	3, 8, 16, 20, 26, 29, 32
4. *a > e/__Ci	:	5, 6, 13, 15, 17, 18, 23, 24, 28, 34, 38, 39
5. *n > Ø/V__V (before 6)	:	5, 12, 13, 15, 26, 28, 32
6. $V_iV_i > V_i$ (before 3)	:	12, 32

7. *w > Ø/u__a   :   14

Discussion. This problem is particularly difficult because Lg. A has added echo vowels and Lg. B has dropped final consonants, producing a misalignment of sound correspondences that can easily lead to false hypotheses about historical development. For example, $t : k$ is not a sound correspondence in sets 2 and 25, but rather the outcome of regular changes to *ukut and *lakat respectively (in Lg. A echo vowels were added and *k disappeared, in Lg. B *k was retained but final consonants were lost). For the same reasons $f : k$ is not a sound correspondence in set 31, but rather the residue of sound changes that (1) lengthened a $C_1VC_2VC_3$ form in Lg. A by adding an echo vowel, and then shortened it to a disyllable again by deleting medial *k and contracting a sequence of like vowels, but (2) shortened the same form to C_1VC_2V in Lg. B. As a result of these changes the original final consonant has become medial in Lg. A, and disappeared in Lg. B, producing the false impression that C_3 in Lg. A and C_2 in Lg. A continue the same structural position in the word.

Perhaps the most challenging feature of this problem is justfying the inference that items 9, 12, 18, 22, 26, 30, 33, 34 and 36 contained a final *k, since this segment disappeared in both languages. However, unless long vowels or clusters of identical vowels are reconstructed for Proto-AB, which the reader is told to avoid, these clusters could only have arisen by the addition of echo vowels after a word-final consonant that subsequently was lost, and the only candidate for this scenario is *k.

Problems of this type expose the fallacy of procedures like 'mass comparison' (Greenberg 1957) and the necessity of establishing sound correspondences before undertaking reconstruction, since without prior reconstruction the sound correspondences in many cases would simply be unstateable.

SOLUTION TO GENETIC RELATIONSHIP PROBLEM 11

1. Lgs. A, B and D are genetically related.
2. The cognate forms are most transparently displayed in the following way, where words marked by identical letters in parentheses are cognate, and those marked by non-identical letters are not.

No.	Lg. A	Lg. B	Lg. C	Lg. D	
01.	fəduh (A)	paruk (A)	pasim (B)	ər (A)	hand
02.	enahi (A)	enaki (A)	musok (B)	ila (A)	head
03.	bohaŋ (A)	bokaŋ (A)	vugu (B)	limak (C)	eye
04.	hanəl (A)	kanar (A)	liner (B)	al (A)	nose
05.	adih (A)	arik (A)	inu (B)	ar (A)	ear
06.	nulon (A)	nuron (A)	silum (B)	luy (A)	mouth
07.	lefa (A)	repa (A)	tayas (B)	yi (A)	earth
08.	fune (A)	pune (A)	kuvan (B)	ul (A)	sky
09.	ədam (A)	aram (A)	lumiŋ (B)	ər (A)	rain
10.	hiben (A)	biki (B)	fuli (C)	ih (A)	eat
11.	baŋo (A)	baŋo (A)	abar (B)	han (A)	drink
12.	abəh (A)	abak (A)	ruram (B)	yima (C)	sleep
13.	hohe (A)	koke (A)	golek (B)	u (A)	speak
14.	lanoh (A)	ranok (A)	nafo (B)	luyu (C)	walk
15.	dudəl (A)	rurar (A)	uvin (B)	rur (A)	laugh
16.	nefon (A)	nepon (A)	mumak (B)	li (A)	cry
17.	obuli (A)	oburi (A)	lurar (B)	uhuy (A)	dream
18.	ŋifit (A)	ŋipit (A)	sukal (B)	ni (A)	wake

3. The recurrent sound correspondences that show this relationship are as follows (underlined numbers indicate correspondences that are incompletely represented in the relevant cognate sets either through lack of cognation or through loss of information in cognate forms):

No.	Lg. A	:	Lg. B	:	Lg. D	
1.	f	:	p	:	Ø	1, 7, 8, 16, 18
2.	ə	:	a	:	ə	1, 4, 9, 12, 15
3.	d	:	r	:	r	1, 5, 9, 15
4.	-VC	:	-VC	:	Ø	1, 4, 5, 6, 9, 10, 14, 15, 16, 18
5.	h	:	k	:	Ø	1, 2, 3, 4, 5, 10, 12, 13, 14
6.	e	:	e	:	i	2, 7, 8, 10, 13, 16
7.	n	:	n	:	l	2, 4, 6, 8, 10, 14, 16
8.	-V	:	-V	:	Ø	2, 7, 8, 11, 13, 17
9.	b	:	b	:	h	3, 10, 11, 12, 17
10.	l	:	r	:	y	4, 6, 7, 14, 15, 17
11.	ŋ	:	ŋ	:	n	11, 18
12.	o	:	o	:	u	3, 6, 11, 13, 14, 16, 17

Discussion. This is a difficult problem, and one in which the statement of sound correspondences is formally quite complex. The principal difficulty is introduced by Lg. D, which shows such extreme phonological erosion that cognates are initially difficult to recognise, not so much because the corresponding segments themselves are radically different, but because so much information has been lost.

The formal statement of correspondences in this problem is also more difficult than in most others. If the relationship were restricted to Lgs. A and B the solution would be far simpler, but the inclusion of Lg. D, with its extreme 'erosion from the right' adds a layer of complexity which introduces a number of additional complications. For example, it seems simpler to state that there are -VC : -VC : -Ø and -V : -V : -Ø correspondences than to represent the former as -C : -C : -Ø, since that would leave the loss of vowels preceding final consonants unstated. If reconstruction were carried out this type of relationship could be explained through ordering (loss of -C, followed by loss of -V), but in a bare statement of correspondences it is best represented as shown here. A second type of complication introduced by the extreme changes in Lg. D arises in stating correspondences that hold between specific segments vs. those that hold between classes of segments. The statement of an $h : k : Ø$ correspondence, for example, overlaps with the statement that there is a -VC : -VC : -Ø correspondence, since the first of these correspondences needs to be stated for both final and non-final positions, but the latter includes the former word-finally, and renders it defective in much the same way we would find if Lg. D lacked a cognate form. Finally, correspond-ences 11 and 12 are each represented by just two comparisons. However, correspondence 12 is the back vowel equivalent of correspondence 6, and the two can be generalised to a statement that mid vowels in the first two languages correspond to high vowels in Lg. D.

SOLUTION TO GENETIC RELATIONSHIP PROBLEM 12

1. Lgs. A and C are genetically related.
2. All forms are cognate except 4, 9 and 16.
3. The recurrent sound correspondences that show this relationship are as follows:

No.	Lg. A	:	Lg. C	
1.	Ø	:	V/#(C)__	1, 3, 5–8, 10–15, 19–21, 23–26
2.	s	:	t/_V	1, 5, 6, 8, 10, 15, 19, 21
3.	-V	:	Ø	1, 2, 10, 22, 24, 25
4.	l	:	n/_V	2, 7, 12, 13, 15, 17
5.	ə	:	V	2, 17, 18, 22
6.	n	:	ŋ/_#	2, 15, 21, 22, 26
7.	r	:	l	3, 8, 18, 20
8.	s	:	h/_#	3, 14, 18, 19, 23, 25
9.	p	:	f	5, 6, 11, 17, 25
10.	o	:	a/uC_	5, 15
11.	l	:	ŋ/_#	5, 11
12.	e	:	a/iC_	6, 20, 26
13.	k	:	Ø/_#	6, 20
14.	k	:	h/_V	7, 10, 18, 21, 23
15.	m	:	ŋ/_#	7, 12, 24
16.	b	:	v	13, 26
17.	d	:	r	22

Discussion. This is an exceptionally difficult problem which reminds us of two very important points: (1) that cognation and phonetic similarity are independent notions, and (2) that although genetic relationship is often apparent 'at a glance' as Joseph Greenberg insisted with his method of 'mass comparison', there are some cases in which a valid genetic relationship is so well disguised by divergent patterns of history that it takes great skill to see the connection. Without systematic mapping of the sound correspondences, who would guess that *su* and *it* 'man' or *ləni* and *nuŋ* 'woman' are both valid cognate sets connecting Lgs. A and C? To some extent the problem here is one of *alignment*: in searching for correspondences one tends to align segments lineally, hence *s* : *i* and *u* : *t* in 'man'. However, for words that originally began or ended with a vowel in this problem a lineal alignment will lead the analyst astray, given changes 1 and 3 above.

It is only when reflexes of proto-forms that contained an initial or final consonant are considered that the alignment issue is alleviated, and the outline of a set of recurrent sound correspondences begins to appear, providing a 'bridge' to deciphering the more recalcitrant cases. But with natural language data the percentage of cognates may be so low and the correspondences so obscure that it eventually becomes impossible to determine whether forms (and hence the languages that carry them) are related or not.

Given the complexity of the sound correspondences in this problem it is helpful to reconstruct proto-forms in order to keep track of the divergent paths of change in the two languages. This is done here to assist in the recognition of recurrence, where Proto-AC = the ancestor of Lgs. A and C:

No.	Proto-AC	Lg. A	Lg. C	
01.	*isu	su	it	man
02.	*luni	ləni	nuŋ	woman
03.	*aras	ras	alah	child
04.	(none)	ppit	parfa	village
05.	*supal	spol	tufaŋ	house
06.	*pisak	psek	fita	fire
07.	*kilum	klum	hinuŋ	to cook
08.	*sunur	snur	tunul	to eat
09.	(none)	kur	lakus	to drink
10.	*kusu	ksu	hut	to sleep
11.	*apul	pul	afuŋ	to talk
12.	*ilim	lim	iniŋ	to walk
13.	*bulut	blut	vunut	big
14.	*tumis	tmis	tumih	small
15.	*sulan	slon	tunaŋ	long
16.	(none)	pru	makat	short
17.	*lumip	ləmip	numif	hot
18.	*rakas	rəkas	lahah	cold
19.	*usis	sis	utih	strong
20.	*rirak	rrek	lila	weak
21.	*sukun	skun	tuhuŋ	black
22.	*dinu	dənu	riŋ	white
23.	*akus	kus	ahuh	red

24.	*mamu	mmu	maŋ	one
25.	*pasi	psi	fah	two
26.	*iban	ben	ivaŋ	three

In most languages phonological erosion proceeds from the 'right' (weakening and ultimately eliminating word endings). In a few languages, however, it proceeds from the left, normally as a result of final stress. Some readers might object that such stress-dependent changes would not work in opposite directions within the same language family, but the classic example of Munda and Mon-Khmer within the Austroasiatic family shows that this has happened (Donegan and Stampe 1983).

In this problem, Lg. A weakens unstressed (non-final) vowels, and loses them entirely in environments where the resulting consonant cluster can be pronounced without an intervening schwa. It does so, however, only after the frontness of an unstressed penultimate vowel has been copied onto a last-syllable low vowel (the conditioning vowel being preserved in Lg. C). A number of the sound correspondences attested here are found only in certain phonologically specified environments, and a full recognition of their regularity requires at least some consideration of ordering relations, as where final high vowels must have been lost in Lg. C before the merger of all word-final nasals as -ŋ. Despite these difficulties and the sometimes limited phonetic similarity between cognate forms, there is overwhelming evidence that Lgs. A and C are genetically related.

SOLUTIONS TO SOUND CHANGE PROBLEMS

SOLUTION TO SOUND CHANGE PROBLEM 1

Proto-Malayo-Polynesian (PMP) to Hawaiian

1. The mergers found in this data are as follows:

   1. *b and *p merged as h (1, 8, 10, 12, 15, 18, 19, 21, 27, 32, 34, 38, 44).

   2. *ə and *-aw merged as o (2, 4, 9, 18, 25–28, 32, 37, 38; there are also two sporadic assimilations of *a to *u in the following syllable, seen in 18 'new', and 41 'inject').

   3. Final consonants merged as zero (2, 4–9, 13, 14, 16, 17, 20, 22–24, 26, 29–31, 33–36, 39–41, 43, 45; this followed *-ay > e, *-aw > o, *-uy > i, and resyllabification of *kahiw (> kaiw) > $kayu$).

   4. *s, *z, and *j merged as Ø or h^1 (3, 5, 7, 14, 20–22, 25, 28, 30, 32, 33, 41).

   5. *R, *q, *y and *h merged as zero (4, 6, 13–19, 23–25, 30, 32, 35, 36, 39–42).

   6. *d, *nd and *l merged as l (1, 2, 5, 8, 11, 13, 17, 22, 26, 29, 30, 35–37, 40).

   7. *-uy and *i merged as i (19).

   8. *ŋ, *ñ and *n merged as n (9, 15, 31, 37–39, 43).

---

1 The palatals *s, *z, *c and *j first merged as *s, which subsequently became *h, and then disappeared sporadically.

2. The split-merger affected PMP *b which (along with *p) became Proto-Polynesian (PPN) *f. Ignoring issues of 'consonant grade', which play little role in the data given here, PMP *bVb and *pVp became PPN *fVf. If the sequence was specifically *faf- it underwent Proto-Eastern Polynesian labial dissimilation to *wah-, as seen in examples 15, 27, 34 and 44. Since *w did not change this led to a split of *b and partial merger with *w. This change did not affect PPN *p or *m, as seen in *papa > Hawaiian *papa* 'board', *pipi > *pipi* 'shellfish sp.', *popo > *po-popo* 'rot, decay', *mama > *mama* 'chew', *mimi > *mimi* 'urine, urinate', etc. (Walsh and Biggs 1966). A similar type of labial dissimiation with much broader scope has been reported for Akkadian in a number of sources, most recently by Suzuki (1998).

3. *q, which became PPN *?, first disappeared. Then *k > ?, and finally *t > *k*. This was a classic drag chain, with the first two changes completed before European contact and the last one still in progress when the Boston missionaries began to establish a practical orthography for Hawaiian in the early decades of the nineteenth century. If *k > ? had preceded loss of glottal stop then both *q and *k would have disappeared, which is not the case; similarly, if *t > *k* had preceded *k > ?, the two phonemes would have merged.

Changes in the order they are encountered in this data are as follows:

Changes	Examples
1. *b > h	1, 12, 15, 18, 27, 32, 34, 44
2. *-ay > -e	1, 32, 42
3. *t > k	2, 4, 7, 10, 12, 24, 31, 42, 45
4. *ə > o	2, 4, 9, 26, 32, 38
5. -C > Ø	2, 4–9, 13, 14, 16, 17, 20, 22–24, 26, 29-31, 33–36, 39–41, 43, 45
6. *s > Ø	3, 7, 20, 30, 32
7. *s > h	22, 28, 30
8. $V_i V_i > \bar{V}$	3, 13, 36
9. *R > Ø	4, 6, 18, 32, 41
10. *z > Ø	5, 14
11. *z > h	41

12. *p > h	8, 10, 19, 21, 38
13. *nd/d > l	8, 13, 17, 26, 29, 35, 40
14. *q (> ʔ) > Ø (before 15)	13, 14, 17, 18, 24, 25, 40, 42
15. *k > ʔ (before 3)	13, 20, 23, 28
16. *y > Ø	13, 36
17. *b > w/__ab	15, 27, 34, 44
18. *h > Ø	16, 19, 23, 35, 39
19. *-uy > i	19
20. *j > Ø	21, 25
21. *j > h	33
22. *-aw > o	25, 27, 28, 37
22. *ŋ > n	31, 37, 39
23. *ñ > n	38
24. *mb > p	45

Discussion. This problem illustrates extreme consonant merger and consequent phoneme reduction. PMP (the immediate ancestor of all Austronesian languages outside the island of Taiwan) had twenty-five consonants, four vowels and four vowel-glide sequences *-ay, *-aw, *-uy and *-iw that monophthongised in many daughter languages. In Hawaiian these are reduced to eight consonants and five vowels (short and long). This extreme reduction of a once globally more typical kind of phoneme inventory has led to jokes that the Polynesians 'tossed phonemes' overboard as they sailed east, and if there had been further landfalls before the Americas they would have ended up speaking only with vowels! Given the extent of merger in Hawaiian (and Polynesian languages more generally), it would be easier to derive the data from Proto-Oceanic, a later proto-language, ancestral to about 460 of the Austronesian languages of the Pacific, but since this language had already undergone some of the mergers seen here it would be less suitable in illustrating the wholesale collapse of phonemic distinctions in Hawaiian.

Like many other Oceanic languages Hawaiian has oral grade and nasal grade reflexes of some obstruents, where the nasal grade was originally a prenasalised stop, fricative or affricate in most cases. The lone instance of *mb > *p* in example 45 illustrates this development here. The varying reflexes of *s as /h/ or zero are distinct from the oral grade/nasal grade contrast, and have been called 'fortis' and 'lenis' reflexes in Ross (1988).

SOLUTIONS

SOLUTION TO SOUND CHANGE PROBLEM 2

Proto-Oceanic (POC) to Arosi

1. POC *s remained a sibilant before high vowels, but changed to /t/ elsewhere:

| *s | > | s/__i,u | 3, 15, 27, 32 |
| | > | t/__a, e, o | 7, 12, 23, 26, 30, 36, 40 |

2. Arosi /s/ derives from POC *s before high vowels, and from *y before low vowels, a type of glide epenthesis that has affected a number of Oceanic languages. Since the palatal glide was historically secondary in the latter case some examples of /s/ may appear to derive from zero or from a word-initial consonant that was lost before *a:

| *Ø > (y/#__a) > | s | 1, 4, 25, 33, 37 |
| *y   > | s | 9, 21 |

3. A prominent shift in Arosi and other closely related languages in the Southeast Solomon Islands is *t > Ø, followed by *s > t/__ a,e,o:

| *t | > | Ø | 1, 5, 11, 13, 19, 27, 31, 33, 39, 41 |
| *s | > | t/__a, e, o | 7, 12, 23, 26, 30, 36, 40 |

A prominent merger is that of POC *l, *r and *R:

*l	>	r	5, 12, 17, 22, 24, 29, 30
*r	>	r	2, 14, 28, 43
*R	>	r	8, 15, 25, 26

Sound changes in this data, in the order that they are encountered, are as follows:

Changes	Examples
1. *q > O (before 2, 12)	1, 9, 14, 18, 33, 37, 38, 40, 41, 43
2. O > y/#__a (before 3)	1, 4, 25, 33, 37
3. *y > s	1, 4, 9, 21, 25, 33, 47
4. *t > O (before 8)	1, 5, 11, 13, 19, 27, 31, 33, 39, 41
5. *C > O/__#	2, 3, 6, 8, 10, 12–15, 20, 21, 24, 26, 27, 29, 31–33, 40, 43
6. *l > r	5, 12, 17, 22, 24, 29, 30
7. *k > ʔ	7, 13, 20, 29, 34
8. *s > t/__V[-hi]	7, 12, 23, 26, 30, 36, 40
9. *R > r	8, 15, 25, 26
10. *p > h	9, 11, 18, 35
11. ñ > n	10, 16, 35, 42
12. ViVi > Vi/__CV	41

Discussion. The addition of an initial sibilant in *qate > *sae*- 'liver' and similar etymologies is most plausibly explained under a hypothesis that *q first disappeared, and that a palatal glide was then added before initial low vowels, after which the change *y > s took place. Palatal glide epenthesis before initial low vowels is a recurrent change in many Oceanic languages (Blust 1990). In most of these no further change has occurred, but in some the added glide has undergone a later sound change (as in Motu of Southeast New Guinea, where *y* was added before initial *a, and this glide then became *l*). What complicates the picture for languages in the Southeast Solomons is the later fortition of *y, to *s* or θ, depending upon the language (Lichtenberk 1988).

Note that palatal glide epenthesis must have preceded loss of *t in Arosi, since otherwise forms that began with *ta- such as 27 and 31, would have acquired the glide and then strengthened it to *s*-.

SOLUTION TO SOUND CHANGE PROBLEM 3

PMP to the Musi dialect of Rejang

1. The sequences -*eCe*- and -*oCo*- developed under two sets of conditions. The first of these is in CVCVC stems where V_1 was *a and V_2 was high, as in examples 9, 12, 14, 15, 18, 22, 24, 45 and 51, or in CVCVC stems where V_1 was high and V_2 was schwa, as in examples 7, 10 or 32. Note that this change did not occur if V_1 high and V_2 was *a, as in *dilaq > *dileʔ* 'tongue' (not **deleʔ), *bulat > *bulət* 'round' (not **bolot), *hisaŋ > *isaŋ* 'gills' (not **eseŋ), *qudaŋ > *udaŋ* 'shrimp' (not **odoŋ), or *ma-iRaq > *miləʔ* 'red' (not **meləʔ), nor if V_1 was schwa and V_2 was high, as in *penuq > *pənoʔ* 'full' (not **ponoʔ).

   The second condition is in CVCVC stems where both vowels were high and agreed in backness, and the last consonant was *q, *l or *R, as in examples 40, 41 and 43. High vowels were lowered before these consonants, and harmonic constraints required that penultimate high vowels with the same value for backness be lowered in response. Note that this change did not occur if the high vowels disagreed in backness, as with *niuR > *nioa* 'coconut palm' (not **neoa), or *putiq > *puteʔ* 'white' (not **poteʔ).

   Apparent exceptions to the first condition are the following:

2: *aluR > *aloa* 'to flow' (expected **oloa; cp. 22)

26. *punay > ponoy 'dove' (expected **punay; cp. 48)

2. There are two conditions under which *a was raised to a high vowel in Rejang, and both are less problematic than the conditions that led to the new vowel sequences -*eCe*- and -*oCo*-. All known cases of penultimate *a > *i* occur in stems of the shape C*a*C*i*, and all known cases of *a > *u* in stems of the shape C*a*C*u*. There are no known exceptions:

5. *tali > *tiləy* 'rope'   21. *batu > *butəw* 'stone'
20. *laRiw (> laRi) > *liləy* 'to run'   30. *sapu > *supəw* 'broom'

25. *baRani (> bani) > *binəy* 'courageous'
32. *waRi > *biləy* 'day'

All known cases of the raising of *a to a high vowel in the ultima occur in the sequence *-ay. Again, there are no known exceptions (note that *q- was lost before this change):

4. *anay > *anie-anie* 'termite'
11. *qatay > *atie* 'liver'
23. *matay > *matie* 'die; dead'

3. *q caused diphthongisation of a preceding vowel, while *k did not, and this provides unambiguous evidence of the source of Rejang -ʔ:

3. *anak > *anaʔ* 'child'   8. *dilaq > *diləaʔ* 'tongue'
15. *manuk > *monoʔ* 'chicken'   17. *pənuq > *pənoaʔ* 'full'
32. *hutək > *otoʔ* 'brain'   36. *daRaq > *daləaʔ* 'blood'
                                  40. *bunuq > *bonoaʔ* 'to kill'
                                  49. *putiq > *puteaʔ* 'white'
                                  50. *m-iRaq (> miRaq) > *miləaʔ* 'red'

Discussion. The development of *-eCe-* and *-oCo-* from earlier sequences in which one vowel was originally high and the other non-high is sufficiently well attested to earn our confidence that it is basically correct, and to raise suspicions that at least some apparent exceptions may be subregularities or products of borrowing. It is clear that this pattern developed only in consonant-final stems, since a very different pattern is attested in CVCV stems in which one vowel was originally high and the other non-high.

The first indication of a possible subregularity is seen in *dilaq > *diləaʔ* 'tongue' and *ma-iRaq > *miləaʔ* 'red', where the final glottal stop has diphthongised the preceding vowel, apparently destroying the conditions for the uniform vowel lowering pattern to apply. The second possible subregularity is more narrowly defined. Stems with uniform vowel lowering to *-eCe-* or *-oCo-* include *-aCi-, *-aCu-, *-iCə-, *uCa- and *-uCə-. The absence of examples with *-iCa- is assumed to be an accidental gap, but there are no examples of the majority pattern of vowel lowering in which the penultimate vowel is schwa, and this pattern is consistent with other examples in McGinn (2005: 57–62), where his examples 33, 34, 76, 109, 129 and 174 meet this structural description but also fail to undergo uniform vowel lowering. It therefore seems likely that this is a structural condition on the change: whereas *iCə and *uCə produced uniform vowel lowering, *əCi or *əCu apparently did not. For the other apparent exceptions it is harder to find evidence of conditioning, although VCVC stems often fail to undergo vowel lowering, suggesting that the preferred canonical shape for this change was CVCVC.

The primary lessons of this problem are (1) how extensive phonemic splitting can be, and (2) how specific the conditions can be for splits. The PMP system of four vowels (*i, *u, *ə, *a) and three diphthongs (*-ay, *-aw, *-uy) developed into six vowels (*i, u, e, o, ə, a*), six diphthongs (*əy, əw, ea, oa, əa, ie*) and one triphthong (*uəw*).

In what is perhaps the most striking example of splitting, *a is a source of all six vowels and two diphthongs: in the sequences *-aCi and *-aCu it became *i* and *u* respectively; before final alveolars it became ə; in the sequence *aCiC it became *e*; in the sequences *aCuC, *uCaC and *uCəC it generally became *o*; before final *q it became *əa*; word-finally it became *-əy*, and before final *k (which became glottal stop), *ŋ, and in some penultimate environments it remained *a*. To avoid unnecessary complications some changes are stated in terms of phoneme sequences rather than individual segments. This is because of vowel harmony constraints that would require questionable ordering if stated separately.

For example, we could ask whether *laŋit became *leŋit* and then *leŋet* 'sky' because mid and high vowels were disfavoured in the same morpheme, or whether the transition from *laŋit to *leŋet was a single change. Although the assimilation of *a to the frontness and height features of a high vowel in the following syllable is a natural and common sound change in the world's languages, this did not happen where the final syllable was open, as in *tali > *tiləy* 'rope' (note that if we assume *tali (> teli) > *teləy*, with subsequent raising of *e to *i it is unclear why *e did not raise in *leŋet*; if we assume that the entire process leading from *tali to *tiləy* had already taken place before *leŋet* appeared we would be claiming, counter-intuitively, that *a > e/__Ci took place in CVCV words before it took place in CVCVC words). Since forms such as 40, 41 and 43 also show vowel harmony triggered by lowering of the last-syllable vowel it is likely that a harmonic condition was imposed when new mid vowels *e* and *o* were created by sound change.

As just seen, many vocalic changes in Rejang take place under very specific conditions. For example, *a > ə took place only before final alveolars (*t, *s, *n), the sequences *aCi and *aCu developed differently in open or closed final syllables, the diphthongs *-ea* and *-oa* developed only before word-final *l and *R, which disappeared (probably after merging as *l*), and also before *q, which is retained as a glottal stop.

The following changes to the vowels and diphthongs of PMP have taken place in Rejang:

Changes	Examples
1. *u, i > əw, əy/__#	1, 5, 16, 20, 21, 25, 29, 30, 34, 47
2. *u, i > oa, ea/__R,l,q#	2, 14, 22, 40, 41, 43, 44, 49
3. *ay, aw > ie, uəw/__#	4, 11, 23, 27, 33, 46
4. *a > i,u/C__Ci,u#	5, 20, 21, 25, 30, 34
5. *a > ə/__n, t, s#	6, 13, 38
6. *iCə, aCi > eCe, *aCu, uCa, uCə > oCo/__C#	7, 9, 10, 12, 14, 15, 18, 22, 24, 26, 32, 45, 51
7. *a > əa/__q#	8, 36, 50
8. *a > əy/__#	19, 28, 31, 35

Many new diphthongs and at least one triphthong were created by splitting of vowels or earlier diphthongs, as with *qatay > *atie* 'liver', or *kasaw > *kasuəw* 'rafter'. Given the general parallelism of developments that affected front and back vowels in Rejang we would expect *-ie* to be *-iəy*, but McGinn (2005) does not report this for any of the five Rejang dialects that he describes. Some types of diphthongisation in this language are quite surprising, as with *-a > -əy*. It seems likely that *-a became *i before this change, since *a and *i merged word-finally, although *a > i word-finally would be a rather odd change in itself. Finally, pronouns as a class are exempted from all of these changes for reasons that remain in dispute (Blust 1984; McGinn 1997).

SOLUTION TO SOUND CHANGE PROBLEM 4

Pre-Kayan to Uma Juman Kayan (Sarawak, Malaysian Borneo)

1. In Uma Juman Pre-Kayan final glottal stop is reflected as zero and Pre-Kayan final vowel is reflected as vowel + glottal stop. In effect, glottal stop and zero have been interchanged in this dialect. In classic Generative phonology this was handled by an 'alpha-switching rule' (Kiparsky 1968).

2. The predictable differences of vowel height (high vowels automatically lowered before final glottal stop) provide a second difference between words that end with a surface high vowel and those that end with an underlying high vowel followed by glottal stop. Since the distinction between these syllable types is still maintained by the vocalic difference it makes the phonemic role of the glottal stop dispensable. However, the Uma Juman data alone provide no basis for seeing how *-a and *-a? could be distinguished if glottal stop were first added to *-a or deleted from *-a?, since either change would produce merger.

Discussion. The general theoretical interest of this problem lies in the relationship between change (1), which added glottal stop after original final vowels, and change (4), which dropped original glottal stop in final position (but not intervocalically). A priori, this fits the description of what in early Generative phonology was called an 'alpha-switching rule': x became y and y became x, avoiding merger. While this initially looks like a case of segment exchange, the reality is both more complex and more natural.

Kayan is spoken in a number of dialects spread over the large island of Borneo, and in the Uma Juman dialect earlier minimal pairs such as *bulu? 'large bamboo sp.' and *bulu 'body hair, feathers', are reflected with two differences, the first as *bulu* and the second as *bulo?*. The lowering of high vowels before a final glottal stop thus provides perhaps the only clue that can be extracted from the data of this dialect about how the apparently simultaneous switch of final glottal stop and zero occurred. What it suggests is that differences in the reflexes of high vowels in the ultima continued to distinguish syllables that originally ended in a glottal stop from those that originally ended in a vowel even after a glottal stop had been added to the latter. To see this we need to have access to relevant data from other dialects, and this is found in Uma Bawang, which has added glottal stop to original final vowels without dropping *-ʔ. In words that contain a low vowel in the ultima the original contrast of *-a vs. *-aʔ appears as UB -aʔ vs. -aaʔ, as in:

Pre-Kayan	Uma Bawang	Uma Juman	
*dua	duaʔ	duaʔ	'two'
*buaʔ	buaaʔ	bua	'fruit'

In words that contain a high vowel in the ultima the orignal contrast of *-i/u vs. *-iʔ/uʔ appears as UB -eʔ, -oʔ vs. -iʔ, -uʔ, as in:

Pre-Kayan	Uma Bawang	Uma Juman	
*puti	puteʔ	puteʔ	'banana'
*putiʔ	putiʔ	puti	'white'
*asu	asoʔ	asoʔ	'dog'
*pusuʔ	pusuʔ	pusu	'heart'

The changes leading to an apparent 'alpha-switch' in Uma Juman Kayan thus consisted of the following steps (Blust 2002a):

1. All Proto-Kayanic vowels were lengthened before final glottal stop.
2. Glottal stop was added after final vowels, producing length contrasts in *i, u* and *a* only before final glottal stop.
3. Short high vowels were lowered before final glottal stop.
4. Final glottal stop was lost after long vowels.

*təlu	*puluʔ	*mata	*tanaʔ	Innovation
təlu	puluuʔ	mata	tanaaʔ	1
təluʔ	puluuʔ	mataʔ	tanaaʔ	2
təloʔ	puluuʔ	mataʔ	tanaaʔ	3
təloʔ	puluu	mataʔ	tanaa	4
three	ten	eye	earth	

The Uma Bawang dialect underwent only changes 1–3, and so does not show an apparent alpha-switch. In this dialect vowel length is distinctive, but only for /a/ before final glottal stop. In addition to the first three changes Uma Juman (and several other dialects) underwent change 4. Since high vowel lowering before final glottal stop and lengthening of final vowels are predictable from context, however, the phonemic shapes of the words for 'three' and 'ten' are /təluʔ/ and /pulu/ (this assumes that one does not accept the 'once a phoneme always a phoneme' principle). There are other problems in Kayan historical phonology, such as why intervocalic *d did not lenite to *r* in forms such as 13 and 15 (possibly because the first syllable was lost prior to lenition), but the reversal of earlier final glottal stop and zero in many Kayan dialects and independently in the closely related Murik (Blust 1974) dominates the discussion of sound change in this language.

SOLUTION TO SOUND CHANGE PROBLEM 5

PMP to Muna (southern Sulawesi, Indonesia)

1. PMP *u in the last syllable has the following reflexes in Muna:

> > i: 4, 18, 20, 21, 32, 40, 56
> > u: 6, 42, 47, 50–53
> > o: 7, 19

   The conditions for this three-way split were essentially that *u was fronted immediately before a palatal glide from PMP *y or *R, it lowered to *o* if it came into contact with a low vowel in the sequence *ahu (> au) > oo*, and remained unchanged elsewhere. Further support for each of these hypotheses is seen in the fronting effects of non-final *R in 13 (*baRah > *waya* > *wea*), 27 (*qabaRa > *qawaya* > *ghowea*), 38 (*daRaq > *raya* > *rea*), 43 (*pəRəs > *poyos* > *feo*), 51 (*zaRum > *dayu* > *deu*) and 57 (*kaRat > *kaya* > *sia*), and the reflex of *-aw as *-o* (5, 26, 41).

2. There is evidence that at least some final consonants affected a preceding vowel before they were lost. This is most clearly seen with *-uR (> -uy) > *i* in 4, 18, 20, 21, 32, 40 and 56, since without this condition *u normally remained a high back vowel.

3. One unusual consonant reflex is *k > *s*, seen in examples 5, 11, 22, 23, 57 and 58. There are two exceptions in this problem: 31 and 44. The first of these has a double irregularity (*s > *s*, *k > *k*) which suggests borrowing, most likely from Malay. *k > *s* must be ordered after *s > *h*, seen in 5, 18, 34 and 36, since the two did not merge.

4. PMP prepenultimate *a became *u* if the last syllable contained *u, as in 32, 40 and 42. This is surprising in that we do not normally expect conditioning between vowels that are separated by an intervening vowel which remains unaffected.

   The sound changes in this data, in the order that they are encountered, are as follows:

Changes	Examples
1. *q > gh	1, 6, 9, 12, 16, 20, 24, 27, 32, 36, 37, 40–42, 46, 47
2. *ə > o (before 6)	1, 3, 6, 9, 11, 12, 14, 22, 27, 28, 35, 36, 39, 41, 44, 54
3. C > Ø/__#	1, 3, 6–14, 16-20, 24, 29–35, 37–39, 43, 44, 47–55, 57
4. *b > w	3, 4, 10, 13, 15, 18, 26, 27, 33
5. *h > Ø (before 10, 13, 16, 24)	3, 7, 10, 19, 23, 45, 50, 55, 56
6. *o > u/u__	3
7. *a/ə > e/__Ci (before 2)	4, 18, 20, 21, 29, 32, 58
8. *-uy > i (before 3, 7)	4, 18, 20, 21, 32, 56
9. *k > s	5, 11, 22, 23, 57, 58
10. *s > h (before 9, 23)	5, 18, 29, 34, 36
11. *wa/aw > o, *ay/əy > e (before 3)	5, 8, 13, 16, 25–27, 34, 38, 40, 41, 43, 46, 51, 55
12. *d > r/[-nas]__V (before 22)	7, 14, 28, 35, 38, 44, 53
13. *au > oo	7, 19
14. *ŋ > n	8, 15, 21, 30
15. *j > y (before 3, 11)	8, 16, 25, 34, 40, 41
16. *ə > Ø/__V	10
17. *i > e/__q# (before 3)	10, 49
18. *a > ə/C)__(C)V(C)V(C) (before 2, 19, 25)	11, 12, 22, 27, 36, 41
19. *əw > u (before 2)	11
20. *p > f	12, 19, 20, 28, 40, 43, 56
21. *R > y (before 3, 8, 11, 27)	13, 18, 20, 27, 32, 33, 36, 38, 42, 43, 51, 57
22. *r > l/__Vl	14
23. *z > s	17, 24, 52
24. *iw > yu/V__	23
25. *ə > u/C__(C)V(C)V(C) (before 2)	32, 40, 42
26. nasal place assimilation	35, 54
27. *y > Ø/i__V	36

Discussion. Muna is interesting in being phonologically innovative in some features, and conservative in others. It is innovative, for example, in losing final consonants, a change that is common to a number of the languages of central and southern Sulawesi, and in developing two new vowels *e* and *o*. On the other hand, it is conservative in retaining a reflex of *q word-initially and the schwa in the environment VC__CV, both of which are rarities in most Austronesian languages outside Taiwan.

Among problems with double reflexes noted by van den Berg (1991: 8) are *p > *p* and *f*, *k > *k* and *s*, *b > *b*, *bh* (bilabial implosive), and *w*, and *s > *s* and *h*. In addition we can add *a > e/__Ci in most forms, but *a > i/__Ci in *hapuy > *ifi* 'fire', and *a > a/__Ci in 30, 31, 37 and 48. Since some of these show stratum-like correlations, as with *kasaw > *saho* 'rafter' (*k > *s*, *s > *h*), next to *sakit > *saki* 'sick, ill' (*s > *s*, *k > *k*, *a > a/__Ci), it is tempting to posit two separate 'speech strata' in Muna, one native and the other borrowed. However, examples such as *pusəj > *puhe* 'navel' show *p > *p*, where *f* is distinctive and surely a native reflex, as well as *s > *h*, which again is surely native. At least some of the double reflexes in Muna, then, appear to be found in native words which may show the effects of 'lexical diffusion' in the manner first suggested by Wang (1969) and later documented in greater detail by Chen and Wang (1975).

SOLUTION TO SOUND CHANGE PROBLEM 6

POC to Leipon (Admiralty Islands, Papua New Guinea)

1. The bilabial trills derive from earlier prenasalised labial stops. More particularly, the bilabial trill developed from [mb] before a rounded vowel, usually *u, and the alveolar trill from [nd] before any vowel. Examples of the former are: 8, 9, 11, 14, 17, 27, 29 and 40. For details on the aerodynamic basis for this change cf. Maddieson (1989a).
2. The low vowel *a was fronted under two conditions, first if there was a high vowel or glide in an adjacent syllable (preceding or following), and, second, if it was the first of two low vowels in successive syllables. In the first case *a became *e*; in the second it became *i*. Examples of *a > *e* are: 1, 2, 4, 6, 7, 10, 15, 16, 19, 21, 23, 25, 27, 33, 36, 39 and 42–45, and examples of *a > *i* are: 7, 19, 23, 24, 33, 36, 38 and 39.

Condition 1. The change *a > *e* is almost always found where there is a high vowel or glide in the following syllable. This is true for 1, 2, 4, 10 (all followed by *u), and for 6, 15, 21, 25, 27, 33, 42, 44 and 45 (all followed by *i or *y). However, cases like *mate > *met* (43) suggest that fronting and raising to *e* occurred if any non-low vowel occupied the next syllable. *a > *e* also occured as an apparent by-product of the second fronting of low vowels, which is noted below.

Condition 2. The change *a > *i* is an example of what has been called 'low vowel dissimilation' in Oceanic languages (Bender 1969; Blust 1996; Lynch 2003). Disyllabic bases which had low vowels in both syllables and retained them after the loss of *-VC dissimilated the first of these to *i* (7, 19, 23, 24, 33, 36, 38, 39), and then fronted the last-syllable vowel to *e* if it did not immediately precede *h* (24, 38). Note that this restriction did not hold in examples 1, 2 and 4, where *a > *e* arose from condition 1.

Many of the vowels that conditioned *a > *e* subsequently disappeared. Given cases like 43 or 45 it is not immediatly apparent why examples like 30 show no fronting of the surviving stem vowel. It is possible that the fronting of low vowels that have come to stand before a final consonant happened after the loss of final vowels was complete, but that words like *met* and *teŋ* could also occur in suffixed form, in which case the conditioning stem vowel survived, whereas this was not possible in common nouns like *das* 'saltwater, sea'.

Recurrent changes in this problem are as follows (N represents a homorganic nasal):

Changes	Examples
1. *a > e if word has *i,u,e* (before 3)	1, 2, 4, 6, 7, 10, 15, 16, 19, 21, 23, 25, 27, 33, 36, 39, 42–45
2. *p > h/V__	1–3, 24, 32, 38, 40, 46, 48
3. V > Ø/__# (before 11)	1–48
4. V > Ø/VC__CV	2, 4, 6, 42
5. C > Ø/__# (before 3)	4, 5, 9, 12–14, 17, 19, 20, 22, 25, 28–31, 34, 37, 41, 44, 45, 47
6. *R > Ø	4, 21, 26, 28, 32
7. *na > N/#__C (before 8, 10, 12, 13)	5–42
8. *r > dr/N__	5, 31
9. *R > y	5, 35
10. *t > d/N__	6, 15, 16, 30, 32
11. *a > i/__Ca (before 1)	7, 19, 23, 24, 33, 36, 38, 39
12. *t > nd/NV__	7, 44
13. *p > br/N__u	8, 9, 11, 14, 17, 27, 29, 40
14. *k > Ø/V__V (before 19)	8, 22, 25, 34
15. *ui > i	8, 26
16. *q > Ø	16, 27, 42
17. *s > c/n__	20, 22, 48
18. *b > p	21, 37
19. *au/oa, ai > o, e	22, 25, 34

Discussion. Like many other languages in Melanesia, the languages of the Admiralty Islands are phonologically highly innovative. Two of the changes in Leipon that merit special notice are the changes that produced the bilabial and alveolar trills, and the fronting of *a if there was a high vowel (front or back) anywhere else in the word.

As noted above, the bilabial trills, which are found in most of the languages spoken on the island of Manus, derive from earlier *mb preceding *u (Maddieson 1989a; Blust 2007). This change affected the initial stops of many nouns, since the unstressed common noun article *na lost its vowel, allowing the nasal to fuse with the initial stop of the base to produce historically secondary prenasalisation (Ross 1988: 332). In a few cases the vowel that conditioned this change has subsequently changed, as with *na puki (> mbuki > *mbruki* > *mbrui* > *bri-* [mb̃i] 'vulva, vagina'), but it is always clear that the bilabial trill arose at a time when it was followed by a high back rounded vowel.

The conditions under which *a fronted are complex. First, as already seen, *a was raised if there was a high vocoid elsewhere in the word. Second, like some other Oceanic languages in Micronesia, the Admiralty Islands and Vanuatu, Leipon shows low vowel dissimilation, a change whereby *a fronted if the following syllable nucleus was also *a (Blust 1996; Lynch 2003). This change must have followed final vowel loss, since etymologies such as *na paRa > *pay* 'firewood shelf', or *sapa > *cah* 'what?' show no fronting. However, it is clear that low vowel dissimilation preceded change 1, since the new high vowel then usually conditioned the raising of the remaining low vowel, as in *na kanase > *kines* 'mullet', *na kamali > *kimel* 'man, male', or *na tama > *time-* 'father' (but not in *na panapa > *pinah* 'needlefish', or *na katapa > *kitah* 'frigate bird').

Again, like many other Austronesian languages in Melanesia, Leipon appears to show a high degree of irregularity in sound change. Some of this may be due to undetected conditioning or borrowing, but many examples resist this type of explanation.

SOLUTION TO SOUND CHANGE PROBLEM 7

POC to Rotuman (central Pacific)

1. The reflexes of POC *p, *t, *k and *l in Rotuman are as follows:

*p	>	h	1, 5, 10, 15, 17, 23, 34
	>	f	7, 12, 18, 22, 24, 27, 33
*t	>	f	1, 2, 6, 13, 14, 16, 23, 36, 39, 42
	>	t	8, 15, 18, 20, 22, 27, 28, 32, 37
*k	>	ʔ	4, 9, 11, 13, 16, 21, 25, 39, 41
	>	k	8, 12, 20, 28, 32
*l	>	l	2–5, 10, 21, 26, 31, 38
	>	r	19, 24, 29, 35

2.   Stratum I: If *p > h, then *t > f (1, 23)

   If *p > h, then *l > l (5, 10)
   If *t > f, then *k > ʔ (13, 16, 39)
   If *t > f, then *l > l (2)
   If *k > ʔ, then *l > l (4)

   Stratum II: If *p > f, then *t > t (18, 22, 27)
   If *p > f, then *k > k (12)
   If *p > f, then *l > r (24)
   If *t > t, then *k > k (8, 20, 28, 32)

These criterial cases show clear stratal associations such that *p > h and *t > t, on the one hand, and *t > f and *k > k, etc., on the other, will not be found in the same lexical item. The stratal inferences based on criterial cases can then be generalised to bases that contain only one diagnostic reflex, as with 3 (*l > l = Stratum I), 6 (*t > f Stratum I), 7 (*p > f Stratum II) or 19 (*l > r = Stratum II).

3. The usual approach for distinguishing native vs. borrowed speech strata is to use reflexes in the most basic vocabulary as marking the native stratum. This does not always yield clear results with Rotuman, since Stratum I includes such uncontroversially basic lexical items as 'stone', 'three', 'five', 'go' and 'moon', but Stratum II includes other lexical items that appear to be nearly as basic, as 'to

hammer, pound' (8), the causative prefix (12), 'to pluck' (18), 'seaweed' (19), or 'body hair, feathers' (24). Moreover, in a few cases there are mixed stratal associations, as with 'shelf' (15).

The clearest clue to the native stratum is the surprising change *t > f, although the present [ʃ] < *t was recorded as [θ] by Hale (1846), and remains an interdental fricative in some Rotuman villages (Vilsoni Hereniko, p.c.). Because this change is unknown in any other Austronesian language lexical items that show it cannot be loans.

4. New vowels are /ɔ/, which developed from *a when followed by a high vowel (either front or back) in the next syllable (1, 27, 33, 34, 38, 39, 41), and /æ/, which developed from *a if the next syllable contained *e (32, 42). Note that there are exceptions to this change in both Stratum I and Stratum II reflexes (22, 36).

The sound changes in this data, in the order that they are encountered, are as follows:

Changes	Examples
1. *p > h	1, 5, 10, 15, 17, 23, 34
2. *a > ɔ/__Cu,i	1, 27, 33, 34, 38, 39, 41
3. *t > f	1, 2, 6, 13, 14, 16, 23, 36, 39, 42
4. *k > ʔ	4, 9, 11, 13, 16, 21, 25, 39, 41
5. *ʔ > Ø (before 4)	6, 7, 30, 36, 42
6. *p > f	7, 12, 18, 22, 24, 27, 33
7. *w > v	11, 32, 38, 40
8. *l > r	19, 24, 29, 35
9. *a > æ/__Ce	32, 42
10. *R > Ø (before 11)	34, 39
11. ViVi > Vi (before 2)	39

Discussion. As described by Biggs (1965), who derived the language from a putative 'Proto-Eastern Oceanic' that is now generally equated with Proto-Oceanic, Rotuman presents a classic case of two speech strata, one native and the other borrowed from an unspecified Polynesian source. This is shown in two ways. First, many proto-phonemes show divergent reflexes in the same immediate environment, as with *tolu > folu 'three' as opposed to *toko > toko 'punting pole', or *sala > sara 'err, be wrong', as opposed to *sala > sala 'path, road'. Second, these double reflexes show clear stratal associations. Biggs

(1965: 390), for example, noted that POC *p, *t, *k and *l each have two distinct reflexes that he assigned to different historical sources, labelled Stratum I and Stratum II:

POC	p	t	k	l
Stratum I	h	f	ʔ	l
Stratum II	f	t	k	r

With only rare exceptions morphemes which contain two of these POC phonemes in the same morpheme will have only Stratum I or Stratum II reflexes, hence *pitu > *hifu* 'seven' draws the reflexes of both *p and *t from Stratum I, while *tapi > *tɔfi* 'sweep' draws the reflexes of the same proto-phonemes from Stratum II, and so on with many other examples. One of the principal concerns of Biggs (1965) was to determine which of these strata is native and which borrowed. Toward this end he appealed to the distinction between basic and non-basic vocabulary. However, as noted above, there is an additional, and in some ways more reliable clue to stratum identification in this language. The Austronesian family contains upwards of 1,200 languages, and Rotuman is the only one to reflect *t as *f*. Given this unique reflex, a form such as *hɔfu* 'stone' < *patu must be native, and this confirms that *p > h also occurs in native words. Likewise, *tolu > *folu* 'three' shows that *l* is the native reflex of *l, and hence *kuli > *ʔuli* 'skin' shows further that ʔ is the native reflex of *k. Rotuman presents particularly clear evidence of speech strata, but similar cases appear in other Austronesian languages, including Ngaju Dayak of southeast Borneo (Dyen 1956), and Tiruray of the southern Philippines (Blust 1992).

SOLUTION TO SOUND CHANGE PROBLEM 8

PMP to Mukah Melanau (Sarawak, Malaysian Borneo)

1. The reflexes of PMP *i, *u and *a in the final syllable of Mukah words are:

*i	>	-əy	2, 6, 39, 65
	>	-iə	9, 13, 17
	>	-eə	12, 70
	>	-i	14, 62, 66
	>	-e	16, 43, 69

*u	>	-əw	3, 31, 53
	>	-o	8, 11, 36, 37, 57
	>	-uə	10, 22, 28, 38, 45, 59
	>	-u	33, 41, 54, 60, 61, 67

| *a | > | -eə | 1, 4, 15, 19, 21, 42, 46, 49 |
| | > | -a | 5, 23–25, 27, 29, 30, 32, 34, 35, 47, 48, 50, 51, 56, 58, 68 |

2. The conditions for splitting of high vowels in Mukah Melanau are complex, and can be summarised as follows:

   2.1. *i and *u developed a mid-central *onglide* in open final syllables.
   2.2. *i and *u developed a mid-central *offglide* before final ʔ (< *k), and *ŋ.
   2.3. Before final *h* from *R the high *front* vowel lowered and developed a mid-central offglide (*i > -eə), but the high *back* vowel simply lowered to /o/.
   2.4. Contrarily, before *h* < *s the high *front* vowel simply lowered (*i > *e*), but the high *back* vowel developed a high front offglide (*a > *ai*, *u > *ui*). However, a similar change in some dialects of Spanish, and in the Chamic languages of Vietnam suggests that it is not the vowel that undergoes breaking, but rather the consonant that develops from *-s to -*ih*. For this reason back vowel reflexes in etymologies such as *panas > *panaih* 'hot', or *qaRus > *auih* 'current' are treated as retentions of the pure vowel.

2.5. Before -ʔ < *q both high vowels lowered.

2.6. In all other environments last-syllable high vowels remained unchanged.

3. The conditions for splitting of *a are somewhat different from those for high vowels, and are best summarised as follows:

3.1. *a was raised and fronted to [e] and developed a mid-central *offglide* before final ʔ < *k and *ŋ.

3.2. Before word-final *h* < *s the low vowel developed a high front offglide (*a > *ai*), much like *u, but this appears to be better treated as a phonetically complex reflex of final *s rather than a vowel breaking process (see 2.4).

3.3. Elsewhere *a remained unchanged in the final syllable.

4. The historical source of Mukah -ʔ can be determined by the development of the preceding vowel, as follows:

4.1. *-ik > *iəʔ*, but *-iq > *eʔ*

4.2. *-uk > *uəʔ*, but *uq > *oʔ*

4.3. *-ak > *eəʔ*, but *-aq > *aʔ*

In Rejang (sound change problem 3) the effect on a preceding vowel of final glottal stop from *k and from *q is almost exactly the reverse of that in Mukah, since *-ik and *-uk show simple lowering to -*eʔ* and -*oʔ*, and *-ak leaves *a unchanged as -*aʔ*, while *-iq and *-uq show both lowering and offgliding of the high vowel to *eaʔ* and *oaʔ*, and *-aq shows raising and offgliding of the low vowel to -*əaʔ*.

5. Breaking of unstressed vowels before final *k and *ŋ is theoretically unexpected, and becomes even more puzzling when it is seen that high vowel never break before *-g.

The sound changes in this data, in the order that they are encountered, are as follows:

Changes   Examples

1. *a > eə/__k,ŋ,R# (before 2, 4)   1, 4, 15, 19, 21, 42, 46, 49
2. *k > ʔ/[- schwa]__#   1, 9, 17, 22, 28, 38, 44, 46, 59
3. *i,u > əy,əw/__#   2, 3, 6, 31, 39, 53, 65
4. *R > h (before 5, 8)   4–6, 8, 12, 18, 19, 30, 36, 41, 47, 54, 57, 59, 66, 70
5. *h > Ø/__V   5, 6, 18, 30, 41, 44, 47, 54, 59, 66
6. *q > ʔ (before 9, 11)   5, 11, 16, 25, 27, 31, 32, 35-37, 41, 42, 48,   52–54, 57, 58, 60, 62, 65, 67–69
7. C > Ø/__C   7, 10, 12, 13, 19, 20, 38, 57, 61, 63
8. *i > eə__h#   12, 70
9. *i/u > e/o/__ʔ# (before 2)   8, 11, 16, 36, 37, 43, 57, 69
10. *a,i,u > eə,iə,uə/__k,ŋ (before 2) 9, 10, 13, 15, 17, 21, 22, 28, 38, 42, 44-46, 49, 59
11. ʔ > Ø/#__ (before 17)   18, 25, 31, 35, 36, 42, 48, 52, 54, 57, 58, 62
12. *ə > a/__a__   18, 30, 47
13. *j > d   20, 31, 34, 52
14. *s > ih/__# (before 19)   23, 33, 43, 47, 54
15. V > ə/__CV(C)V(C) (before 17, 22)   26, 31, 35, 36, 50, 51, 57, 58, 62, 69
16. *n > ñ/__i   27, 55, 57
17. *ə > Ø/#__   29, 31, 35, 36, 40
18. *z > j   41, 48, 56
19. *ii > i (before 8)   43
20. *uə > u (before 10)   44
21. *ʔ > Ø/ə__V (before 22)   58, 62
22. *ə > Ø/__V   58, 62, 69

Discussion. Although superficially similar to phonologically more conservative languages such as Malay, the Melanau languages show a large number of innovations. The most striking of these undoubtedly are those that affect vowels before final *k (> ʔ), *ŋ and *R (> h). Before *-k and *-ŋ the high vowels underwent a process of breaking or diphthongisation, developing a mid-central offglide that is still largely predictable in the synchronic grammar. Before glottal stop, and h from *R they lowered to [e] and [o]. There is a complication: *k subsequently became ʔ, but since breaking occurred before this change the reflexes of high vowels before PMP final *k and *q are distinct: *-ik > *iə?*, *-uk > *uə?*, but *-iq > *e?*, *uq > *o?*.

In Mukah, but not most other Melanau dialects, *a underwent raising, fronting and breaking in the same three environments, producing [eə] as the realisation of *a* before final *k, *ŋ and *h* (< *R). Word-final *s also became *-ih*, but since the orthographic vowel in this unit is extrametrical, and did not lower it is probably best treated as a glide.

Given the regularity of high vowel breaking before final *k and *ŋ it is tempting to propose the generalisation that this process happened before final velars. However, breaking did not occur before /g/, making it cumbersome to state this process in terms of phonologial features: /hig/ = [hig] 'budge, move slightly', /duhig/ = [duhig] 'mythical forest monster', /pajug/ = [paʤug] 'foot', /tug/ = [tug] 'ball of the heel' (Blust 1988).

SOLUTION TO SOUND CHANGE PROBLEM 9

POC to Tangoa (Vanuatu)

1. The Tangoa reflexes of POC *p, *b, *bʷ, *m and *mʷ are as follows (final consonants were lost):

*bʷ	>	p	1
*p	>	v	2, 23, 25, 26, 36
	>	p̃	20
	>	ṽ	30, 34, 44
*m	>	m̃	3–5, 12, 15, 32, 33, 35, 39, 45, 48
	>	m	39
*b	>	p	8, 16, 37
	>	p̃	21
*mʷ	>	m	14, 18

2. Bilabials became apico-labials when not in contact with a rounded vowel or consonant. There are three apparent exceptions in the data given here, namely 26, 36, and the last consonant of 39. The latter may be because apico-labials occur as syllable onsets, but not as codas, although a generalisation is hampered by the rarity of final consonants in this language. The other two exceptions remain unexplained.

3. POC *k shows two reflexes for which conditions cannot yet be stated:

*k	>	h	11, 15, 19, 20
	>	x	22, 40, 41, 48

Recurrent changes between POC and Tangoa are as follows:

Changes	Examples
1. *bʷ > p	1
2. *p > v (before 1)	2, 23, 25, 26, 36
3. *m > m̈/__V[-round] (before 10)	3–5, 12, 15, 32, 33, 35, 39, 45, 48
4. *q > Ø (before 5, 14)	7, 9, 26, 28, 29, 38
5. *ai > e	7, 9
6. *b > p	8, 16, 37
7. *R > Ø (before 14)	10, 14, 19, 41
8. *k > h	11, 15, 19, 20
9. C > Ø/__#	11, 14, 20, 24–28, 31, 42, 43, 47, 48
10. *mʷ > m	14, 18
11. *p > p̈/__V[-round]	20
12. *b > p̈/__V[-round]	21
13. *k > x	22, 40, 41, 48
14. ViVi > Vi	26, 38, 41
15. *p > v̈/__V[-round]	30, 34, 44

Discussion. The most remarkable feature of this data is the appearance of apico-labial (also called linguo-labial) stops, nasals and fricatives, a trait that is widespread in the languages of East Santo and North Malakula (Tryon 1976: 52; Maddieson 1989b). These typologically unique segments evolved from *p, *v and *m before non-round vowels. This is especially clear before *a, where all three apico-labials appear as reflexes of bilabial or labiovelar consonants. Before *i and *e the evidence is more mixed, some reflexes showing apico-labials, as with *bebe > p̈ēp̈ē 'butterfly', but others showing labio-dentals, as with *pisa > visa 'how many?'. One other developmental feature of these consonants is noteworthy: labiovelar stops and nasals (*bʷ, *mʷ) are never reflected as apico-labials, presumably because the apico-labials were innovated and spread among territorially contiguous or near-contiguous languages prior to the reduction of labiovelars to simple labials.

SOLUTIONS

SOLUTION TO SOUND CHANGE PROBLEM 10

Proto-Admiralty (PADM) to Seimat

1. Seimat *h* reflects PADM *p and *r, as follows:

*p	>	h	1, 13–17, 19, 20
*r	>	h	18, 20, 22–24, 32

Vowels are nasal following *h* < *r, but oral following *h* < *p.

2. Seimat *w* reflects PADM *w and *m^w, as follows:

*w	>	w	9, 24, 25, 27
*m^w	>	w	21, 26, 28, 29

Vowels are nasal following *w* < *m^w, but oral following *w* < *w.

3. The reflex that is perhaps phonetically most surprising in the data given here is *dr > *k*, seen in examples 21, 33, and 34.

　　The following changes from PADM to Seimat appear in this data set:

Changes	Examples
1. *p > h (before 6)	1, 13–17, 19, 20
2. –V > Ø	1–3, 6, 13–15, 19, 20, 23, 25, 26, 28–30, 32, 33, 35
3. *q > Ø (before 14)	2, 7–9, 11, 12, 19, 23, 29, 32
4. *k > Ø (before 11)	3–5, 31
5. *y > Ø	6, 19
6. *b > p	6, 30
7. *s > x	10–12, 16
8. *ñ > n	15, 35
9. *r > h (before 10)	18, 20, 22–24, 32
10. V > Ṽ/h__ (before 1)	18, 20, 22, 24
11. *dr > k	21, 33, 34
12. *m^w > w	21, 26, 28, 29
13. V > Ṽ/*m^w__ (before 12)	21, 26, 28, 29
14. ViVi > Vi	29

Discussion. This problem is interesting for the conditions under which phonemic vowel nasality arose. While vowel nasality generally spreads from coda to nucleus in Indo-European languages such as English or French, allophonic nasality in Austronesian languages is typically onset driven (Blust 1997). This was true in the history of Seimat, and remains so in the contemporary language after nasal consonants. Phonemically nasalised vowels in Seimat occur only after w and h.

In the first environment contrastive nasality developed from allophonic nasality after nasal consonants, followed by the merger of *w and *m^w as w- (*wa- > wa-, but *m^{w}a- > $w\tilde{a}$-). In the second environment vowel nasality developed through what Matisoff (1975) somewhat tongue-in-cheek called 'rhinoglottophilia', a laryngeal setting in which vowels are sometimes nasalised as a result of incidental velic lowering following glottal stop, h and pharyngeal fricatives. In Seimat this is complicated by the fact that h has two sources: *p and *r, and rhinoglottophilia is found only after h from *r. It is likely that *r > h occurred first, followed by rhinoglottophilia, and that *p > f > h is a more recent change, with no nasality developing after the new h. Alternatively, it is possible that there was some phonetic difference between h from the two sources that contributed to this difference in nasalisation behaviour. Finally, although it initially appears that the locus of nasality in Seimat is on the vowel that follows w or h there is morphological evidence that it is the glide that is phonemically nasalied, and this contributes nasal colouring to the following vowel, much as nasal consonants do (Blust 1998).

SOLUTION TO SOUND CHANGE PROBLEM 11

Pre-Iban to Iban (Sarawak, Malaysian Borneo)

1. The reflexes of final nasals in Iban are as follows:

*-m	>	m ~ w	3
	>	w	14, 28, 33
	>	m	38, 40, 42, 46
*-n	>	y	1, 10, 34, 39
	>	n	16, 20, 24, 30, 36, 43, 45
	>	n ~ y	37
	>	w	23
*-ŋ	>	y	5, 7, 15, 19, 26, 31, 41
	>	ŋ	6, 11, 22, 44
	>	ŋ ~ w	9

2. There has been a general tendency in Iban to replace word-final nasals with glides. This is far from consistent, but has happened too often to avoid calling it a sound change.

    Generally, *m is replaced with *w* (written -*u*), while *-n and *-ŋ are replaced by *y* (written -*i*). However, *-n and *-ŋ are sometimes replaced by *w* (9, 23), although no cases are known in which *y* replaces *-m. In addition, all cases of *-n or *-ŋ > *y* occur after *a, or less commonly schwa (which may already have merged with *a at the time of this change). However, although no cases are known of *-n or *-ŋ > *y* following high vowels, there are a number of cases where the sequences *-an and *-aŋ have not changed.

3. Reflexes of the fricatives and affricates in Iban are as follows:

*j	>	j	1, 26, 29, 31, 33, 35, 40, 42, 47
	>	d	29, 35, 47
*s	>	t	4, 12, 25
	>	s	4, 12, 21, 23, 25, 27, 39
*c	>	t	8, 13, 45
	>	c	8, 13, 45

These divergent reflexes are products of sibilant dissimilation, in which the first of two identical or non-identical sibilants becomes the corresponding stop (*d* for *j* and *t* for both *s* and *c*).

The following changes can be found in this data set:

Changes	Examples
1. *n > y/a__#	1, 10, 34, 37, 39
2. V > Ø/Ci__Ci	2, 11, 18, 21
3. *ə > a/__C# (before 6)	3, 5, 9, 14, 23, 25, 28, 33, 38, 40, 46
4. *m > w/ə__# (before 3)	3, 14, 28, 33
5. *s > t/__Vs	4, 12, 25
6. *ŋ > y/a__#	5, 7, 15, 19, 26, 31, 41
7. *c > t/__V(n)c	8, 13, 45
8. *j > d/__Vj	29, 35, 47

Discussion. There are at least two theoretically interesting sound changes in Iban. The first is the set of changes that transform word-final nasals in many words into glides. While this development is somewhat unexpected in itself, the environment in which it occurs is even more surprising. In general, word-final alveolar and velar nasals became *y*, and *m became *w* following *a, but no change occurred after high vowels. Nothofer (1988: 50ff.) tried to show that reflexes of final nasals differ after *a or *ə, suggesting that *-an and *-aŋ became -*ay*, while *-əm, *-ən, and *-əŋ became -*aw*. In some cases this works, but there are a number of exceptions which he suggests may be due to borrowing from Malay, a far more prestigious and regionally influential language. Borrowing from Malay may also be the reason that examples such as 6, 11, 16, 20, 22, 24, 30, 36, 38, 40 and 42–46 show no lenition of final nasals. However, the existence of doublets with and without nasal lenition, as in 3, 9 and 37, suggests that this may instead be a change in progress which has been completed in some lexical items but not others.

The second phonological innovation in Iban that is noteworthy is sibilant dissimilation, a change that affected pre-Iban *s, *c and *j (voiceless alveolar fricative, voiceless alveolar affricate and voiced alveolar affricate respectively), if any of these sounds were followed in the next syllable by a member of the same class. Due to constraints against dissimilar sibilants in the same morpheme this generally means that *s and *c dissimilate to *t*, and that *j dissimilates to *d* when an identical segment is the onset of the following syllable. However, rare forms such as Iban *tuci* 'pure; faultless', a borrowing of Malay *suci* 'pure' (ultimately from Sanskrit), suggest that sibilant dissimilation in Iban was triggered by *any* sibilant as the onset of the following syllable. A similar historical change is found in Ngaju Dayak of southeast Borneo and in some dialects of Kayan in central Borneo, neither of which is closely related to Iban, although all three languages may have been in contact at an earlier time.

SOLUTION TO SOUND CHANGE PROBLEM 12

PMP to Javanese (Java, Indonesia)

1. The new Javanese phonemes /o/ and /e/ arose from crasis (fusion) of *a with *u or *i respectively across a syllable boundary, although a parallel change happened sporadically next to a glide. Examples are (x/y = both orders are represented):

*a/u, wa	>	o	1, 3, 10, 12, 17, 22, 24, 28, 35, 36, 38, 40, 45, 46
*a/i	>	e	14, 15, 42

It is unclear why a schwa that came to be prevocalic through consonant loss acquired a rounding feature, but this appears to be true for 1, 24 and 38.

2. Although some PMP forms had vowel sequences, and so presented no obstacle to contraction, in other forms *h and *R had to drop before this was possible, as follows:

*h	>	Ø	3, 17, 22, 30, 45
*R	>	Ø	1, 4, 10, 12, 15, 19, 24–26, 34, 38, 42, 46

The consonant that has since disappeared, but which stayed long enough to prevent vowel crasis, is *q (probably a uvular stop in PMP that became glottal stop in pre-Javanese and then /h/ in Old Javanese):

*q	>	Ø	5, 18, 31, 43

3. In some forms the stative prefix *a-* was fossilised, creating a new disyllabic base. In others the new monosyllabic base was reduplicated. In both cases these processes operated to restore a favoured disyllabic canonical shape that had been lost as a result of regular sound change:

loss of morpheme boundary:	1, 24, 28, 36
reduplication:	3, 4, 12, 15, 17, 25, 26, 42

SOLUTIONS

In some of the latter reduplication may not be obvious, as with (3) *duha > rua > ro > roro > *loro* (with regular liquid dissmilation), (4) *baRa (> baa > ba > wa) > *wawa*, or (25) *daRa (> daa > da > ra > rara) > *lara* (again with regular liquid dissmilation).

4. Javanese shows double reflexes of *b, *d and *R. Part of this is undoubtedly due to centuries of borrowing from Malay, but some forms are difficult to account for in this way. Unconditioned phonemic splits include the following:

*b	>	b	1, 2, 16, 27, 33, 37
	>	w	4, 6, 9, 13, 30, 35, 38
*d	>	d	20
	>	l	3, 25
	>	r	3, 17, 23, 25, 29, 34, 45
	>	ḍ	8, 17, 21, 32
*R	>	Ø	1, 4, 10, 12, 15, 19, 24–26, 29, 34, 38, 42, 46
	>	r	7, 8, 11, 16

Discussion. This problem is included for several reasons. First, it provides evidence for how the phonemic typology of a language can change over time, in this case how the inherited vowel system was expanded as a result of vowel fusions. Noteworthy sound changes in native Javanese vocabulary are the loss of *h or *R, and fusion of an original or resulting vowel sequence; where the vowels were identical the result was a single vowel of the same quality, but where they differed they generally fused to produce new vowels *e* and *o*.

Second, it shows how reduplication, which is normally considered part of morphology, can be used for purely canonical reasons. Like many other Austronesian languages, Javanese favours a disyllabic canonical shape for base morphemes, and where a base reduced to a monosyllable through regular sound change the lost disyllabism was often restored through various mechanisms, most commonly reduplication. In these cases reduplication has no other function. Where this resulted in sequences of *rVr liquid dissimilation altered the first segment to a lateral: *baRa (> baa > waa) > *wawa* 'ember', *paRih (> pai > pe) *pe, pepe* 'stingray', *duha (> dua > rua > ro > roro) > *loro* 'two', *daRa (> raRa > raa > ra > rara) > *lara* 'young girl, virgin', etc. Moreover, in a smaller number of cases the morpheme boundary that once distinguished certain bases from their stative forms has been lost for the same reason, as with *abot* 'heavy', *atos* 'hard', *alon* 'slow', or *adoh* 'far, distant', all of which are dictionary entries in the modern language.

Third, Javanese is included here because of its relevance to the Regularity Hypothesis and the possible role of borrowing. Javanese shows an apparent unconditioned phonemic split of *b, *d and *R. In many cases *b > *w*, *d > *l/r* and *R > Ø are confined to what is almost certainly native vocabulary, and *b > *b*, *d > *ḍ* (post-alveolar) and *R > *r* to demonstrable or probable loans from Malay. Malay has been a lingua franca in western Indonesia since at least the seventh century, and it is therefore not surprising that it is the source of many loanwords in languages throughout the region.

SOLUTION TO SOUND CHANGE PROBLEM 13

PMP to Chamorro (western Micronesia)

1. Chamorro shows final devoicing with reflexes of *R, which became /k/ in coda position (symbolised with __$ here, since it includes all syllable codas regardless of position in the word), but /g/ elsewhere:

*R	>	k/__$	2, 33, 37, 47, 54
	>	g/elsewhere	7, 9, 18, 23, 27, 32, 36

2. Chamorro /gʷ/ reflects *[w] as a syllable onset from any source, phonemic or phonetic. Prior to this change /w/ must have been added before initial vowels, and *h must have been lost. A parallel fortition affected [j] from any source, phonemic (where it was /y/) or phonetic (where it was phonemic zero), giving rise to the novel affricate /dz/:

*w	>	gʷ/__V	3, 8, 29
Ø > w	>	gʷ/#__V	11, 20–22, 24–26, 41
*y	>	dz/__V	31, 37, 38, 47
Ø > y/i__a,u	>	dz/__V	26, 54

3. The /g/ : /gʷ/ contrast is neutralised before rounded vowels, where only /g/ appears:

*w	>	g	12, 23, 28, 51

4. PMP *l became /t/ as a syllable coda, but remained unchanged as an onset. This change had to follow syncope of vowels in the environment VC__CV:

*l	>	t/__$	5, 10, 29, 53
	>	l/elsewhere	6, 13, 30, 34, 44, 47, 51

5. The merger of PMP *d and *k as /h/ in onset position and zero in coda position is unusual, as shown here:

*d	>	h	4, 11, 27, 28, 30, 31, 33, 48
	>	Ø	51
*k	>	h	16, 21, 24, 29, 38, 52
	>	Ø	35, 46, 49, 50

The following changes are found in this problem. Where two forms of the same base are given the change is cited only for the first form. Note that PMP *j probably was a voiced velar stop with palatal offglide ([gʲ]), that *y was a palatal glide, and that Chamorro strengthened phonetic glides whether or not they were phonemic.

Changes

1. *q- > Ø/#__
2. *z > ch
3. *p > f (before 13)
4. *u,i > o,e/__CC
5. *R > g (before 6)

6. *g > k/__$
7. *w/y ([w,j]) > gʷ, dz /__V (before 17)

8. *d > h (before 22)

9. *-q-, -q > ʔ

10. *l > t/__$
11. V> Ø/VC__CV (before 4, 10, 14)
12. *ə > u (before 4)

13. *b > p

14. *j > d/C__ (before 19)
15. *h > Ø/__V (before 16, 18, 20)
16. Ø > [w]/u__V, a__u, > [j]/i__V (before 7)

Examples

1–10, 39, 40, 42, 43, 53
1, 12–14, 42
2, 6, 15–18, 20, 39, 53
14, 44, 48
2, 7, 9, 18, 23, 27, 32, 33, 36, 37, 47, 54
2, 33, 37, 47, 54
3, 8, 11, 12, 19–26, 28, 29, 31, 37, 38, 41, 47, 51, 54
4, 11, 27, 28, 30, 31, 33, 48, 51
4, 12, 15, 18, 27, 36, 40, 41, 44, 45
5, 10, 29, 53
5, 10, 36, 39, 40, 44, 45
6, 14, 18, 19, 32–34, 39, 43, 48, 49
7, 14, 32, 36, 37, 41, 46, 49, 50
10
11, 20, 22, 24, 28, 51

11, 12, 26, 28, 37, 38, 41, 51, 54

17. $*g^w > g/\_\_u/o$ 12, 19, 23, 28, 51

18. $*k > h$ (before 6, 22)   16, 21, 24, 29, 35, 38,
                                                         46, 49, 50, 52

19. $*j > ?$ 17, 30, 34

20. $\emptyset > w/\#\_\_$ (before 1, 7)   19–26

21. $*\text{-uy} > i$ 20

22. $*h > \emptyset/\_\_\#$ 35, 46, 49, 50

23. $*i > y/CVC\_\_V\#$ (before 7)   37, 38

24. $*hC > CiCi$ 46, 50

---

2. Ordering that increases the phonetic plausibility of some changes
   would include 1. $*h > \emptyset$ before glides could develop and undergo
   fortition in words such as *duha, *dahun, or *hapuy, and 2. $*d > h$
   probably passed through a stage $*d (> r) > h$, although there is no
   direct evidence for this.

Discussion. One reason for including this problem is to provide examples
of what are sometimes called 'excresent' consonants. There actually was only
one of these: *w* was added before initial vowels. This *w along with *y then
underwent fortition to *gw* and *dz* respectively (written *gu* and *y* in the standard
orthography). What is noteworthy about this change in Chamorro (and similar changes in a number of the languages of Borneo) is that it affected all
phonetic glides, whether they were phonemic or not. It is clear that glide
fortition could not have occurred until *h was lost, since otherwise this consonant would have blocked glide formation. Without such an ordering it might
be assumed erroneously that *h is the source of *gw* in e.g. *duha > *hugwa* 'two',
or *hapuy > *gwafi* 'fire', but this clearly is not the case. The change *q (uvular
stop) to zero in initial position almost certainly went through intermediate
glottal stop (the reflex of *q in other positions). It is likely that words which
begin with a vowel in Chamorro have an automatic glottal onset, as this
blocked the accretion of initial *w*.

Another change that merits some attention in Chamorro is medial vowel
syncope. In many Austronesian languages unstressed vowels delete between
consonants that are themselves flanked by vowels, hence/VC__CV. This
change is seen in examples 5, 10, 36, 39, 40, 44 and 45, where it invariably
affects schwa, but inconsistently affects other vowels (cf. examples 7, 8, 9 and

16, which show no syncope despite similar conditions). Medial vowel syncope produced some new closed syllables, increasing the number of forms in which the somewhat surprising change *l > t/__$ took place. Chamorro shows devoicing before a syllable boundary in the sequence *R > g > k, and it seems likely that *l > t passed through a stage *l > d, although the substitution of t for syllable-final l also occurs in many Spanish loanwords (Blust 2000a).

Finally, the ordering of *b > p and *g > k/__# is unclear. If *b > p occurred first there would have been only one voiced stop in the language at the time of final devoicing. On the other hand, it is possible that final devoicing affected both labial and velar stops, and that *b as an onset was later devoiced through a separate change. Whichever ordering is chosen, it is clear that *d > h had to precede final devoicing, since otherwise it would have merged with *t (and *l).

SOLUTION TO SOUND CHANGE PROBLEM 14

PMP to Palauan

1. PMP *R became Palauan *r* before dentals (5, 25, 32, 46), but *s* elsewhere (4, 17, 19, 38, 41, 43, 44).
2. The second source of Palauan ŋ- is zero (5, 13, 19, 24, 27, 28, 32, 35, 40, 44). The addition of an initial velar nasal followed *h > Ø. Whether this change was phonological or morphological is debatable (Blust 2009, 2012a; Reid 2010; Blevins and Kaufman 2012).
3. The order of the first set of phonemes was:

   1. *y > r
   2. *l > y
   3. *n > l

   This led to a shift in the phonetic value of each phoneme without reduction of the phoneme inventory; if 3 had preceded 2, or 2 had preceded 1 merger would have occurred. The order of the second set of phonemes was:

   1. *t > ð
   2. *s > t
   3. *R > s

   Again, this produced shift, and any change in the order would have led to merger, with consequent reduction of the phoneme inventory.
4. The two forms that show consonant metathesis are *Ratus (> taRus) > ðart 'hundred', and *ŋipən (> piŋən) > wíŋəl 'tooth'.

5. Changes in the order they are encountered in this data are as follows (note that pre-Palauan stress was penultimate, and that V̌ indicates an unstressed vowel):

Changes	Examples
1. *n > l	1, 8, 11, 13, 20, 23, 27, 29, 33, 35, 37, 47, 49, 51, 53, 55, 56

SOLUTIONS

2. V̆ > Ø (before 17)	1–3, 5–12, 14–18, 20–33, 36, 38–41, 44–47, 49, 50, 53–55
3. *t > ð (before 4)	2, 5–7, 14, 18, 22, 23, 25, 31, 32, 46, 48
4. *s > t (before 6, 13)	3, 11, 16, 25, 46
5. *d > r (before 20)	4, 10, 20, 34, 41, 45, 47, 52
6. *R > s/__[-dental]	4, 17, 19, 38, 41, 43, 44
7. V̆ > ə	4, 11, 13, 19, 32, 35, 37, 42, 3, 51, 53, 54, 56
8. *q > ʔ	4, 7, 15, 16, 21, 30, 38, 42, 47, 48, 50
9. Ø > ŋ/#__V	5, 13, 19, 24, 27, 28, 32, 35, 40, 44
10. *R > r/__[+dental]	5, 25, 32, 46
11. *l > y (before 1)	6, 9, 12, 17, 20, 21, 31, 36, 7, 42, 45
12. *-ay/uy > e/o/i (before 2, 15)	7, 8, 11, 18, 21, 27
13. *j > s	9, 15, 21, 39, 45
14. *h > Ø (before 9)	10, 13, 24, 32, 44, 54
15. *p > w (before 17)	14, 24, 26, 33, 34, 38, 43, 48, 49, 51, 52
16. *ŋ > Ø/C__#	15, 39
17. *wa-/-aw/-əw > o (before 2)	16, 24, 33, 34, 36, 43, 48, 52
18. *y > r (before 11)	17, 50, 54
19. *z > d (before 5)	20, 41, 47
20. rl > ll	47
21. *ə́ > o	21, 25, 42, 56
22. Ø > y,w/i,u__V (before 2)	23, 28, 30, 53
23. *ə́ > e	37, 49, 52
24. *ñ > n (before 1)	37, 49
24. *j > k/__C	55

Discussion. The history of Palauan consonants is remarkable for extensive shifting, and the history of the vowels for extensive neutralisation or deletion in unstressed position. All PMP consonants except *b, *k, *m and *ŋ have either been lost or shifted. As a result it is one of the few reported languages with no n (Maddieson 1984: 69). Extensive shifting is responsible for the large number of ordering requirements in this data: *y > r had to precede *l > y, and this in turn had to precede *n > l; likewise, *t > ð had to precede *s > t, and this in turn had to precede *R > s (when not preceding a dental), and *j > s.

All PMP final vowels were lost. This includes the diphthongs *-ay, *-aw and *-uy, which presumably monophthongised to -e, -o and -i before deleting. Since *p became /w/, and the resulting sequences wa- and -aw/əw contracted to a mid-back vowel that was not lost this change must have followed loss of final vowels, and we must assume that *-aw > -o occurred twice, once before and once after the loss of final vowels. The phonological development in *sawaq > tao? 'channel' suggests that where both -aw and wa- options were available in the same form, vowel coalescence favoured the tautosyllabic sequence.

Unstressed vowels before a final consonant were sometimes lost and sometimes reduced to schwa under conditions that are difficult to state. Similarly, prepenultimate vowels were sometimes lost (21, 36), sometimes reduced to schwa (11, 32, 43, 53, 54), and in one case retained (8). One difficult complication involves reflexes of *-Vp, as in *dapdap to róro (34), *qatəp to áðo (48) or *dəpa to réo (52): does the final o represent a fusion of the vowel + w, or loss of the unstressed vowel and vocalisation of postconsonantal [w] as [o]? The similar reflex in initial position, as with *paniki > olik suggests fusion.

A feature of Palauan historical phonology that is especially noteworthy is its addition of a velar nasal before words that earlier began with a vowel. While it is tempting to see such a change as morphological, there is no convincing evidence that this is the case, since ŋ was added to nouns, pronouns and verbs without any apparent syntactic or semantic consequence. Since Palauan regularly lost original final vowels (which were unstressed), it is impossible to see whether a velar nasal would also have been added word-finally had the vowels survived to the time that this change took place. Remarkably, however, many loanwords from Spanish and English and a few from Japanese that have a final vowel in the lending language show an added -ŋ: banderáŋ 'flag' (Spanish bandera), belatóŋ 'plate, dish' (Spanish plato), stoáŋ 'store', tóktaŋ 'doctor' (both from an English dialect lacking postvocalic /r/), kámaŋ 'sickle' (Japanese kama), etc. (Blust 2009).

Some sound changes in Palauan are determined by very specific conditions, as where *R (probably an alveolar trill) became r preceding dentals, but s elsewhere, and where *j (probably [gʲ]) normally became s, but appears as k when preceding another consonant in *ŋajan > ŋakl 'name'. Probably in the same category is the loss of ŋ postconsonantally: although Palauan has developed a very large number of word-final consonant clusters as a result of unstressed vowel syncope, it does not tolerate word-final clusters that end with a velar nasal, hence the cluster reductions seen in *qajəŋ 'charcoal' > ?as 'soot, ink of squid, pencil lead', and *ijuŋ > *ús* 'nose' (cp. *ʔəsəŋ-él* 'its sepia, its lead' and *isŋ-él* 'his/her/its nose', where *-ŋ is retained in non-final position, either through schwa epenthesis or as a non-final cluster).

Finally, some changes appear to involve unconditioned phonemic splits, as with reflexes of stressed schwa, sometimes as *o* and sometimes as *e*, with no obvious condition.

SOLUTION TO SOUND CHANGE PROBLEM 15

PMP to Taba, Buli, Numfor and Munggui

1. Reflexes of *k and final vowels are as follows:

	Taba	Buli	Numfor	Munggui
1. *k	k	Ø	Ø	Ø
2. -V	Ø	Ø	Ø	V

The loss of *k and of final vowels is shared by Buli of South Halmahera and Numfor of West New Guinea, but these changes must have taken place in different orders, since Buli preserves a vowel that preceded final *k, while Numfor does not.

2. One way to account for such change in early Generative phonology was through the notion of rule reordering (Kiparsky 1968), where one possible type of change was for a language with rules in the order x,y to simply reorder them as y,x.

3. Another way to explain the facts is by diffusion of sound changes along a dialect chain in opposite directions, overlapping in the middle area.

4. The diffusion explanation accounts for both differences of ordering in the changes that took place, and for the fact that one of the changes has the distribution ABC and the other BCD, showing that Lgs. A and D each share one of the changes with its nearest neighbour, but not the other.

Discussion. If we number the two relevant changes as (1) *k > Ø, and (2) *-V > Ø, then it is clear that Numfor has undergone these changes in the order 1, 2, while Buli has experienced them in the opposite order, 2, 1.

This problem is included in order to discuss the claim in early Generative approaches to historical linguistics that sound change is rule change, and that one possible type of rule change is rule reordering. While claims of rule reordering must be evaluated on a case-by-case basis, it is clear that few unambiguous examples of a change that requires this type of explanation exist. The original examples, which were conveniently summarised by King (1969: 51ff.) assume dialect continuity, but it is by no means certain that this is always, or for that matter, ever the case. In the example at hand there are at least two persuasive reasons to reject rule reordering in favour of a diffusionist model. First, rule reordering would artificially limit the data considered to Buli and Numfor, even though change 1 is also shared with Munggui in the extreme east, and change 2 with Taba in the extreme west of the distribution area. Treating these shared innovations as independent would be unconvincing, since this would have to be done twice, once for Munggui and another time for Taba.

The most comprehensive account of the facts is obtained by hypothesising that change 1 (loss of *k) began in the far east, and that innovation 2 (loss of final vowels) began in the far west of an earlier dialect chain, and that these innovations then spread in opposite directions, overlapping in the central region. Since the loss of final vowels began in the west it reached Buli first, and since loss of *k began in the east it reached Numfor first. This hypothesis assumes that the two innovations were roughly contemporaneous, or, if they were not, that they spread at different rates so that the loss of final vowels reached Buli before it reached Numfor (and never extended as far as Munggui), and that the loss of *k reached Numfor before it reached Buli (and never extended as far as Taba).

The second reason why rule reordering is untenable as an explanation for this data set is that rule reordering is possible only with conditioned changes. Most features of synchronic phonologies reflect conditioned changes, which give rise to complementation, alternation or neutralisation. By contrast, unconditioned changes produce restructuring, and leave no trace in the synchronic grammar. In the case at hand it is possible (though as yet unconfirmed) that the loss of final vowels in South Halmahera-West New Guinea languages has produced synchronic alternations in which stems lack final vowels when unsuffixed, but have them under suffixation. However, even if this is the case it seems clear that *k > Ø in Buli and Numfor was unconditioned, and therefore left no trace in the synchronic grammar of any language that experienced it. Without at least two interacting rules in a synchronic grammar the idea of rule reordering becomes meaningless, and it must be assumed that this is the case in the example at hand.

SOLUTION TO SOUND CHANGE PROBLEM 16

PAN to Thao (central Taiwan)

1. Reflexes of PAN *C, *d, *z and *S in Thao are as follows:

   *C   > c: 5, 10, 19, 24, 25, 46, 52–54
            > sh: 7, 49
            > lh: 44, 45, 47
            > s: 48

   *d   > s: 9, 12, 14, 16, 23, 30, 36, 43, 48
            > lh: 20, 32
            > sh: 21, 28

   *z   > lh: 13
            > s: 17, 26, 50, 55

   *S   > sh: 3, 7, 8, 15, 18, 21, 22, 28, 33–35, 41, 49
            > s: 14
            > Ø: 25

2. The unconditioned reflexes are: *C > *c*, *d > *s*, *z > *s* and *S > *sh*. The conditions for splitting are as follows:

   2.1
   *C became *sh* if there was an *sh* (< *S) later in the word.
   *C became *lh* if there was an *r* (< *l) later in the word.
   *C became *s* if there was an *s* (< *d) later in the word.

   2.2
   *d became *lh* if there was an *lh* (< *R) later in the word.
   *d became *sh* if there was an *sh* (< *S) later in the word.

   2.3
   *z had almost certainly merged with *d before sibilant assimilation began in Thao; it thus behaved like *d in becoming *lh* if there was an *lh* later in the word.

2.4

*S became *s* if there was an *s* (< *d) later in the word.

*S disappeared unpredictably in some lexical items.

3. This is hard to demonstrate, although certain tendencies are clear. The following statements appear certain:

3.1

c and *sh* may not occur in the same phonological word. If the expected sequence is *c...sh* the result is *sh...sh*. No reflexes of *SVC (expected *sh...c*) are known.

3.2

c and *s* apparently may not occur in the same phonological word. In the one known case, where the expected sequence was *c...s* the result is *s...s*.

3.3

s and *lh* may not occur in the same phonological word. If the expected sequence is *s...lh* the result is *sh...sh*. No reflexes of *RVd (expected *lh...s*) are known. Reflexes of *d and *z behave the same in this respect, presumably because these phonemes merged before the assimilatory tendencies shown here began.

3.4

s and *sh* may not occur in the same phonological word. If the expected sequence is *s...sh* the result is *sh...sh*, and if the expected sequence is *sh...s* the result is *s...s*.

The tendency seen in these cases is an avoidance of dissimilar sibilants within the same phonological word, where 'sibilant' includes *c*, *s*, *lh* and *sh*. One can see this as a type of sibilant harmony. However, *z* (voiced postdental or interdental fricative) can co-occur with *s* or *lh*, as in examples 9, 11 and 16, and *lh* and *sh* can co-occur in the same word, as in examples 15 and 18. This makes it particularly hard to generalise about an underlying principle governing the full set of assimilating forms. Moreover, the surprising cases of expected *c...r* becoming *c...lh* in examples 44, 45 and 47 are difficult to reconcile with the other cases of assimilation cited here.

4. This raises the question of what to call a natural class that includes [θ], [s], [ɬ], and [ʃ], since it is larger than what would normally be called 'sibilants', but smaller than the class of voiceless fricatives, since Thao also has [f] and [h].
5. Last-syllable schwa became *u* before a final labial consonant (37, 39, 42, 43), but *i* elsewhere (19, 25, 28, 31, 33, 35, 45, 49).

The following changes can be found in the data given:

Primary changes	Examples
1. *l > r	1, 17, 31, 36, 39, 42, 44–47
2. *s > t (before 7, 11)	2, 31, 51
3. *S > sh	3, 7, 8, 15, 18, 21, 22, 28, 33–35, 41, 49
4. *b > f	4, 11, 15, 35, 39
5. *C > c	5, 10, 19, 24, 25, 46, 52–54
6. *N > z	6, 9, 16, 26, 34
7. *d > s	9, 12, 14, 16, 23, 30, 36, 43, 48
8. *R > lh	11, 13, 15, 18–20, 25, 27, 29, 32, 34, 37, 41, 52
9. *j > z	11, 33, 38
10. *ə > Ø/C_CVC	15, 22, 25, 36, 40, 45, 49
11. *z > s	17, 26, 50, 55
12. *ŋ > n	18, 31, 46, 47
13. *ə > i/__[-labial]#	19, 25, 28, 31, 33, 35, 45, 49
14. *ə > u/__[+labial]#	37, 39, 42, 43

Secondary changes	Examples
15. *C > c > sh/_VCVsh	7, 49
16. *z > s > lh	13
17. *S > sh > s/__Vs	14
18. *d > s > lh/__Vlh	20, 32
19. *d > s > sh/__VCVsh	21, 28
20. *C > c > lh/__V(CV)l (before 1)	44, 45, 47
21. *C > c > s/__VCVs	48

Discussion. Most Austronesian languages have only two fricatives, *s* and *h*, and some have only *s*. Thao is exceptional in having seven: *f, c, z, s, lh, sh* and *h*, and as the data given here show, this has played a crucial role in conditioned sound change. Perhaps the most notable feature of Thao historical phonology is the multiple reflexes of phonemes that became fricatives, as shown above. What has operated in each of these cases is a principle of 'sibilant assimilation' or 'sibilant harmony', but one in which the category 'sibilant' must be defined much more widely than is customary in phonological theory.

First, while *S became *sh* in non-conditioning environments, it assimilated to *s* from *d in *Sidi > *sisi* 'serow, wild goat'. Second, while *C normally became *c*, it assimilated to *sh* from *S in *CaqiS > *shaqish* 'sew' or *CəkəS > *shkish* 'slender bamboo' and to *s* from *d in *Cukud > *sukus* 'punting pole' (*C > *lh* when *r* from *l followed later in the word is more puzzling). Third, while *d became *s* when unconditioned, it assimilated to *lh* from *R in *diRi > *lhilhi* 'stand', and *daRa > *lhalha* 'Formosan maple', and to *sh* in *daqiS > *shaqish* 'face' or *dakəS > *shakish* 'camphor laurel'. Finally, while *z also normally became *s*, it became *lh* when followed by *lh* from *R in *zaRum > *lhalhum* 'sew', and *Sidi > *sisi* (expected **shisi*) shows that the avoidance of *s* and *sh* in the same word can be brought about by assimilation to *sh...sh* or *s....s*, depending on order.

These assimilations require recognition of a natural class unlike any currently recognised, namely one that includes [s], [ʃ], [θ] and [ɬ] as members of a harmonic set (barring sibilant harmony *CaqiS > *shaqish* 'sew' would have become **cakish*, *Cukud > *sukus* 'punting pole' would have become **cukus*, *diRi > *lhilhi* 'stand' would have become **silhi*, *daqiS > *shaqish* 'face' would have become **saqish*, etc.).

Thao sibilant harmony has the following traits: (1) in most cases it is regressive, but in a minority of cases it is progressive, (2) it operates both on adjacent syllables and at a distance, (3) as regressive interference it affects the voiceless postdental fricative *c*, but not its voiced counterpart *z*, as seen in examples 9 (*s*VC*Vz*), 16 (*s*V*z*VC), 26 (C*Vs*V*z*) and 33 (*sh*V*z*VC), none of which shows interference effects; however, as progressive interference it can optionally affect *z*, as in *baRuj > *falhuz ~ falhulh* 'dove sp.', (4) *f* sometimes is heard as [h] or a voiceless lateral fricative, but this does not appear to be a product of sibilant harmony; the fricatives *f* and *h* thus appear to be exempt from the interference effects common to the other Thao sibilants (Blust 2003: 31), (5) the voiceless lateral can trigger assimilation, but is never assimilated to another fricative. Generically similar but independent histories of sibilant assimilation are attested in two other Formosan languages, Saisiyat and Paiwan (Blust 1995). Finally, although the class of segments affected by this change in Thao

SOLUTIONS

includes the sibilants *s* and *sh*, and in this respect shows interference effects very similar to those seen in the English tongue-twister 'She sells sea shells by the seashore', it is larger than this class, and might (perhaps less felicitously) be called 'voiceless coronal fricative assimilation/harmony'.

As noted above, somewhat confounding attempts to generalise about motivations for assimilation, Thao shows a pattern whereby the expected voiceless postdental sibilant has become *lh* under the influence of a lateral later in the word (44, 45, 47), a change that presumably occurred before *l > *r*.

One last conditioned change in Thao affects the schwa, which could not occur in open final syllables in Proto-Austronesian. This vowel normally disappeared when not in a final syllable, but became *u* before final labials, and *i* before other final consonants.

SOLUTION TO SOUND CHANGE PROBLEM 17

Levei (Admiralty Islands, Papua New Guinea)

1. Levei -ŋ derives from the following sources:

*r	>	-ŋ	1, 5, 44
*m	>	-ŋ	7, 16
*l	>	-ŋ	8, 9, 11, 17, 23, 45, 53
*n	>	-ŋ	14, 31
*dr	>	-ŋ	26
*ñ	>	-ŋ	42
*ŋ	>	-ŋ	46

The generalisation appears to be that *r, *l and *dr merged as *-l, and that this lateral then merged with *n and *ñ as *-n before all final nasals merged as -ŋ. Note that example 19 shows unexplained loss of the final syllable (expected **ronohuŋ).

2. The reflexes of Proto-Manus *t are:

*t	>	-k	10, 20, 28, 37, 41, 49
	>	-h	32, 34, 38
	>	(-)t-	36, 40, 46, 50
	>	s	44, 51, 52, 54

*t > k happened only word-finally (hence in coda position). *t > h also happened word-finally. All examples follow high vowels, but this cannot be accepted as a condition, since some examples of *t > k also follow high vowels, as 10. *t > s happened only before a high front vowel.

3. Levei -p reflects *w and *y, including the automatic transitional glides between a high or mid vowel and a following vowel of equal or lesser height:

*w	>	-p	3, 4, 29
*y	>	-p	12, 13, 15, 18, 24, 27, 33, 35

It is conceivable that the glides *w and *y first merged as *w, which then underwent glide fortition to -*p*. However, this is a speculation that assumes merger and fortition only word-finally, since both glides are retained as onsets in 6, 47, 53 and 54.

Recurrent changes from Proto-Manus to Levei in the order they are encountered are:

Changes	Examples
1. *ku-, pu-, bu- > kʷi-, pʷi-	1, 23, 27, 39
2. *r > l (before 3)	1, 5, 26, 44
3. *l > n/__# (before 4)	1, 5, 8, 9, 11, 17, 23, 26, 44, 45, 53
4. *n > ŋ/__#	1, 5, 7–9, 11, 14, 16, 17, 23, 26, 31, 44, 45, 53
5. V > Ø/__# (before 3, 6, 9, 12, 13, 19, 20)	1–20, 23, 24, 26–29, 31–38, 41–49, 51–54
6. *s > h/__# (before 16)	2, 47
7. *a > e/__Ci	3, 44, 46?
/__y (before 9)	13, 18, 33, 35
8. *k > ʔ/V__V	3, 39
9. *w[w], y[j] > p/__#	3, 4, 12, 13, 15, 18, 24, 27, 29, 33, 35
10. Ø > [w]/o,u__V, [j]/i,e__V (before 9)	4, 12, 13, 15, 24, 25, 38
11. *p > h/V__V (before 5)	6, 19, 30, 36, 43, 48
12. *m > n/__# (before 4)	7, 16
13. *t > k/__#	10, 20, 28, 37, 41, 49
14. *a > o	11, 19, 28, 41, 49, 50
15. *ñ > n (before 4)	16, 42, 49
16. *s > r	19, 20
17. *ŋ > n/__V	19, 20, 22
18. *dr > c/__V	21, 25, 31
19. *dr > r/__# (before 2)	26
20. *t > h/__#	32, 34, 38
21. *t > s/__i	44, 51, 52, 54

Discussion. This problem is included for several reasons. First, it raises the issue of irregularity in sound change, particularly in connection with reflexes of *t that came to be final, but also with the often unpredictable reflexes of vowels, as with changes 7 and 14, which are recurrent, but not regular. Contrary to the Regularity Hypothesis, *t is reflected as *k* in some forms and *h* in others in essentially the same environment, and no plausible hypothesis of borrowing is available. A similar problem arises in connection with the transfer of rounding from *u to an adjacent (usually labial) consonant, causing the resulting unrounded back vowel to front. In this data set *ku- became *kwi-* in item 1, but not in 17, 32 or 38, and *pu- or *bu- became *pwi-* in 23, 27 and 39, but not in 10, 13 or 26. In other cases, as with *balu > *pwaŋ* 'pigeon' the change of a labial to a labiovelar appears to be unconditioned. Both of these processes are recurrent in the Oceanic group of Austronesian languages, where they are commonly sporadic (Lynch 2002).

A second reason for including this problem is to illustrate the issue of 'telescoping', which leads to sometimes quite radical divergence between sound change and reflex. This process can be seen in examples such as 1, 5, 8, 9, 11, 17, 23, 26, 44, 45 and 53, where *l, *r (an alveolar flap or trill) and *dr (a prenasalised alveolar trill) that came to be word-final probably first merged as -*l*, and this word-final liquid then merged with *n, as shown by cognates in closely related languages (Lindrou *kun* 'cooking pot', *kon* 'village', *ban* 'pigeon', *san* 'path, road', *kun* 'breadfruit', *bun* 'moon', *bur* 'banana'). The change of *l to *n* only word-finally is known from other languages, including Thai, and several languages of Borneo, as Bintulu and Kiput. This *n*, from any source, then merged with *m and *ŋ as a final velar nasal.

A third reason for including this problem is to illustrate the occurrence of reflexes for which a 'telescoping' explanation appears problematic, most notably the surprising merger of *w and *y as -*p*, a change that affected not only *w and *y, but also glides of similar quality that occurred as automatic transitions between a high vowel and a following unlike vowel, as in *ia ([ija]) > *ip* '3s', or *kalia ([kalija]) > *kalip* 'grouper'. Although Goddard (2007) has claimed that this change could have come about through merger of *w and *y as *w*, followed by fortition to *p*, this seems unlikely, since both glides are reflected without change in non-final position (Blust 2005). Cases like this therefore raise the question of whether all sound changes are phonetically motivated.

SOLUTION TO SOUND CHANGE PROBLEM 18

PMP to Bario Kelabit (Sarawak, Malaysian Borneo)

1. The voiced aspirates of Bario Kelabit continue earlier geminates that resulted from two mechanisms, as follows:

   Gemination after stressed schwa: 1, 3, 6, 8, 9, 11, 20, 24, 26

   Assimilation of medial consonant clusters: 10, 12, 18, 26, 33

   Note that where gemination is fully predictable after stressed schwa in the contemporary language it is left unmarked, as with /təluh/ ([təl:uh]) 'three' or /pəpag/ ([pəp:ag]) 'slap', and that either gemination after stressed schwa or assimilation of medial consonant clusters could have played a part in some forms.

2. PMP *l became /r/ in Bario Kelabit if followed by /r/ in the next syllable; otherwise it remained a lateral:

*l	>	l	2, 4, 34, 35
	>	r	21, 25, 29

3. PMP *t became /s/ immediately preceding *i; otherwise it did not change:

*t	>	t	2, 4, 7, 9, 14, 15, 18, 19, 21, 38, 39
	>	s/__i	5, 17, 36

The following changes are observable in the data given here:

Changes	Examples
1. *h > Ø (before 2)	1, 6, 24, 29
2. $V_i V_i$ > V_i (before 3)	1, 6, 24, 31
3. Ø > ə/#__CV(C)# (before 4)	1, 6, 24
4. C > C:/ə__V(C)# (before 15)	1, 3, 6, 8, 9, 11, 20, 24, 26
5. *bb,*dd > b^h, d^h	1, 3, 6, 8-12, 18, 20, 24, 26, 33
6. *R > r	1, 19, 21, 25, 29–32, 36
7. *q > Ø/#__ (before 9)	2, 3, 5, 7, 11, 21, 34, 35

8. V > ə/__CV(C)V(C) (before 9)   2, 3, 5, 11, 21, 31, 34, 36, 37

9. *ə> Ø/#__CV(C)V(C)   2, 3, 5, 11, 21, 34

10. *j > d (before 16)   3, 11, 35

11. *-aw, -ay > o, e   3, 7, 32

12. Ø > h/V__# (before 11, 19)   4, 9, 11, 14, 16, 23, 28, 30, 31, 37–39

14. *t > s/__i (before 8)   5, 17, 36

15. *q > ʔ/V__   6, 17, 20, 22, 23, 36, 38, 39

16. $C_1C_2 > C_2C_2$ (before 5)   8, 10, 12, 15, 18, 26, 27, 33

17. *a > ə/__C_iC_i (before 4)   10, 12, 27

18. *tt > t, *pp > p, *kk > k   15, 27, 40

19. *s > Ø (before 14)   19, 22, 25, 34

20. *l > r/__Vr   21, 25, 29

21. *a > ə/__h   23, 30, 37, 39

Discussion. The comparative problem presented by Kelabit (and other languages of northern Sarawak) is one that can only be understood in the light of phonetic theory. Like many other Austronesian languages Kelabit disfavours monosyllabic content morphemes. When PMP disyllables became monosyllables as a result of regular sound change this violation of canonical form was repaired through schwa epenthesis. Stressed schwas (in the penult) then automatically geminated most or all following consonants, a process that is attested in the history of a number of Austronesian languages in insular Southeast Asia, and which remains part of the synchronic grammar of Kelabit. However, aerodynamic constraints make it difficult to maintain voicing throughout a geminate obstruent, and earlier *bb, *dd, *jj and *gg therefore underwent terminal devoicing, producing a new series of true voiced aspirates. It is important to note that these are phonetically distinct from the murmured stops of languages such as Hindi, which are often mislabelled 'voiced aspirates' (Ladefoged 1971: 9).

This process apparently began with loss of *h and coalescence of a resulting sequence of like vowels, or unlike vowels one of which was schwa. The disyllables *bahaR, *bahaq and *buhək then became monosyllabic content morphemes *baR, *baq and *buk. Schwa epenthesis restored the favoured disyllabism, and all consonants automatically geminated after stressed schwa, whether it was epenthetic or inherited from PMP, hence *əbbaR, *əbbaq, *əbbuk, *qaləjaw > ələddaw > ələddaw > əddaw, *qapəju > pəddu, etc. Gemination also came about through the complete assimilation of the first of two consonants in sequence, generally in PMP reduplicated monosyllables such as *dakdak or *bunbun. While gemination remained allophonic with other consonants after penultimate (stressed) schwa, the terminal devoicing of voiced geminate obstruents gave rise to a new series of phonemes that are distinct from the plain voiced obstruents. In forms like *tutuk* or *kukud* the presumed earlier gemination of voiceless stops after vowels other than schwa was simply lost. In other languages within the North Sarawak group the voiced aspirates evolved into implosive stops, voiceless stops or fricatives, and occasionally into plain voiced obstruents.

There is some residual ambiguity about the source of gemination in forms such as *dəmdəm, where the doubling of the medial obstruent could have occurred either through lengthening after schwa (following cluster reduction) or through complete assimilation of the first consonant. In *qaləjaw > *ədho* 'day', both options initially appear possible, but examples such as 11, 21, 34 or 36 show that although medial schwa syncope is a rule of the synchronic grammar this rule was not innovated until after the reduction of original trisyllables with *qa- to disyllables. The only option left, then, is to propose a derivation in which *q is lost word-initially, prepenultimate vowels merge as schwa, initial schwa is dropped three or more syllables from the end of the word, and gemination leading to a voiced aspirate develops after the stressed penultimate schwa. However, this leaves the disappearance of *l unexplained.

SOLUTION TO SOUND CHANGE PROBLEM 19

Proto-North Sarawak (PNS) to Long Terawan Berawan

1. The phonetic glides in the sequences *-ua- and *-ia- were strengthened to a voiced bilabial stop /b/ and a voiced palatal affricate /j/, as follows:

[w]	>	b	1, 5, 8, 80
[j]	>	j [dʒ]	6, 52, 79

2. Phonemic geminates developed from the onsets of open final syllables:

*CV#	>	C:Vh#	3, 10, 12, 13, 15, 17, 18, 20, 22, 23, 28, 29, 31, 32, 35, 40, 44, 49, 53, 55, 57, 64, 66, 67, 71, 74

   Gemination in this environment must be ordered before the addition of word-final *h* (see previous examples), and before the loss of PNS word-final *ʔ and *R:

*CVʔ#	>	CV#	4, 34, 43, 48, 58, 77
*CVR#	>	CV#	19, 47, 78

3. The glottal stop did not geminate, even though it met all other conditions, as shown in examples 54 and 81.

4. PNS *a raised to *i* immediately after a voiced stop, to əi immediately after a voiced stop and before final glottal stop, to [ə] when originally word-final or preceding *s and not following a voiced stop, and generally remained [a] elsewhere. Raising to ə apparently preceded glide fortition, as this bled examples from raising to *i* (52, 79):

*a	>	i	1, 5, 6, 10, 11, 13, 16, 24–26, 29, 30, 32, 38, 44, 45, 58, 59, 62, 66, 71, 75
	>	ə	3, 7, 17, 38, 52, 54, 64, 79
	>	əi	8, 51
	>	a	13–15, 17, 23, 25, 28, 31, 40–43, 45, 49, 50, 54, 58, 60, 61, 63, 64, 69, 72, 74, 76, 77, 80

Exceptions include (30), which shows raising to *i* at a distance, sporadic loss in (36) and sporadic change of *l to /d/ in (62) before raising to *i*.

5. Reflexes of *b, *d and *R in all positions are as follows. Where the initial syllable of a trisyllable has been lost, as in (5) or (6) the form is ignored:

*b-	>	b	7, 16, 18, 25, 29, 30, 34, 44, 45, 51, 53, 66, 68, 71
*-b-	>	k	8, 9, 12, 28, 32, 35, 53
*-b	>	m	36, 50
*d-	>	l	1
	>	d	22, 24, 37, 38, 78
*-d-	>	r	40, 47, 57, 61, 63, 69
*-d	>	n	33, 39, 42, 46, 62, 65, 73
*R-	>	g	11, 12, 56, 58
	>	Ø	75
*-R-	>	k	5–7, 10, 13, 22, 37, 44, 51, 70
*-R	>	Ø	9, 19, 21, 47, 78

The most unusual features of this pattern are the merger of *b and *R medially as /k/, and the merger of voiced stops with the homorganic nasals word-finally.

Discussion. Some of the innovations in this language are theoretically unexpected, and raise questions about the nature of sound change. The first innovation highlighted here is *b > *k*/V__V. Berawan is the only language in the entire Austronesian family in which *b and *R have merged (other than as zero) in any position. The reflexes of *R shed light on how this may have happened through intervocalic devoicing – again, a theoretically unexpected development, but one for which there is abundant evidence both in this language and in Kiput, also spoken in northern Sarawak (Blust 2002b). The non-final reflexes of *R suggest that *b became *g* between vowels and then underwent intervocalic devoicing, which affected only -*g*- < *b/R, since *d had previously become *r*. The replacement of voiced stops by the homorganic nasals word-finally is also surprising, but can be seen as a phonetically motivated alternative to final devoicing (Blust 2016b). Finally, the developments from *bəRuaŋ > *kəbiŋ* and *duRian > *kəjin* are not immediately obvious, but follow these steps:

	*bəRuaŋ 'bear'	*dəRian 'durian'	
1.	*bəguaŋ	*dəgian	(*R > g)
2.	*bəkuaŋ	*dəkian	(intervocalic devoicing)
3.	*kuaŋ	*kian	(loss of the first syllable in trisyllables)
4.	*kəbaŋ	*kəjan	(glide fortition + high vowel centralisation)
5.	*kəbiŋ*	*kəjin*	(low vowel fronting)

The fact that *R is reflected as *k-* in these forms shows that it was not yet initial at the time of intervocalic devoicing. The loss of the first syllable in trisyllables is irregular, but recurrent, also being reflected in a number of stative verbs that earlier were marked by the prefix *mə-* (< PAN *ma-), which has since been lost.

One other feature of these and some other comparisons that must be understood in order to recognise the sometimes quite opaque reflexes of well-established proto-forms is glide fortition. Like several other languages of northern Sarawak, Long Terawan Berawan has strengthened both phonemic glides and the automatic transitions in sequences such as *ia* or *ua*. In the latter case the high vowel that triggered the glide is centralised to schwa, so that *ia > əji*, and *ua > əbi*. It is clear that glide fortition preceded low vowel fronting, but postdated intervocalic devoicing.

Another surprising change that is unique to the four dialects of Berawan is the gemination of consonants that were earlier onsets of open final syllables. If the syllable was closed gemination did not occur, as seen in minimal pairs such as *bulu > bulluh* 'body hair, feather' vs. *buluʔ > bulu* 'large bamboo sp.'. As illustrated by this example, after gemination, but before the loss of final glottal stop, a glottal fricative was added after final vowels, somewhat masking the earlier condition on gemination.

A third puzzling change that is shared in a similar form with several other languages of northern Sarawak, as Miri (see sound change problem 20) is low vowel fronting, a process that resembles Adjarian's law in some dialects of Armenian, but presents even greater challenges to phonetic theory. Details differ in theoretically important ways in other North Sarawak languages, but low vowel fronting in Long Terawan Berawan raised *a to a high front vowel immediately following a voiced obstruent, including voiced obstruents that derived from glide fortition.

A major reason for including this problem in the workbook is because it raises the important and neglected question of whether all sound changes are phonetically motivated. In particular, the apparently simultaneous fortition of glides and centralisation of the high vowel that triggered them seems to involve two distinct phonological processes as part of a single phonological innovation. While such complex articulatory adjustments are not explicitly ruled out in most discussions of sound change, this is primarily because they are not mentioned, since they are rare or absent in Indo-European languages and other language families for which good historical documentation is available.

Equally puzzling is why gemination would affect the onsets of final syllables only if they are open. In several languages of northern Sarawak word-final vowels automatically lengthen, but it is unclear why this would trigger lengthening of a preceding consonant (if anything, arguments from isochrony suggest that onsets of final *closed* syllables would be geminated, since the nuclei of these syllables are short). For further discussion of this change see Blust (2017).

SOLUTION TO SOUND CHANGE PROBLEM 20

Proto-North Sarawak (PNS) to Miri

1. Reflexes of PNS last-syllable high vowels in Miri are:

*i	>	ay	2, 40, 45, 47–50
*u	>	aw	41, 44, 46

2. Last-syllable *a and *ə (which probably had already merged as *a) were fronted to /e/ if a voiced obstruent preceded it, even if another, unaffected vowel intervened. The symbol *b* in the following schema represents any voiced obstruent, and V any vowel):

*a	>	e/b__	3, 5, 6, 8, 12, 15, 16, 18, 20, 23, 24, 27, 29, 31, 33, 34
	>	e/bVCa(C)	9, 11, 13, 21, 25, 32, 37, 43

3. Blocking consonants play a significant role in apparent exceptions to low vowel fronting in Miri. The blocking consonants include all voiceless stops except glottal stop, and presumably all nasals, although examples of /m/ are unattested:

n:	7, 19
p:	10
t:	14, 42, 46
ŋ:	22, 35
k:	26, 36

   For the absence of blocking effects by a glottal stop see (32).

4. In Long Terawan Berawan low vowels were fronted in any syllable immediately after a voiced obstruent. In Miri *a fronted to *e* only if it occurred in the ultima and a voiced obstruent was found earlier in the word, except that blocking consonants provide specific limitations on application of the change, as noted above. For further details on these developments see Blust (2000b).

   The changes in Miri, in the order in which they are encountered in the data, are as follows:

Change	Examples
1. Ø > h/V__# (before 2, 10)	1, 2, 4–6, 10, 13, 15, 19, 23, 27, 36, 39, 41, 45, 46
2. *i,u > ay,aw/__C# (before 10)	2, 40, 41, 44–50
3. *a > e/[+obs, +voice](VC)__(C)# (before 8)	3, 5, 6, 8, 9, 11–13, 15, 16, 18, 20, 21, 23–25, 27, 29, 31–34, 37, 43
4. [j,w] > j, b/__V (before 3, 6, 10)	5, 6, 12, 15, 18, 31, 34
5. Ø > [j,w]/i,u__V (before 4)	6, 12, 15, 18, 31, 34
6. *u,i > ə/__j, b	6, 15, 18
7. *R > r	9, 11, 13, 21, 35, 44
8. CV > Ø/__j, b	12, 31, 34
9. *dʰ,bʰ > s,f	20, 24 27, 33
10. *s > Ø	21, 37, 38, 44, 47, 50
11. *ə > a/__(C)# (before 3)	29, 33, 38, 42, 43

Discussion. The first change documented here (addition of *h* after final vowels) is common to a number of languages in northern Sarawak, as well as to a few Austronesian languages elsewhere, including Tboli and Tausug of the southern Philippines. The second change (diphthongisation of high vowels in the ultima) is also common to many languages in northern Sarawak, to some of the languages of southern Sumatra, and to the Chamic languages of Vietnam, where the nucleus is usually mid-central and the change normally affects only final vowels (hence *-i/u > -əy/əw*). The ordering of these changes may seem arbitrary. In other languages of the region *h* was added after final vowels, but not after diphthongs, a consideration that favours ordering change (1) first.

The third change is theoretically the most interesting, and the challenge is to recognise how it is conditioned (and what might motivate this type of conditioning). The examples given here and many others like them show that low vowels were fronted in Miri only if a voiced obstruent was found earlier in the word. The condition under which this change took place is surprising, but similar changes are attested in other languages in northern Sarawak, independently in a number of Austronesian languages in northeast Luzon, Philippines, and are part of Adjarian's law in Armenian, where *a, *o and *u fronted following original voiced obstruents in the Van and Kirzan dialects, among others (Vaux 1992, 1998; Blust 2000b). The distribution of these innovations in an Indo-European language and in two widely separated groups of Austronesian languages thus suggests that vowel fronting after voiced obstruents is phonetically motivated, although the nature of the phonetic mechanism giving rise to this phenomenon remains in dispute (Vaux 1992, 1998; Garrett 1998).

Three features of low vowel fronting in Miri deserve attention. First, as already noted, low vowels front only if there is a prior voiced obstruent in the word. These include *b, *d, *j, *g, *bʰ and *dʰ, and it is clear that *a was fronted before these two voiced aspirates changed to voiceless fricatives *f* and *s*. Second, low vowel fronting is blocked by an intervening supraglottal voiceless stop or nasal: *bakaw > *bakaw* (**bakew) 'mangrove', *butan > *butan* (**buten) 'coconut', *danaw 'lake' > *danaw* (**danew) 'pond', *dəpa > *dəpah* (**dəpeh) 'fathom', but *daʔan > *daʔen* 'branch', etc. Third, and most strikingly, low vowel fronting passes over penultimate *a, as in *daraʔ > *dareʔ* 'blood', *bara 'shoulder' > *bareh* 'arm', or *daʔan > *daʔen* 'branch', a pattern that is hard to reconcile with phonetic explanations that have been proposed for Adjarian's law in Armenian. Attempts to remedy this problem by appeals to dissimilation or other types of secondary change have so far proved unconvincing. Stress in Miri is generally final (although there is some evidence that it is variable), and it may turn out that low vowel fronting affects only stressed vowels.

The fourth change is stated in phonetic rather than phonemic terms because glide fortition affected not only the phonemic glides *y and *w, but also the automatic transitional glides in vowel sequences such as *ia or *ua. Possibly as part of the same change as glide fortition, the high vowel that triggered glide formation was centralised to schwa. In several cases, including examples 12, 31 and 34, an entire first syllable has been lost after glides were strengthened. In other words, the changes *buaq > *beʔ* 'fruit', *diaʔ > *jeʔ* 'good', etc., must have passed through a stage in which disyllables were preserved after glide fortition, but these words were then truncated by loss of CV-: *buaq (> bəbaʔ > bəbeʔ) > *beʔ*, *diaʔ (> dəja ʔ > dəjeʔ) > *jeʔ*). Finally, it is clear that glide fortition must have preceded low vowel fronting, since *a is usually fronted following the strengthened reflexes of both [j] and [w]).

The frequent, but irregular change *s > Ø must have followed the addition of *h* after final vowels, since words that originally ended with *s now end with a glide, and if the loss of *s had occurred first bot*-i and *-is should be reflected as -ayh. However, this presents something of a paradox, since ordering change 1 before change 10 makes it difficult to account for the loss of final *s through normal phonetic processes (*s > h > Ø). Instead, it is hard to find alternatives to the hypothesis that *-s > Ø was a one-step change. Also puzzling is the retention of *s as a sibilant in 45 and 49; this may be due to borrowing from Brunei Malay.

The relationship between schwa and *a* in Miri is somewhat complex. The two sounds are clearly in free variation in prepenultimate syllables, with *a* preferred in careful speech. In the penult there is good evidence for contrast, and in the ultima only the low vowel is attested. Rather than assuming that both *a and *ə underwent a process that is restricted to low vowels in other Austronesian languages it is most plausible to assume that *a and *ə merged in the ultima before low vowel fronting.

SOLUTION TO SOUND CHANGE PROBLEM 21

POC to Chuukese

1. *t   >   Ø/__i   1, 16
                  Ø/__u   3, 10, 26, 39, 47
                  Ø/__e   7, 45
                  Ø/__o   15, 46
   *t   >   s/__a   2, 8, 9, 27, 30, 32
                  s/__o   5
                  s__u   19, 40

Since both *t > Ø and *t > s occurred preceding u and o, but with loss being more frequent, the change *t > s in these environments can be considered an exception to the regular (or at least statistically predominant) pattern of change.

2. *s   >   t/__i   9, 21
                  t/__a   13, 33
                  t/__u   29
                  Ø/__a   28

For the avoidance of merger see the discussion below.

3. Problem sets are 3, 9, 11, 22, 32 and 39. For 3 and 39 the penultimate vowel has been lengthened even though the original final vowel is still present in the independent (non-suffixed) form. For 9, 11, 22 and 32, *aa was fronted but not raised by a following *i, while a short vowel was both fronted and raised. This is unexplained unless lengthening of the penultimate vowel preceded loss of the final *i, and hence that 'compensatory lengthening' was not compensatory.

4 The Chuukese labiovelars developed from earlier *m and *p adjacent to *u or *o. In some cases, as 4, 41 and 43 the rounding of the vowel was transferred to the labial consonant, producing a labiovelar consonant and a front unrounded vowel:

   *um   >   imʷ   4
          >   umʷ   23, 31, 48

*mu	>	m^{w}i	41
*pu	>	p^{w}i	43
*mo	>	m^{w}ɨ	47

This was not completely consistent, as seen in examples 35, 36, 42 and 46.

The following recurrent changes from POC to Chuukese can be found in this data set. Where affixed forms occur statements of sound change are made in relation to the base morpheme, as with loss of final vowels:

Changes

1. *t > Ø/__ V[-low] (before 5, 17)

2. V$_1$ > V$_1$V$_1$/(C)__CV(C)# (before 3, 22)

3. V > Ø/__#

4. *t > s/__a,o,u
5. *u > w/V__#
6. *R > Ø
7. *m,p > m^w,p^w/u,o__ (before 8)
8. *u > i/adjacent to m^w,p^w
9. C > Ø/__# (before 3)

10. *q > Ø (before 17)
11. *a > ɔ/__Co
12. *k > s/__i
13. *l > n

14. *a >æ /#(C)__Ce,i(C)#

15. *s > t
16. *u > ɨ
17. Ø > w/#__ɨ,u,o

Examples

1, 3, 7, 10, 15, 16, 26, 39, 45–47

1a, 2a, 3a, 4a, 5, 6a, 7, 8a, 9a, 10, 11a, 12, 13, 16, 17–22a, 23–25, 27, 28, 31, 32a, 35–39a, 42–47

1a, 2a, 4a, 5, 6a, 8a, 9a, 10, 11a, 12, 13, 16–22a, 23–28, 30–32a, 33–35 37, 38, 40, 42–45, 47, 48

2, 5, 8, 9, 19, 27, 30, 32, 40
3a, 36, 39a, 46
4, 25, 27
4, 23, 31, 41, 43, 47, 48
4, 41, 43
4–6, 9, 11, 13, 18, 23, 24, 28, 31, 33, 34, 42, 43, 47, 48

5, 7, 13, 23, 24, 26, 48
5, 37
6, 38, 44
6, 11, 15, 17, 20, 28, 30–32, 37, 43, 44

7, 9a, 11a, 12, 16, 22a, 25, 32a, 45

9, 13, 21, 29, 33
10, 13–15, 24, 27, 29, 47
13, 15, 18, 23, 24, 35, 42, 46, 48

18. *i,o > i/__Cu   19, 26, 47
19. *p > f/__a,i   16, 19, 22, 25, 39
20. V > Ø/C*i*__C*i* (before 3)   21, 29, 40
21. *p > Ø /__o,u (before 3, 5, 17)   35, 36, 42, 46
22. *a > e /#(C)__C*i*CV(C)#   9b, 11b, 22b, 30, 32b, 33

Discussion. Chuukese historical phonology is characterised by extensive conditioned change, especially in the vowels, and in this respect it resembles most other Oceanic languages of Micronesia (Bender et al. 2003a, 2003b). Dyen (1949) was the first to show how the nine vowels of Chuukese developed from the four vowels of Proto-Austronesian, and thus in demonstrating the adequacy of the reconstructed vowel system.

Labiolvelars *mw* and *pw* developed from *m and *p adjacent to a rounded vowel. In some cases, as with *Rumaq > *iimw* 'house', *muri > *mwiri-* 'afterwards', *puliq > *pwiin* 'cowrie shell' and *motus > *mwii-* 'break off' rounding appears to have been transferred from *u to the adjacent labial consonant. A similar, but historically independent change in the word for 'house' is seen in a number of other Oceanic languages.

Among its many consonant changes Chuukese shows both *t > *s* and *s > *t*, an apparent 'alpha-switch' that is seen in the same morpheme in *tasik> *sææt* 'sea, saltwater'. Bender et al. (2003a) reconstruct Proto-Micronesian (PMC) *taSi, Proto-Chuukic (PCK) *tadi 'saltwater'. However, PMC *t almost always became PCK *s before low vowels, and both PMC *s and *S became PCK *t before any vowel. Given the observation that a similar crossover is found in all Chuukic languages the steps that led to *t/s interchange are unclear. In the closely related Pohnpeic languages, which also show an *s/t switch, *t > *j* (voiced palatal affricate) > *s*, thus allowing *s > *t* to take place before *j completed the change to *s*, and it is likely that a similar explanation holds for Chuukese (Kenneth Rehg, p.c.).

Finally, there are some irregularities that are not accounted for by the reconstructions. For example, although POC *t nearly always appears as Chuukese *s* before a low vowel, it is reflected unpredictably as zero or *s* before other vowels. Bender et al. (2003a, 2003b) account for this by positing PMC *t (> Ø) and *T (> *s*), both reflecting POC *t, but without stateable conditions or further explanation. Similarly, *u does not always unround when labials become velars, as seen by comparing 4a, 41 or 43 with 23 or 31, and the change *k > s/__i is straightforward in 38 and 44, but requires the previous irregular fronting of *u in 6.

SOLUTION TO SOUND CHANGE PROBLEM 22

Proto-Kelabit-Lun Dayeh (PKLD) to Sa'ban (northern Sarawak, Malaysian Borneo)

1. Sa'ban shows no evidence of erosion from the right; rather it shows a seemingly sporadic loss of initial consonants, with the following examples of unpredictable change (consonants are counted as lost only if they leave no trace in the form of gemination, devoicing of sonorants, etc.):

C-	>	Ø	4, 7–10, 13, 14, 17, 19, 21, 22, 26, 31, 32, 35, 36, 38, 39, 51, 52
	>	C-	3, 5, 6, 11, 12, 15, 16, 18, 20, 23–25, 27, 29, 33, 34, 37, 40–50, 53–62, 64–67

With vowels there appears to be more patterning: in the penult *a is always retained as a vowel of some quality, while high vowels and schwa almost always drop (although there are some exceptions), as follows:

*a	>	V	1–8, 17–21, 23, 31, 32, 36, 37, 39, 47, 48, 57, 63, 64
	>	Ø	(none)
*ə	>	ə	24, 49
	>	Ø	9–12, 33, 40, 42–44, 58–60, 74
*i	>	i	13, 50, 75
	>	e	25, 38, 51, 76–78
	>	Ø	26–30, 55, 56
*u	>	w	14, 22, 68
	>	Ø	14, 15, 16, 24, 34, 35, 41, 45, 46, 52–54, 61, 62, 65–67, 69–73

Note that *i was usually retained only if it lowered to /e/ (six of the nine cases), and that *u was retained only when it became initial and prevocalic, where it semivocalised to /w/.

2. Reflexes of the plain voiced obstruents are as follows:

Changes			Examples
1. *b-	>	b	3, 5, 6, 12, 15, 16
2. *b-	>	Ø	4, 7, 8, 13, 14
3. *bV-	>	Ø	9, 10
4. *bVCi-	>	CiCi	11
5. *-b-	>	b	1, 13, 61
6. *-b	>	p	59, 68
7. *d-	>	Ø	17, 19, 21, 22
8. *d-	>	l	18, 20
9. *-d-	>	d	3, 17, 18, 45, 62, 63, 70
10. *-d	>	t	34, 36, 66, 67
11. *g-	>	j	23, 24
12. *g-	>	p	25, 64
13. *gV-	>	Ø	26
14. *-g-	>	j	2
15. *-g	>	p	2, 25, 44, 53, 76

Unsurprising changes in this series include final devoicing and *d > *l* (although normally we would expect this to go through *d > r > *l*, which evidently has not happened here). Surprising changes include *g > *j* in non-final position and *g > *p* word-finally. The latter change would be less bizarre if it were *-g > -b > -*p*. However, in a few cases *g has also become Sa'ban *p* word-initially, as in examples 25 and 64.

3. Both the geminates and voiceless sonorants arose from deletion of a penultimate vowel. In the case of geminates this was followed by complete assimilation of the first consonant of the resulting cluster to the second, and in the case of voiceless sonorants it was followed by a voiceless stop devoicing following nasals and liquids, as follows:

CVC-	>	CC-	11, 34, 42, 44, 45, 54, 58, 61, 62, 67
	>	vl. sonorant	26, 27, 29, 33, 43, 53, 55, 56, 59, 60, 65, 66

Note the different behaviour of very similar proto-forms, as (10) and (11), the first one losing *bə-, but the second losing only the schwa, and then assimilating the resulting cluster to form an initial geminate. It can be assumed that all geminates (which occur only word-initially) arose as consonant clusters that were either identical

SOLUTIONS

at that point, as with (34), or that became identical through complete assimilation, as with *bs > ps > ss-in (11), *ps > *ss-* in (42), etc. Clusters remained intact if they were pronounceable without alteration of the member segments, as with *bl-* (12, 15), *br-* (16), *mr-* (40), *pl-* (46, 48), or with only place assimilation, as with (41).

4. Low vowel fronting in Sa'ban generally targets only a last-syllable *a, as in Miri (cf. examples 17–21, where it skips over an *a in the penult to front an identical proto-vowel in the following syllable). However, even this may be conditioned, as a penultimate low vowel following initial *b is fronted in examples 3 and 6.

Discussion. Sa'ban has an extraordinarily rich, challenging, fascinating and in some ways exasperating historical phonology. Although many changes seem to show complex conditioning, others defy attempts to perceive regularity, and some are simply odd. The changes in Sa'ban are too numerous and complex for us to make a meaningful attempt to list them all here (cf. Blust 2001b for a detailed account). However, several features of the historical phonology of this language stand out in striking contrast to those of most other Austronesian languages.

First, although so-called 'erosion from the right' is common in many languages, giving rise to final devoicing of stops, merger of final stops as glottal stop and final nasals as -ŋ, and eventually to loss of final consonants entirely, Sa'ban instead shows 'erosion from the left'. In some cases this has resulted in the loss of only the initial consonant. In others it has resulted in loss of the initial (C)V-. This change almost certainly began with a shift of primary stress from penultimate to final position, thus weakening vowels preceeding the final syllable. However, even given stress shift erosion from the left is surprising for several reasons. In nearly all Austronesian languages spoken in the southern Philippines and western Indonesia prepenultimate (hence pretonic) vowels weaken in a fixed order, reflexes of *a first merging with schwa, and then reflexes of *i and *u following at a later date. By contrast, in Sa'ban high vowels and schwa are the first to drop, with low vowels strongly resisting deletion, or even weakening to schwa. Another peculiarity of this change, even if it is attributed to stress shift, is that the initial consonant drops in many cases without loss of the following vowel, as in *batu > *ataw* 'stone', *bibiR > *ibiəl* 'lip', *dara? > *areə?* 'blood', *kapal > *apal* 'thick', *liməh > *emah* 'five', or *matəh > *atah* 'eye'. Yet another peculiarity is that, unless it was first semivocalised, *u is always lost syllable-initially, whether it was originally preceded by a consonant or not, whereas *i is often retained, although frequently lowered to *e*.

Second, Sa'ban has developed several new vowels (not seen in this data), as well as a range of new consonants, including voiceless nasals and liquids, and initial consonant clusters that did not previously exist. Tautomorphemic initial clusters include *bl-, br-, mp-, nt-, ŋk-, mr-, pl-* and *pr-*. Other consonant clusters that arose through loss of the first-syllable vowel produced voiceless sonorants. This happened most often when a voiceless stop came to immediately precede a nasal or liquid, as in *tina-n > hna-n 'his/her mother', *kəmuʔ > hmuʔ 'short', *pənuʔ > hnoʔ 'full, of a container', *siri > hray 'straight', *tərur > hrol 'egg', or *tulud > hlut 'to fly'.

Other derived clusters produced geminates. The full recorded range of these (only partially illustrated in the data set given here) is: *bbʰ > pp-, *bdʰ > ss-, *bt > tt-, *bk > kk-, *by > jj-, *ddʰ > ss-, *kk > kk-, *ll > ll-, *mn > nn-, *dk > kk-, *pdʰ > ss-, *pp > pp-, *pt > tt-, *pd > dd-, *rm > mm-, *rr > rr-, *tbʰ > pp-, *tk > kk-, *tb > bb-, *td > dd-, *tk > kk-, *tp > pp-, and *tt > tt-. Yet another peculiarity of this language is that although a number of new heterorganic consonant clusters arose in medial position as a result of syncope in the environment VC__CV, geminates were produced only word-initially.

Another striking change that is only incompletely illustrated in this data is low vowel fronting: the reflex of *a was fronted to *i, e* or *əi* if there was a voiced obstruent earlier in the word. Although this change is found in a number of other languages in northern Sarawak they are all geographically and genetically separated from Sa'ban, and it is almost certain that low vowel fronting in Sa'ban is historically independent from the change in other languages of the region. In Sa'ban the conditioning consonant was lost in many cases after the reflex of *a was fronted, and in these and other cases it is clear that fronting skipped an adjacent low vowel to target a low vowel in the last syllable.

Equally odd is the change *g > *j-, -j-, -p* (with occasional *p-* reflexes in initial position). While the labial reflexes in final position can be attributed to a change *g > b* followed by final devoicing, the occasional reflex *g > p-* suggests that this was a single-step change.

Finally, as can be seen in comparing etymologies such as *baka > aka 'wild pig' and *bakul > bakol 'basket', *bədʰək > sək 'nasal mucus' and *bədʰuk > ssuək 'coconut monkey', or *dadan > adin 'old, long time' and *dadaŋ > ladeəŋ 'heat of a fire', it is clear that many PKLD phonemes have split. The search for possible conditions for these splits has proved frustrating, and it must be concluded that in addition to its many strange features Sa'ban historical phonology shows massive irregularity. Because Sa'ban shares about 83 per

SOLUTIONS

cent of its basic vocabulary with Bario Kelabit, which reflects PKLD virtually unchanged, this bewildering variety of sound changes must have taken place over a comparatively short time span. Perhaps the rapidity of innovation led to many sound changes overlapping in time, and this may have been a factor in the large number of irregularities that have been observed.

SOLUTION TO SOUND CHANGE PROBLEM 23

PMP to Hawu (Lesser Sunda Islands, eastern Indonesia)

1. The following vowel changes are encountered in the data in the order listed:

Changes	Examples
1. *iCe > əC*i*	1
2. *uCa > əC*u*	2, 5, 7–9, 12, 14, 16, 19
3. *uCa > əC*o*	3
4. *iCa > əC*i*	4, 6, 10, 11, 13, 15, 17, 18
5. *ə > a/__#	25, 30, 34

2. Hawu appears to show regular vowel metathesis, but only if the first vowel is higher (less sonorous) than the second.
3. This is an entirely open question at this point!

Discussion. This change is puzzling, as it seems to combine unrelated phonological processes in a single innovation: (1) regular metathesis of the vowels in adjacent syllables if the first is high and the second is non-high, and (2) centralisation of the non-high vowel to schwa. There is no obvious way that this could be the result of two distinct, ordered changes, since if metathesis preceded centralisation *buta (> batu) > ɓədu 'blind' should show the same vowel pattern as *batu > wadu 'stone', and if centralisation preceded metathesis last syllable *a should have centralised in forms that did not metathesise, but this did not happen (*mata > mada 'eye', *nanaq > nana 'pus', etc.).

The preliminary conclusions that the data seem to support, then, are: (1) that this is the first case of *regular* vowel metathesis ever reported; (2) it seems to involve two unrelated phonetic processes in a single change (metathesis, and changing of any non-high vowel to schwa); and (3) conditions governing its occurrence are theoretically puzzling (it happens only if the first vowel is higher than the second). For further details on this unusual development cf. Blust (2012b).

SOLUTION TO SOUND CHANGE PROBLEM 24

Pre-Sundanese to Sundanese

1. Consonant changes include the following:

Changes	Examples
1. *w > c/#___	1
2. *h > Ø/V$_x$___V$_y$	1, 10
3. *R > Ø	1, 12
4. *w > nc/V___V	2, 4, 6–8
5. *ʔ > h	2, 7, 9, 15, 26
6. *h > ʔ/V$_i$___V$_i$	9, 25, 26
7. *b > c/#___	9, 11–14, 17–20, 22, 27
8. *b > nc/V___V	16
9. *l > r/_Vl	20
10. *Nb > Nc/V___V	23, 24, 27

2. The most startling consonant change in Sundanese is *b/w- > c, and *-(N)b/w- > -nc-.

Discussion. The major reason for including this problem is the unexpected reflex of both *w and *b in this relatively well-studied language, a change first noted by Nothofer (1975). Faced with such a radical difference in the feature composition of either [b] or [w] on the one hand, and [ʄ] or [nʄ] on the other, one is inclined to assume intermediate steps leading from proto-phoneme to reflex. However, a hypothesis of this kind would require a number of steps for which there is neither internal nor comparative evidence. It is possible that *b > c passed through a transitional stage with w, but if so the words in question would have to be regarded as Javanese loans, since Sundanese otherwise reflects *b only as b (Nothofer 1975: 123). Moreover, such an explanation is impossible for *mb > -nc-, since the cluster -mw- is unknown in any language of western Indonesia.

While the great majority of sound changes show clear evidence of phonetic motivation, then, cases such as this raise the controversial prospect that some sound changes may be products of a conscious and deliberate manipulation of language by its speakers, rather than of the phonetic mechanisms that give rise to sound changes that are cross-linguistically recurrent.

SOLUTIONS

SOLUTIONS TO PHONOLOGICAL RECONSTRUCTION PROBLEMS

SOLUTION TO RECONSTRUCTION PROBLEM 1

No.	Lg. A	Lg.		B
01.	*tamti	tanhi	tamti	earth
02.	*tomfat	tomfat	tumfa	stone
03.	*esemti	ehenhi	isimti	water
04.	*corak	corak	cura	river
05.	*fentara	fentara	fintara	tree
06.	*garsil	garhil	garsi	leaf
07.	*tisin	hihin	tisi	house
08.	*donte	donte	dunti	path
09.	*lintam	lintam	linta	forest
10.	*arondar	arondar	arunda	fruit
11.	*sunbi	humbi	sunbi	flower
12.	*ilamu	ilamu	ilamu	seed
13.	*kositi	kohihi	husiti	person
14.	*sembor	hembor	simbu	man
15.	*samkek	haŋkek	samki	woman
16.	*otif	ohif	uti	child
17.	*kasi	kahi	hasi	son
18.	*inkil	iŋkil	inki	daughter

1. Recurrent changes in Lgs. A and B in the order in which they are encountered are:

Change	Examples
Lg. A	
1. nasal place assimilation (before 3)	1, 3, 11, 15, 18
2. *t > s/__i (before 3)	1, 3, 7, 13, 16
3. *s > h	1, 3, 6, 7, 11, 13–17
Lg. B	
1. *e,o > i,u	2–5, 8, 10, 13–16
2. -C > Ø	2, 4, 6, 7, 9, 10, 14–16, 18
3. *k > h/[-nas]__V	13, 15, 17

Discussion. It is very difficult to begin this problem by trying to reconstruct item 1 first, as the form in Lg. A has been affected by three sound changes, and disentangling these all at once can be quite difficult. As a result, in approaching a set of data such as this it is best to start with comparisons that require no assumptions about change, as number 12. Then go on to comparisons that require one assumption about change, as numbers 5 or 9. Comparison 12 gives us no information about change, but numbers 5 and 9 suggest two preliminary hypotheses:

Hypothesis 1: mid vowels were raised in Lg. B.
Hypothesis 2: final consonants were lost in Lg. B.

This enables us to reconstruct the following forms with no further assumptions about change:

02. *tomfat
04. *corak
05. *fentara
08. *donte
09. *lintam
10. *arondar
12. *ilamu

Next, go on to comparisons that require one additional assumption, as 6, which leads to a third hypothesis:

Hypothesis 3: *s became *h* in Lg. A. This enables us to reconstruct:

06. *garsil
14. *sembor
17. *kasi

Next, note that *t* in Lg. B sometimes corresponds to *t* in Lg. A, and sometimes to *h*. What are the conditions for this correspondence? This leads to a fourth hypothesis:

Hypothesis 4: *t > s/__i in Lg. A (ordered before *s > *h*).

This enables us to reconstruct the following forms with no further assumptions about change:

07. *tisin
16. *otif

The next sound correspondence that we find is *k* in Lg. A corresponding to *h* in Lg. B, which leads to Hypothesis 5:

Hypothesis 5: *k became *h* in Lg. B.

This enables us to reconstruct two more forms without further assumptions about change:

13. *kositi
17. *kasi

Finally, we assume nasal place assimilation in Lg. A (ordered before *t > s/__i). This enables us to reconstruct the remaining five forms:

01. *tamti
03. *esemti
11. *sunbi
15. *samkek
18. *inkil

This problem is constructed to illustrate some of the most basic types of phonological processes in sound change: nasal place assimilation (the adjustment of a nasal consonant to the place of articulation of an immediately following obstruent), lenition (weakening of a consonantal constriction, as with *k > *h* or *s > *h*), palatalisation (the fronting of alveolar or velar consonants to palatals before, or sometimes after, front vowels) or its variant assibilation (*t > *s/__i*), vowel raising (as in the Great Vowel Shift in the history of English), loss of final consonants. Moreover, it draws attention to the crucial role of ordering in historical phonology. In most remaining problems sound changes will be listed in the order they are encountered in the data. However, as a strategy for beginning a problem that is initially recalcitrant, it is useful to follow the approach illustrated here, beginning with reconstructions that require the fewest assumptions about change, and working step-by-step towards those that require more complex hypotheses.

SOLUTION TO RECONSTRUCTION PROBLEM 2

No.	Proto-ABC	Lg. A	Lg. B	Lg. C	
01.	*tisaw	tizaw	diho	tisu	one
02.	*lumo	rumo	lumo	lumu	two
03.	*pajan	pajan	paja	padan	three
04.	*saloti	saroti	halodi	saluti	head
05.	*ñenu	ñenu	nenu	ninu	hair
06.	*kuber	huber	kube	kubir	ear
07.	*gonay	konay	gone	guni	eye
08.	*ucewa	ucewa	usewa	usiwa	nose
09.	*eliray	eriray	elire	iliri	mouth
10.	*rawraw	rawraw	roro	ruru	tooth
11.	*torosi	torozi	dorohi	turusi	earth
12.	*dedeŋ	deden	dede	didiŋ	water
13.	*botbot	botbot	bobo	butbut	stone
14.	*siŋe	sine	hiŋe	siŋi	tree
15.	*duŋat	dunat	duŋa	duŋat	sky
16.	*ilaya	iraya	ilea	ilia	rain
17.	*dayday	dayday	dede	didi	star
18.	*tatir	tatir	dadi	tatir	moon
19.	*cakcak	cahcah	sasa	saksak	lightning
20.	*guroŋ	kuron	guro	guruŋ	thunder
21.	*rasaŋ	razan	raha	rasaŋ	storm
22.	*tugan	tukan	duga	tugan	flood
23.	*june	june	june	duni	sand
24.	*tañak	tañah	dana	tanak	mud

1 Recurrent changes in Lgs. A, B and C in the order they are encountered are:

Change	Examples
Lg. A	
1. *s > z/V__V	1, 11, 21
2. *l > r	2, 4, 9, 16
3. *k > h (before 4)	6, 19, 24

4. *g > k   7, 20, 22
5. *ŋ > n   12, 14, 15, 20, 21

Lg. B
1. *t > d   1, 4, 11, 18, 22, 24
2. *s > h (before 6)   1, 4, 11, 14, 21
3. *aw/ay > o/e (before 5)   1, 7, 9, 10, 16, 17
4. C > Ø/__$ 3, 6, 12, 13, 15, 18–22, 24
5. *ñ > n   5, 24
6. *c > s   8, 19

Lg. C
1. *aw/ay > o/e (before 2)   1, 7, 9, 10, 16, 17
2. *o,e > u,i   1, 2, 4–14, 16, 17, 20, 23
3. *j > d   3, 23
4. *ñ > n   5, 24
5. *c > s   8, 19

2. The consonants and vowels of Proto-ABC are:

Consonants   **Vowels**

p   t   c   k   i   u
b   d   j   g
m   n   ñ   ŋ   e   o
     s
     l   a
     r
w   y

Discussion. This is a relatively simple problem, as there are no unusual changes, indeterminacies in direction of change, or other special complications. Although there are only two examples each of *c, *j and *ñ, the reflexes of these phonemes pattern in the same way, and so provide mutually confirmatory evidence for an original palatal series. Among the more complex correspondences are those involving mid and high vowels, but even here the patterns are clear: for $i : i : i$ and $u : u : u$ there is no choice but to posit *i and *u. For $e : e : i$ and $o : o : u$ this choice no longer exists, and so forces a choice of something different, the most plausible alternatives being *e and *o. For *ay* : *e* : *i* and *aw* : *o* : *u* the reconstruction must differ from both of the preceding, and so leads naturally to sequences *ay and *aw. The monophthongisation of tautosyllabic *ay and *aw is a common type of sound change; the similar change across a syllable boundary is much less common, but is attested in languages such as Toba Batak of northern Sumatra.

The ordering relationships are also simple and straightforward: in Lg. A *k > *h* must precede *g > *k*, since otherwise the two stops would have merged as *h*; in Lg. B *s > *h* had to precede *c > *s* for the same reason; in Lg. C *aw, ay > *o, e* is ordered before *o, *e > *u, i*, since the reverse of this would force us to assume that an identical raising of mid vowels had occurred twice in the history of the language, first for *o, *e, and later for the similar mid vowels that resulted from monophthongisation of *aw and *ay. In this case the ordering is motivated not by logical necessity, but by simplicity (Occam's razor).

SOLUTION TO RECONSTRUCTION PROBLEM 3

No.	Proto-AB	Lg. A	Lg. B	
01.	*popok	fofok	pupuk	stone
02.	*sunar	hunar	sunal	earth
03.	*kantay	katay	hante	tree
04.	*ule	ule	uli	branch
05.	*ləmət	ləmat	lomot	leaf
06.	*natal	natal	natal	root
07.	*tisəp	tihaf	tisop	grass
08.	*kino	kino	hinu	water
09.	*impət	ipat	impot	rain
10.	*aŋaw	aŋaw	aŋo	cloud
11.	*təpək	təfak	topok	sky
12.	*əlaŋ	əlaŋ	olaŋ	sun
13.	*wakor	wakor	wahul	moon
14.	*lipay	lifay	lipe	star
15.	*ekul	ekul	ihul	house
16.	*lukoŋ	lukoŋ	luhuŋ	roof
17.	*kusəp	kuhaf	husop	floor
18.	*opər	ofar	upol	door
19.	*luŋke	luke	luŋki	person
20.	*ulap	ulaf	ulap	man
21.	*mərəs	mərah	molos	woman
22.	*tunaw	tunaw	tuno	child
23.	*lampis	lapih	lampis	fish
24.	*roŋkup	rokuf	luŋkup	dog

1. Recurrent changes in Lgs. A and B in the order they are encountered are:

Change	Examples
Lg. A	
1. *p >f/[-nas]___ (before 3)	1, 7, 11, 14, 17, 18, 20, 24
2. *s > h	2, 7, 17, 21, 23
3. C > Ø/__C	3, 9, 19, 23, 24
4. *ə > a/__C#	5, 7, 9, 11, 17, 18, 21

Lg. B
1. *o/e > u/i (before 4, 5)   1, 4, 8, 13, 15, 16, 18, 19, 24
2. *r > l   2, 13, 18, 21, 24
3. *k > h/[-nas]__V   3, 8, 13, 15–17
4. *-ay/aw > e/o   3, 10, 14, 22
5. *ə > o   5, 7, 9, 11, 12, 17, 18, 21

Discussion. This is a relatively simple problem. Correspondences such as *f* : *p*, *h* : *s*, or *k* : *h* are easily resolved as lenitions of *p and *s in Lg. A, and of *k in Lg. B, either unconditionally or under conditions that are familiar from many of the world's languages (lenition of stops being more likely before vowels, and more likely to be blocked when the stop is prenasalised). The most challenging part of this problem probably is the reconstruction of *ə, as this involves two distinct correspondences, *ə* : *o* in the penult (where it is clearly distinct from *o), and *a* : *o* in the ultima (where it is clearly distinct from *a). An important methodological lesson illustrated by this feature is that sound correspondences that are in complementary distribution are to be treated as conditioned reflexes of the same proto-phoneme, just as phones that are in complementary distribution are to be treated as allophones of the same phoneme.

SOLUTION TO RECONSTRUCTION PROBLEM 4

No.	Proto-Tarawan	Taraw	Ikung	Sawe	
01.	*taya?	daya	taya	tara?	one
02.	*homel	omel	homey	omel	two
03.	*idam	iram	idam	idam	three
04.	*sibuŋ	sivuŋ	hibuŋ	sibuŋ	sun
05.	*kima	kima	kima	kima	star
06.	*yumo	yumo	yumo	rumo	wind
07.	*hius	yus	hiuh	ius	water
08.	*ŋiwi	ŋivi	ŋiwi	ŋiwi	grass
09.	*?ukub	ukuv	ukub	?ukup	stone
10.	*ŋurut	ŋurut	ŋurut	ŋulut	earth
11.	*ratis	rasis	ratih	latis	tree
12.	*u?ud	ur	uud	u?ut	bark
13.	*birol	virol	biroy	bilol	leaf
14.	*ayag	ayag	ayag	arak	flower
15.	*deŋu	reŋu	deŋu	deŋu	fruit
16.	*tawas	davas	tawah	tawas	rotten
17.	*mulat	mulat	muyat	mulat	angry
18.	*lisuk	lisuk	yihuk	lisuk	painful
19.	*bui?	vui	bui	bui?	swollen
20.	*?asom	asom	ahom	?asom	eat
21.	*wa?at	vat	waat	wa?at	drink
22.	*dabaw	ravaw	dabaw	dabo	walk
23.	*lewak	levak	yewak	lewak	sleep
24.	*tisab	sisav	tihab	tisap	think
25.	*uhay	way	uhay	ue	no/not
26.	*ratus	radus	ratuh	latus	because
27.	*ake	ake	ake	ake	perhaps
28.	*himas	imas	himah	imas	when

1. Recurrent changes in Taraw, Ikung and Sawe in the order they are encountered are:

Change	Examples

Taraw
1. *t > d/__V   1, 16, 26
2. *ʔ > Ø (before 8)   1, 9, 12, 19–21
3. *h > Ø (before 5)   2, 7, 25, 28
4. *d > r   3, 12, 15, 22
5. *b > v   4, 9, 13, 19, 22, 24
6. *i/u > y/w/#__V   7, 25
7. *t > s/__i (before 1)   11, 24
8. $V_1V_1 > V_1$ 12, 21

Ikung
1. *ʔ > Ø   1, 9, 12, 19–21
2. *l > y   2, 13, 17, 18, 23
3. *s > h   4, 7, 11, 16, 18, 20, 24, 26, 28

Sawe
1. *y > r/__V   1, 6, 14
2. *h > Ø   2, 7, 25, 28
3. *b,d,g > p,t,k/__#   9, 12, 14, 24
4. *r > l (before 1)   10, 11, 13, 26
5. *-aw/ay > o/e   22, 25

2. Phoneme inventory:

Consonants

	t	k	ʔ
b	d	g	
m	ŋ		
	s		h
	l,r		
w	y		

Vowels

i		u
e		o
	a	

3. Typological peculiarities: see Discussion.

Discussion. The reconstructions and sound changes in this problem do not require extensive discussion. Taraw shows lenition of *b and *d, and the only feature of this change that might occasion surprise is that it happens not only to syllable onsets but also to codas. Sawe shows final devoicing, which is found in many languages globally.

As for the inventory, it is not unusual for phoneme systems to lack /p/, which often lenites to *f, h* or zero. However, systems without /n/ are extremely rare (Maddieson 1984). Austronesian, with nearly 20 per cent of the world's languages, presents two examples: Palauan in western Micronesia, where *n has shifted to /l/, and Ontong Java/Luangiua, a Polynesian Outlier in the Solomon Islands, where *n has merged with /ŋ/. Consequently, both of these languages have /m/ and /ŋ/, but no /n/.

SOLUTION TO RECONSTRUCTION PROBLEM 5

No.	Proto-ABC	Lg. A	Lg. B	Lg. C	
01.	*lilliput	liliput	rilliput	rilliput	mythical country
02.	*linaraŋu	lilaranu	rinaraŋu	rirayanu	hailstone
03.	*rilolo	rilolo	riroro	yiroro	butterfly
04.	*ayato	ayaro	ayato	azayo	ghost
05.	*irrutup	irurup	irrutup	irruyup	shadow
06.	*ritoro	riroro	ritoro	yiyoyo	whirlwind
07.	*ŋallu	nalu	ŋallu	nallu	centipede
08.	*liliput	liliput	ririput	ririput	mushroom species
09.	*littolo	litolo	rittoro	rittoro	elf
10.	*rolollo	rololo	rorollo	yorollo	echo
11.	*raŋu	ranu	raŋu	yanu	stone
12.	*liroro	liroro	riroro	riyoyo	firefly
13.	*rittolo	ritolo	rittoro	yittoro	earthworm
14.	*liriput	liriput	ririput	riyiput	rainbow
15.	*lina	lila	rina	rira	rain
16.	*zinayak	zilayak	rinayak	zirazak	cannibal
17.	*rinna	rina	rinna	yinna	ant
18.	*rozorozo	rozorozo	rorororo	yozoyozo	bumblebee

1. Recurrent changes in Lgs. A, B and C in the order they are encountered are:

Change	Examples
Lg. A	
1. $C_iC_i > C_i$	1, 5, 7, 9, 10, 13, 17
2. *n > l/V__V (before 1, 3)	2, 15, 16
3. *ŋ > n	2, 7, 11
4. *t > r/V__V (before 1)	4–6
Lg. B	
1. *l > r	1–3, 8–10, 12–15
2. *z > r	16, 18

Lg. C

1. *l > r	1–3, 8–10, 12–15
2. *n > l/V__V (before 1, 4)	2, 15, 16
3. *r > y (before 1)	2–6, 10–14, 17, 18
4. *ŋ > n	2, 7, 11
5. *y > z (before 3)	4, 16
6. *t > r/V__V (before 3)	4–6

Discussion. This problem is included primarily to dazzle the eye with a number of similar but distinct forms. In keeping with its fanciful theme the data given here could hardly be an accurate reflection of phoneme frequency. They do, however, suggest some features of sound change in natural languages, in particular the tendency for geminates to resist lenitions that affect their singleton counterparts. In counting examples of changes it should be noted that *lina in comparisons 2 and 15 and *raŋu in comparisons 2 and 11 are repetitions of the same morphemes.

SOLUTION TO RECONSTRUCTION PROBLEM 6

No.	Proto-ABC	Lg. A	Lg. B	Lg. C	
01.	*piŋod	hiŋod	finot	piŋo	head
02.	*saray	sagay	salay	saɣe	eye
03.	*amuŋ	amuŋ	amun	amu	nose
04.	*butik	busik	putih	buti	ear
05.	*duɾi	duli	tuli	ɾuɾi	tooth
06.	*kənap	kənah	hənaf	kona	hand
07.	*ŋulu	ŋulu	nulu	ŋulu	elbow
08.	*tokaw	tokaw	tohaw	toko	belly
09.	*nesir	nesig	nesil	nesi	leg
10.	*waɾa	wala	wala	waɾa	water
11.	*udag	udag	utak	uɾa	stone
12.	*lilip	lilih	lilif	lili	grass
13.	*rulat	gulat	lulat	ɣula	hill
14.	*payas	hayas	fayas	paya	rain
15.	*aɾab	alab	alap	aɾa	wood
16.	*sage(l,ɾ)	sagel	sakel	sage	fire
17.	*ɾəfay	ləhay	ləfay	ɾofe	smoke
18.	*uriti	ugisi	uliti	uɣiti	ashes
19.	*tupək	tuhək	tufəh	tupo	hole
20.	*guan	guan	kuan	gua	snake
21.	*tiur	siug	tiul	tiu	bird
22.	*gabuŋ	gabuŋ	kapun	gabu	wing
23.	*uko(l,ɾ)	ukol	uhol	uko	feather
24.	*fikan	hikan	fihan	fika	egg

1. Recurrent changes in Lgs. A, B and C in the order they are encountered are:

Change   **Examples**

Lg. A
1. *p > f (before 2)   1, 6, 12, 14, 19
2. *f > h   1, 6, 12, 14, 17, 19, 24
3. *r > g   2, 9, 13, 18, 21

4. *t > s/__i   4, 18, 21
5. *ɾ > l   5, 10, 15, (16), 17, (23)

Lg. B
1. *p > f   1, 6, 12, 14, 19
2. *ŋ > n   1, 3, 7, 22
3. *b,d,g > p,t,k   1, 4, 5, 11, 15, 16, 20, 22
4. *r > l   2, 9, 13, 18, 21
5. *k > h (before 3)   4, 6, 8, 19, 23, 24
6. *ɾ > l   5, 10, 15, (16), 17, (23)

Lg. C
1. *C > Ø/__#   1, 3, 4, 6, 9, 11–16, 19–24
2. *r > γ   2, 13, 18
3. *-ay/aw > e/o (before 1)   2, 8, 17
4. *d > ɾ   5, 11
5. *ə > o   6, 17, 19

Discussion. This problem raises several questions. The first regards the change *p > *h* in Lg. A. Historical linguists sometimes use the word 'change' loosely for both change (an immediate transition from one state to another) and 'reflex' (the by-product of one or more changes). The reflex of Proto-ABC *p in Lg. A is *h*, but this does not necessarily correspond to a single change. Many languages exhibit various stages in the lenition sequence *p > *f* > *h* > zero (or just the last three parts of this sequence if *f* derives from some other source, as with Latin to the Romance languages). In the present case the fact that Proto-ABC *p and *f both became Lg. A *h* also favours the account that *p > *f*, and that *f from both sources then lenited to *h*.

    A second question may arise with respect to the *g* : *l* : γ correspondence. Since two of these reflexes are in the rear of the vocal tract (velar and uvular), while the third is much further forward (alveolar), a phoneme must be proposed that could plausibly produce both alveolar and velar/uvular reflexes. The most likely candidate for such a segment is an alveolar trill, since alveolar trills can become uvular (as in the history of French), and so give rise to uvular or velar consonants. Proto-ABC is thus reconstructed with two rhotics: a trill (*r) and a flap (*ɾ), not unlike modern Spanish. Although the IPA symbols [r] and [ɾ] have been adopted for the reconstructions in this problem, it is not common for historical linguists to use IPA symbols in reconstructions. Rather, typographical convenience often dictates the choice of symbols for proto-phonemes, so that the trill:tap contrast in this language might equally well be represented as *R vs. *r. It should be kept in mind that in most other problems in this workbook the symbol *r* is used indifferently for a tap or trill, as these two sounds are free variants in many languages.

A third question may arise with respect to the phoneme reconstructed as schwa. Since it is centrally located within the vowel space, a schwa can change to almost any other vowel. Austronesian languages, for example, show either conditioned or unconditioned changes of *ə > *a* (Isnag, Kapampangan, Banjarese, Makasarese), *ə > *e* (Malagasy, southern dialects of Ilokano), *ə > *o* (Subanon, Toba Batak, Proto-Oceanic), *ə > *i* (Tagalog when not adjacent to a syllable with *u*/*o*), *ə > *u* (Bisayan languages, Chamorro). If unambiguous evidence already exists for the reconstruction of each of these other vowels, a highly diverse vowel correspondence which overlaps with one or more of them is likely to point to an original mid-central vowel.

Finally, a parenthesis notation has been adopted to represent ambiguity in the choice of proto-segments. This is seen in *sage(l,ɾ) 'fire', and *uko(l,ɾ) 'feather', where the absence of information from Lg. C makes it impossible to determine whether the original final segment was a lateral or a rhotic flap. It should be noted in passing that a second type of ambiguity arises where information has been lost in a critical witness (where 'critical witness' means a language needed in order to know what might have happened before loss obliterated the record). In the present problem, did changes such as *r > γ or *d > *r* take place before the loss of final consonants in Lg. C (in which case the list of examples should include 1, 9 and 21), or after the loss of final consonants (in which case examples 1, 9 and 21 are irrelevant as illustrations of *r > γ or *d > ɾ)? To complicate matters further, without more information we cannot be certain that either of these changes was unconditioned. In the light of such multiple uncertainties the general convention has been adopted in this workbook of counting all examples of a sound change where a segment has disappeared without a trace as segment loss, without speculation about possible changes that occurred prior to obliteration of the record. For this reason the change *r > γ under Lg. C does not include examples 9 and 21, and the change *d > ɾ does not include example 1.

SOLUTION TO RECONSTRUCTION PROBLEM 7

No.	Proto-ABC	Lg. A	Lg. B	Lg. C	
01.	*sipak	sipak	sifah	hibak	hand
02.	*biraŋ	biraŋ	biraŋ	bilaŋ	foot
03.	*unus	unus	unus	unuh	knee
04.	*pusud	pusut	fusut	puhud	elbow
05.	*ubi	uvi	ubi	ubi	head
06.	*tukal	tukal	tuhal	tugal	hair
07.	*rasam	rasam	rasam	laham	eye
08.	*kalub	kalup	halup	kalub	nose
09.	*duŋu	duŋu	duŋu	duŋu	ear
10.	*iduk	iruk	iduh	iduk	mouth
11.	*surup	surup	suruf	hulup	tooth
12.	*baŋit	baŋit	baŋit	baŋit	tongue
13.	*dilap	dilap	dilaf	dilap	skin
14.	*pudi	puri	fudi	pudi	breast
15.	*atap	atap	ataf	adap	liver
16.	*labu	lavu	labu	labu	blood
17.	*bukas	bukas	buhas	bugah	water
18.	*badag	barak	badak	badag	earth
19.	*damar	damar	damar	damal	stone
20.	*arat	arat	arat	alat	river
21.	*lipid	lipit	lifit	libid	mountain
22.	*nalib	nalip	nalip	nalib	sky
23.	*dabag	davak	dabak	dabag	sun

1. Recurrent changes in Lgs. A, B and C in the order they are encountered are:

Change	Examples
Lg. A	
1. *b/d/g > p/t/k/__#	4, 8, 18, 21–23
2. *b/d > v/r/V__V	5, 10, 14, 16, 18, 23

Lg. B
1. *p/k > f/h (before 2)   1, 4, 6, 8, 10, 11, 13–15, 17, 21
2. *b/d/g > p/t/k/__#   4, 8, 18, 21–23

Lg. C
1. *s > h   1, 3, 4, 7, 11, 17
2. *p/t/k > b/d/g/V__V   1, 6, 15, 17, 21
3. *r > l   2, 7, 11, 19, 20

Discussion. In Lg. A *r and *d merged intervocalically as /r/ (2, 10, 11, 14, 18, 20); in addition, voiced and voiceless stops merged word-finally in both Lg. A and Lg. B (4, 6, 18, 21–23). Finally, in Lg. C voiced and voiceless stops merged intervocalically (1, 6, 15, 17, 21) and *r and *l merged in all positions (2, 6–8, 11, 13, 16, 19–22).

This is a very basic problem in which most reconstruction decisions can be made quickly by appeal to majority rule ($s : s : h$ // $r : r : l$ // $p : f : p$ // $v : b : b$), most natural development ($-t : -t : -d$ // $-p : -p : -b$ // $-k : -k : -g$), or both. Probably the most challenging sound correspondence is $p : f : b$ intervocalically (1, 21), but even this is quickly resolved in favour of *p, since the reconstruction of *b would imply intervocalic devoicing, and would conflict with the $v : b : b$ correspondence for which *b must be posited.

SOLUTION TO RECONSTRUCTION PROBLEM 8

No.	Proto-AB	Lg. A	Lg. B	
01.	*darakit	darak	rākit	head
02.	*ilaru	ilar	ilau	hair
03.	*tarip	tar	taip	eye
04.	*duris	dur	ruis	ear
05.	*munisa	munis	munisa	nose
06.	*akarun	akar	akaun	mouth
07.	*satilik	satil	satilik	tooth
08.	*kurudu	kurud	kūru	tongue
09.	*kuludu	kulud	kuluru	hand/arm
10.	*kuduru	kudur	kurū	body
11.	*pasiti	pasit	pasiti	foot/leg
12.	*tamus	tam	tamus	cloud
13.	*ratali	ratal	atali	water
14.	*rurutus	rurut	ūtus	sky
15.	*rutis	rut	utis	rain
16.	*ukuka	ukuk	ukuka	earth
17.	*tarira	tarir	taia	tree
18.	*ilara	ilar	ilā	grass
19.	*timanu	timan	timanu	fish
20.	*kuru	kur	kū	bird
21.	*iradat	irad	iarat	feather
22.	*duruku	duruk	rūku	dog

1. Recurrent changes in Lgs. A and B in the order they are encountered are:

Change	Examples
Lg. A	
1. *-V > Ø	1–22
2. *-C > Ø (before 1)	1, 3, 4, 6, 7, 12, 14. 15, 21

Lg. B

1. *r > Ø (before 2, 3)	1–4, 6, 8, 10, 13–15, 17, 18, 20–22
2. *d > r	1, 4, 8, 9, 10, 21, 22
3. ViVi > V̄	1, 8, 10, 1, 18, 20, 22

Discussion. Most problems in this workbook use artificial data, but this problem is more artificial than most, as it is designed to illustrate an important point of method in approaching the process of phonological reconstruction. The student who insists on what might be called 'serial reconstruction', where an explanation is sought for the first cognate set before moving to the second, and an answer to the second before moving to the third, will be frustrated with this set of data. How can /r/ correspond to /k/ in the first example, to /u/ in the second, and to who knows what in the third?

The point illustrated here is that a satisfactory reconstruction will be more likely to come quickly if one begins with comparisons that require minimal assumptions about change. In comparing *munis* to *munisa* (05), for example, we need only assume that Lg. A lost final vowels, and so posit *munisa, whereas comparing *darak* to *rākit* appears to involve too many changes to permit reconstruction without first doing considerably more groundwork. Following this procedure we can also reconstruct *pasiti (11), *ukuka (16), and *timanu (19). We then notice that examples such as *satil* : *satilik* (07) and *tam* : *tamus* (12) are identical except for the last -VC. By ordering the loss of final consonants before the loss of final vowels all of these forms can be explained from reconstructions that are essentially identical to the reflexes in Lg. B.

Once this much has been established, comparisons such as *ilar* : *ilau* (02), or *tar* : *taip* (03) become more transparent. Since we know that Lg. A has lost -V in some forms and -VC in others we can supply the lost segments in (02) and (03) and posit *ilaru and *tarip respectively, which in turn forces us to recognise the change *r > Ø in Lg. B. Keeping this single change in mind for Lg. B we can reconcile *akar* and *akaun* under the proto-form *akarun (06), *ratal* and *atali* (13) under *ratali, *rurut* and *ūtus* under *rurutus (14), *rut* and *utis* under *rutis (15), *tarir* and *taia* under *tarira (17), *ilar* and *ilā* under *ilara (18), and *kur* and *kū* under *kuru (20). The remaining comparisons now yield their secrets easily: *darak* : *rākit* must reflect *darakit, with *r > Ø in Lg. B followed by *d > r, and so on with all other examples that have not already been considered. Surprisingly, then, this problem, which appears virtually insoluble at first glance, involves only two sound changes in each language (three in Lg. B if the fusion of a sequence of identical vowels into a single long vowel is counted as a separate change).

What makes this problem difficult is an assumption that students are likely to carry into the analysis, namely that segments in corresponding positions correspond etymologically. It is this assumption that makes the comparison *darak* : *rākit* in the first example so difficult to process at first sight: a correspondence /d/ : /r/ is not problematic, but /r/ : /k/ and /k/ : /t/ are much more challenging. Moreover, the latter 'correspondences' are not recurrent, and there is no obvious way when considering this comparison in this light that the vowel length in Lg. B can be explained. It is for this reason that the whole matter becomes more tractable if one postpones these more complex comparisons and moves on to cases like *munis* : *munisa* as a first step in doing the reconstruction. In this way a set of firmly established hypotheses about change in one or the other language is established as a foundation upon which to build hypotheses about more complex cases such as *darak* : *rākit*. Stated another way, when faced with a very difficult set of forms that appear to be cognate one should begin by attacking at the weakest point – that is, those comparisons that require minimal assumptions about change. In this way the entire complex set of interconnecting phonological relationships will come apart like a ball of yarn that is unwound by pulling on a single string at a time.

SOLUTION TO RECONSTRUCTION PROBLEM 9

No.	Proto-Abaic	Abai	Soxun	Otile	
01.	*tilápa	təlapa	siráha	tilafa	water
02.	*supát	səpat	suhát	huva?	sky
03.	*mókay	mokay	móxay	moke	earth
04.	*súpat	supat	súhat	hufa?	tree
05.	*kúfan	kufan	xúhan	kufaŋ	root
06.	*iták	ətak	itáx	ida?	stone
07.	*tafín	təfin	tahín	taviŋ	dust
08.	*átola	atola	átora	atola	river
09.	*ítar	itar	ítar	itar	boat
10.	*rukáw	rəkaw	ruxáw	rugo	oar
11.	*atupú	təpu	atuhú	atuvu	rapids
12.	*itár	ətar	itár	idar	waterfall
13.	*kepú	kəpu	xehú	kevu	rainbow
14.	*isuté	səte	isuté	ihude	morning
15.	*lútip	lutip	rúsih	luti?	evening
16.	*ótum	otum	ótum	otuŋ	night

1. Recurrent changes in Abai, Soxun and Otile in the order they are encountered are:

Change	Examples
Abai	
1. stress is fixed on penult	1–16
2. V > ə/__(CV)CV́ (before 1, 3)	1, 2, 6, 7, 10–14
3. *ə > Ø/__CVCVC#	11, 14
Soxun	
1. *t > s/__i	1, 15
2. *l > r	1, 8, 15
3. *p > f (before 4)	1, 2, 4, 11, 13, 15
4. *f > h	1, 2, 4, 5, 7, 11, 13, 15
5. *k > x	3, 5, 6, 10, 13

Otile
1. stress is fixed on initial   1–16
2. *p > f (before 4)   1, 4
3. *s > h   2, 4, 14
4. *f, t, k > v, d, g/__V́   2, 6, 7, 10–14
5. *p, t, k > ʔ/__#   2, 4, 6, 15
6. *-ay,aw > e,o   3, 10
7. *m, n > ŋ/__#   5, 7, 16

Discussion. This problem is relatively straightforward once it is determined that Proto-Abaic had phonemic stress, and that the inherited stress
conditioned certain sound changes in Abai and Otile before it became fixed
in each of these languages. This is particularly evident in the case of minimal
pairs distinguished only by the placement of the accent, as with *supát 'sky'
and *súpat 'tree', or *ítar 'boat' and *itár 'waterfall'. Pretonic vowels in Abai
were weakened to schwa, and this schwa was then lost in initial position in the
antepenult. Soxun shows several natural lenitions, including a feeding relationship between *p > *f* and *f* > *h*. The most complicated set of changes
occurs in Otile, which has reduced the number of possible syllable codas to
just /ʔ/ and /ŋ/, monophthongised the sequences *-ay and *-aw, voiced all
obstruents before a stressed vowel, and then lenited *p and *s.

SOLUTION TO RECONSTRUCTION PROBLEM 10

No.	Proto-ABC	Lg. A	Lg. B	Lg. C	
01.	*praktum	pratum	praktum	prattũ	bread
02.	*sortino	sodino	surtiru	sottĩlo	wheat
03.	*unanino	unanino	urariru	ũlãlĩlo	oats
04.	*klotru	kloru	krutru	klottu	cow
05.	*grumbe	grumbe	grumbi	grũbe	milk
06.	*rimanaŋ	rimanaŋ	rimaran	rĩmãlã	sky
07.	*otrasu	orazu	utrasu	ottasu	rain
08.	*nuptini	nutini	ruptiri	luttĩli	water
09.	*blaraso	blarazo	brarasu	blaraso	flood
10.	*muktoni	mutoni	mukturi	sogoku	ditch
11.	*salakon	salagon	sarakur	salakõ	hill
12.	*razante	razande	razarti	razãtte	grass
13.	*dumaru	dumaru	urasi	dũmaru	tree
14.	*enonam	enonam	iruram	ẽlõlã	bark
15.	*sortine	sodine	surtiri	sottĩle	head
16.	*amanutu	amanudu	amarutu	ãmãlutu	eye
17.	*tampuŋi	tambuŋi	tampuni	tãppũni	ear
18.	*ogunama	ogunama	ugurama	ogũlãma	nose
19.	*serinom	serinom	sirirum	serĩlõ	skin
20.	*aradomu	aradomu	aradumu	aradõmu	hand
21.	*lundine	lundine	rurdiri	lũdĩle	liver
22.	*kopraŋa	koraŋa	kuprana	koppãna	lungs
23.	*lambesa	lambesa	rambisa	lãbesa	blood

1. Recurrent changes in Lgs. A, B and C in the order they are encountered are:

Change   **Examples**

Lg. A
1. C_1[-nas]C_2 > C_2/V__V   1, 2, 4, 7, 8, 10, 15, 22
2. *p,t,k,s > b,d,g,z/vd__vd (before 1)   2, 7, 9, 11, 12, 15–17

Lg. B

1. *o,e > u,i	2–5, 7, 9–12, 14, 15, 18–23
2. *n > l/ (before 1, 4)	2, 3, 6, 8, 10–12, 14–16, 18, 19, 21
3. *l > r	4, 9, 11, 21, 23
4. *ŋ > n	6, 17, 22

Lg. C

1. C_1C_2 > voiceless geminate/V__	1, 2, 4, 7, 8, 12, 15, 17, 22
2. V > Ṽ/__N (before 3, 4, 5)	1–3, 5, 6, 8, 11–23
3. C > Ø/__#	1, 6, 11, 14, 19
4. *n > l (before 6)	2, 3, 6, 8, 14–16, 18, 19, 21
5. N > Ø/__b,d (before 1)	5, 21, 23
6. *ŋ > n	17, 22

Discussion. This is a relatively easy problem. Probably the most difficult aspect is in stating the gemination rule for Lg. C, since the innovative geminate is sometimes a doubling of the second consonant in a cluster and sometimes of the first. In the solution adopted here this is expressed informally as postvocalic consonant clusters that contained a voiceless stop became voiceless geminate stops. Alternatively, gemination in Lg. C could be expressed by complementary rules: C_1C_2 > C_2C_2/V__ (for items 1, 2, 8, 12, 15, 17), and C_1C_2 > C_1C_1/V__ (for items 4, 7, 22). However, this formulation misses a useful generalisation, since what matters in determining the dominant member of a cluster appears to be consonant 'strength' (= degree of obstruction of the airstream) rather than position. The failure of prenasalised voiced stops to produce geminates parallel to the voiceless ones can be attributed to the universal problem of how to maintain voicing through exceptionally long closures.

SOLUTION TO RECONSTRUCTION PROBLEM 11

No.	Proto-ABC	Lg. A	Lg. B	Lg. C	
01.	*pusuk	pusu	fuhu?	puuku	earth
02.	*mane	mane	mane	mane	grass
03.	*kutil	kuti	?utir	kutili	root
04.	*raras	rara	rarah	raraa	worm
05.	*wayar	waya	wayar	wayara	beetle
06.	*tapin	tapi	tafin	tapini	water
07.	*luluk	lulu	ruru?	luluku	river
08.	*sasap	sasa	hahaf	aapa	rain
09.	*sapa	sapa	hafa	apa	flood
10.	*tiap	tia	tiaf	tiapa	sky
11.	*ulus	ulu	uruh	uluu	sun
12.	*susu	susu	huhu	uu	egg
13.	*nunuk	nunu	nunu?	nunuku	chicken
14.	*asap	asa	ahaf	aapa	feather
15.	*lipas	lipa	rifah	lipaa	bird
16.	*koris	kori	?orih	korii	fish
17.	*samir	sami	hamir	amiri	snake
18.	*nasiŋ	nasi	nahiŋ	naiŋi	house
19.	*leka	leka	re?a	leka	roof
20.	*piŋi	piŋi	fiŋi	piŋi	door
21.	*misas	misa	mihah	miaa	floor
22.	*pusal	pusa	fuhar	puala	hearth

1. Recurrent changes in Lgs. A, B and C in the order they are encountered are:

Change	Examples
Lg. A	
1. C > Ø/__#	1, 3–8, 10, 11, 13–18, 21, 22
Lg. B	
1. *p > f	1, 6, 8–10, 14, 15, 20, 22
2. *s > h	1, 4, 8, 9, 11, 12, 14–18, 21, 22

3. *k > ?   1, 3, 7, 13, 16, 19
4. *l > r   3, 7, 11, 15, 19, 22

Lg. C
1. *s > Ø   1, 4, 8, 9, 11, 12, 14–18, 21, 22
2. V*i*C > V*i*CV*i*   1, 3–8, 10, 11, 13–18, 21, 22

Discussion. This is a relatively easy problem, in that Lg. A shows only a
single change, and so preserves all phonemes of the proto-forms except the
final consonants, and Lg. C shows only two changes. The hardest part is
perhaps understanding that Lg. A has lost all final consonants and Lg. C has
added echo vowels, initially creating some uncertainty about the shape of
proto-forms. This is particularly true where Proto-ABC had a medial *s,
which was lost in Lg. C, and a final consonant, which was lost in Lg. A, giving
rise to misaligned sound correspondences, as in (8) *sasa* : *aapa* 'rain', (14) *asa* :
aapa 'feather', (18) *nasi* : *naiɲi* 'house', (21) *misa* : *miaa* 'floor', or (22) *pusa* : *puala*
'hearth'. Despite this minor complication there are no ordering requirements
(apart from assuming that *s > Ø passed through *s > *h* and *h > Ø), and
little else to create difficulty in finding a satisfactory solution.

SOLUTION TO RECONSTRUCTION PROBLEM 12

No.	Proto-ABC	Lg. A	Lg. B	Lg. C	
01.	*kulak	ʔulaʔ	hula	kurak	grass
02.	*hanupa	hanupa	honufa	anufa	earth
03.	*ruru	luru	ruru	ruru	water
04.	*tikapu	tiʔapu	tihofu	tikafu	rat
05.	*tomuru	tomuru	tomuru	tomuru	owl
06.	*tapis	tapis	tefis	tafis	feather
07.	*arun	arun	orun	arun	fish
08.	*lihek	liheʔ	lihe	riek	frog
09.	*hupak	hupaʔ	hufa	ufak	snake
10.	*pahiri	pahiri	fehiri	fairi	eagle
11.	*reraki	leraʔi	rerehi	reraki	hawk
12.	*kanup	ʔanup	honuf	kanuf	pig
13.	*laruk	laruʔ	loru	raruk	dog
14.	*kilala	ʔilala	hilala	kirara	tree
15.	*imiri	imiri	imiri	imiri	forest
16.	*lehiki	lehiʔi	lehihi	reiki	village
17.	*marurus	malurus	morurus	marurus	river
18.	*kanih	ʔanih	heni	kani	bridge
19.	*pasimi	pasimi	fesimi	fasimi	mountain
20.	*luruh	luruh	luru	ruru	cloud

1. Recurrent changes in Lgs. A, B and C in the order they are encountered are:

Change	Examples
Lg. A	
1. *k > ʔ	1, 4, 8, 9, 11–14, 16, 18
2. *r > l/__Vr	3, 11, 17
Lg. B	
1. *k > h (before 2)	1, 4, 8, 9, 11–14, 16, 18
2. *h > Ø/__#	1, 8, 9, 13, 18, 20
3. *a > o,e/__Cu,i	2, 4, 6, 7, 10–13, 17–19

4. *p > f   2, 4, 6, 9, 10, 12, 19

Lg. C
1. *l > r   1, 8, 13, 14, 16, 20
2. *h > Ø   2, 8–10, 16, 18, 20
3. *p > f   2, 4, 6, 9, 10, 12, 19

Discussion. This is a rather simple problem, with most changes occurring in Lg. B. The only real complications are the dissimilation of *rVr sequences in Lg. A, which complicates the correspondences of liquid phonemes, and the partial assimilation of *a to a high vowel in the following syllable in Lg. B, which complicates the reconstruction of *oCu and *eCi in examples 5 and 16. However, in both cases the conditions for these changes are clear, and should not present a problem in distinguishing *l from *r or *a from *e or *o. Perhaps the greatest difficulty is in distinguishing *rVr from *lVr, since the first of these dissimilated to *lVr* in Lg. A, and *l became *r* in Lg. C, producing the following correspondences, which leaves only Lg. B to distinguish the two:

	Lg. A	Lg. B	Lg. C
*rVr >	lVr	rVr	rVr
*lVr >	lVr	lVr	rVr

Here we must fall back on the basic principle that in many-to-one correspondences which are found in the same environment it is the language that makes distinctions not shown in the others that is most likely to reflect the original state of affairs (in this case Lg. B), since otherwise we would be forced to recognise an unconditioned phonemic split.

SOLUTION TO RECONSTRUCTION PROBLEM 13

No.	Proto-ABC	Lg. A	Lg. B	Lg. C	
01.	*kabata	xafata	kavata	ʔabata	earth
02.	*rasiŋ	rasiŋ	rahiŋ	rasiŋ	clay
03.	*pilak	filax	pilak	hilaʔ	mud
04.	*urani	urani	urani	urani	stone
05.	*tudap	tutaf	turap	tudah	hill
06.	*lanisa	lanisa	laniha	lanisa	tree
07.	*gupit	xufit	ɣupit	guhit	trunk
08.	*nayasa	nadᶻasa	nayaha	naasa	branch
09.	*siruki	siruxi	hiruki	siruʔi	leaf
10.	*lepika	lefixa	lepika	lehiʔa	fruit
11.	*dawap	tagʷaf	rawap	daah	bird
12.	*magulu	maxulu	maɣulu	magulu	snake
13.	*piʔat	fiʔat	piat	hiʔat	fish
14.	*bisan	fisan	vihan	bisan	dog
15.	*tinas	tinas	tinah	tinas	sky
16.	*siapa	siafa	hiapa	siaha	cloud
17.	*igaka	ixaxa	iɣaka	igaʔa	sun
18.	*ukub	uxuf	ukuv	uʔup	moon
19.	*yulug	dᶻulux	yuluɣ	uluk	star
20.	*hakulin	haxulin	akulin	haʔulin	rain
21.	*tihapa	tihafa	tiapa	tihaha	house
22.	*orosim	orosim	orohim	orosim	person
23.	*ʔukal	ʔuxal	ukal	ʔuʔal	man
24.	*pinid	finit	pinir	hinit	woman
25.	*watoʔ	gʷatoʔ	wato	atoʔ	child
26.	*pakig	faxix	pakiɣ	haʔik	old
27.	*rusud	rusut	ruhur	rusut	strong
28.	*sarib	sarif	hariv	sarip	weak

1. Recurrent changes in Lgs. A, B and C in the order they are encountered are:

Change	Examples
Lg. A	
1. *k > x	1, 3, 7, 9, 10, 12, 17, 18, 19, 20, 23, 26
2. *b > p (before 3)	1, 14, 18, 28
3. *p > f	1, 3, 5, 7, 10, 11, 13, 14, 16, 18, 21, 24, 26, 28
4. *d > t	5, 11, 24, 27
5. *g > k (before 1)	7, 12, 17, 19, 26
6. *y > dᶻ	8, 19
7. *w > gʷ	11, 25
Lg. B	
1. *b > v	1, 14, 18, 28
2. *s > h	2, 6, 8, 9, 14–16, 22, 27, 28
3. *d > r	5, 11, 24, 27
4. *g > γ	7, 12, 17, 19, 26
5. *ʔ > Ø	13, 23, 25
6. *h > Ø (before 2)	20, 21
Lg. C	
1. *k > ʔ	1, 3, 9, 10, 17, 18, 20, 23, 26
2. *p > h (before 5)	3, 5, 7, 10, 11, 13, 16, 21, 24, 26
3. *y > Ø	8, 19
4. *w > Ø	11, 25
5. *b/d/g > p/t/k/__#	18, 19, 24, 26–28

Discussion. This problem is relatively simple, since all sound correspondences are forced toward a particular proto-phoneme because of the improbability that a sound change would take place in the opposite direction. Thus, for the $x : k : ʔ$ correspondence in (1) neither *x > k nor *ʔ > k is as likely as *k > x or *k > ʔ. Similarly, in (2) *s > h is a change known from many languages, while *h > s is unattested in natural language data as an unconditioned sound change. Likewise, the correspondence $f : p : h$ in (3) shows the familar lenition sequence *p > f > h > Ø found in many language families.

Somewhat more challenging are the $f : w : b$ correspondence in (1), the $t : r : d$ correspondence in (5) and the $dz : y : \emptyset$ correspondence in (8) or the $gw : w : \emptyset$ in (11). However, common directions of sound change again suffice to lead us through each of these, since *b > f or *b > w is far more likely than *f > b or *w > b (although the latter is attested in a few languages), the $t : r : d$ correspondence cannot go back to *t, which produced $t : t : t$, or to *r, leaving *d as the only plausible choice, and $dz : y : \emptyset$ or $gw : w : \emptyset$ are correspondences we would expect from glide fortition in one language and glide elision in another, not from lenition of *dᶻ or *gʷ.

SOLUTION TO RECONSTRUCTION PROBLEM 14

No.	Proto-ABC	Lg. A	Lg. B	Lg. C	
01.	*tabih	təbe	tavi	tapeh	earth
02.	*ikuh	io	iku	ixoh	water
03.	*pərat	fərat	poraʔ	palat	wind
04.	*ilis	ilih	ilis	ilih	rain
05.	*lapoh	ləfo	lapo	lapoh	cloud
06.	*homaŋ	omaŋ	homaŋ	homaŋ	storm
07.	*dawəh	dəwə	rawo	tawah	mountain
08.	*kiso	iho	kiso	xiso	river
09.	*munti	munti	muti	mudi	stone
10.	*biləs	biləh	vilos	pilah	tree
11.	*ŋureh	ŋura	ŋure	ŋuleh	forest
12.	*rukih	rue	ruki	luxeh	house
13.	*aŋkuʔ	əŋko	akuʔ	aguh	village
14.	*tuləp	tuləf	tuloʔ	tulap	person
15.	*sompu	hompu	sopu	sobu	man
16.	*kahus	əuh	kahus	xahuh	woman
17.	*lidiʔ	lide	liriʔ	litih	child
18.	*kənes	ənah	kones	xaneh	dog
19.	*hepik	afe	hepiʔ	hepix	bird
20.	*tenuh	tano	tenu	tenoh	eat
21.	*ukam	uam	ukaŋ	uxam	drink
22.	*parin	fərin	pariŋ	palin	sleep
23.	*rəntək	rəntə	rotoʔ	ladax	dream
24.	*puʔiʔ	fue	puʔiʔ	puhih	wake up
25.	*usuk	uho	usuʔ	usux	stand
26.	*kota	ota	kota	xota	walk

1. Recurrent changes in Lgs. A, B and C in the order they are encountered are:

Change	Examples
Lg. A	
1. *a > ə/#(C)__ (before 7)	1, 5, 7, 13, 16, 22
2. *i,u > e,o/__h,ʔ# (before 3, 6, 8)	1, 2, 12, 13, 17, 19, 20, 24, 25
3. *h > Ø (before 6)	1, 2, 5–8, 11, 12, 16, 18, 19, 20, 23–26
4. *k > h/[-nas]__ (before 2, 3)	2, 8, 12, 16, 18, 19, 21, 23, 25, 26
5. *p > f/[-nas]__	3, 5, 14, 19, 22, 24
6. *s > h	4, 8, 10, 15, 16, 18, 25
7. *e > a	11, 18–20
8. *ʔ > Ø	13, 17, 24
Lg. B	
1. *b,d > v,r	1, 7, 10, 17
2. *h > Ø	1, 2, 5–7, 11, 12, 16, 19, 20
3. *ə > o	3, 7, 10, 14, 18, 23
4. *p,t, k > ʔ/__#	3, 14, 19, 23, 25
5. $C_1C_2 > C_2$	9, 13, 15, 23
6. *m,n > ŋ/__#	21, 22
Lg. C	
1. *b,d > p,t	1, 7, 10, 17
2. *i,u > e,o/__h# (before 5, 9)	1, 2, 12, 20
3. *k > x	2, 8, 12, 16, 18, 19, 21, 23, 25, 26
4. *ə > a	3, 7, 10, 14, 18, 23
5. *r > l	3, 11, 12, 22, 23
6. *s > h/__#	4, 10, 16, 18
7. *p,t,k > b,d,g/N__ (before 6, 8)	9, 13, 15, 23
8. $C_1C_2 > C_2$	9, 13, 15, 23
9. *ʔ > h	13, 17, 24

Discussion. The principal difficulty in this problem is the sets of overlapping vowel correspondences. The first vowel correspondence that is encountered is /ə/ : /a/ : /a/ in the first syllable of cognate set 1. Although it is possible that the original vowel was something other than *ə or *a there is little basis for assuming this. It therefore seems best to try to motivate a choice between these two proto-vowels. Comparison with example 3 and other items shows that the correspondences /ə/ : /a/ : /a/ and /a/ : /a/ : /a/ are in complementary distribution, the former occurring in initial syllables, and the latter in final syllables. It therefore seems best to reconstruct *a for the first of these sound correspondences, and to posit a conditioned change of *a > ə in non-final syllables.

The second vowel correspondence that is encountered in the first cognate set is /e/ : /i/ : /e/, and although majority rule may initially give the impression that this derives from *e, it can be seen that this correspondence is in complementary distribution with /i/ : /i/ : /i/ in items 4 or 9. It is therefore best to reconstruct *i for this correspondence, and to posit a conditioned sound change that lowered *i to e before a final h (which subsequently disappeared in Lg. A). The correspondence /o/ : /u/ : /o/ in comparison 2 parallels that of /e/ : /i/ : /e/ in comparison 1, and strengthens the hypothesis that high vowels lowered before final h in Lgs. A and C (with subsequent loss of the conditioning factor in Lg. A).

The sound correspondence /ə/ : /o/ : /a/ is distinct from any considered so far, and since it contrasts with /o/ : /o/ : /o/ in other comparisons and cannot be assigned to *a, it is best assigned to *ə. The correspondence /i/ : /i/ : /i/ in cognate set 4 initially appears to contradict /e/ : /i/ : /e/ in example 1, since Lg. C has a final h in both cases. However, Lg. B has final zero in comparison 1, but -s in comparison 4, and the absence of lowering before final h in this example can thus be attributed to ordering: high vowels lowered before final h, and *s then produced new instances of final h which did not trigger lowering. Supporting evidence for this interpretation appears in items 4 and 16, where high vowels also did not lower before final h from *s in Lgs. A or C.

The only other vowel correspondence that requires comment is /a/ : /e/ : /e/ in cognate sets 11, 18 and 19. Here *a can be excluded, since it has already been reconstructed for /ə/ : /a/ : /a/ (in initial or penultimate syllables) and /a/ : /a/ : /a/ (in final syllables). This leaves *e as the only viable choice, and forces us to conclude that in Lg. A *e > a.

SOLUTION TO RECONSTRUCTION PROBLEM 15

No.	Proto-ABCD	Lg. A	Lg. B	Lg. C	Lg. D	
01.	*liman	riman	liman	liman	limaŋ	hand
02.	*tunuʔ	tunuʔ	tono	tunu	tonoʔ	finger
03.	*kilay	hiray	kele	kilay	kele	nail
04.	*ikur	ihur	eko	ikuh	ekoh	joint
05.	*patik	fasik	patik	ranut	patiʔ	duck
06.	*sunir	hunir	hone	sunih	soneh	goose
07.	*ruki	ruhi	huki	huki	huki	mouth
08.	*ulip	urif	ulip	tamal	uliʔ	lip
09.	*uruk	pinuk	uhuk	uhuk	uhuʔ	tooth
10.	*liaw	riaw	leo	liaw	pisih	tongue
11.	*iris	irih	ihih	ihis	eheh	lip
12.	*tisiʔ	sihiʔ	tehe	tisi	teseʔ	saliva
13.	*nukaʔ	nuhaʔ	nuka	nuka	nukaʔ	head
14.	*pəsir	fəhir	pohe	pəsih	poseh	hair
15.	*tilit	sirit	arak	tilit	poloʔ	ear
16.	*kutun	hutun	kutun	kutun	kutuŋ	nose
17.	*susur	huhur	hoho	susuh	sosoh	neck
18.	*limət	rimət	lemot	limət	lemoʔ	arm
19.	*tapay	tafay	tape	tapay	tape	back
20.	*arut	arut	ahut	ahut	ahuʔ	boat
21.	*əray	əray	ohe	əhay	ohe	paddle
22.	*miruʔ	miruʔ	meho	mihu	mehoʔ	swim
23.	*sipas	hifah	hipah	sipas	sipah	float
24.	*ripaw	rifaw	hepo	hipaw	kala	drift
25.	*kalus	haruh	kaluh	kalus	kaloh	sink
26.	*sapiʔ	hafiʔ	hape	sapi	sapeʔ	drown
27.	*ulam	uram	ulam	ulam	ulaŋ	die
28.	*rukəp	ruhəf	hokop	hukəp	hokoʔ	bury

1. Recurrent changes in Lgs. A, B, C and D in the order they are encountered are:

Change	Examples
Lg. A	
1. *l > r	1, 3, 8, 10, 15, 18, 25, 27
2. *k > h/__V	3, 4, 7, 13, 16, 25, 28
3. *p > f	5, 8, 14, 19, 23, 24, 26, 28
4. *t > s/__i	5, 12, 15
5. *s > h (before 4)	6, 11, 12, 14, 17, 23, 25, 26
Lg. B	
1. *u,i > o,e/__ʔ,h# (before 2, 3, 6, 7)	2, 4, 6, 12, 14, 17, 22, 26
2. V > [-hi]/__(C)o,e	2–4, 6, 10, 12, 17, 18, 22, 24, 28
3. *ʔ > Ø	2, 12, 13, 22, 26
4. *-ay,aw > -e,o (before 2)	3, 10, 19, 21, 24
5. *r > h (before 1, 6)	4, 6, 7, 9, 11, 14, 17, 20–22, 24, 28
6. *h > Ø/__# (before 7)	4, 6, 14, 17
7. *s > h	6, 11, 12, 14, 17, 23, 25, 26
8. *ə > o (before 2)	14, 18, 21, 28
Lg. C	
1. *ʔ > Ø	2, 12, 13, 22, 26
2. *r > h	4, 6, 7, 9, 11, 14, 17, 20–22, 24, 28
Lg. D	
1. *n,m > ŋ/__#	1, 16, 27
2. *u,i > o,e/__ʔ,h# (before 3, 6)	2, 4, 6, 11, 12, 14, 17, 22, 25, 26
3. V > [-hi]/__(C)o,e	2–4, 6, 11, 12, 17, 18, 22, 28
4. *-ay > -e (before 3)	3, 19, 21
5. *r > h (before 2)	4, 6, 7, 9, 11, 14, 17, 20–22, 28
6. *p,t,k > ʔ/__#	5, 8, 9, 18, 20, 28
7. *s > h/__# (before 2)	11, 23, 25
8. *ə > o	14, 18, 21, 28

Note: forms not from the reconstructions are: Lg. A, no. 9, (*pinuk*), Lg. B, no. 15, (*arak*), Lg. C, nos. 5 and 8 (*ranut, tamal*) and Lg. D, nos. 10, 15 and 24 (*pisih, poloʔ, kala*).

Discussion. This is a relatively easy problem, since Lg. C has undergone only two changes, and provides much information about the earlier state of affairs. The major complication is that Lgs. B and D do not permit high vowels to co-occur with mid vowels in the same morpheme, and this has led to harmonic adjustments that increase the number of vowel correspondences. Ordering is also extremely important, since high vowels lower before word-final glottal stop and *h*, but the latter derives from both *r and *s in Lgs. B and D, with the difference that lowering before final laryngeals occurred before *s > *h* in Lg. B, but after this change in Lg. D.

SOLUTION TO RECONSTRUCTION PROBLEM 16

No.	Proto-ABC	Lg. A	Lg. B	Lg. C	
01.	*tápin	tepin	tapiŋ	tápin	head
02.	*ilák	irak	ila?	ilák	hair
03.	*úti	uti	uti	úri	eye
04.	*ipás	ifas	ipa	ipáh	ear
05.	*úlup	ulup	ulu?	úlup	nose
06.	*akúm	oxum	akuŋ	akúm	mouth
07.	*sípis	sipis	sipi	hípih	tooth
08.	*alán	aran	alaŋ	alán	tongue
09.	*ukú	uxu	uku	ukú	neck
10.	*lápal	rapan	lapal	lápal	shoulder
11.	*sálat	salat	sala?	hálat	hand
12.	*hákap	hakap	aka?	ákap	foot
13.	*ítip	itip	iti?	írip	man
14.	*átil	etin	atil	áril	woman
15.	*lákut	rokut	laku?	lákut	child
16.	*sukí	suxi	suki	hukí	father
17.	*híli	hili	ili	íli	mother
18.	*lupín	lufin	lupiŋ	lupín	house
19.	*pákis	fekis	paki	pákih	door
20.	*tulám	turam	tulaŋ	tulám	floor
21.	*kúas	xuas	kua	kúah	hearth
22.	*titák	titak	tita?	tirák	window

1. Recurrent changes in Lgs. A, B and C in the order they are encountered are:

Change	Examples
Lg. A	
1. stress becomes fixed	1–22
2. *a > e/o/__(C)i/u	1, 6, 14, 15, 19
3. *l > r/__V́ (before 1)	2, 8, 10, 15, 20
4. *p,k > f,x/__V́ (before 1)	4, 6, 9, 16, 18, 19, 21
5. *l > n/__#	10, 14

Lg. B

1. stress becomes fixed	1–22
2. *m,n > ŋ/__#	1, 6, 8, 18, 20
3. *p,t,k > ʔ/__#	2, 5, 11–13, 15, 22
4. *s > h/__# (before 5)	4, 7, 19, 21
5. *h > Ø	4, 7, 12, 17, 19, 21

Lg. C

1. *t > r/V__V	3, 13, 14, 22
2. *s > h	4, 7, 11, 16, 19, 21
3. *h > Ø (before 2)	12, 17

Discussion. This problem raises the issue of suprasegmental conditioning, a factor in sound change that was first clearly brought to the attention of linguists in the statement of 'Verner's law' (Verner 1875), which accounted for a number of cases previously treated as exceptions to Grimm's law.

The details of the present problem differ from those of that classic case, but it should be clear that /p : p : p/ and /f : p : p/ are in complementary distribution, the former occurring after and the latter before a stressed vowel. A parallel complementation is seen in the sound correspondences /k : k : k/ and /x : k : k/. Finally, two prevocalic correspondences involve liquids, /r : l : l/ (2, 8, 10, 15, 20) and /l : l : l/ (5, 11, 17, 18). These are also found to be non-contrastive, the former occurring before and the latter after a stressed vowel. If these correspondences are attributed to *l the proto-language will have a single liquid phoneme with one allophone. If instead they are attributed to *r it will be seen that *r is found only in non-final position but that *l must be reconstructed word-finally in items 10 and 14. Since the symbols *r and *l would then be in complementary distribution it would be necessary to unite them as a single proto-phoneme, and since there is no real option except to reconstruct *l word-finally this would have to be the symbol chosen for both sets of correspondences.

SOLUTIONS

SOLUTION TO RECONSTRUCTION PROBLEM 17

No.	Proto-ABC	Lg. A	Lg. B	Lg. C	
01.	*kilaru	kirru	cilar	kilalu	road
02.	*penaka	pekka	penak	penaga	hill
03.	*kusit	kuhit	kušit	kuhi?	meadow
04.	*lenapo	leppo	lenap	lenabo	grass
05.	*toloŋ	toloŋ	toloŋ	toloŋ	tree
06.	*ampaki	akki	ampac	appagi	branch
07.	*cirita	sitta	cirit	silida	root
08.	*tamiki	takki	tamic	tamigi	leaf
09.	*simiteŋ	hitteŋ	šimiteŋ	himideŋ	water
10.	*mukiso	musso	mucis	mugiho	wind
11.	*uluro	urro	ulur	ululo	sky
12.	*rucinu	runnu	rucin	lusinu	sun
13.	*soika	hoika	soik	hoiga	cloud
14.	*iras	irah	iras	ilah	river
15.	*hakiti	atti	hacit	agidi	rain
16.	*umala	ulla	umal	umala	man
17.	*cotaki	sokki	cotac	sodagi	woman
18.	*lohak	loak	lohak	loa?	child
19.	*puntilu	pullu	puntil	puttilu	give
20.	*kiacep	kiasep	ciacep	kiase?	think
21.	*sambuka	hakka	sambuk	hambuga	eat
22.	*iŋgapa	ippa	iŋgap	iŋgaba	sleep
23.	*silihu	hiliu	šilihu	hiliu	dream
24.	*toŋkato	totto	toŋkat	tokkado	wake up
25.	*siman	himan	šiman	himaŋ	yawn

1. Recurrent changes in Lgs. A, B and C in the order they are encountered are:

Change	Examples
Lg. A	
1. V > Ø/VC__CV (before 2)	1, 2, 4, 6–12, 15–17, 19, 21–24
2. $C_1C_2 > C_2C_2$ (before 3)	1, 2, 4, 6–12, 15–17, 19, 21–24
3. *s > h (before 5)	3, 9, 10, 13, 14, 21, 23, 25
4. C > Ø/__C (before 1)	6, 19, 21, 22, 24
5. *c > s	7, 12, 17, 20
6. *h > Ø (before 3)	15, 18, 23
Lg. B	
1. *k,s > c,š /__i (before 2)	1, 3, 6, 8–10, 15, 17, 20, 23, 25
2. –V > Ø	1, 2, 4, 6–8, 10–13, 15–17, 19, 21–24
Lg. C	
1. *r > l	1, 7, 11, 12, 14, 16
2. *p,t,k > b,d,g/V__V	2, 4, 6–10, 13, 15, 17, 21, 22, 24
3. *s > h (before 7)	3, 9, 10, 13, 14, 21, 23, 25
4. *p,t,k > ʔ/__#	3, 18, 20
5. *n > ŋ/__#	5, 25
6. *mp,nt,ŋk > pp,tt,kk	6, 19, 24
7. *c > s	7, 12, 17, 20
8. *h > Ø (before 3)	15, 18, 23

Discussion. Probably the most difficult feature of this problem is the mismatch in phoneme correspondence slots that is created by medial vowel syncope in Lg. A, which produced numerous geminates, and final vowel loss in Lg. B, so that comparisons such as Lg. A *killu* : Lg. B *cilar*, or Lg. A *musso* : Lg. B *mucis* provide no immediate clue to which phonemes correspond. Lg. C, which preserves all syllables from the proto-language, helps with this situation, so that it can gradually be untangled. The sound changes themselves are all quite natural, and widely attested in the world's languages.

SOLUTION TO RECONSTRUCTION PROBLEM 18

No.	Proto-Makuan	Mok	Kuma	Ilaka	
01.	*patik	pahik	fahik	kepede	man
02.	*sunbi	hunbi	sumbi	kiubbi	woman
03.	*tita	hita	tiha	ketede	child
04.	*ramti	ramhi	hanti	keledde	house
05.	*utia	uhia	uhia	keodee	chicken
06.	*alu	alu	aru	keolo	dog
07.	*tara	tara	taha	ketele	bird
08.	*satuŋ	hatuŋ	sahuŋ	keodo	water
09.	*bari	bari	bahi	kebele	tree
10.	*idap	idap	ihaf	keere	root
11.	*kasap	kahap	kasaf	kekee	stone
12.	*tapi	tapi	tafi	tebe	drink
13.	*suru	huru	suhu	ulu	eat
14.	*taŋtaŋ	taŋtaŋ	tantaŋ	tadda	walk
15.	*rasi	hari	hasi	lee	speak
16.	*lisua	lihua	risua	leoo	sit
17.	*siba	hiba	siba	ebe	stand
18.	*unda	unda	unda	oddo	black
19.	*tinti	hinhi	tinti	tiddi	white
20.	*rapu	rapu	hafu	lobo	red
21.	*dumpat	dumpat	dumfat	dobbo	yellow
22.	*padis	padih	fahis	pere	green/blue

1. Recurrent changes in Mok, Kuma and Ilaka in the order they are encountered are:

Change	Examples
Mok	
1. *t > s/__i (before 2)	1, 3–5, 19
2. *s > h	1–5, 8, 11, 13, 15–17, 19, 22

Kuma

1. *p > f	1, 10–12, 20–22
2. *t > d/V__V (before 3)	1, 3, 5, 8
3. *d > r/V__V (before 4)	1, 3, 5, 8, 10, 22
4. *r > h (before 6)	1, 3–5, 7–10, 13, 15, 20, 22
5. nasal place assimilation	2, 4, 14
6. *l > r	6, 16

Ilaka

1. HL/LH/HM/MH/ML > MM	1, 3–6, 8–10, 12, 15–18, 20–22
2. *p,t > b,d/[+voice]__[+voice] (before 5)	1, 3–5, 8, 12, 14, 19–21
3. C > Ø/__#	1, 8, 10, 11, 14, 21, 22
4. *s > Ø	2, 8, 11, 13, 15–17, 22
5. *NC$_i$ > C$_i$C$_i$	2, 4, 14, 18, 19, 21
6. *r > l (before 8)	4, 7, 9, 13, 15, 20
7. *ea > æ	7, 11
8. *d > r/V__V (before 2)	10, 22

2. The form that shows metathesis is item 15 in Mok.

Discussion. A major source of complexity in this problem is that *t has conditioned reflexes in all three languages. In Mok *t became *s* before a high front vowel, a type of change (assibilation) that is common in Austronesian, as well as in Finnic languages. In Kuma *t became *r* intervocalically, a type of flapping like that in American English. In both languages these changes were followed by further lenition (*s > h in Mok, a sound change found in many languages, *r > h in Kuma, a less common type of sound change, but one found in e.g. the northeastern dialect of Brazilian Portuguese, where it affects the trilled rhotic of the standard language). This resulted in the following correspondences, all originating from simple or prenasalised *t:

	Initial	Intervocalic	Postnasal
Before *i*	h : t : t	h : h : d	h : t : dd
Before other vowels	t : t : t	t : h : d	t : t : dd

SOLUTIONS

The problem with these six sets of sound correspondences is to recognise that they are in complementary distribution, and therefore must be assigned to a single proto-phoneme. A careful analysis of the sound correspondences will also show that the changes to *t in this problem are constructed so as to present the false impression that item number 3 in Mok (*hita* 'child') has transposed the consonants. The true example of metathesis (*hari* 'speak' in Mok) is well concealed, since comparison with *hasi* in Kuma superficially suggests that these languages retain the same original order of consonants. However, analysis of the sound correspondences exposes this as impossible.

A second, if somewhat more obvious source of complexity in this problem is the appearance of a nominal prefix in Ilaka which must be separated from the base before the sound correspondences can be properly understood.

A third source of complexity is the mutual assimilation of high-low or low-high vowels in adjacent syllables, producing mid vowels in Ilaka that agree in frontness with the Proto-Makuan high vowels. The result is a system of vowel harmony in which all vowels within a word must be high, mid, or low. Although it is not a focus of the present analysis, this constraint on vowel co-occurrence has also given rise to allomorphy in the nominal prefix /ke-/ or /ki-/, the underlying shape of which is indeterminate on the basis of the evidence given here.

Most other aspects of this problem have a more straightforward solution. The temptation to posit *tida rather than *tita for (3) is thwarted by the *d* : *h* : *r* correspondence in (10) and (22), and the *d* : *d* : *d* correspondence in (21), both of which require *d, and so eliminate this possibility in (3).

SOLUTIONS

SOLUTION TO RECONSTRUCTION PROBLEM 19

No.	Proto-ABCD	Lg. A	Lg. B	Lg. C	Lg. D	
01.	*beřin	beřen	biřin	belin	biri	sun
02.	*pukul	fukul	pugul	pukun	pugu	rain
03.	*parnak	fanak	pannak	panhak	parna	cloud
04.	*řiuk	řiuk	řiuk	liuk	riu	sky
05.	*salpo	safo	sappu	xanpo	salbu	wind
06.	*kurtiŋ	kutiŋ	huttiŋ	kuthiŋ	kurdi	earth
07.	*etur	etoř	idur	etuh	idu	water
08.	*kalpit	kafit	happit	kanpit	kalbi	grass
09.	*rontu	řoto	ruttu	hontu	rundu	flower
10.	*sipal	sifal	sibal	xipan	siba	stone
11.	*muton	mutun	mudun	muton	mudu	bird
12.	*pogos	fogos	pugus	pogox	pugu	feather
13.	*iboř	ibuř	ibuř	ibol	ibu	snake
14.	*lelpem	lefem	lippim	nenpem	lilbi	house
15.	*impat	ifat	ippat	impat	imba	person
16.	*urmol	umul	ummul	umhon	urmu	man
17.	*odin	oden	udin	odin	udi	woman
18.	*rameti	řamete	ramidi	hameti	ramidi	child
19.	*serti	sete	sitti	xethi	sirdi	hand
20.	*siřte	siti	sitti	xilte	sirdi	root
21.	*sorup	sořof	surup	xohup	suru	tree
22.	*ilur	iluř	ilur	inuh	ilu	leaf

1. Recurrent changes in Lgs. A, B, C and D in the order they are encountered are (MH = mid-high, MM = mid-mid, HM = high-mid, HH = high-high):

Change	Examples
Lg. A	
1. vowel harmony: MH > MM, HM > HH	1, 7, 9, 11, 13, 16–21
2. *p > f	2, 3, 5, 8, 10, 12, 14, 15, 21
3. C > Ø/__C	3, 5, 6, 8, 9, 14–16, 19, 20
4. *r > ř	7, 9, 18, 21, 22

Lg. B
1. *e,o > i,u   1, 5, 7, 9, 11–14, 16–21
2. *p,t,k > b,d,g/V__V   2, 7, 10, 11, 18
3. $C_1C_2 > C_2C_2$ 3, 5, 6, 8, 9, 14–16, 19, 20
4. *k > h/#__   6, 8

Lg. C
1. *ř > l   1, 4, 13, 20
2. *l > n (before 1)   2, 5, 8, 10, 14, 16, 22
3. *r > h (before 4)   3, 6, 7, 9, 16, 18, 19, 21, 22
4. *hC > Ch   3, 6, 16, 19
5. *s > x   5, 10, 12, 19–21

Lg. D
1. *e,o > i,u   1, 5, 7, 9, 11–14, 16–21
2. *ř > r   1, 4, 13, 20
3. C > Ø/__#   1–4, 6–8, 10–17, 21, 22

Discussion. This is a moderately difficult problem. Perhaps the greatest challenge is the reconstruction of the vowels, since the harmonic height adjustment in Lg. A and the general raising of mid vowels in Lgs. B and D creates a much wider range of vowel correspondences than would otherwise exist. The development of the vowels in Lg. A requires particular attention, since high and mid vowels are not tolerated in the same word, and this constraint is satisfied by adjusting the height of the second vowel to that of the first, regardless of which is higher.

One other complication that causes some difficulty in this problem is the existence of two rhotics in the proto-language, one a tap and the other a trill. The distinction between these is lost in Lgs. A and D, in the first case through merger as the tap and in the second case through merger as the trill. Languages B and C retain the distinction, the first of these in its original phonetic form, and in the second with changes in articulation.

Finally, consonant clusters reduce in Lg. A, produce geminates in Lg. B, and metathesise *h*C to C*h* in Lg. C, all of which increases the difficulty of inferring their original shapes.

SOLUTION TO RECONSTRUCTION PROBLEM 20

No.	Proto-ABC	Lg. A	Lg. B	Lg. C	
01.	*pitak	piraʔ	pitak	fidaʔ	many
02.	*raŋis	raŋih	lanis	laŋis	few
03.	*andip	adiʔ	andip	andif	alone
04.	*hiraŋ	iraŋ	hilan	hilaŋ	how many?
05.	*saku	hagu	saku	saʔu	when?
06.	*awat	agʷaʔ	oat	aat	how?
07.	*muntu	mutu	mundu	muttu	where?
08.	*sisilan	hihilan	sisilan	sisinaŋ	what?
09.	*buret	bureʔ	bulit	bulet	alive
10.	*timpo	tipo	timbu	dippo	dead
11.	*uzal	usal	udal	uzan	road
12.	*kalita	kalira	kalita	ʔanida	dust
13.	*buyut	buzuʔ	buyut	buut	weeds
14.	*raraku	raragu	lalaku	lalaʔu	locust
15.	*ŋeri	ŋeri	nili	ŋeli	cricket
16.	*luɲisi	luɲihi	lunisi	nuɲisi	honeybee
17.	*lubus	luvuh	lubus	nubus	ant
18.	*modan	moran	muran	modaŋ	dog
19.	*kulum	kulun	kulum	ʔunuŋ	forest
20.	*zipor	sivor	divul	zifon	tree
21.	*suhuk	huuʔ	suhuk	suhuʔ	branch
22.	*pihis	piih	pihis	fihis	leaf
23.	*isim	ihin	isim	isiŋ	fruit
24.	*wayan	gʷazan	wean	aaŋ	eat
25.	*humbaŋ	ubaŋ	humban	humbaŋ	drink
26.	*kohuz	kous	kuhud	ʔohuz	sleep
27.	*ibas	ivah	ibas	ibas	wake up
28.	*duyal	duzal	ruyal	duan	sit
29.	*hatis	arih	atis	adis	stand
30.	*saŋkup	hakuʔ	saŋgup	sakkuf	talk
31.	*idus	iruh	irus	idus	walk
32.	*tunaya	tunaza	tunea	dunaa	fall

1. Recurrent changes in Lgs. A, B and C in the order they are encountered are:

Change	Examples
Lg. A	
1. *p,t,k > b,d,g/V__V (before 4, 9)	1, 5, 12, 14, 20, 29
2. *b,d > v,r/V__V	1, 12, 17, 18, 20, 27, 29, 31
3. *p,t,k > ʔ/__#	1, 3, 6, 9, 13, 21, 30
4. *s > h (before 7)	2, 5, 8, 16, 17, 21–23, 27, 29–31
5. *N > Ø/__C	3, 7, 10, 25, 30
6. *h > Ø (before 3)	4, 21, 22, 25, 26, 29
7. *w > gʷ	6, 24
8. *z > s (before 8)	11, 20, 26
9. *y > z	13, 24, 28, 32
Lg. B	
1. *r > l (before 7)	2, 4, 9, 14, 15, 20
2. *ŋ > n/__[-cons]	2, 4, 15, 16, 25
3. *aw,ay > o,e	6, 24, 32
4. *p,t,k > b,d,g/N__	7, 10, 30
5. *e,o > i,u (before 3)	9, 10, 15, 18, 20, 26
6. *z > d	11, 20, 26
7. *d > r/[-nas]__ (before 6)	18, 28, 31
Lg. C	
1. *p > f/[-nas]__	1, 3, 20, 22, 30
2. *(-)t- > d/[-nas]__	1, 10, 12, 29, 32
3. *k > ʔ/[-nas]__	1, 5, 12, 14, 19, 21, 26
4. *r > l	2, 4, 9, 14, 15, 20
5. *w,y > Ø	6, 13, 24, 28, 32
6. *mp,nt,ŋk > pp,tt,kk	7, 10, 30
7. *m,n > ŋ/__# (before 8)	8, 18, 19, 23, 24
8. *l > n (before 4)	8, 11, 12, 16, 17, 19, 28

Discussion. For several of the sound correspondences encountered in this problem the 'majority rule' principle is of no avail. Rather, the solution is forced by a consideration of similar but distinct correspondences found in the same environment. The correspondence $r : t : d$ in the first cognate set, for example, could in principle derive from either *t or *d, but the matter is resolved in favour of *t once the $r : r : d$ correspondence is seen in number 18, since this can only plausibly be attributed to *d. Confidence in this solution is reinforced by other observations: the reconstruction of *-d- in this word would force us to posit intervocalic devoicing – an attested, but rare type of sound change. Furthermore, the intervocalic reflexes of *p and *k also show a pattern of assimilation to neighbouring vowels in either voicing, or both the voicing and continuant features.

Other details of this problem that may delay reconstruction are the correspondences $h : z : s$ and $s : d : z$. Because both of these correspondence sets contain s and z, the distinction between them must be based entirely on the presence of h in the former vs. d in the latter. Since *s > h is an extremely common sound change in many language families the odds favour *s as the source of the first correspondence, leaving something very similar to *s as the source of the second correspondence. Since *d has already been pre-empted it is ruled out, and the fact that d is one of the reflexes of this proto-phoneme also suggests that it was voiced. The only plausible choice, then, is *z.

Finally, the correspondence $z : y : Ø$ (or $z : Ø : Ø$) cannot reflect *z, since this symbol has already been chosen to represent the correspondence $s : d : z$. This leaves us with a proto-phoneme that was equally likely to undergo fortition or lenititon, a hallmark of the glides in many language families. A plausible source for $z : y : Ø$, then, would be *y, and this choice is further supported by reflexes of *w, which undergo fortition in Lg. A, partial fusion with adjacent vowels in Lg. B, and loss in Lg. C.

SOLUTION TO RECONSTRUCTION PROBLEM 21

No.	Proto-Loniu-Lou	Wuvulu	Loniu	Lou	
01.	*palu	palu	pan	pol	dove sp.
02.	*lisa	lita	lis	lis	nit, louse egg
03.	*taliŋa-	ʔalia	taliŋa-	teliŋa-	ear
04.	*cala	tala	can	sal	path
05.	*ñatu	naʔu	ñat	not	tree sp.
06.	*nohu	nofu	noh	noh	stonefish
07.	*laŋo	lao	laŋ	laŋ	housefly
08.	*sake	tae	sak	sak	climb
09.	*loto	loʔo	lot	lot	abscess
10.	*taŋi	ʔai	taŋ	teŋ	cry, weep
11.	*kutu	uʔu	kut	kut	louse
12.	*ahi	afi	ah	eh	fire
13.	*peka	bea	pek	pek	fruit bat
14.	*natu-	naʔu	natu-	notu-	child
15.	*kani	ani	kan	ken	eat
16.	*manu	manu	man	monmon	bird
17.	*tasi	ʔaki	tas	tes	saltwater
18.	*mati	maʔi	mat	met	low tide
19.	*mate	maʔe	mat	mat	die, dead

1. Recurrent changes in Loniu and Lou in the order they are encountered are:

Change	Examples
Loniu	
1. V > Ø /__# (before 2)	all but 3, 14
2. *l > n/__#	1, 4
Lou	
1. *a > e, o/__Ci, u (before 2)	1, 3, 5, 10, 12, 14–18
2. V > Ø /__#	all but 3 and 14
3. *c > s	4
4. *ñ > n 5	

Discussion. The first question this solution raises is how we can reconstruct final vowels for Proto-Loniu-Lou (PLL) when neither language retains them. Loniu and Lou have five correspondences with identical vowels, *a* : *a*, *e* : *e*, *o* : *o*, *i* : *i*, *u* : *u*, and for these we have no choice but to posit *a, *e, *o, *i and *u. However, there are also two vowel correspondences with dissimilar segments:

Loniu *a* : Lou *e*
Loniu *a* : Lou *o*

The question arises, then, whether it is necessary to posit two additional vowels *ɛ and *ɔ (or something similar) in penultimate position. This approach would miss an important generalisation, namely that the sixth and seventh vowels would be posited in penultimate position only where Wuvulu has *a* followed by a high vowel in the next syllable. Perhaps the most obvious examples of this correlation are seen in the words for 'ear' and 'child', which have preserved a last-syllable high vowel in Loniu and Lou due to obligatory suffixation. A solution that accounts for the correspondences Wuvulu *aCi* : Loniu *a* : Lou *e*, and Wuvulu *aCu* : Loniu *a* : Lou *o* by regressive height assimilation in items 3 and 14 can then be extended to other examples of this correspondence, forcing the conclusion that final high vowels must have been retained in the ancestor of Loniu and Lou (and other languages of the eastern Admiralty Islands).

This reconstruction raises another point of method. If *a, *e, *o, *i and *u are posited for PLL and every vowel could occur in either syllable of a two-syllable form, there are twenty-five possible combinations of vowels in two-syllable words:

1. aCi	6. eCi	11. oCi	16. iCi	21. uCi
2. aCu	7. eCu	12. oCu	17. iCu	22. uCu
3. aCe	8. eCe	13. oCe	18. iCe	23. uCe
4. aCo	9. eCo	14. oCo	19. iCo	24. uCo
5. aCa	10. eCa	15. oCa	20. iCa	25. uCa

Only patterns 1 and 2 could leave a trace of the earlier final high vowel. If a final vowel is reconstructed in e.g. *palu (pattern 2), but not in *lis (pattern 20), or *cal (pattern 5), it implies that final vowels were lost *only when it was not possible for them to leave a trace on the surviving penultimate vowel*. It is obvious that this cannot be a condition on sound change, but must instead be a condition on the nature of evidence (direct vs. indirect). If we take the Regularity Hypothesis seriously, then, we must reconstruct final vowels for items 1–19, and hypothesise that *all* final vowels disappeared following the break-up of

PLL, since to do otherwise would introduce unconditioned phonemic splits that correlate with the difference between conditions that preserved a trace vs. those that did not.

Why must we assume that the loss of final vowels was independent (hence a 'drift') in Loniu and Lou? This follows from the need to assume chronological ordering to explain the *a* : *e* and *a* : *o* vowel correspondences. In Loniu a single change took place: (1) loss of final vowels. In Lou two changes took place: (1) regressive height assimilation, and (2) loss of final vowels. If change (2) had preceded change (1) in Lou we would have no way to account for *e* or *o* corresponding to Loniu *a* just in those cases where Wuvulu has -*aCi* or -*aCu*. Final vowels must, therefore, have been present in PLL and must have persisted in Lou at least until regressive height assimilation had taken place.

This problem illustrates the need for 'inverted reconstruction' (Anttila [1972, 1989] 2009), or 'reconstruction from the top down' (Blust 1972: 1) in dealing with conditioned changes where the condition has been lost by subsequent change. The best-known example of this principle is undoubtedly Verner's law, which is often cited as important in showing the role of suprasegmental conditioning, but which is equally important in showing how inverted reconstruction can fill gaps that a strictly inductive approach will leave unfilled.

In addition, the loss of final vowels must have happened *independently* in Loniu and Lou, since in Lou this change had to follow the partial assimilation of *a to a high vowel in the next syllable, a change that did not take place in Loniu.

Finally, the reconstruction of final vowels that left no trace (all patterns except 1 and 2) provides a general lesson in scientific method. The philosopher Karl Popper argued that the essential distinction between statements that are part of science and those that are assigned to what he called 'metaphysics'depends on falsifiability. If a statement can be falsified it is subject to the hypothetico-deductive method and is part of the discourse of science. If it cannot be falsified it remains in the shadowy domain of metaphysics. In Popper's terms, then, the reconstruction of final vowels in forms such as *lisa 'nit, louse egg', *nohu 'stonefish' or *laŋo 'housefly' is not part of science. However, rejecting this reconstruction entails rejecting the Regularity Hypothesis, and it clearly seems preferable to argue that some statements which cannot be falsified are speculations pure and simple, but others follow from the application of general principles.

A similar problem arises in connection with the reconstruction of final consonants in Proto-Oceanic (POC), a descendant of Proto-Malayo-Polynesian (PMP) that was itself ancestral to around 460 Austronesian languages of the

Pacific. About 90 per cent of these languages have lost final consonants, but the others retain them either through the addition of an echo vowel, or through the addition of a fixed supporting vowel -*a*. It follows that POC must have retained PMP final consonants, but for many cognate sets relevant forms are available only in an Oceanic language that has lost final consonants and a non-Oceanic language that has retained them. Compare the following:

No.	PMP	POC	Mussau	Fijian	
1.	*bulan	*pulan	ulana	vula	'moon'
2.	*uRat	*uRat	ueta	ua	'vein'
3.	*laŋən	*laŋon	—	laŋo	'roller for canoe'
4.	*laŋit	*laŋit	—	laŋi	'sky'

In 1 and 2 final consonants can be posited for POC on the basis of 'inductive' evidence, since at least some Oceanic languages (such as Mussau) preserve reflexes of them. However, in comparisons 3 and 4 final consonants can be posited for POC only by enforcing the Regularity Hypothesis: *if* a reflex of these forms (or others like them) were available in a language that retains PMP final consonants, it should provide direct evidence, and so permit the POC final consonant to be inferred inductively.

SOLUTION TO RECONSTRUCTION PROBLEM 22

No.	Proto-ABCD	Lg. A	Lg. B	Lg. C	Lg. D	
01.	*xʷɛtəs	hʷɛtəs	hʷɛtəs	xʷɛtəs	wetɨs	snow
02.	*ʔitnɔh	itnɔh	ʔitnɔh	hitnɔh	ʔitnoʔ	ice
03.	*qtil	qtil	qtin	ʔčil	qtil	freeze
04.	*snɛhʷa	nɛhʷa	snɛhʷa	snɛhʷa	snewa	storm
05.	*wahɔ	wahɔ	wahɔ	wahɔ	aʔo	wind
06.	*nxul	nhul	nhun	nxul	nxul	fog
07.	*skʷakʷə	kʷakʷə	sxʷaxʷə	skʷakʷə	sgʷagʷɨ	rain
08.	*faxʷəl	fahʷəl	hahʷən	faxʷəl	fawɨl	fire
09.	*ihʷə	ihʷə	ihʷə	ihʷə	iwɨ	bird
10.	*ayuq	ayuq	ayuq	ayuʔ	auq	fish
11.	*suqox	suqoh	suqoh	suʔox	suqox	seal
12.	*wuʔuf	wuuf	wuʔuh	wuhuf	uʔuf	whale
13.	*yumʔə	yumə	yumʔə	yumhə	umʔɨ	bear
14.	*ʔəmɛs	əmɛs	ʔəmɛs	həmɛs	ʔɨmes	dog
15.	*hloxʷ	hlohʷ	hlohʷ	hloxʷ	ʔlow	ivory
16.	*sxɛkʷ	hɛkʷ	shɛxʷ	skɛkʷ	sxegʷ	stone
17.	*xose	hose	hose	xose	xose	bone
18.	*uhqan	uhqan	uhqan	uhʔan	uʔqan	skin
19.	*fuhiʔ	fuhi	huhiʔ	fuhih	fuʔiʔ	fat
20.	*mextɔ	mehtɔ	mehtɔ	mextɔ	mexto	blood
21.	*lɛhəm	lɛhəm	lɛhəm	lɛhəm	leʔim	hair/fur
22.	*snaws	naws	snaws	snaws	snaws	water
23.	*nuqma	nuqma	nuqma	nuʔma	nuqma	land
24.	*ɛwɛhʷ	ɛwɛhʷ	ɛwɛhʷ	ɛwɛhʷ	ewew	house
25.	*afkʷax	afkʷah	ahxʷah	afkʷax	afgʷax	village
26.	*txal	thal	than	tkal	txal	person
27.	*kʷəʔɔh	kʷɔɔh	xʷəʔɔh	kʷəhɔh	gʷɨʔoʔ	man
28.	*hʷin	hʷin	hʷin	hʷin	win	woman
29.	*foyɛq	foyɛq	hoyɛq	foyɛʔ	foeq	child
30.	*laqəm	laqəm	laqəm	laʔəm	laqim	food
31.	*tikʷə	tikʷə	tixʷə	čikʷə	tigʷɨ	eat
32.	*nilqəs	nilqəs	nilqəs	nilʔəs	nilqɨs	drink

1. Recurrent changes in Lgs. A, B, C and D in the order they are encountered are:

Change	Examples
Lg. A	
1. *x^w > h^w	1, 8, 15
2. *ʔ > Ø	2, 12–14, 19, 27
3. *s > Ø/__C	4, 7, 16, 22
4. *x > h	6, 11, 16, 17, 20, 25, 26
Lg. B	
1. *x^w > h^w (before 4)	1, 8, 15
2. *l > n/__#	3, 6, 8, 26
3. *x > h	6, 11, 16, 17, 20, 25, 26
4. *k^w > x^w	7, 16, 25, 27, 31
5. *f > h	8, 12, 19, 25, 29
Lg. C	
1. *ʔ > h (before 2)	2, 12–14, 19, 27
2. *q > ʔ	3, 10, 11, 18, 23, 29, 30, 32
3. *t > č/__i	3, 31
4. *x > k/C__	16, 26
Lg. D	
1. *x^w > w	1, 8, 15
2. *ɛ/ɔ > e/o	1, 2, 4, 5, 14, 16, 20, 21, 24, 27, 29
3. *ə > ɨ	1, 7–9, 13, 14, 21, 27, 30–32
4. *h > ʔ	2, 5, 15, 18, 19, 21, 27
5. *h^w > w	4, 9, 24, 28
6. *k^w > g^w	7, 16, 25, 27, 31
7. *y > Ø	10, 13, 29

Discussion. This problem may look more difficult than it actually is because of the large number of marked segments it contains, including labialised glottal fricatives, labialised velar stops and fricatives, tense/lax vowel contrasts, and difficult consonant clusters. Although some segments can be reconstructed without hesitation (e.g. *q, *h^w, *w), others are considerably more difficult, as with *x^w or *x. In the end everything should emerge clearly after some tedious labour to distinguish sound correspondences, particularly where these are in complementary distribution because of conditioning in highly restricted environments, as with $h : h : k : x$ in 16, and 26 (where *x becomes a stop immediately after an obstruent), as against $h : h : x : x$ in 6, 11, 17 or 25 (where *x remains unchanged in initial position or following a sonorant). One feature of this problem that makes it easier than some is the limited need for ordering relations.

SOLUTION TO RECONSTRUCTION PROBLEM 23

No.	Proto-ABCD	Lg. A	Lg. B	Lg. C	Lg. D	
01.	*paŋus	honus	faʔuh	vuŋus	paŋuʔu	fish
02.	*tutuk	tutuh	turuʔ	tutuk	tuluku	frog
03.	*inat	ilat	inat	inat	inala	snail
04.	*suraga	suraga	hulago	suraka	ʔulaga	worm
05.	*tilip	tiyih	tilif	silif	tilipi	snake
06.	*pisum	hisum	fihup	visuŋ	piʔumu	spider
07.	*ruŋu	runu	luʔu	ruŋu	luŋu	rain
08.	*sago	sago	hago	saku	ʔago	water
09.	*waki	wehi	waʔi	viki	aki	river
10.	*mekun	mehul	meʔut	mikuŋ	mekunu	grass
11.	*basir	besir	wahil	pisir	vaʔili	tree
12.	*hakat	ahat	aʔat	hakat	ʔakala	branch
13.	*aluk	oyuh	aluʔ	uluk	aluku	leaf
14.	*kuna	hula	ʔuno	kuna	kuna	root
15.	*subil	subiy	huil	supil	ʔuvili	bark
16.	*oniti	oliti	oniri	unisi	onili	eat
17.	*gulan	guyal	gulat	kulaŋ	gulana	drink
18.	*lidas	yidas	lirah	litas	liraʔa	walk
19.	*pihan	hial	fiat	vihaŋ	piʔana	sit
20.	*adik	edih	ariʔ	itik	ariki	stand
21.	*puhiŋ	huin	fuiʔ	vuhiŋ	puʔiŋis	sleep
22.	*ayap	eah	ayaf	ayaf	apa	dream
23.	*maku	mohu	maʔu	muku	maku	talk
24.	*supa	suha	hufo	suva	ʔupa	breathe
25.	*bitis	bitis	wirih	pisis	viliʔi	black
26.	*iwan	iol	iwat	ivaŋ	iana	white
27.	*alam	ayam	alap	alaŋ	alama	red
28.	*ŋatin	netil	ʔarit	ŋisiŋ	ŋalini	yellow
29.	*wiat	wiat	wiat	viat	iala	green
30.	*kawin	hewil	ʔawit	kiviŋ	kaini	blue
31.	*salay	saye	halay	salay	ʔala	tall
32.	*raru	roru	lalu	riru	lalu	short
33.	*gusep	guseh	guhef	kusif	guʔepe	when?
34.	*awat	oat	awat	avat	ala	where?

1. Recurrent changes in Lgs. A, B, C and D in the order they are encountered are:

Change	Examples
Lg. A	
1. *p > h	1, 5, 6, 19, 21, 22, 24, 33
2. *a > o,e/__Cu,i (before 8)	1, 9, 11, 13, 20, 23, 28, 30, 32
3. *ŋ > n	1, 7, 21, 28
4. *k > h	2, 9, 10, 12–14, 20, 23, 30
5. *n > l (before 3)	3, 10, 14, 16, 17, 19, 26, 28, 30
6. *l > y (before 5)	5, 13, 15, 17, 18, 27, 31
7. *h > Ø (before 1, 4)	12, 19, 21
8. *aw,wa > o, *ay > e (before 6)	22, 26, 31, 34
Lg. B	
1. *p > f (before 8)	1, 5, 6, 19, 21, 22, 24, 33
2. *ŋ > k (before 5)	1, 7, 21, 28
3. *s > h	1, 4, 6, 8, 11, 15, 18, 24, 25, 31, 33
4. *t > r/V__V	2, 16, 25, 28
5. *k > ʔ	1, 2, 7, 9, 10, 12–14, 20, 21, 23, 28, 30
6. *r > l (before 4, 9)	4, 7, 11, 32
7. *a > o/__#	4, 14, 24
8. *m,n,ŋ > p,t,k/__#	6, 10, 17, 19, 21, 26–28, 30
9. *b,d > w,r (before 11)	11, 15, 18, 20, 25
10. *h > Ø (before 3)	12, 19, 21
11. *w > Ø/u__V	15
Lg. C	
1. *p > w (before 3, 7)	1, 5, 6, 19, 21, 22, 24, 33
2. *a > o,e/__Cu,i (before 8)	1, 9, 11, 13, 20, 23, 28, 30, 32
3. *b,d,g > p,t,k	4, 8, 11, 15, 17, 18, 20, 25, 33
4. *t >s/__i (before 3)	5, 16, 25, 28
5. *v > f/__#	5, 22, 33
6. *m,n > ŋ/__#	6, 10, 17, 19, 26–28, 30
7. *w > v (before 5)	1, 5, 6, 9, 19, 21, 22, 24, 26, 29, 30, 33, 34
8. *o,e > u,i	1, 8–11, 13, 16, 20, 23, 28, 30, 32, 33

Lg. D

1. *s > h (before 7)	1, 4, 6, 8, 11, 15, 18, 24, 25, 31, 33
2. ViC > ViCVi (before 3, 5)	1–3, 5, 6, 10–13, 15, 17–22, 25–30, 33, 34
3. *t > r/V__V (before 4)	2, 3, 12, 16, 25, 28, 29, 34
4. *r > l (before 6)	2, 4, 7, 11, 12, 16, 25, 28, 29, 32, 34
5. *w,y > Ø (before 8)	9, 22, 26, 29–31, 34
6. *b,d > v,r	11, 15, 18, 20, 25
7. *h > ʔ	1, 4, 6, 8, 11, 12, 15, 18, 19, 21, 24, 25, 31, 33
8. ViVi > Vi	22, 31, 34

Discussion. This is a moderately difficult problem largely because of the oddity of some of the sound correspondences, as with $n : ʔ : ŋ : ŋ$ in number 1, or $e : a : i : a$ in number 9. However, these should not cause long delays. Since glottal stops and fricatives have few change options apart from becoming the other glottal consonant or disappearing, it seems clear that the first correspondence points to an original nasal, and since $l : n : n : n$ is most plausibly derived from *n this leaves *ŋ as the best choice. For a correspondence similar to this in natural language data cf. Hawaiian *lani*, Tahitian *raʔi*, Maori *raŋi*, Samoan *laŋi* < Proto-Polynesian *laŋi 'sky, heaven', with *ŋ/k merger in Tahitian before *k > ʔ. The complex vowel correspondence occurs only where a reflex of *i appears in the next syllable (hence *aCi > eCi), and was followed in Lg. C by raising of all mid vowels, whether these were original or derived, as can be seen by comparing 9 with 10.

SOLUTION TO RECONSTRUCTION PROBLEM 24

No	Proto-ABC	Lg. A	Lg. B	Lg. C	
01.	*londu	lodu	luddu	rond	garden
02.	*u(l,r)pat	upat	uppat	urufət	weeds
03.	*huap	uap	huap	uəf	grass
04.	*kantir	kandih	kassil	kantər	flower
05.	*salahi	salai	salehi	sar	fruit
06.	*sahak	sak	sahak	saək	seed
07.	*a(l,r)na	ana	anna	aran	tree
08.	*utile	utile	usili	utir	wood
09.	*rimbus	hibus	libbus	rimbəs	vine
10.	*korop	kohop	kulup	korəf	forest
11.	*u(l,r)nay	une	unnay	urun	lake
12.	*rampi	hambi	lappi	ramp	river
13.	*a(l,r)kiŋ	akiŋ	akkiŋ	arakən	water
14.	*tedin	terin	tidin	tedən	shore
15.	*ludur	luruh	ludul	rudər	fish
16.	*halim	alim	helim	arəm	stone
17.	*maŋkit	maŋgit	makkit	maŋkət	boulder
18.	*simaw	simo	simaw	sim	sand
19.	*duahan	ruan	duahan	duən	earth
20.	*parur	pahuh	polul	farər	house
21.	*ti(l,r)bas	tibas	sibbas	tiribəs	village
22.	*aruna	ahuna	oluna	arun	man
23.	*so(l,r)mil	somil	summil	soromər	woman
24.	*iŋgu	igu	iggu	iŋg	child
25.	*pe(l,r)tik	petik	pissik	feretək	sun
26.	*dadap	rarap	dadap	dadəf	moon
27.	*lerutay	lehute	lilutay	rerut	star
28.	*karinu	kahinu	kelinu	karin	meteor
29.	*amahu	amau	amohu	am	lunar halo
30.	*mateŋ	mateŋ	matiŋ	matəŋ	fog

1. Recurrent changes in Lgs. A, B and C in the order they are encountered are:

Change	Examples

Lg. A

1. $C_1C_2 > C_2$ (before 3)   1, 2, 7, 9, 11, 13, 21, 23–25
2. *h > O (before 4, 7)   3, 5, 6, 16, 19, 29
3. *p,t,k > b,d,g/N__   4, 12, 17
4. *r > h (before 7)   4, 9, 10, 12, 15, 20, 22, 27, 28
5. ViVi > Vi 6,   19
6. *-ay,-aw > -e,-o   11, 18, 27
7. *(-)d- > r (before 1)   14, 15, 19, 26

Lg. B

1. *o,e > i,u (before 5)   1, 8, 10, 14, 23, 25, 27, 30
2. $C_1C_2 > C_2C_2$ 1, 2, 4, 7, 9, 11–13, 17, 21, 23–25
3. *t > s/__i (before 1, 2)   4, 8, 21, 25
4. *r > l   4, 9, 10, 12, 15, 20, 22, 27, 28
5. *a > e,o/__(C)i,u   5, 16, 20, 22, 28, 29

Lg. C

1. *l > r   1, 5, 8, 15, 16, 23, 27
2. V > Ø/__#   1, 5, 7, 8, 11, 12, 18, 22, 24, 27–29
3. Vi(l,r)C > VirViC (before 4)   2, 7, 11, 13, 21, 23, 25
4. *p > f/[-cons]__   2, 3, 10, 20, 25, 26
5. V > ə/__C# (before 2)   2–4, 6, 9, 10, 13–17, 19–21, 23, 25, 26, 30
6. *h > Ø (before 7)   3, 5, 6, 16, 19, 29
7. *ai,au > ay,aw/__# (before 8)   5, 29
8. *ay,aw > e,o/__# (before 2)   5, 11, 18, 27, 29

2. Examples 2, 7, 11, 13, 21, 23 and 25 are ambiguous for *l or *r, since Lg. A shows deletion, and Lg. B shows complete assimilation to a following stop, leaving only Lg. C, where *l and *r have merged.

Discussion. This is a problem of greater than average difficulty. As noted above, the feature that is most difficult to reconstruct is the medial consonant cluster *lC or *rC (or perhaps both *lC and *rC), leaving the shape of the seven proto-forms that contain this cluster indeterminate. In addition, these changes skew the sound correspondences so as to make the initial alignment

SOLUTIONS

of forms unclear, as seen in *u(l,r)pat > *upat* : *uppat* : *uruʃət* 'weeds', *a(l,r)kiŋ > *akiŋ* : *akkiŋ* : *arakəŋ* 'water', or perhaps even more obscurely in *a(l,r)na > *ana* : *anna* : *aran* 'tree'.

One other detail that requires attention is the monophthongisation of *-ay and *-aw before final vowels were deleted in Lg. C. This also affected sequences of *-ai* and *-au* derived from *-ahi and *-ahu after deletion of *h. Most other changes are relatively straightforward, although Lgs. A and C are both rather innovative.

SOLUTION TO RECONSTRUCTION PROBLEM 25

No.	Proto-ABC	Lg. A	Lg. B	Lg. C	
01.	*kutup	kutuʔ	hudu	kuptu	eat
02.	*tanim	taniŋ	dali	tamni	drink
03.	*ulus	uhuih	uru	ulsu	talk
04.	*saŋat	saŋaʔ	sana	saŋta	sleep
05.	*akan	akaŋ	aha	akna	dream
06.	*ŋuro	ŋulo	nuro	ŋuro	wake up
07.	*risək	lisoʔ	risə	riskə	stand up
08.	*user	usel	use	usre	sit down
09.	*putiŋ	putiŋ	fudi	putŋi	walk
10.	*wakili	wakihi	vahiri	wakli	give
11.	*sipaŋ	sipaŋ	sifa	sipŋa	pick up
12.	*ulun	uhuŋ	uru	ulnu	wait
13.	*sadaŋ	sadaŋ	sara	sadŋa	village
14.	*kilir	kihil	hiri	kilri	house
15.	*torok	toloʔ	doro	torko	door
16.	*kənit	koniʔ	həli	kənti	window
17.	*pelu	pehu	feru	pelu	roof
18.	*natal	natah	lada	natla	floor
19.	*dulin	duhiŋ	ruri	dulni	road
20.	*puduta	puduta	furuda	putta	dust
21.	*siwit	siwiʔ	sivi	siwti	fire
22.	*utak	utaʔ	uda	ukta	smoke
23.	*bakuŋ	bakuŋ	wahu	bakŋu	ashes
24.	*inaŋ	inaŋ	ila	iŋna	sparks
25.	*tibəs	tiboih	diwə	tipsə	hearth
26.	*sədəp	sodoʔ	sərə	səptə	cooking pot
27.	*amas	amaih	ama	amsa	water
28.	*ukuŋ	ukuŋ	uhu	ukŋu	steam
29.	*palira	pahila	farira	palra	burn

1. Recurrent changes in Lgs. A, B and C in the order they are encountered are:

Change	Examples
Lg. A	
1. *p,t,k > ʔ/__#	1, 4, 7, 15, 16, 21, 22, 26
2. *m,n > ŋ/__#	2, 5, 12, 19
3. *l > h (before 5)	3, 10, 12, 14, 17–19, 29
4. *s > ih/__#	3, 25, 27
5. *r > l	6–8, 14, 15, 29
6. *ə > o	7, 16, 25, 26
Lg. B	
1. *k > h	1, 5, 10, 14, 16, 23, 28
2. *t > d	1, 2, 9, 15,18, 20–22, 25
3. C > O/__# (before 4,5,6,7)	1–5, 7–9, 11–16, 18, 19, 21–28
4. *n > l (before 6)	2, 5, 12, 16, 18, 19, 24
5. *l > r (before 4)	3, 10, 12, 14, 17–19, 29
6. *ŋ > n	4, 6, 9, 11, 13, 23, 24, 28
7. *p > f	9, 11, 17, 20, 26, 29
8. *w > v	10, 21
9. *d > r	13, 19, 20, 26
10. *b > w	23, 25
Lg. C	
1. ViC > ViCVi/__#	1–5, 7–9, 11–16, 18, 19, 21–28
2. V > Ø/VC__CV (before 3, 4)	1–5, 7–16, 18–29
3. *tp,tk,dp > pt,tk,pd	
*nm,nŋ > mn,ŋn	1, 2, 22, 24, 26
4. voicing assimilation	20, 25, 26

Discussion. This is a complex problem. The major trap is in Lg. C, which appears to have undergone -VC metathesis in many forms. However, closer inspection of examples such as 10, 20 and 29, which are original trisyllables, shows that this language added echo vowels, and then underwent syncope in the environment VC__CV, a change that affected both original trisyllables and original disyllables that ended with a consonant.

To further complicate matters, derived consonant clusters in the order coronal-non-coronal *did* undergo metathesis, provided that they had the same value for nasality, a change that is well attested in Tagalog and several other Austronesian languages, and which shows the same dispreference for this consonant sequence as English, which solves it through place assimilation

(Blust 1971a). This is seen in examples 1, 2, 22 and 24. Together with voicing assimilation in derived clusters and a wide array of changes in Lgs. A and B, there is much here to puzzle over before settling on a clear solution.

Finally, because final consonants were lost in Lg. B various changes that affected consonants in non-final position, as *k > *h*, *t > *d*, *n > *l* and *p > *f* are moot in word-final position: did these changes occur before or after final consonant loss? There is no basis for ordering here, so the choice as to which came first is essentially arbitrary, and I have chosen here to include final consonants in the statement of these changes in Lg. B, although there is no direct evidence to decide the issue.

SOLUTION TO RECONSTRUCTION PROBLEM 26

No.	Proto-ABC	Akman	Birina	Coshon	
01.	*lupat	luhaʔ	hugʷat	rupat	sun
02.	*pinaw	hino	inaw	pinaw	hot
03.	*panad	hanaʔ	anar	panat	moon
04.	*mulut	muluʔ	muhut	murut	cold
05.	*ayab	ayaʔ	ajav	ap	star
06.	*sirud	siluʔ	sirur	sirut	wind
07.	*balam	balaŋ	vaham	baram	fire
08.	*pupaʔ	huha	ugʷa	pupaʔ	tree
09.	*tian	tiaŋ	tijan	tian	water
10.	*runip	luniʔ	runi	runip	fish
11.	*laway	lawe	hagʷay	ray	sand
12.	*turib	tuliʔ	turiv	turip	earth
13.	*taʔup	tauʔ	tau	taʔup	mud
14.	*wali	wali	gʷahi	ari	man
15.	*sipa	siha	sija	sipa	woman
16.	*winuʔ	winu	gʷinu	inuʔ	child
17.	*kuap	kuaʔ	kugʷa	kuap	dog
18.	*nipuk	nihuʔ	nijuk	nipuk	bird
19.	*tapu	tahu	tau	tapu	eat
20.	*liaŋ	liaŋ	hijaŋ	riaŋ	sleep
21.	*dariʔ	dali	rari	dariʔ	wake up
22.	*piʔat	hiaʔ	iat	piʔat	cold
23.	*uig	uiʔ	ugʷig	uik	itchy
24.	*apari	ahali	ari	apari	tired
25.	*wuyak	wuyaʔ	gujak	uak	bored
26.	*dugag	dugaʔ	rugag	dugak	dark
27.	*riwuŋ	liwuŋ	riguŋ	riuŋ	light
28.	*buʔi	bui	vui	buʔi	fear
29.	*liʔan	liaŋ	hian	riʔan	fight
30.	*kubaw	kubo	kuvaw	kubaw	kill
31.	*lupuk	luhuʔ	huk	rupuk	die

1. Recurrent changes in Akman, Birina and Coshon in the order they are encountered are:

Change	Examples

Akman

1. *p > h   1–3, 8, 15, 18, 19, 22, 24, 31
2. *p,t,k > ʔ/__# (before 1)   1, 3–6, 10, 12, 13, 17, 18, 22, 23,
                                           25, 26, 31
3. *aw,ay > o,e/__#   2, 11, 30
4. *b,d,g > p,t,k/__# (before 2)   3, 5, 6, 12, 23, 26
5. *r > l   6, 10, 12, 21, 24, 27
6. *m,n > ŋ/__#   7, 9, 29
7. *ʔ > Ø (before 2)   8, 13, 16, 21, 22, 28, 29

Birina

1. *l > h   1, 4, 7, 11, 14, 20, 29, 31
2. *p > Ø (before 1, 3, 7)   1–3, 8, 10, 13, 15, 17–19, 22, 24, 31
3. Ø > w,y/u,i__V (before 4)   1, 8, 9, 15, 17–20, 23
4. *w,y > gʷ,j/__V (before 6, 8)   1, 5, 8, 9, 11, 14–20, 23, 25, 27
5. *b,d > v,r   3, 5–7, 12, 21, 26, 28, 30
6. *ʔ > Ø   8, 13, 16, 21, 22, 28, 29
7. ViVi > Vi (before 3)   24, 31
8. *gʷ > g/__u   19, 25, 27

Coshon

1. *l > r   1, 4, 7, 11, 14, 20, 29, 31
2. *b,d,g > p,t,k/__#   3, 5, 6, 12, 23, 26
3. *y,w > Ø/__V (before 4)   5, 11, 14, 16, 25, 27
4. ViVi > Vi   5, 11

2. Sound changes that might initially appear 'unnatural' (prior to work-ing out ordering relationships) are *p > *gw* (1, 8) and *p > *j* (15) in Birina. However, as explained below, this is due to a sequence of phonetically natural developments.

Discussion. This problem is more difficult than most. Its complexity arises largely from one change overlaying another. This is seen perhaps most clearly where *p has disappeared in Birina, giving rise to intervocalic vowel sequences that contained a phonetic transitional glide [w] or [j], as in *lupat > *luat* ([luwat]), or *sipa > *sia* ([sija]). All phonetic glides, both those that were inherited from Proto-ABC and those that developed later, then underwent fortition to /gʷ/ and /j/ ([ʤ]), giving rise to the odd sound correspondences $h : gw : p$ or $h : j : p$.

Other correspondences that may be challenging in this problem are $l : h : r$ and $w : g : \emptyset$. In the first of these $l : r : r$ is best attributed to *r, leaving only l and h as possible sources of this correspondence, and since *h > l is implausible we are left with *l (note that *l > h occurs in some Austronesian languages, including Kadazan Dusun of Sabah, where it is regular, and Tagalog, where it is sporadic). In the second correspondence glide fortition has produced g rather than gw from *w, but the neutralisation of the $g : gw$ contrast before rounded vowels is seen in languages such as Chamorro (Blust 2000a).

Finally, note that the ordering of *p > $\emptyset$ before *l > h in Birina is proposed on the assumption that *p > $\emptyset$ would most naturally have been a three-step change, *p > f > h > $\emptyset$, and if *p > h had preceded *l > h *p and *l would have merged, which did not occur. This forces us to assume that *l > h did not occur until the h from *p had first been lost.

SOLUTION TO RECONSTRUCTION PROBLEM 27

No.	Proto-KST	Kulak	Saru	Toto	
01.	*kape	kap	kawi	kapi	man
02.	*saruki	sɔrüc	haruki	sarki	woman
03.	*rotina	röcin	rutina	rutna	child
04.	*maniɛ	mɛni	manie	manii	person
05.	*dimalu	jimɔl	dimalu	dimaru	chief
06.	*arop	arop	arup	arup	village
07.	*atet(o,u)	atet	atitu	attu	field
08.	*leŋasu	leŋɔs	liŋahu	riŋasu	earth
09.	*tonel	tonel	tunil	tunir	stone
10.	*lamisi	lɛmiš	lamihi	ramsi	water
11.	*pokalu	pokɔl	wukalu	pukaru	river
12.	*sɔrodi	sɔröj	horudi	surdi	grass
13.	*usati	usɛc	uhati	usati	tree
14.	*waku	wɔk	waku	oku	animal
15.	*tɛgia	tɛji	tegia	tigia	fat, grease
16.	*karudi	kɔrüj	karudi	kardi	meat
17.	*nɛnute	nɛnut	nenuti	ninti	blood
18.	*lawik	lɛwik	lawik	roik	eat
19.	*lasuɔ	lɔsu	lahuo	rasuu	drink
20.	*asɔki	asɔc	ahoki	aski	walk
21.	*latase	latas	latahi	ratasi	sleep
22.	*kaseŋ	kaseŋ	kahiŋ	kasiŋ	sit
23.	*pikin(o,u)	picin	wikinu	piknu	stand
24.	*akep(o,u)	akep	akiwu	akpu	dark
25.	*tawa	taw	tawa	toa	night
26.	*tilisa	cilis	tiliha	tirsa	star
27.	*kete	ket	kiti	kiti	moon
28.	*takɛti	takɛc	taketi	takti	sun
29.	*sipadi	šipɛj	hiwadi	sipadi	comet
30.	*lelɛp	lelɛp	lilep	ririp	eclipse
31.	*walo	wal	walu	oru	rain

1. Recurrent changes in Kulak, Saru and Toto in the order they are encountered are:

Change	Examples
Kulak	
1. V > O/__#	1–5, 7, 8, 10–17, 19–21, 23–29, 31
2. *a > ɔ,ɛ /__(C)u,i (before	1, 3, 2, 4, 5, 8, 10, 11, 13, 14, 16, 18, 19, 29
3. *u > u, *o,ɔ > o/__Ci (before 1)	2, 3, 12, 16, 20
4. *k > c/__i (before 1)	2, 20, 23
5. *t > c/__i (before 1)	3, 13, 26, 28
6. *d > j/__i (before 1)	5, 12, 16, 29
7. *s > š/__i (before 1)	10, 29
8. *g > j/__i (before 1)	15
Saru	
1. *p > w/__V	1, 11, 23, 24, 29
2. *e,o > i,u (before 4)	1, 3, 6–9, 11, 12, 17, 21, 22, 24, 27, 30, 31
3. *s > h	2, 8, 10, 12, 13, 19–22, 26, 29
4. *ɛ,ɔ > e,o	4, 12, 15, 17, 19, 20, 28, 30
Toto	
1. *e,o > i,u (before 2, 5)	1, 3, 4, 6–9, 11, 12, 15, 17, 19–22, 24, 27, 28, 30, 31
2. *i,u > Ø/VC__CV	2, 3, 7, 10, 12, 16, 17, 20, 23, 24, 26, 28
3. *ɛ,ɔ > e,o (before 1)	4, 12, 15, 17, 19, 20, 28, 30
4. *l > r	5, 8–11, 18, 19, 21, 26, 30, 31
5. *wa, aw > o	14, 18, 25, 31

Discussion. This is a difficult problem. Ordering relationships are important, but in general these are clear. In Kulak, for example, all palatalisations of consonants and fronting or rounding of vowels had to precede the loss of final vowels, since otherwise there would have been no conditioning factor present at the time these changes occurred. Similarly, *a > ɔ,ɛ /__(C)u,i had to precede *u,o > ü/__Ci, since we would not expect the change *a > ɔ to be conditioned by a front rounded vowel, as in *saruki > sɔrüč. Where the final vowel could otherwise have been either mid or high, but no palatalisation of consonants or vocalic assimilation took place, the absence of these trace effects forces the conclusion that the lost final vowel in Kulak was mid rather than high, as in *kape (since *kapi would have produced Kulak **kɛp).

In this problem the history of mid vowels is particularly complex. In Toto all mid and high vowels have merged, eliminating this language as a witness for non-low vowels. Saru has merged tense mid vowels with high vowels, but preserves lax mid vowels as a distinct category (altered to their tense counterparts). Kulak preserves the distinction between vowels of all three heights, but since it has lost final vowels and developed new lax mid vowels by partial assimilation, it must be used with caution in comparisons with the other two languages. As noted in example 1, Kulak alone allows us to reconstruct *-e, but only by a process of elimination (the non-fronting and raising of original penultimate *a). For similar reasons examples 17 and 21 must be posited with *-e, and example 31 with *-o, since *-i would have palatalised the preceding consonant, and both high vowels would have had assimilatory effects on the original penultimate vowel.

Finally, because trace effects of high vowels in the last syllable are visible only on preceding vowels that are either low or back, words that had a front vowel in the penult and have word-final -*u* in Saru and Toto are ambiguous for final *o or *u (7, 23, 24). Note that a similar ambiguity for *e, i does not exist in any of the examples given here, since palatalisation affects so many onsets of word-final syllables (all coronal obstruents and velar stops). However, in principle this could be true for correspondences of the form -*ep* : -*ipi* : -*ipi* (< *-ep(e,i)), -*ip* : -*ipi* : -*ipi* (< *-ip(e,i)), -*el* : -*ili* : -*iri* (< *el(e,i)), and so on, where neither palatalisation of the consonant nor assimilatory effects on the penultimate vowel would provide clues to the character of the lost/merged final vowel.

SOLUTION TO RECONSTRUCTION PROBLEM 28

No.	Proto-ABC	Lg. A	Lg. B	Lg. C	
01.	*payak	haak	feaxa	payah	chicken
02.	*kulu	kuyu	xulu	hul	duck
03.	*ampaw	abaw	ampo	apaw	pig
04.	*rarap	lalah	larafa	rarap	dog
05.	*sukampi	sukabi	uxampi	huhap	flea
06.	*tarom	talom	tarumu	ʔaron	cricket
07.	*lurud	yulut	lurudu	lurud	man
08.	*sulaki	suyaki	ulaxi	hulah	woman
09.	*turana	tulana	turana	ʔuran	child
10.	*kiŋkit	kigit	xiŋkiti	hikiʔ	house
11.	*raruŋ	laluŋ	larunu	raruŋ	roof
12.	*pentas	hedas	fintaa	petah	door
13.	*kawas	kaas	xoaa	hawah	floor
14.	*leday	yeray	lide	leday	fire
15.	*sintab	sidap	intaba	hitab	cook
16.	*lilin	yiyin	lilini	lilin	pot
17.	*rintuk	liduk	rintuxu	rituh	ladle
18.	*puŋkil	hugin	fuŋkili	pukil	soup
19.	*ŋori	ŋoli	nuri	ŋor	meat
20.	*unadi	unari	unadi	unad	grass
21.	*liwis	yiis	liwii	liwih	tree
22.	*dampag	rabak	dampaga	dapag	leaf
23.	*puyud	huut	fuyudu	puyud	branch
24.	*tawal	taan	toala	ʔawal	flower
25.	*runtum	ludum	runtumu	rutun	fruit
26.	*baŋkayar	bagaal	baŋkeara	bakayar	sun
27.	*puraŋi	hulaŋi	furani	puraŋ	moon
28.	*utor	utol	uturu	uʔor	star
29.	*pitun	hitun	fitunu	piʔun	storm
30.	*biruri	biluli	biluri	birur	hail

1. Recurrent changes in Lgs. A, B and C in the order they are encountered are:

Change	Examples

Lg. A

1. *p > h	1, 4, 12, 18, 23, 27, 29
2. *y,w > Ø/V__V (before 3)	1, 13, 21, 23, 24, 26
3. *l > y (before 6)	2, 7, 8, 14, 16, 21
4. *p,t,k > b,d,g/N__ (before 1, 5)	3, 5, 10, 12, 15, 17, 18, 22, 25, 26
5. N > Ø/__C	3, 5, 10, 12, 15, 17, 18, 22, 25, 26
6. *r > l (before 8)	4, 6, 7, 9, 11, 17, 19, 25–28, 30
7. *b,d,g > p,t,k/__# (before 8)	7, 15, 22, 23
8. *d > r__V (before 4)	14, 20, 22
9. *l > n/__# (before 3, 6)	18, 24

Lg. B

1. *p > f/[-nas]__	1, 4, 12, 18, 23, 27, 29
2. *ay,aw > e,o (before 4)	1, 3, 13, 14, 24, 26
3. *k > x/[-nas]__	1, 2, 5, 8, 10, 13, 17
4. $V_1C > V_1CV_1/$__# (before 6)	1, 4, 6, 7, 10–13, 15–18, 21–26, 28, 29
5. *r > l/__Vr	4, 11, 30
6. *s > Ø	5, 8, 12, 13, 15, 21
7. *e,o > i,u (before 2)	6, 12, 14, 19, 28
8. *ŋ > n	11, 19, 27

Lg. C

1. *k > h/[-nas]__ (before 3)	1, 2, 5, 8, 10, 13, 17
2. V > Ø/__#	2, 5, 8, 9, 19, 20, 27, 30
3. C > Ø/__C	3, 5, 10, 12, 15, 17, 18, 22, 25, 26
4. *s > h	5, 8, 12, 13, 15, 21
5. *t > ʔ/[-nas]__ (before 3)	6, 9, 10, 24, 28, 29
6. *m > n/__#	6, 25

2. The four correspondences that include /l/ in at least one language are as follows:

	Lg. A	Lg. B	Lg. C
(1)	y	l.	l
(2)	l	l	r
(3)	l	r	r
(4)	n	l	l

(1) reflects *l as syllable onset, and (2) reflects *r as syllable onset preceding *Vr. This produced liquid dissimilation from *rVr to /Vr in Lg. B. (3) reflects *r where liquid dissimilation did not apply, and (4) reflects *l as syllable coda. Proto-ABC *l and *r suffice to account for all four sound correspondences, since (1) and (4) are in complementary distribution, as are (2) and (3).

Discussion. This is a difficult problem. In addition to numerous sound changes in all three languages, many of which must be ordered, there is fairly intricate conditioning in some cases, as with the correspondence $l : l : r$, found only in the first reflexes of *r in *rarap, *raruŋ and *biruri, all of which show liquid dissimilation (apart from the more general change *r > l in Lg. A).

In other cases conditioning must be stated in terms of a single exceptional environment, as with *p > f/ [-nas]__ in Lg. B to account for the fact that *p lenited everywhere except where it was prenasalised. Alternatively, one might avoid the statement of conditions by ordering change 4 in Lg. A (*p,t,k > b,d,g/N__) before *p > h. However, although the same result is achieved, it overlooks the fact that lenitions of simplex consonants are often blocked with their prenasalised counterparts, and the use of conditions rather than ordering in this case therefore draws attention to a natural process of change.

Finally, reflexes such as *p > h or *s > Ø presumably represent sequences of changes with intermediate steps *p (> f) > h and *s (> h) > Ø. However, since the proto-language had no *f or *h there is no need to include these steps in the statement of reflexes, as this would largely duplicate the pattern for the reflex and require an ordering relationship, as with *p > f/ [-nas] : 1, 4, 12, 18, 23, 27, 29 before f > h : 1, 4, 12, 18, 23, 27, 29 in Lg. A, or *s > h : 5, 8, 12, 13, 15, 21, before h > Ø : 5, 8, 12, 13, 15, 21 in Lg. B.

SOLUTION TO RECONSTRUCTION PROBLEM 29

No.	Proto-ABC	Lg. A	Lg. B	Lg. C	Gloss
01.	*uba	fà	ua	uba	water
02.	*(d,r)aduk	tùk	raruk	lalku	eye
03.	*atup	túf	atup	aptu	snake
04.	*tedup	tùf	tirup	telpu	belly
05.	*pekis	kíx	pikis	peksi	die
06.	*bitiŋ	tíŋ	wisiŋ	bitŋi	arrow
07.	*mapat	fát	mapat	mapata	cloud
08.	*anim	nim	anim	amni	spirit
09.	*atep	téf	atip	atepe	sleep
10.	*bagen	kèn	wagin	bagene	pig
11.	*pakis	kíx	pakis	paksi	rice field
12.	*(d,r)opal	fál	rupal	lopala	waterfall
13.	*kuden	tèn	kurin	kulene	village
14.	*poki	kí	puki	poki	navel
15.	*tanom	nom	tanum	tanomo	headhunting
16.	*batak	ták	watak	bataka	axe
17.	*okop	kóf	ukup	okopo	earthquake
18.	*batik	tík	wasik	bakti	night
19.	*gugas	kàx	gugat	gugasa	star
20.	*subik	fik	suik	supki	lunar halo
21.	*tete	té	titi	tete	comet
22.	*kuruŋ	ruŋ	kuruŋ	kulŋu	chief
23.	*masi	xí	masi	masi	noble
24.	*suŋap	ŋaf	suŋap	suŋapa	slave
25.	*piris	rix	piris	pilsi	enemy
26.	*(d,r)olut	lut	rulut	loltu	captive
27.	*(d,r)idip	tìf	ririp	lilpi	war
28.	*gagus	kùx	gagus	gaksu	peace
29.	*nabut	fùt	nawut	naptu	corpse
30.	*(d,r)usuŋ	xúŋ	rusuŋ	lusŋu	ghost
31.	*enum	num	inum	emnu	dream

1. Recurrent changes in Lgs. A, B and C in the order they are encoun-
    tered are:

Change	Examples
Lg. A	
1. V > O/#__	1–31
2. *b,d,g > p,t,k (before 3)	1, 2, 4, 10, 13, 19, 20, 27–29
3. *p > f	1, 3, 4, 7, 9, 12, 17, 20, 24, 27, 29
4. V > V+low tone/b,d,g__ (before 2)	1, 2, 4, 10, 13, 19, 20, 27–29
5. C > O/#__ (before 1)	2, 4–7, 10–16, 18–30
6. V > V+high tone/p,t,k,s__ (before 2)	3, 5–7, 9, 11, 12, 14, 16–18, 21, 23, 30
7. *s > x	5, 11, 19, 23, 25, 28, 30
Lg. B	
1. *b,d > w,r (before 2)	1, 2?, 4, 6, 10, 12?, 13, 16, 18, 20, 26?, 27?, 29, 30?
2. *w > Ø/u__V	1, 20
3. *e,o > i,u	4, 5, 9, 10, 12–15, 17, 21, 26, 31
4. *t > s/__i (before 3)	6, 18
Lg. C	
1. *d > r (before 5)	2?, 4, 12?, 13, 26?, 27?, 30?
2. ViC > ViCVi/__# (before 3)	2–13, 15–20, 22, 24–31
3. *i,u > Ø/VC__CV	2–6, 8, 11, 18, 20, 22, 25–31
4. *b,g > p,k/__vl.	20, 28, 29
5. *r > l	2, 4, 12, 13, 22, 25–27, 30
6. C[+cor]C[-cor] > C[-cor]C[+cor]	3, 18, 31

2. Reconstructions with ambiguous segments are (2) *(d,r)aduk 'eye',
    (12) *(d,r)opal 'waterfall', captive, war, and (30) *(d,r)usuŋ 'ghost'. In
    each of these Lg. A has lost the initial CV-, thus providing no
    information on the quality of the initial consonant, and Lgs. B and
    C reflect *d and *r identically.

3. The loss of initial syllables in Lg. A implies final stress in Proto-ABC, but vowel syncope in the environment VC__CV after the addition of echo vowels in Lg. C favours a pattern of initial stress. These can be reconciled by assuming that if Proto-ABC stress was initial it shifted to the final syllable before erosion from the left in Lg. A, or if it was originally final it shifted to the initial syllable before medial vowel syncope in Lg. C.

Discussion. Among other things, this problem attempts to replicate registrogenesis – the initial, and one of the major features of tonogenesis. In registrogenesis the voicing of syllable-initial stops first creates breathy voice and then lowers the pitch on a following vowel, generally with concomitant loss of the original voicing contrast in stops. Low-pitch vowels in Lg. A thus all reflect vowels immediately after voiced stops that have since devoiced, and high-tone vowels reflect vowels immediately after voiceless stops. For purposes of this problem syllables not meeting either of these conditions are left with no tone mark, since the particular development that such syllables undergo depends in sometimes unpredictable ways on the syllable coda.

Other features of this problem that present obstacles to reconstruction are the loss of the initial syllable of Lg. A, and the addition of echo vowels and subsequent syncope of unstressed high vowels in medial position (VC__CV) in Lg. B. As noted above, these changes provide contrary indications of the earlier placement of stress, suggesting that whatever it was in Proto-ABC, it had shifted in either Lg. A or Lg. C before these innovations occurred. Finally, Lg. C shows metathesis of derived clusters of coronal stops with the same value for nasality in items 3, 18 and 31, a change that is found in Tagalog and a number of other Austronesian languages as part of a language-universal tendency to eliminate such clusters either by assimilation or by transposition.

SOLUTION TO RECONSTRUCTION PROBLEM 30

No.	Proto-NKP	Nsam	Kuni	Palu	
01.	*ma-saki	nsek	saxi	matehi	red
02.	*m-apanu	mapm	afnu	mawonu	strong
03.	*m-apu	mop	afu	mowu	rotten
04.	*lanitu	lant	lantu	renitu	smell
05.	*kila	kil	xila	hira	to eat
06.	*ma-pilu	mpil	filu	mewiru	long
07.	*untu	unt	utu	undu	to drink
08.	*aŋka	aŋk	aka	aŋga	dog
09.	*m-atuka	matk	atxa	motuha	big
10.	*ma-kalu	ŋkol	xalu	mahoru	heavy
11.	*m-asuki	mask	asxi	motuhi	angry
12.	*kamiki	kaŋk	xaŋxi	hemihi	to run
13.	*ma-sula	nsul	sula	motura	sick
14.	*sampu	samp	sapu	tombu	water
15.	*ulapi	ulp	ulfi	urewi	snake
16.	*lasaku	lask	lasxu	ratohu	to sleep
17.	*m-uli	mul	uli	muri	deep
18.	*m-iŋka	miŋk	ika	miŋga	dark
19.	*anusi	ans	ansi	onuti	person
20.	*tampa	tamp	tapa	tamba	man
21.	*inika	iŋk	iŋxa	iniha	woman
22.	*ati	et	ati	eti	child
23.	*sunupa	sump	sumfa	tunua	house

1. Recurrent changes in Nsam, Kuni and Palu in the order they are encountered are:

Change	Examples
Nsam	
1. V > Ø/__CV[+stress] (before 2)	1, 6, 10, 13
2. nasal place assimilation	1, 2, 10, 12, 13, 21, 23
3. *a > e,o/__Ci,u (before 4)	1, 3, 10, 22
4. V > Ø/__#	1–23
5. V[-stress] > Ø/VC__CV (before 2, 3, 4)	2, 4, 9, 11, 12, 15, 16, 19, 21, 23

SOLUTIONS

Kuni
1. loss of stative prefix   1–3, 6, 9–11, 13, 17, 18
2. *p, k > f, x/[-nas]__ (before 4)   1–3, 5, 6, 9–12, 15, 16, 21, 23
3. V > Ø/VC__CV (before 5)   2, 4, 9, 11, 12, 15, 16, 19, 21, 23
4. N > Ø/__C   7, 8, 14, 18, 20
5. nasal place assimilation   12, 21

Palu
1. *s > t   1, 11, 13, 14, 16, 19, 23
2. *a > e,o/__(C)(C)i/u   1–4, 6, 9–16, 19, 22
3. *p > w   2, 3, 6, 15, 23
4. *l > r   4–6, 10, 13, 15–17
5. *k > h   5, 9–12, 16, 21
6. *p,t,k > b,d,g/N__ (before 3, 5)   7, 8, 14, 18, 20
7. *w > Ø/u__a   23

2. Stress fell on the first syllable of the lexical base.
3. The stative prefix was *ma- before consonant-initial bases and *m-
   before vowel-initial bases.

Discussion. This is a difficult problem for several reasons. First, some of
the forms show radically different shapes, especially Nsam as compared
with the others. However, systematic attention to sound correspondences
and natural sound changes should enable the better students to provide
adequate reconstructions and determine innovations in individual languages.
Second, it must be assumed that Proto-Nsam-Kuni-Palu (Proto-NKP) adjectives or stative verbs were prefixed with *ma- (*m- before vowel-initial
bases), a prefix that is retained in Nsam and Palu, but lost in Kuni. Third,
ordering is imporant in Nsam and Palu to account for changes as regular
developments. Prenasalised stops in many languages are resistant to lenition
processes that affect the corresponding simplex stops in initial or intervocalic positions. In Kuni *p and *k lenited to *f* and *x* except when following
a nasal. However, medial vowel syncope and nasal place assimilation then
produced a new generation of homorganically prenasalised consonants
after lenition had occurred, with the result that Kuni has both postconsonantal stops and postconsonantal fricatives. Finally, although some changes
are common to many languages, their scope may differ cross-linguistically.
The partial assimilation of *a to a following high vowel is common to many

natural languages, but in some languages it is blocked by an intervening consonant cluster, while in others it is not. This is the case in the present problem, where the change $*a > e,o/\_Ci,u$ occurs in both Nsam and Palu, but is blocked by a sequence of consonants in Nsam.

SOLUTION TO RECONSTRUCTION PROBLEM 31

No.	Proto-ABC	Lg. A	Lg. B	Lg. C	
01.	*kihaz	sihaz	hizas	kɛz	head
02.	*rayak	ayak	razak	rɛak	hair
03.	*nunu	lul	nunu	nunu	brain
04.	*ulkin	ursil	ukkin	ulkin	eye
05.	*suad	suad	uvat	sɔd	ear
06.	*kapahu	kawah	habau	kapɔ	mouth
07.	*ŋiuz	niuz	ŋizus	ŋüz	nose
08.	*lohuk	rohuk	louk	lʊk	chin
09.	*risahi	isah	rizai	risɛ	neck
10.	*kirvuz	sivuz	hivvus	kirvuz	shoulder
11.	*zireg	zieg	zirek	zireg	back
12.	*uŋua	unua	uŋuva	uŋɔ	arm
13.	*ponoti	wolot	ponodi	ponoti	bone
14.	*siŋia	sinia	iŋiza	siŋɛ	blood
15.	*raiv	aiv	raif	rɛv	earth
16.	*silab	sirab	ilap	silab	water
17.	*pantot	waltot	pattot	pantot	mountain
18.	*savinu	savil	avinu	savinu	tree
19.	*tomoka	tomoka	tomoha	tomoka	forest
20.	*eriap	eiaw	erizap	erɛp	grass
21.	*uruad	uad	uruvat	urɔd	vine
22.	*natu	lat	nadu	natu	stone
23.	*tupa	tua	tuba	tupa	river
24.	*uhoki	uhos	uvohi	ʊki	wind
25.	*zahag	zahag	zak	zag	storm
26.	*puil	wuir	puvil	pül	flood
27.	*sihin	sihil	in	sin	to swim
28.	*warak	wak	varak	warak	to drown
29.	*paisu	wais	paizu	pɛsu	to rescue

1. Recurrent changes in Lgs. A, B and C in the order they are encountered are:

Change	Examples
Lg. A	
1. *k > s/__i (before 4)	1, 4, 10, 24
2. *r > Ø (before 5, 8)	2, 9–11, 15, 20, 21, 28
3. *n > l (before 7)	3, 4, 13, 17, 18, 22, 27
4. *i,u > Ø/__#	3, 6, 9, 13, 18, 22, 24
5. *l > r (before 3)	4, 8, 16, 26
6. *p > w (before 9)	6, 13, 17, 20, 23, 26, 29
7. *ŋ > n	7, 12, 14
8. V*i*V*i* > V*i*	21, 28
9. *w > Ø/u__V	23
Lg. B	
1. *k > h/[-cons]__V (before 8)	1, 6, 10, 19, 24
2. *h > Ø (before 1, 3, 9)	1, 5, 6, 8, 9, 14, 16, 18, 24, 25, 27, 29
3. Ø > y,w/i,u__V (before 4)	1, 5, 7, 12, 14, 20, 21, 24, 26
4. *y,w > z,v	1, 2, 5, 7, 9, 14, 20, 21, 24, 26, 28, 29
5. *b,d,g,z > p,t,k,s/__#	1, 5, 7, 10, 11, 15, 16, 21, 25
6. $C_1C_2 > C_2C_2$ (before 1)	4, 10, 17
7. *s > h (before 2)	5, 9, 14, 16, 18, 27
8. *p,t,s > b,d,z/V__V (before 7)	6, 9, 13, 22, 23, 29
9. V*i*V*i* > V*i*	25, 27
Lg. C	
1. *h > Ø (before 2, 3, 5, 6)	1, 6, 8, 9, 24, 25, 27
2. *ia,ai,ay > ɛ	1, 2, 9, 14, 15, 20, 29
3. *ua,au,aw > ɔ	5, 6, 12, 21
4. *iu,ui > ü	7, 26
5. *ou,uo > ʊ	8, 24
6. V*i*V*i* > V*i*	25, 27

SOLUTIONS

Discussion. This is a relatively difficult problem, starting with the first example, where it may prove hard to determine what the proper sound correspondences are between *sihaz* in Lg. A and *hizas* in Lg. B, since these forms contain the same five phonemes in different orders, tempting the unwary to assume that the proto-form was something like *sihaz with a complex series of metatheses in Lg. B. The actual correspondences are quite different, with $s : h$ going back to *k-, as confirmed by Lg. C, where the k- could hardly have derived from either of the other sounds.

Other traps that make this problem among the more difficult ones in this book are the fortition of phonetic glides [w] and [j] in Lg. B. Where this happened after the loss of *h the correspondences can initially be confusing, as in example 1, where $h : z$ reflects *h, not through a direct change *h > z, which would be phonetically implausible, but through loss of *h followed by fortition of the glide that developed automatically between a high front vowel and a following unlike vowel. Such changes are well attested in various Austronesian languages, as with Proto-Malayo-Polynesian *duha > Chamorro *hugwa* 'two', where the intervocalic consonant of the Chamorro word developed after *h > Ø, and the automatic insertion of [w]/u__a.

Finally, Lg. C adds to the complications by developing several new vowels from the crasis of two unlike vowels after the loss of an intervening consonant.

SOLUTIONS

SOLUTION TO RECONSTRUCTION PROBLEM 32

No.	Proto-ABCD	Lg. A	Lg. B	Lg. C	Lg. D	
01.	*lambut	labu	lambut	labuʔ	lamutu	grass
02.	*igam	igã	igam	igaŋ	iɣama	sky
03.	*kifanu	əfanu	tilap	kifonu	hifanu	cloud
04.	*santuka	hətua	sattuk	satuka	sanduha	rain
05.	*milaŋ	milã	milaŋ	bakuŋ	milaa	water
06.	*torum	torũ	torum	toruŋ	torumu	earth
07.	*noapu	napu	noap	noopu	noafu	fire
08.	*ekahu	au	ekah	ekohu	ehahu	sand
09.	*umpila	pila	uppil	upila	umbila	river
10.	*pundak	puda	pundak	pudaʔ	funaha	man
11.	*saŋkup	haku	sakkup	sakuʔ	saŋgufu	woman
12.	*tapin	tapĩ	tapin	tepiŋ	tafini	child
13.	*dundun	dudũ	dundun	duduŋ	rununu	head
14.	*kentil	eti	kettil	keti	hendili	hair
15.	*fakuŋ	faũ	fakuŋ	fokuŋ	fahuu	eye
16.	*impoho	poo	ippoh	ipoho	imboho	nose
17.	*naŋgat	naga	naŋgat	nagaʔ	naɲata	ear
18.	*biŋbiŋ	bibĩ	biŋbiŋ	bibiŋ	vimii	mouth
19.	*alapar	lapar	alapar	alapa	alafara	tooth
20.	*lamuŋ	lamũ	lamuŋ	lomuŋ	lamuu	hand
21.	*hambin	abĩ	hambin	habiŋ	hamini	elbow
22.	*sualu	halu	sual	suolu	amuhu	back
23.	*kumbaŋka	əbaka	kumbak	kubaka	humaŋga	belly
24.	*rudup	rudu	rudup	ruduʔ	rurufu	leg
25.	*ibarak	bara	ibarak	ibaraʔ	ivaraha	heart
26.	*siali	hali	sial	sieli	siali	liver
27.	*gangan	gagã	gangan	gagaŋ	ɣaɲana	lungs
28.	*lamari	ləmari	lamar	lameri	lamari	blood
29.	*ubiraŋ	birã	ratul	ubiraŋ	uviraa	vein
30.	*goran	gorã	goran	goraŋ	ɣorana	brain
31.	*tumtum	tutũ	tuttum	tutuŋ	tundumu	gall
32.	*hiŋat	iŋa	hiŋat	hiŋaʔ	hiata	bone

1. Recurrent changes in Lgs. A, B, C and D in the order they are encountered are:

Change	Examples
Lg. A	
1. N > O/__C	1, 4, 9–11, 13, 14, 16–18, 21, 23, 27, 31
2. C > O/__#	1, 2, 5, 6, 10–15, 17–21, 24, 25, 27, 29–32
3. V > Ṽ/__N# (before 2)	2, 5, 6, 12, 13, 15, 18, 20, 21, 27, 29–31
4. *k > h/[-nas]__V (before 1, 9)	3, 4, 8, 10, 14, 15, 23, 25
5. *h > O (before 7, 8)	3, 4, 8, 14–16, 21, 23, 32
6. V > ə/__(C)V(C)V(C) (before 8)	3, 4, 7–9, 16, 19, 22, 23, 25, 26, 28, 29
7. *s > h	4, 11, 22, 26
8. ə > O/#__(C)V(C)V(C) (before 5)	7, 8, 9, 16, 19, 22, 25, 29
Lg. B	
1. N+vl. stop > vl. geminate	4, 9, 11, 14, 16, 23, 31
2. V > Ø/__#	4, 7–9, 16, 22, 23, 26, 28
3. CiCi > Ci/__#	23
Lg. C	
1. N > Ø/__C	1, 4, 9–11, 13, 14, 16–18, 21, 23, 27, 31
2. *p,t,k > ʔ/__#	1, 10, 11, 17, 24, 25, 32
3. *m,n > ŋ/__#	2, 6, 12, 13, 21, 27, 30, 31
4. *a > o,e/__(C)u,i (before 1)	3, 7, 8, 12, 15, 20, 22, 26, 28
5. *l,r > Ø/__#	14, 19
Lg. D	
1. *mb,nd,ŋg > m,n,ŋ (before 5)	1, 10, 13, 17, 18, 21, 23, 27
2. V₁C > V₁CV₁/__# (before 6)	1, 2, 5, 6, 10–15, 17–21, 24, 25, 27, 29–32
3. *g > γ/[-nas]__	2, 27, 30
4. *k > h	3, 4, 8, 10, 14, 15, 23, 25

5. *p,t,k > b,d,g/N__ (before 4, 7)　　　4, 9, 11, 14, 16, 23, 31
6. *ŋ > Ø/__V (before 1)　　　　　　　5, 15, 18, 20, 29, 32
7. *p > f　　　　　　　　　　　　　　7, 10–12, 19, 24
8. *d > r/[-nas]__　　　　　　　　　　13, 24
9. *b > v[-nas]__　　　　　　　　　　18, 25, 29
10. nasal place assimilation (before 1, 5)　18, 27, 31

Discussion. This is a difficult problem which raises several questions. The changes in Lg. A require fairly complex ordering. Since vowels were nasalised preceding word-final nasals that disappeared when all final consonants were lost, but not before syllable-final nasals in the penult or antepenult that were also lost through a separate change, we must order the loss of syllable-final nasals in the penult/antepenult (change 1) before vowel nasalisation (change 3), but the loss of word-final nasals (change 2) after vowel nasalisation.

The failure of *k to lenite in Lg. A in items 11 and 23 requires reference to both conditioning and ordering, since lenition normally affects singleton stops but not their prenasalised or geminate counterparts, leaving the prenasalised *k in these two words unafffected by change 4. Change 1 introduces new instances of *k* into Lg. A, but since this is after lenition has run its course these are unaffected by that change.

Finally, change 8 must be ordered before change 5 to show why a reflex of the weakened antepenultimate vowel is preserved word-initially in items 3 and 23, but not in 8, 9, 16, 25 or 29. The schwas of the latter items were initial when prepenultimate initial schwa was deleted, while those of the former were 'protected' by *h* < *k that later disappeared.

The changes in Lgs. B and C are relatively straightforward, and require little ordering. The only complication to note is that change 4 in Lg. C must be ordered before change 1 to account for the fact that anticipatory low vowel raising occured across a single intervening consonant, but not across an intervening consonant cluster.

In describing the changes of Lg. D one might want to combine *b > *v*, *d > *r* and *g > γ as distinct reflexes of a single innovation leniting voiced stops, but it is not always clear when it is justified to generalise in this way. Since this lenition did not take place when a voiced stop was prenasalised, each of these changes is stated as conditioned. However, there is an alternative which would make it possible to dispense with marking conditions, namely if changes 3, 8 and 9 preceded change 5, which introduced new instances of *mb*, *nd* and *ŋg* after the original ones had been lost by change 1. The choice among these alternatives is essentially arbitrary.

Finally, there are issues of complementation in this problem that – if this were natural language data – could only be resolved by considering a more extensive corpus. It can be seen that [b] and [v], [d] and [r] and [g] and [ɣ], for example, form three sets of complementary phones, the stops occuring after a nasal and the continuants elsewhere, suggesting that they be united as /b/, /d/, /g/ in a phonemic orthography. Despite the looseness of the phonetic/phonemic distinction in Lg. D the complementation of the correspondences leads inevitably through the comparative method to the reconstruction of single phonemes in the proto-language, one simple and the other prenasalised. This is a reminder that even before the phonemic principle was recognised in synchronic linguistics it was an unstated but inherent part of the comparative method.

SOLUTION TO RECONSTRUCTION PROBLEM 33

No.	Proto-ABC	Lg. A	Lg. B	Lg. C	
01.	*tisum	cumu	tisuŋ	titumə	bird
02.	*mana	mala	mana	marə	feather
03.	*ula	ula	ua	urə	rain
04.	*akap	ahapa	āf	akapə	clothing
05.	*mahal	mala	mā	maharə	horse
06.	*kihim	himi	īŋ	kihimə	dog
07.	*basat	bata	vasa?	batatə	pig
08.	*masan	mala	masaŋ	matarə	rope
09.	*ulin	ulili	uiŋ	urirə	land
10.	*puhuk	puhu	fū	puhukə	house
11.	*dian	jala	diaŋ	diarə	door
12.	*suru	uru	suru	turə	roof
13.	*dihal	jala	dia	diharə	road
14.	*tiaha	ca	tiā	tiahə	dust
15.	*imut	imutu	imu?	imutə	to eat
16.	*halus	alu	auh	harutə	to sleep
17.	*dasa	da	dasa	datə	to dream
18.	*ritas	rita	ritah	ritatə	afraid
19.	*pasi	pai	fasi	patə	worried
20.	*tunak	tulaha	tuna	turakə	desperate
21.	*titi	titi	titi	titə	panicky
22.	*kihi	hi	ī	kihə	dead
23.	*kubaŋ	hubaŋa	uvaŋ	kubaŋə	ghost

1. Recurrent changes in Lgs. A, B, and C in the order they are encountered are:

Change

Lg. A

1. *s > h (before 2)
2. *h > Ø (before 3, 6, 7)
3. *ti,di > c, j/__V
4. $V_1C > V_1CV_1/$__#

Examples

1, 7, 8, 12, 16-19
1, 5-8, 10, 12-14, 16-19, 22
1, 11, 13, 14
1, 4-11, 13, 15, 16, 18, 20, 23

5. *n > l   2, 8, 9, 11, 20
6. *k > h   4, 6, 10, 20, 22, 23
7. $V_i V_i > V_i$ 5–8, 10, 14, 17, 18, 22

Lg. B
1. *m,n > ŋ/__#   1, 6, 8, 9, 11
2. *l > h (before 3)   3, 5, 9, 13, 16
3. *h > Ø (before 9)   3–6, 9, 10, 13, 14, 16, 20, 22, 23
4. *k > h (before 3)   4, 6, 10, 20, 22, 23
5. *p > f   4, 10, 19
6. $V_i V_i > \bar{V}$ 4–6, 10, 14, 22
7. *b > v   7, 23
8. *t > ʔ/__#   7, 15
9. *s > h/__#   16, 18

Lg. C
1. *s > t   1, 7, 8, 12, 16–19
2. $V_1 C > V_1 C V_1$/__# (before 3)   1, 4–11, 13, 15, 16, 18, 20, 23
3. V > ə/__#   1–23
4. *n > l (before 5)   2, 8, 9, 11, 20
5. *l > r   2, 3, 5, 8, 9, 11, 13, 16, 20

Discussion. This problem is initially difficult because it may take a while to align the sound correspondences. In comparing *cumu* to *tisuŋ* (01), or *mala* to *masaŋ* (08), for example, it may not immediately be clear that the medial segments do not correspond (although their phonetic dissimilarity is likely to cause puzzlement if it is assumed that they do). Once it is recognised that *s disappeared and that echo vowels were added after original final consonants in Lg. A it can be seen that the true correspondences are /m/ : /ŋ/ (< *-m) and /l/ : /ŋ/ (< *-n).

An additional complication arises from the palatalisation of *t and *d before *iV, as this created new segments *c* and *j* in Lg. A that correspond to *t* and *d* respectively in the other languages. The correspondence *c* : *t* : *t* is then in complementary distribution with *t* : *t* : *t*, and *j* : *d* : *d* is in complementary distribution with *d* : *d* : *d*. Both sets of complementary correspondences occur before *i, but the one with a palatal obstruent in Lg. A is found only before prevocalic *i.

SOLUTION TO RECONSTRUCTION PROBLEM 34

No.	Proto-ABCD	Lg. A	Lg. B	Lg. C	Lg. D	
01.	*lahuk	lauk	hahu	hou?	auh	fish
02.	*ratas	latah	rata	latah	yatos	water
03.	*ayun	ayut	aru	oyuŋ	aun	wave
04.	*hesam	ehap	heha	ehaŋ	esom	sky
05.	*irup	ilup	iru	iluf	iuf	wind
06.	*tula	tula	tuha	tuha	tuo	earth
07.	*usiŋ	uhik	uhi	uhiŋ	usiŋ	grass
08.	*pohol	pool	foho	foh	fo	stone
09.	*maru	malu	maru	molu	mayu	wake
10.	*uyas-a	uyah-a	mu-ura	m-uyah	uos-o	wash
11.	*inur-a	inul-a	mu-ilu	mu-lahaf	inuy-o	drink
12.	*sapel-a	hapel-a	mu-hafe	mu-hafeh	safe-o	eat
13.	*haŋati	aŋati	hanasi	aŋesi	limu	walk
14.	*panim	panim	fali	feniŋ	fanim	fire
15.	*sulat	hulat	huha	huha?	suot	smoke
16.	*rahum	laup	rahu	louŋ	yaum	ash
17.	*tiap	tiap	sia	siaf	tiof	hearth
18.	*kayali-a	kayali-a	mu-harahi	mu-mutuk	hai-o	burn
19.	*anuŋ	anuŋ	alu	onuŋ	anuŋ	rubbish
20.	*nitaŋ	nitak	lita	nitaŋ	nitoŋ	house
21.	*oyala	pukap	oraha	oyaha	oao	roof
22.	*tikuŋ-a	tikuk-a	sihu	sihuŋ	tihuŋ-o	work
23.	*ŋatik	ŋatik	nasi	ŋesi?	sihif	sleep
24.	*uŋan	uŋan	una	uŋaŋ	etom	dream
25.	*ramak	lamak	rama	lama?	yamoh	shadow

1. Recurrent changes in Lgs. A, B, C and D in the order they are encountered are:

Change   **Examples**

Lg. A
1. *h > Ø (before 3)   1, 4, 8, 13, 16
2. *r > l   2, 5, 9, 11, 16, 25

3. *s > h   2, 4, 7, 10, 12, 15
4. *m,n,ŋ > p,t,k/[-nas]__#   3, 4, 7, 16, 20, 22

Lg. B
1. *l > h (before 6)   1, 6, 15, 18, 21
2. C > Ø/__#   1–5, 7, 8, 10–12, 14–17, 19, 20, 22–25
3. *y > r   3, 10, 18, 21
4. *s > h (before 8)   4, 7, 12, 15
5. *p > f   8, 12, 14
6. *n > l (before 7)   11, 14, 19, 20
7. *ŋ > n   13, 23, 24
8. *t > s/__i   13, 17, 22, 23
9. *k > h   18, 22

Lg. C
1. *l > h (before 5)   1, 6, 8, 12, 15, 21
2. *a > e,o/__Ci,u   1, 3, 9, 13, 14, 16, 19, 23
3. *h > Ø (before 1, 6, 9)   1, 4, 8, 13, 16
4. *t,k > ʔ/__#   1, 15, 23, 25
5. *r > l   2, 5, 9, 16, 25
6. *s > h (before 10)   2, 4, 7, 10, 12, 15
7. *m,n > ŋ/__#   3, 4, 14, 16, 24
8. *p > f   5, 8, 12, 14, 17
9. ViVi > Vi 8
10. *t > s/__i   13, 17, 22, 23
11. *k > h/__V   22

Lg. D
1. *l > h (before 2)   1, 6, 8, 12, 15, 18, 21
2. *h > Ø (before 3, 8)   1, 4, 6, 8, 12, 15, 16, 18, 21
3. *k > h   1, 18, 22, 25
4. *r > y   2, 5, 9, 11, 16, 25
5. *a > o/__(C)#   2, 4, 6, 10–12, 15, 17, 18, 20, 21, 22, 24, 25
6. *y > Ø (before 4, 8)   3, 10, 18, 21
7. *p > f   5, 8, 12, 14, 17
8. ViVi > Vi 8, 18

Discussion. This is a relatively difficult problem, with numerous innovations in most languages. One feature that may seem unusual is the change of
nasals to voiceless stops word-finally in Lg. A. However, changes of this type

SOLUTIONS

are found in several Mon-Khmer languages of the Malay peninsula, as well as in a number of the Austronesian languages of western Indonesia which have developed 'preploded' final nasals – that is nasals preceded by an oral vowel with orality persisting into the onset of the nasal consonant. In such languages, typified by the Land Dayak (Bidayuh) languages of southern Sarawak, allophonic vowel nasality is onset driven, and various consonants (usually the glides *y* and *w*, the laryngeals ʔ, *h*, and sometimes *l*) are transparent to nasal spreading. Final syllables that have a nasal onset prevent preplosion of final nasals due to nasalisation of the immediately preceding nucleus. A number of languages that had preploded final nasals -ᵖm, -ᵗn or -ᵏŋ have simplified these to voiceless stops, and the development of final voiceless stops from earlier nasals unless the final syllable has a nasal onset is a clear indication of earlier nasal preplosion (Blust 1997).

Another change which may seem odd is the shift of *a to /o/ in the last syllable, which occurs in Lg. D. Again, a number of languages in Indonesia show a change that is similar, although not identical to this, shifting *a > /o/ only in word-final position. In Javanese, which provides the best-known case, final *a became /ɔ/, and this rounded vowel then triggered rounding of a low vowel in a preceding syllable, hence *lima > *limɔ* 'five' and *mata > *mɔtɔ* 'eye'.

Note that the change *r > y in Lg. D is counted for item 5, because to count it as zero would obscure the fact that phonetically the same change took place in this form as in items 2, 9, 11, 16 and 25. The only difference is that the glide is now predictable intervocalically after /i/, and so need not be written in forms such as /iuf/.

Finally, although all four languages use some form of affixation to mark transitive verbs, Lgs. A and D use suffixation, while Lgs. B and C use prefixation, creating an uncertainty as to which, if either, of these affixes was present in Proto-ABCD. Even though the data suggest a priori that both *mu- and *-a can be reconstructed, a preliminary inspection of exclusively shared innovations will show that *mu- is found only in languages that form a single branch of the family, and must therefore be considered an innovation in relation to *-a, which is found in languages that show no subgrouping connection.

SOLUTION TO RECONSTRUCTION PROBLEM 35

No.	Proto-ABCD	Lg. A	Lg. B	Lg. C	Lg. D	
01.	*talam	talãp	talã	talab	talaŋ	grass
02.	*kepã	kefã	kipã	kepa	kepa	tree
03.	*nuyus	nuyuh	nuyu	nuzu?	nujuh	earth
04.	*alom	alõp	alũ	alob	aloŋ	stone
05.	*hiul	hiul	hiu	izul	hiju	water
06.	*kũiŋ	kũĩk	kũĩ	kuvig	kugʷiŋ	sky
07.	*sanid	hanit	sani	?anid	hani?	rain
08.	*ãhar	ãhar	ãha	aar	aha	storm
09.	*mitan	mitãt	mitã	mitad	mitaŋ	cloud
10.	*liap	liaf	lia	lizap	lija?	hand
11.	*wato	wato	watu	vato	gʷato	arm
12.	*hua	hua	hua	uva	hugʷa	elbow
13.	*abun	avũt	abũ	abud	abuŋ	knee
14.	*saras	harah	sara	?ara?	harah	house
15.	*rawik	rawik	rawi	ravik	ragʷi?	wall
16.	*lupĩh	lufĩh	lupĩ	lupi	lupih	roof
17.	*utab	utap	uta	utab	uta?	dog
18.	*bisek	vihek	bisi	bi?ek	bihe?	ant
19.	*palug	faluk	palu	palug	palu?	fly
20.	*gulũs	gulũh	gulũ	gulu?	guluh	see
21.	*odat	orat	uda	odat	oda?	hear
22.	*dasuŋ	rahũk	dasũ	da?ug	dahuŋ	eat
23.	*iŋuh	iŋuh	iŋu	iŋu	iŋuh	drink
24.	*yabet	yavet	yabi	zabet	jabe?	sleep
25.	*papah	fafah	papa	papa	papah	dream

1. Recurrent changes in Lgs. A, B, C and D in the order they are encountered are:

Change	**Examples**
Lg. A	
1. V > Ṽ/__N# (before 2)	1, 4, 6, 9, 13, 22
2. *m,n,ŋ > b,d,g/__# (before 3)	1, 4, 6, 9, 13, 22
3. *b,d,g > p,t,k/__#	1, 4, 6, 7, 9, 13, 17, 19, 22
4. *p > f (before 3)	2, 10, 16, 19, 25
5. *s > h	3, 7, 14, 18, 20, 22
6. *b,d > v,r/__V	13, 18, 21, 22, 24
Lg. B	
1. V > Ṽ/__N# (before 2)	1, 4, 6, 9, 13, 22
2. C > Ø/__#	1, 3–10, 13–25
3. *e,o > i,u	2, 4, 11, 18, 21, 24
4. *h > Ø/__#	16, 23, 25
Lg. C	
1. *m,n,ŋ > b,d,g/__#	1, 4, 6, 9, 13, 22
2. *Ṽ > V	2, 6, 8, 16, 20
3. *y,w > z,v	3, 5, 6, 10–12, 15, 24
4. *s > h (before 5)	3, 7, 14, 18, 20, 22
5. *h > ʔ	3, 7, 14, 18, 20, 22
6. Ø > y,w/i,u__V (before 3)	5, 6, 10, 12
7. *h > Ø (before 4)	5, 8, 12, 16, 23, 25
Lg. D	
1. *m,n > ŋ/__#	1, 4, 9, 13
2. *Ṽ > V	2, 6, 8, 16, 20
3. *y,w > j, gʷ	3, 5, 6, 10–12, 15, 24
4. *s > h	3, 7, 14, 18, 20, 22
5. Ø > y,w/i,u__V (before 3)	5, 6, 10, 12
6. *l,r > Ø/__#	5, 8
7. *b,d,g > p,t,k/__# (before 8)	7, 17, 19
8. *p,t,k > ʔ/__#	7, 10, 15, 17–19, 21, 24

2. The inventory of Proto-ABCD phonemes and their distributions within the word is as follows:

Consonants   Vowels

p   t   k   i   u
b   d   g
m   n   ŋ   e   o
     s   h
     l   a
     r
w   y   Plus nasalisation of at least some vowels

Discussion. One of the challenges in this problem is to use shared phonological features to reconstruct final nasals. Lgs. B and D distinguish final nasals from final stops, but provide no information about place features. Lgs. A and C reflect final nasals as stops, but preserve information about place of articulation. By combining the place features of the stop reflexes in Lgs. A and C with the nasality implied by Lgs. A, B and D we are able to reconstruct *-m, *-n and *-ŋ, as distinct from the corresponding voiced or voiceless stops. An additional complication is that nasalised vowels in Lgs. A and B reflect original nasal vowels in some words, but -VN sequences in others. This in turn raises a perennial question in phonological analysis: if Proto-ABCD had phonemic vowel nasality but automatically nasalised vowels before a final nasal, should vowel nasality be indicated in the latter environment (the 'once a phoneme always a phoneme' principle), or should it be derived contextually?

A second issue that emerges in this problem concerns glide fortition. Lgs. C and D have strengthened phonemic glides in examples 3, 11, 15 and 24, a type of change found in a number of the world's languages. However, both languages also strengthened phonetic glides in examples 5, 6, 10, and 12, a type of change that is less common, but occurs in several Austronesian languages, including Chamorro and various languages of northern Sarawak (Blust 2000a). Should these be treated as separate changes, or united as a single change that altered all phonetic glides to obstruents, whether or not they were also phonemic? They are treated here as a single change, since it is clear that the phonetic glides must have been present between a high vowel and a following unlike vowel at the time phonemic glides were strengthened, and any change that affected the latter would therefore potentially have affected the former.

SOLUTIONS

A third issue is seen in connection with the reconstruction of *-s. The correspondence $h : \emptyset : \text{?} : h$ (3, 14, 20) may initially seem to support Proto-ABCD *-ʔ. However, the instructions state that Proto-ABCD did not have a glottal stop. This forces us to consider *-h, but the correspondence $h : \emptyset : \emptyset : h$ in 16, 23 and 25 is an equally good or better candidate for *-h, forcing us to consider other alternatives. Attention to the data shows that this correspondence is in complementary distribution with non-final $h : s : \text{?} : h$, which must reflect *s. Both correspondences can thus be subsumed under *s, with *s > h in Lg. A, loss of final consonants in Lg. B, *s (> h) > ʔ in Lg. C, and *s > h in Lg. D.

SOLUTIONS TO INTERNAL RECONSTRUCTION PROBLEMS

SOLUTION TO INTERNAL RECONSTRUCTION PROBLEM 1

Toba Batak (northern Sumatra, Indonesia)

1. The underlying forms of the reduplicated or affixes words that were given are:

(a) andok-andok 'rice sack'
(b) otok-otok 'shrub with yellow blossoms'
(c) maŋ-kakkaŋ-i 'hold s.t. tightly between the legs'
(d) anak 'child' : par-anak-on 'relation between father and child'
(e) lapuk 'mold, fungus' : lapuk-on 'mouldy, mildewed'
(f) m-urak 'be ashamed' : ka-urak-on 'disgrace, scandal'
(g) m-oltuk-oltuk 'tasty (of fruits, sweet potatoes)'
(h) tar-tuktuk 'stumble, knock against' : ma-nuktuk-i 'knock on, pound on'

2. [h] and [k] are in complementary distribution in Toba Batak.
3. [h] and [k] also alternate in Toba Batak, making this an alternation of allophones.

Discussion. The phones [h] and [k] are in complementary distribution in Toba Batak, and so belong to a single phoneme /k/. In general [h] appears as syllable onset and [k] as syllable coda. However, [k] can also occur as a syllable onset when geminated (hence when following a written nasal within a morpheme). In this position it appears to contrast with [h], but never does, since [h] may only follow a nasal across a morpheme boundary. One of the lessons that this problem teaches, then, is the relevance of boundaries to statements of phonological distribution.

In American Structuralism phonological alternations were called 'morpho-phonemic alternations', but that term hardly seems appropriate in cases like this, where the alternation is between allophones, not phonemes. One could in theory distinguish the two as 'morphophonemic alternation' and 'morpho-phonetic alternation', but a more general description of the process is captured by the term 'phonological alternation', which covers both types without distinction.

SOLUTION TO INTERNAL RECONSTRUCTION PROBLEM 2

Western Bukidnon Manobo (southern Philippines)

1. The underlying forms of [əmutaʔ] 'a contribution', [əpuʔan] 'line of descent' and [bəlakan] 'crossroads' are: /amut-aʔ/, /apuʔ-an/, and /balak-an/. The surface forms result from neutralisation of prepenultimate /a/ and schwa as a mid-central vowel.

2. The underlying forms of [məvantug] 'famous', [bəvərəkaʔ] 'many-coloured' and [məvavaʔ] 'short' are: /mə-bantug/, /ba-barək-aʔ/ and /mə-bavaʔ/. The surface forms result from lenition of intervocalic /b/ to [v], and neutralisation of prepenultimate /a/ to schwa. In addition, the first syllable of [bəvərəkaʔ] is most likely a partial reduplication.

3. The underlying forms of [bunsuzan] 'area at foot of ladder', [məzakəl] 'many' and [məzəsən] 'strong' are: /bunsud-an/, /mə-da-kəl/ and /mə-dəsən/. The surface forms result from lenition of intervocalic /d/ to [z].

4. The underlying forms of [məɣəvuʔ] 'weak, fragile', [guyɣuy] 'trampled sword grass' and [ləmbaɣan] 'crossroad' are: /mə-gəvuʔ/, /guyguy/ and /ləmbag-an/, with surface forms resulting from lenition of intervocalic /g/ to a voiced velar fricative. In the case of [guyɣuy] it is assumed that this is a historical reduplication that retains its integrity as a reduplication in the synchronic grammar, and that glides and vowels function in identical ways to define the environment for lenition.

5. The underlying forms of [bəlvəlayan] 'a toy', [kəhilawan] 'humanity' and [təkawən] 'a thief' are: /bal-baləy-an/, /kə-hiləw-an/ and /takəw-ən/. Although the vowel-glide sequence in these forms historically contained *a, these have been restructured to -/əy/ and -/əw/. Under suffixation these innovative vowel-glide sequences return to their historical values (or more accurately, have preserved them).

6. The retention of the prepenultimate low vowel in [barasbaras] 'do something thoroughly', [sandigsandig] 'lean back on something' or [savuŋsavuŋ] 'bangs in the hair' is due to the stress pattern. Stress is penultimate on the base, and as a result historical low vowels in the antepenult merged/neutralised with schwa. However, in reduplications each iteration of the base form carries stress. In effect, then, it is more accurate to describe the alternations of [a] and [ə] as exemplifying a process of pretonic neutralisation rather than prepenultimate neutralisation.

SOLUTION TO INTERNAL RECONSTRUCTION PROBLEM 3

Samoan (western Polynesia)

1. The classic solution favoured by linguists (e.g. Bloomfield 1933: 219) is to propose an invariant suffix -*ia* by assigning the unpredictable thematic consonant to the base, hence:

01.	/inum/	
02.	/utuf/	
03.	/afāt/	
04.	/salan/?	
05.	/uan/?	
06.	/fana?/	
07.	/taŋis/	
08.	/tofuŋ/	
09.	/pulut/	
10.	/uluf/	
11.	/manatul/	
12.	/tūl/	
13.	/tā/	
14.	/tautalaŋ/	
15.	/fulis/	
16.	/?eli/	+ a
17.	/tanum/	
18.	/tunu/	+ a
19.	/aton/	?
20.	/tau/	

This simplifies the description of suffixation, since now there is a single form -*ia*. Early work in Generative Grammar which adopted this position sometimes pointed out that the thematic consonant that is assigned to the base matches a historical segment. In many cases this is true, as seen by comparing /inum/ with Proto-Oceanic *inum 'to drink', /utuf/ with *qutup 'submerge to fill', or /afāt/ with *apaRat 'west monsoon'. However, in other cases the thematic consonant does not match the historical final, as with /fana?/ next to POC *panaq 'to shoot' (Samoan ? reflects *k), or /aton/ next to POC *qatop 'thatch', where the expected thematic consonant in Samoan would be /f/.

Another problem with the single-shape solution to describing what is sometimes called the -Cia suffix in Samoan and other Polynesian languages is seen in examples such as 4, 5 and 19, where instead of the expected -Cia shape, what is clearly the same suffix has the shape -iCa. In every case this is -ina, implying that expected -nia underwent regular metathesis to -ina. If the suffix is to be represented consistently as -ia, cases such as these must be accompanied by a synchronic rule of metathesis between the initial /n/ of the suffix and the following vowel (/ua-nia/ > [uaina], etc.).

In addition to these problems we need to consider cases such as 16 and 18, in which the suffix surfaces as a single vowel -a. In examples such as 16 this can be attributed to fusion of two identical vowels in sequence (/ʔeli-ia/ > [ʔelia]), but examples such as 18 require the deletion of the first suffixal vowel whether the vowels are identical or not.

2. Native speakers of Polynesian languages, to the extent they have been tested, reject the single-shape solution out of hand, since it requires base forms with closed syllables, which runs contrary to their perception (based on surface forms) that no word may end in a consonant. For the classic discussion of the two positions, both by linguists, but one of whom was also a native speaker of Maori, cf. Hohepa (1967) and Hale (1968).

SOLUTION TO INTERNAL RECONSTRUCTION PROBLEM 4

Seimat (Admiralty Islands, Papua New Guinea)

1. The underlying forms of bases 1–18 in section A are identical to the possessed forms less the possessive suffix, hence surface [min] = underlying /mina/, surface [sus] = underlying /susu/, etc.
2. The synchronic rule relating these forms is final vowel deletion, the product of a historical change that has remained in the synchronic grammar:

$$V > \emptyset / \_\_ \#$$

/mina/ > [min] 'hand' : /mina-n/ > [minan] 'his/her hand'
/susu/ > [sus] 'breast' : /susu-n/ > [susun] 'her breast', etc.

(A)

No.	Base	3sg. possessed form	
01.	mina	mina-n	hand
02.	susu	susu-n	breast
03.	puto	puto-n	navel
04.	uti	uti-n	penis
05.	patu	patu-n	head
06.	kawã	kawã-n	forehead
07.	pula	pula-n	eye
08.	awa	awa-n	mouth
09.	nisu	nisu-n	tooth
10.	xohe	xohe-n	gums
11.	leho	leho-n	tongue
12.	kinawe	kinawe-n	neck
13.	taxiŋa	taxiŋa-n	ear
14.	uku	uku-n	head hair
15.	kakau	kakau-n	blood
16.	atolu	atolu-n	brain
17.	mapua	mapua-n	sweat
18.	lohu	lohu-n	friend

3. The underlying shapes of the continuative forms in section (B) contain a final vowel that is preserved in the first iteration but lost in the last because of the historical, and arguably synchronic, rule of final vowel deletion.

4. Whether the nouns in section (B) should also be seen as still containing an underlying final vowel because they are reduplications that pattern much like continuative verbs, is a much more difficult question (see discussion below).

(B)

No.	Base	Continuative form	
01.	ikoik		mussel
02.	suhusuh		conch shell
03.	pakapak		shrimp
04.	solisol		tidal wave
05.	ponapon		swamp
06.	hatuhat		4-cornered fish
07.	uliul		side board of canoe
08.	paŋapaŋ		moon
09.	konokon		prow of canoe
10.	taŋi 'to cry'	taŋitaŋi	be crying
11.	aŋi 'to eat'	aŋiaŋi	be eating
12.	mutu 'vomitus'	mutumutu	be vomiting; to vomit
13.	tasutas		nasal mucus
14.	utuut		corner
15.	axaax		fireplow
16.	hatahat		storage shelf
17.	kuhukuh		*Alocasia* taro
18.	silisil		tuna sp.
19.	tioti		large barbelled fish
20.	kawakaw		bamboo
21.	paxapax		sandfly
22.	kioki		kingfisher
23.	unu 'to drink'	unuuunu	be drinking
24.	hoŋo 'to hear'	hoŋohoŋo	be hearing
25.	siwisiw		black hummingbird
26.	laŋalaŋ		to sail
27.	paku 'song; to sing'	pakupaku	be singing

SOLUTIONS

28.	leŋeleŋ		to fight, of animals
29.	hilehil		to fight in war
30.	telei 'to kill'	teletele	be killing
31.	ha-puta 'to drop'	putaputa	to fall; be falling
32.	manuman		drift on a current

Discussion. Positing underlying forms with a final vowel for the bases in section (A) is not controversial because there are phonological alternations, and hence some surface forms that reflect the underlying final vowel. This enables us to state in simple terms which vowel appears in the possessive forms, but the material in section (B) raises more difficult questions for a synchronic analysis.

While the continuative forms of verbs preserve the vowel of the last syllable of the base much like the possessive forms of nouns, they do so through a process of reduplication that is still active in the language (and this suggests that verbs that were recorded only in reduplicated form, such as *laŋalaŋ* or *manuman* probably have synchronic CVC base forms (*laŋ*, *man*, etc.)). The most vexing question is what to propose as underlying forms for nouns that show historical reduplication – a process that presumably has ceased to function in the language for this word class, as with *ikoik* 'mussel', *suhusuh* 'conch shell', or *pakapak* 'shrimp'. While a majority view probably would consider the underlying shapes of such words identical to their surface forms, as with unreduplicated nouns that historically lost the final vowel (*hat* < Proto-Oceanic *patu* 'stone', *uh* < *quraŋ* 'lobster', *laŋ* < *laŋo* 'housefly', etc.), it could be argued that apocope (loss of final vowels) remains an active process in the language, and that these reduplications do not differ formally from those for continuative verbs. Given this interpretation one could argue (although much more controversially) that the underlying forms for mussel, conch shell and shrimp still contain the final vowel, hence *ikoiko, suhusuhu, pakapaka*, etc.

SOLUTION TO INTERNAL RECONSTRUCTION PROBLEM 5

Kapampangan (Central Luzon, Philippines)

No.	Base	Verb
01.	abú 'ash'	man-abú 'become ash'
02.	águs 'current'	mVm-águs 'to flow'
03.	ámbun 'dew'	mVm-ámbun 'be about to rain'
04.	ágiʔ 'spiderweb'	man-ágiʔ 'remove cobwebs'
05.	ínaʔ 'weakness'	mVm-ínaʔ 'grow weak'
06.	íkab 'belch'	man-íkab 'to belch'
07.	áŋin 'wind'	mVm-áŋin 'to blow, of the wind'
08.	ampíl 'a stack'	man-ampíl 'to stack (dishes)'
09.	urúd 'haircut'	man-urúd 'get a haircut'
10.	úna 'first'	mVm-úna 'go first, be first'
11.	atád 'escort'	mVm-atád 'to escort'
12.	apán 'bait'	man-apán 'put out bait'
13.	igpit 'tight'	man-igpit 'to tighten'
14.	íkat 'a braid'	mVm-íkat 'to braid'
15.	ulíʔ 'go home'	man-ulíʔ 'to go home'
16.	iʔ 'urine'	mVm-íʔ 'to urinate'
17.	úkyat 'climbing'	mVm-úkyat 'to climb'
18.	ípus 'servant'	man-ípus 'to serve'
19.	úlu 'medicine'	man-úlu 'curer'
20.	urán 'rain'	mVm-urán 'to rain, be raining'
21.	úpa 'rent'	man-úpa 'to rent'
22.	útak 'brain'	mVm-útak 'to use one's brain'
23.	ísip 'think'	man-ísip 'to think'
24.	íŋat 'caution'	mVm-íŋat 'to beware'

1. There are two prefixes in items 1–24 which are semantically difficult to distinguish, but which show differing formal properties that mark them as distinct.
2. *man-* has a single allomorph, occurring in this fixed shape regardless of the initial vowel of the base. By contrast, *mVm-* copies the first vowel of the base, and so occurs with allomorphs *mam-*, *mim-* and *mum-*.

3. What is surprising is that these prefixes behave differently with regard to assimilatory allomorphy, even though they are very similar in shape.
4. The problem of underlying forms is taken up in the following discussion.

Discussion. Like many other Philippine languages, Kapampangan has a number of verbal prefixes. Two of these are illustrated here: *man-* and *mVm-*. Both prefixes appear to be found only before bases that begin with a vowel. Whereas *man-* has a single invariant shape *mVm-* shows a vowel that copies the first vowel of the base (/a/, /i/ or /u/).

Perhaps the most surprising feature of this behaviour is that assimilatory behaviour is normally assumed to be phonetically conditioned, but here there is no phonetic difference in the conditions which produce assimilatory allomorphy in *mVm-*, but not in *man-*. Before bases which begin with /a/ the two prefixes have the same vowel, and no difference of behaviour is discernible, but before bases which begin with a high vowel the matter is different, since *mVm-* surfaces as *mim-* or *mum-*, while *man-* always surfaces as *man-*. It would be satisfying to be able to state a single underlying shape for *mVm-*, but given three allomorphs, all of which appear to be conditioned, there is little basis for favouring one shape over the others, and we are left with no choice but to posit an underlying prefix with an underspecified vowel.

SOLUTION TO INTERNAL RECONSTRUCTION PROBLEM 6

Thao (central Taiwan)

No.	(A)	(B)
01.	apa 'carry on the back'	um-apa 'to carry on the back'
02.	ishur 'prying up'	um-ishur 'to pry something up'
03.	utaq 'vomit'	um-utaq 'to vomit'
04.	liliz 'following'	um-liliz 'to follow someone, to tail'
05.	rinuz 'earthquake'	um-rinuz 'to shake, of an earthquake'
06.	zai 'advice'	um-zai 'to advise'
07.	ca-capu 'broom'	c<um>apu 'to sweep'
08.	hurhur 'barking'	h<um>urhur 'to bark'
09.	kawar 'wall hook'	k<um>awar 'to hang on a hook'
10.	lhipir 'a fold'	lh<um>ipir 'to fold, as paper or cloth'
11.	qucquc 'binding'	q<um>ucquc 'to tie, bind'
12.	siraq 'a kiss'	s<um>iraq 'to kiss, to lick'
13.	shuruz 'pull'	sh<um>uruz 'to pull'
14.	tiktik 'hacking, chopping'	t<um>iktik 'to hack, to chop'
15.	patash 'tattoo; writing'	p<um>atash 'to write'
16.	pushizi 'separation'	p<um>ushizi 'to separate'
17.	fariw 'buying'	fariw 'to buy'
18.	fuilh 'inform'	fuilh 'to inform'
19.	qpit 'pinching'	q<um>pit 'to pinch'
20.	qtut 'a fart'	q<un>tut 'to fart'
21.	shkash 'fear'	sh<uŋ>kash 'to fear'
22.	shqa 'bequeath'	sh<uŋ-qa [ʃúNqa] 'to bequeath'
23.	shnara 'burn'	sh<u>nara 'to burn'
24.	cnit 'wring out'	c<u>nit 'to wring out'
25.	shrak 'untying'	sh<un>rak [ʃúndrak] 'to untie'
26.	kriuʔ 'stealing, theft'	k<un>riuʔ [kúndreuʔ] 'to steal'

1. The underlying form of the Thao Actor Voice affix is best represented as -/um/-.
2. The phonetic factors which condition the rich allomorphy of this affix are discussed below.

SOLUTIONS

Discussion. In most cases -/um/- attaches immediately before the first vowel of the base, causing it to surface as a prefix in vowel-initial bases, and an infix in most others. Thao does not allow -/um/- to appear as an infix in bases that begin with a liquid or the voiced interdental fricative /z/; instead these are treated like vowel-initial bases. To generalise, then, -/um/- is prefixed to any voiced base-initial segment, whether vowel or consonant. Moreover, an unstressed word-initial vowel in the antepenult drops, leaving the surface form of the affix as *m-*.

In bases that begin with a voiceless obstruent, /h/ or /lh/ the Actor Voice affix is infixed before the first base vowel and the unstressed infixal vowel is lost, leaving the surface form of the affix as *-m-*.

In bases that begin with /p/ the affixed word acquires a highly disfavoured shape, namely one that contains the sequences *pVm* or *bVm* (PAN *b became Thao /f/, thus eliminating this possibility). When morphological processes create this type of sequence many Austronesian languages eliminate it by a process of pseudo nasal substitution (*pVmV-* > *mV-* and *bVmV-* > *mV-*), creating *p/m* pairs like Thao *patash* : *matash*.

Bases that begin with /f/ (< *b) take a zero allomorph of the Actor Voice infix, and so are unchanged in this construction.

Finally, bases that begin with a consonant cluster (the result of historical syncope) maintain the full -VC- shape of the infix if the second consonant of the cluster is a stop. However, the infixal nasal undergoes place assimilation to the following consonant producing surface forms [um], [un], [uŋ] and [uN] (the latter with a uvular nasal that is not a phoneme in the language). If the second consonant in the cluster is a nasal the nasal of the affix drops, leaving just the vowel to surface as *-u-*, as in *sh<u>nara* or *c<u>nit*, and if the second consonant is a rhotic the full VC form of the affix remains, but a transitional stop is inserted between the affixal nasal and the liquid consonant of the base, as in *sh<un>rak* [ʃúndrak] or k<un>riu? [kúndreu?].

SOLUTION TO INTERNAL RECONSTRUCTION PROBLEM 7

Sangir (northern Sulawesi, Indonesia)

1. The underlying forms of the instrumental nouns are given in column B.
2. The most straightforward derivations are those in which the base morpheme begins with a voiceless obstruent *p, t, k* or *s*, since these undergo no change in intervocalic position. Bases that begin with a voiced stop show ordinary lenitions to the base-initial consonant, and are therefore only moderately opaque. Bases that begin with *l* show an unexplained fortition of the liquid to a voiced stop in the reduplicant, and those that begin with a vowel or *h-* show a puzzling addition of *l-* to the reduplicated vowel.
3. For a fuller account of how this system might have developed see the discussion.

No.	Actor voice (A)	Instrumental noun (B)
01.	maŋaki 'extend a fishline'	/a-aki/ 'extension piece on fishline'
02.	mamaŋgo 'to beat'	/ba-baŋgo/ 'a cudgel'
03.	mamuaŋ 'fasten with transverse pin'	/ba-buaŋ/ 'transverse pin'
04.	dumǝka? 'to stick, adhere'	/da-dǝka?/ 'plaster, paste'
05.	mǝndupa 'to hammer'	/da-dupa/ 'a hammer'
06.	maŋǝkiŋ 'give a brideprice'	/a-ǝkiŋ/ 'a brideprice'
07.	maŋǝmmu? 'wipe off'	/a-ǝmmu?/ 'dustcloth, washcloth'
08.	mǝŋgata? 'carry under the arm'	/ga-gata?/ 'bamboo tongs'
09.	mǝhimadǝ? 'use a gouging tool'	/a-himadǝ?/ 'gouging tool'
10.	maŋiki? 'to tie'	/a-iki?/ 'anything used for tying'
11.	maŋǝtuŋ 'seize with pincers'	/ka-kǝtuŋ/ 'pincers'
12.	mǝlau? 'to mix'	/la-lau?/ 'tool used for mixing'
13.	mǝlǝdaŋ 'to file the teeth'	/la-lǝdaŋ/ 'a tooth file'
14.	mamaŋkulǝ? 'hit with stick'	/pa-paŋkulǝ?/ 'stick used for hitting'
15.	mamǝgoŋ 'tie round the middle'	/pa-pǝgoŋ/ 'belt'
16.	manapu 'to sweep'	/sa-sapu/ 'broom'
17.	suminda? 'to breathe'	/sa-sinda?/ 'anything that assists breathing'

SOLUTIONS

18.   manapisə? 'to sift'   /ta-tapisə?/ 'a sieve'
19.   manubuŋ 'knock down fruit'   /ta-tubuŋ/ 'fruiting pole'
20.   maɲuhasə? 'to wash'   /a-uhasə?/ 'water used for
                                            washing'

Discussion. The basic pattern used to form instrumental nouns can be called 'Ca- reduplication'. Essentially, this involves copying the first consonant of the base followed by the fixed vowel /a/, and prefixing this reduplicant to the base form. The most straightforward derivations are those in which the instrumental noun is formed by copying the base-initial consonant plus the fixed vowel /a/, with no further changes. This is seen most clearly with bases that begin with the voiceless obstruents *p, t, k* and *s*, since these undergo no phonological processes when placed in intervocalic position, although they undergo homorganic nasal substitution following the active verb prefix *maŋ-*.

The next most transparent derivations are those for bases that begin with a voiced obstruent *b, d* or *g*, since these show Ca- reduplication followed by lenition of the stop in intervocalic position: /b/ > [w], /d/ > [r] and /g/ > [ɣ] (written *gh*). Since the copied base-initial consonant in the Ca- reduplicant does not lenite this provides a clear indication of the underlying shape of this segment in the base itself. In addition, although bases with *b-* undergo nasal substitution, those with *d-* and *g-* show a pattern of nasal accretion, and so provide a second indication of the shape of the base-initial consonant without lenition in the Actor Voice form.

The third category of derivations are those that begin with *l-*, and these are more obscure than the preceding two categories, since the liquid of the reduplicant undergoes fortition to *d-*, even though that of the base is unchanged. While the consonant of the reduplicant preserves phonological information that is lost in bases that begin with a voiced obstruent, then, this relationship is reversed for bases that begin with *l*. Since Sangir allows /Vl/ sequences within a morpheme, there is no obvious reason why it should dissimilate such sequences in instrumental nouns formed by Ca- reduplication. Again, the active verb form preserves the base-initial consonant unchanged, and this provides another piece of evidence that the underlying form of the base is preserved in the shape of the base itself rather than in the 'copy' that appears in the reduplicant.

Undoubtedly the most puzzling derivations are instrumental nouns formed from bases that begin with a vowel. Here the fixed vowel /a/ is invariant, but unlike the situation for many other languages that have a related process of Ca- reduplication, instrumental nouns in Sangir must begin with a consonant. The consonant that is added is *l*, which historically derives from **y*. Again, the motivation for this development is obscure, since vowel-initial *base forms* are commonplace in Sangir. Equally puzzling, bases that begin with *h-* (< **R*, probably a velar or uvular trill) drop the *h-* and add *l-*, behaving in effect as though they begin with a vowel.

Comparative evidence shows that this system evolved from invariant Ca- reduplication. The most likely innovation which could have created imbalance in Sangir is the lenition of voiced stops in intervocalic position, as this is a natural change that affected the language generally. Once this happened the initial consonants of the base and reduplicant would have differed, opening the way for other phonologically more arbitrary manipulations. The most straightforward of these produced a *da-* pattern for bases that begin with *l-* (initial *r-* does not occur in native forms), somewhat mimicking the *d ~ r* alternations seen with *d*-initial bases. And, then, through a much more obscure extension of the alternation pattern seen with bases that begin with a voiced obstruent or *l-*, bases that began with a vowel or *h-* acquired an excrescent consonant so that all instrumental nouns now have an onset.

SOLUTION TO INTERNAL RECONSTRUCTION PROBLEM 8

Bario Kelabit (Sarawak, Malaysian Borneo)

1. The underlying forms of the affixed words in column B are given below, with morpheme boundaries indicated.

No	A	B	
01.	atur	ŋ-atur	an order; to order
02.	pudut	ŋ-pudut	a shape; to shape
03.	bilaʔ	ŋ-bilaʔ	to split
04.	tərəm	ŋ-tərəm	to sink; force under water
05.	dalan	ŋ-dalan	path; to walk
06.	kiluʔ	ŋ-kiluʔ	a bend; to bend
		k<əm>iluʔ	to meander (river)
07.	laak	ŋ-laak	cooked; to cook
08.	raʔit	ŋ-raʔit	raft; travel by raft
09.	taban	taban-ən	elopement; to elope
10.	badil	badil-ən	gun; be shot
11.	irup	irup-an	drink; watering hole
12.	arəg	arəg-ən	fragment; broken to bits
13.	taʔut	pə-taʔut	fear; to frighten
		p<in>ə-taʔut	was frightened
14.	piŋur	tə-piŋur	echo; echoing back and forth
		t<in>ə-piŋur	was used to make echoes
15.	təbʰək	t<in>əbʰək	pierce mark; was pierced by
16.	tələn	t<in>ələn	swallow; was swallowed by
17.	təbʰar	ŋ-təbʰar	wages; to pay
		təbʰar-an	Pay him! (imper.)
18.	təbʰəŋ	ŋ-təbʰəŋ	felling of trees; to fell
		təbʰəŋ-ən	Fell it! (imper.)
19.	ulud	ulud-ən	words; will tell (near future)
20.	əbʰaʔ	ŋ-əbʰaʔ	water; to add/remove water
		əbʰaʔ-ən	Add/remove water! (imper.)
21.	kədʰa	ŋ-kədʰa	able to take pain; to suffer
	kədʰa-an		suffering
22.	turuʔ	t<in>uruʔ	an order; was ordered by s.o.
23.	kəkəb	kəkəb-ən	lid; be covered by s.o.

24.	agag	agag-ən	rice sieve; to sift
25.	uit	əm-uit	way of bringing; to bring
26.	turun	t<əm>urun	descent; to descend
27.	ələg	əm-ələg	cessation; to stop
		ləgʰən	be stopped by s.o.
28.	bəbʰəd	bəbʰəd-ən	bundle; tie by winding round
		b<in>əbʰəd	was tied by winding round
29.	gətəp	gətəp-ən	bite mark; be bitten by
30.	bəlih	ŋ-bəlih	buying; to buy
	bəlih-ən		Buy it! (imper.)

2. The synchronic phonological processes that produce these results are discussed below.

Discussion. The Bario dialect of Kelabit has a particularly rich synchronic phonology, with some typologically rather unusual alternations. In the order in which they are encountered in this data set, the phonological processes that operate to convert underlying representations to their surface forms are as follows:

1. *Nasal substitution*. The active verb prefix ŋ-, which appears unchanged before vowel-initial bases, assimilates to the place of a following stop, which then deletes. This is the familiar process of *nasal substitution* that is common to many of the languages of the Philippines, western Indonesia/Malaysia, and such geographical outliers as Malagasy in Madagascar and Palauan and Chamorro in western Micronesia; it affects items 2–6, 17, 18, 21 and 30. Before liquids (and nasals) the prefix remains unchanged, and a schwa is inserted between it and the initial consonant of the base, as in items 7 and 8.
2. *Prepenultimate vowel neutralisation*. Within morphemes all vocalic oppositions are neutralised as schwa in prepenultimate position, with the optional exception of /i/ in the passive-perfective infix -*in*-. This is seen in items 9–12, 19, 20, 24 and 27.
3. *Deletion of prepenultimate initial schwa*. If an underlying schwa or a schwa that results from neutralisation becomes initial in the antepenult as a result of suffixation it is dropped, as in items 11, 12, 19, 20, 24, 25 and 27.
4. *Conversion of plain voiced stops to surface voiced aspirates*. Following a stressed schwa plain voiced stops become surface voiced aspirates (stress is

penultimate, and so shifts rightward under suffixation; Blust 2016a). This affects items 12, 23, 27 and 28.

5. *Schwa syncope.* Schwa is deleted /VC__CV (must apply after 3 above). This affects items 13–16 and 28. Note that schwa syncope is blocked if one of the consonants in the environment is phonetically geminate, as in items 18 or 29. Schwa syncope is also blocked before a voiced aspirate, which reflects a historical geminate, and is longer than singleton consonants in the contemporary language, as in items 23 or 28 (*bəbəd^hən*). However, schwa syncope occurs in items 14–16 and 28 (*bib^həd*) in a similar environment. The reason for this difference is not yet understood.

6. *Assibilation.* Historically *t > s/__i in Kelabit, and this remains a synchronic process in the language in bases that take the infix -*in*-, as seen in items 14–16 and 22.

7. *Cluster reduction.* Consonant clusters resulting from schwa syncope were retained at the juncture between the antepenult and penult, but were reduced by deletion of the nasal at the juncture between the penult and ultima. In bases that contain a penultimate schwa this resulted in a pattern of incipient ablaut (ə in the base, *i* in the passive-perfective).

8. *Gemination.* Consonants other than voiced stops are automatically geminated after a stressed penultimate schwa, as seen in items 16, 27, 29 and 30. Plain voiced stops in this environment become surface voiced aspirates, as described in 4 above.

9. *Deaspiration.* Underlying voiced aspirates surface as their plain voiced counterparts when they no longer follow a stressed schwa, as seen in items 20, 21 and 28. This is particularly clear in item 28, where the underlying *b^h* surfaces as [b], and the underlying *d* surfaces as [*d^h*] as a result of rightward stress shift following suffixation.

10. *h-deletion.* An -*h* was added after final vowels in many of the languages of northern Sarawak, including Kelabit. This segment is found in no other position in Kelabit, and under suffixation it deletes.

SOLUTION TO INTERNAL RECONSTRUCTION PROBLEM 9

Mukah Melanau (Sarawak, Malaysian Borneo)

1. There are two active verb affixes: *məŋ-* and *-um-*.
2. There is one passive verb affix: *-in-*.

Discussion. Like many other problems in internal reconstruction, this one requires the analyst to look for evidence of complementation. It is clear from the forms under (1) and (2) that *mə-* and *m-* are allomorphs of the same prefix, as are *nə-* and *n-*, the longer form occurring in stems that begin with a voiced obstruent, and the shorter one in stems that begin with a vowel. Since Mukah has a general morpheme structure constraint that disallows prevocalic schwa we can assume that the shape of these prefixes is *mə-*, *nə-*, and that *m-*, *n-* are reduced by schwa deletion.

The forms under (5) show that there must be a distinct active verb prefix *məŋ-*, since both this and *m-* (/mə-/) occur with vowel-initial bases. The active forms under (4) can then be interpreted as containing realisations of *məŋ-* in stems with a voiceless obstruent initial, undergoing a process of homorganic nasal substitution much like the well-known process in languages such as Malay/Indonesian or Tagalog.

This brings us to pattern (3), in which an innovative process of verbal ablaut is used to mark voice distinctions. It is clear that this pattern is in complementary distribution with the other considered above, since with only a few exceptions that can be safely ignored ablaut is confined to stems that contain a penultimate schwa. Perhaps the surest indication of historical identity is seen in the passive voice, where both *nə-/n-* and *i*-ablaut mark a passive that is obligatorily perfective. The problem at this point is how to relate ablaut to patterns of affixation that perform the same function, since *nə-* and *n-* are prefixed, while ablaut is essentially a form of infixation. However, as noted above, the prefixes *mə-* and *nə-* as used by speakers born around 1955 were infixes *-əm-* and *-ən-* in the speech of persons born around 1915 (a feature that may have disappeared from the language community altogether by now). Since *-ən-* and *i*-ablaut almost certainly have the same historical source we must find some way to account for the fact that they share no phonemic substance. If both mechanisms for marking the passive had begun as *-in- the neutralisation of vocalic oppositions as schwa in prepenultimate syllables would have changed *-in- to *-ən-* in infixed words that remained trisyllabic. In stems that contain penultimate schwa, however, this would not be the case. Consider the following example, based on the verb stem *səsəp 'sucking':

*s-in-əsəp
s-in-səp   (medial schwa syncope)
sisəp   (cluster reduction)

Since schwa is not permitted in the environment VC__CV, and consonant clusters are disallowed in Mukah Melanau, each of these historical processes can be justified by synchronic phonotactic constraints, and in this way all three allomorphs of the passive voice (nə-, n- and -i-) can be derived in a straightforward manner from -/in/-. A parallel argument holds for the active voice, in which mə-, m- and -u- can similarly be derived from -/um/-. As it happens, comparative reconstruction leads to the same conclusion, since *-um- marked the Actor Voice in Proto-Austronesian, and *-in- marked perfective aspect, but functioned as a portmanteau morpheme in patient voice constructions, marking perfective aspect and passive as an inseparable unity.

SOLUTION TO INTERNAL RECONSTRUCTION PROBLEM 10

(Artificial data)

1. Items 4, 10, 14 and 16 should be reconstructed tentatively as *ruvat, *palud, *rilit and *ited. The final consonants of 4 and 14 are voiceless, while those of 10 and 16 are voiced. If the evidence of synchronic alternations were not available all of these forms would be reconstructed with *-t.

2. Items 7, 8, 19, 20 and 21 should be reconstructed tentatively as *ulub, *osup, *lakip, *inab and *neɣtip. The final consonants of 7 and 20 are voiced, while those of 8, 19 and 21 are voiceless. Because Lgs. B and C distinguish the reflexes of *b and *p word-finally the *b/p distinction would be reconstructed correctly whether synchronic alternations were available or not.

3. *d has been reconstructed so far only in final position, and to this we can add postconsonantally in item 6. On the other hand, *r is reconstructed only in initial position. Since the tentative reconstructions of *d and *r are in complementary distribution they should be united as *d. Similarly, *b and *v are in complementary distribution, since *b is reconstructed only in final position and postconsonantally, while *v is reconstructed only in initial position. This leads us to unite tentative *d and *r as a single proto-phoneme *d and to unite tentative *b and *v as a single proto-phoneme *b, leading us to change *ruvat and *rilit to *dubat and *dilit.

4. Since there is clearly a *t/d distinction word-finally that is recoverable when suffixed forms are available, it follows that a *t : t : t* correspondence in final position without access to suffixed forms must be indeterminate for *t or *d, as in 18 and 22, which we should reconstruct as *sena(d,t) and *kusu(d,t) respectively.

Discussion. This problem combines comparative and internal reconstruction in a single process. In the first stage of the reconstruction it should be recognised that some words ending in *p* or *t* alternate under suffixation, while others do not. This forces us to reconstruct different finals in e.g. 4 and 10 or 7 and 8. One of these finals is voiced and the other voiceless. The voiceless finals point fairly clearly to *-p and *-t; the voiced finals are somewhat more problematic, pointing to either voiced continuants or voiced stops. Since -*t* is an unlikely development of a voiced continuant *-d must be considered a more plausible alternative. The alternation of *-t* and -r then follows from two natural and common sound changes: final devoicing of obstruents and the change of voiced stops to continuants before a vowel.

The solution for *-d suggests a parallel solution for the *-p/v* alternation, hence *-b, again with word-final devoicing, and *b > *v*/V__V, followed by *v > *w* in Lg. C. A second piece of evidence that this is the correct solution is seen in the retention of *b and *d as stops in postconsonantal position in 5, 6 and 23, and a third piece of evidence is seen in the different reflexes of *-p and *-b (but not of *-t and *-d) in absolute final position.

The first-round reconstructions for the correspondences /v : v : w/ and /r : r : r/ word-initially and intervocalically presumably were *v and *r. It should now be recognised that *v and *b are in complementary distribution, as are *r and *d: the continuants occur only word-initially and intervocalically, and the stops only postconsonantally and finally. So, both distribution and alternation point to *b and *d in environments where none of the daughter languages have preserved voiced stops.

This leaves two forms (18, 22) as ambiguous for *(d,t), since the reconstruction of the final stop is based on the correspondence /t : t : t/ with no alternation.

SOLUTIONS TO SUBGROUPING PROBLEMS

SOLUTION TO SUBGROUPING PROBLEM 1

No.	Proto-ABCD	Lg. A	Lg.B	Lg. C	Lg. D	
01.	*kutil	ʔutil	util	kuril	kulil	fish
02.	*isara	ihara	iara	isara	isala	water
03.	*nak	naʔ	na	nak	nak	earth
04.	*popat	popat	fofaʔ	popat	popat	rain
05.	*uruʔ	uruʔ	uru	uru	ulu	cloud
06.	*situ	hitu	itu	siru	silu	wind
07.	*lami	lami	lami	lami	lami	man
08.	*narit	narit	nariʔ	narit	nalit	woman
09.	*helu	helu	elu	helu	helu	child
10.	*mumaŋ	mumaŋ	mumaŋ	mumaŋ	mumaŋ	house
11.	*alas	alah	ala	alas	alas	forest
12.	*sutup	hutup	utuʔ	surup	sulup	walk
13.	*rumun	rumun	rumuŋ	rumun	lumun	speak
14.	*kurom	ʔurom	uroŋ	kurom	kulom	sleep
15.	*atar	atar	atar	arar	alal	bathe
16.	*ʔaku	ʔaʔu	au	aku	aku	black
17.	*tiʔan	tiʔan	tiaŋ	tian	tian	white
18.	*tetu	tetu	tetu	teru	telu	red
19.	*lahik	lahiʔ	lai	lahik	lahik	green
20.	*sapiʔ	hapiʔ	afi	sapi	sapi	grass

1. Recurrent changes in Lgs. A, B, C and D in the order they are encountered are:

Change	Examples
Lg. A	
1. *k > ʔ	1, 3, 14, 16, 19
2. *s > h	2, 6, 11, 12, 20
Lg. B	
1. *k > ʔ (before 2)	1, 3, 14, 16, 19
2. *ʔ > Ø (before 6)	1, 3, 5, 14, 16, 17, 19, 20
3. *s > h (before 4)	2, 6, 11, 12, 20
4. *h > Ø	2, 6, 9, 11, 12, 19, 20
5. *p > f/__V	4, 20
6. *p,t > ʔ/__#	4, 8, 12
7. *m,n > ŋ/__#	13, 14, 17
Lg. C	
1. *t > r/V__V	1, 6, 12, 15, 18
2. *ʔ > Ø	5, 16, 17, 20
Lg. D	
1. *t > r/V__V (before 2)	1, 6, 12, 15, 18
2. *r > l	1, 2, 5, 6, 8, 12–15, 18
3. *ʔ > Ø	5, 16, 17, 20

2. The family tree has two primary branches: AB and CD. The first group is based on two innovations: (1) merger of *k and *ʔ, and (2) merger of *s and *h. The second group is also based on two mergers: (1) merger of *t and *r intervocalically (followed by *r > *l* in Lg. D), and (2) merger of *ʔ and zero.

Discussion. As noted above, these four languages appear to form coordinate branches AB and CD. The AB group is justified by two exclusively shared innovations:

1. merger of *k and *ʔ
2. merger of *s and *h

The CD group is also supported by two shared innovations:

1. merger of *t and *r intervocalically (followed by *r > *l* in Lg. D)
2. merger of *ʔ and zero

The second of these changes is shared with Lg. B, but since *k and *ʔ merged in Lgs. A and B it is simplest to assume *k > ʔ in Proto-AB, followed by ʔ > Ø in Lg. B, rather than assume *ʔ > Ø in Lg. B and then a two-step change leading to loss of *k in the same language. Since *k did not lenite in Lgs. C or D, we must conclude that the loss of *ʔ in Lg. B was independent of the similar change in Lgs. C and D.

In both cases one innovation provides relatively weak subgrouping evidence (*s > *h* in the AB group, *ʔ > Ø in the CD group). However, the second innovation in each group is relatively strong, and the combined evidence is sufficient to propose both groups, although not with a high level of confidence.

SOLUTION TO SUBGROUPING PROBLEM 2

No.	Proto-ABC	Lg. A	Lg. B	Lg. C	
01.	*anaŋ	anaŋ	anaŋ	anaŋ	frog
02.	*ketup	kitup	ketuf	keruh	willow tree
03.	*rampid	rampid	rampit	rapit	swamp
04.	*nunum	nunum	nunun	nunuŋ	cattail
05.	*lalag	lalag	lalak	lalak	fish
06.	*futol	futul	futol	hurol	bird
07.	*hopuŋ	upuŋ	hofuŋ	hohuŋ	eagle
08.	*sapat	apat	safat	sahat	hawk
09.	*untik	untik	untik	utik	snake
10.	*samar	amar	samar	samar	lizard
11.	*ulub	ulub	ulup	ulup	earthworm
12.	*lerat	lirat	lerat	lerat	maggot
13.	*pani	pani	fani	hani	tree
14.	*kasid	kaid	kasit	kasit	root
15.	*olan	ulan	olan	olaŋ	branch
16.	*kuham	kuam	kuhan	kuhaŋ	leaf
17.	*uluk	uluk	uluk	uluk	sun
18.	*sintab	intab	sintap	sitap	star
19.	*kunip	kunip	kunif	kunih	moon
20.	*mapug	mapug	mafuk	mahuk	wind
21.	*tamas	tama	tamas	tamas	rain
22.	*fitun	fitun	fitun	hiruŋ	stone

1. Recurrent changes in Lgs. A, B and C in the order they are encountered are:

Change	Examples
Lg. A	
01. *e/o > i/u	2, 6, 7, 12, 15
02. *h > Ø	7, 8, 10, 14, 16, 18, 21
03. *s > h (before 2)	8, 10, 14, 18, 21

Lg. B
01. *p > f/[-nas]__ (before 2)   2, 7, 8, 13, 19, 20
02. *b/d/g/ > p/t/k/__#   3, 5, 11, 14, 18, 20
03. *m > n/__#   4, 16

Lg. C
01. *t > r/V__V (before 3)   2, 6, 22
02. *p > f/[-nas]__ (before 4, 7)   2, 7, 8, 13, 19, 20
03. C > Ø/__C   3, 9, 18
04. *b/d/g/ > p/t/k/__#   3, 5, 11, 14, 18, 20
05. *m > n/__# (before 6)   4, 16
06. *n > ŋ/__#   4, 15, 16, 22
07. *f > h   2, 6, 7, 8, 13, 19, 20, 22

2. There is evidence for a BC subgroup.

Discussion. This is a relatively simple problem. Languages B and C form a rather clear subgroup based on the following exclusively shared innovations:

1. merger of *p and *f except following a nasal, where lenition did not occur (followed by *f > *h* in Lg. C)
2. final devoicing
3. merger of *m and *n word-finally (followed by *n > ŋ in Lg. C)

In many cases cognate forms in Lgs. B and C do not *look* more similar than those in Lg. A, but this is not the basis for determining subgroups, since similarity of form can be due to common retentions, which have no value for subgrouping. The identical forms *samar* for Lgs. B and C in number 10, for example, do not indicate a specially close relationship, since they are straightforward retentions of Proto-ABC *samar. The identical forms *ulup*, in 11, on the other hand, *do* have subgrouping value in that the direction of change must have been from *ulub to *ulup* and not the reverse, since final voicing of obstruents is almost unknown as a sound change, while final devoicing is commonplace. In other cases changes in Lg. C after its separation from Lg. B obscured the closer relationship of these two languages, as with number 22, where the forms in Lgs. A and B differ in a single segment, while those in Lgs. B and C differ in two. In all such cases the key to a proper subgrouping is to

SOLUTIONS

determine the direction of change by appeal to well-known pathways, and by a process of elimination in treating the correspondences at hand. Thus in 22 *t > r/V__V is a known type of sound change, while *r > t/V__V is not, and the sound correspondence n : n : ŋ must reflect *-n, since the correspondence ŋ : ŋ : ŋ in number 7 can only reflect *ŋ.

SOLUTION TO SUBGROUPING PROBLEM 3

No.	Proto-Jalish	Aki	Jali	Suya	Rian	Elis
01.	*salin	halin	halit	sarin	aliŋ	halin
02.	*pati	fahi	fati	paʔi	hai	pati
03.	*pataŋ	fataŋ	fatak	paʔaŋ	hataŋ	pataŋ
04.	*busak	fuhak	buhak	busak	huak	buhak
05.	*asam	ahan	ahap	asam	aaŋ	aham
06.	*sitip	hihif	hitif	siʔip	iih	hitip
07.	*umati	umahi	umati	umaʔi	umai	umati
08.	*kuran	kulan	kurat	kuhan	kulaŋ	kuran
09.	*sabat	hafat	habat	sabaʔ	ahat	habat
10.	*upuŋ	ufuŋ	ufuk	upuŋ	uhuŋ	upuŋ
11.	*talis	talih	talih	ʔaris	tali	talih
12.	*tiram	hilan	tirap	ʔiham	ilaŋ	tiram

1. Recurrent changes in Aki, Jali, Suya, Rian and Elis in the order they are encountered are:

Change	Examples
Aki	
1. *s > h	1, 2, 4–7, 9, 11, 12
2. *p > f	2, 3, 6, 10
3. *t > s/__i (before 1)	2, 6, 7, 12
4. *b > p (before 2)	4, 9
5. *m > n/__#	5, 12
6. *r > l	8, 12
Jali	
1. *s > h	1, 4–6, 9, 11
2. *m,n,ŋ > p,t,k__#	1, 3, 5, 8, 10, 12
3. *p > f (before 2)	2, 3, 6, 10
Suya	
1. *l > r	1, 11
2. *t > ʔ	2, 3, 6, 7, 9, 11, 12

3. *r > h (before 1)   8, 12

Rian
1. *s (> h) > Ø (before 3)   1, 2, 4–7, 9, 11, 12
2. *m/n > ŋ/__#   1, 5, 8, 12
3. *p (> f) > h   2–4, 6, 9, 10
4. *t > s/__i (before 1)   2, 6, 7, 12
5. *b > p (before 3)   4, 9
6. *r > l   8, 12

Elis
1. *s > h   1, 4–6, 9, 11

2. Aki and Rian form a subgroup apart from the other three languages, each of which appears to form a primary branch of the Jalish family. The evidence for an Aki-Rian group is as follows:

(a) *s > h (with further lenition h > Ø in Rian)
(b) merger of *l and *r
(c) merger of *p and *b
(d) *t > s/__i (before 1)
(e) *m/n > n/__# (with subsequent merger of word-final *n and *ŋ in Rian).

Discussion. Subgrouping can be complicated by borrowing between geographically contiguous language communities, and in some cases by drift. In other cases the shared innovations may be of such a common type that they either are not exclusively shared by the languages for which a subgrouping relationship is claimed, or they carry too little weight to be of genuine value as markers of exclusively shared history. For these reasons Brugmann (1884) proposed that subgroups should be based on a 'mass' of exclusively shared sound changes. In the case at hand the evidence for a subgroup containing just Aki and Rian is rather strong, since they share four innovations exclusively of the other languages to which they are related.

Jali and Elis also show *s > *h*, but there are two reasons why these changes are most convincingly treated as convergent. First, the phonetically most plausible development in Aki and Rian requires *t > *s/__i* before *s > *h* (with loss of *h in Rian after its separation from Aki). Since Jali and Elis do not show assibilation of *t, the change *s > *h* in these languages must have been historically independent from that in Proto-Aki-Rian.

In addition, Jali shares the change *p > *f* with Aki and Rian (with subsequent *f > *h* in Rian). However, the latter languages also show *b > *f* (with subsequent *f > *h* in Rian), and so have merged *p and *b, while Jali has not. There are two possibilities here: (1) *p > *f* (a common sound change in many language families) has happened independently in Proto-Aki-Rian and pre-Jali, or (2) Aki, Jali and Rian shared a common ancestor in which *p became *f*, and at a later date *b underwent a similar change in Proto-Aki-Rian. If the latter interpretation is accepted, then in addition to a well-supported Proto-Aki-Rian we must also recognise a weakly defined Proto-Aki-Jali-Rian with immediate descendants Proto-Aki-Rian and Jali.

SOLUTION TO SUBGROUPING PROBLEM 4

No.	Proto-ABCD	Lg. A	Lg. B	Lg. C	Lg. D	
01.	*natum	natuŋ	nadum	nadum	narum	star
02.	*mahir	mair	mahir	maʔil	maʔir	moon
03.	*timan	timaŋ	siman	siman	siman	night
04.	*pasan	pasaŋ	pahan	paʔan	paʔan	dark
05.	*paʔi	pai	paʔi	paʔi	paʔi	wind
06.	*pihin	piiŋ	pihin	piʔin	piʔin	rain
07.	*semas	simas	hemah	ʔemaʔ	ʔemaʔ	storm
08.	*ulap	ulaʔ	ulap	ulap	urap	hail
09.	*ratal	ratal	radal	ladal	rarar	stone
10.	*luko	luku	lugo	lugo	rugo	water
11.	*pusik	pusiʔ	puhik	puʔik	puʔik	house
12.	*labur	lapur	labur	labul	ravur	roof
13.	ʔisim	isiŋ	ʔihim	ʔiʔim	ʔiʔim	door
14.	*kura	kura	kura	kula	kura	floor
15.	*mulas	mulas	mulah	mulaʔ	muraʔ	tree
16.	*akon	akuŋ	agon	agon	agon	leaf
17.	*riteŋ	ritiŋ	rideŋ	lideŋ	rireŋ	branch
18.	*siŋap	siŋaʔ	hiŋap	ʔiŋap	ʔiŋap	bird
19.	*larek	lariʔ	larek	lalek	rarek	nest
20.	*tuʔuk	tuuʔ	tuʔuk	tuʔuk	tuʔuk	laugh
21.	*tanip	taniʔ	tanip	tanip	tanip	cry
22.	*puhat	puaʔ	puhat	puʔat	puʔat	speak
23.	*titiŋa	titiŋa	sisiŋa	sisiŋa	sisiŋa	wash
24.	*hopu	upu	hobu	ʔobu	ʔovu	clean

1. Recurrent changes in Lgs. A, B, C and D in the order they are encountered are:

Change	Examples
Lg. A	
1. *m/n > ŋ/__#	1, 3, 4, 6, 13, 16
2. *h > Ø	2, 6, 22, 24
3. *ʔ > Ø	5, 13, 20

4. *e/o > i/u   7, 10, 16, 17, 19, 24
5. *p/t/k > ?/__#   8, 11, 18–22

Lg. B
1. *p/t/k/ > b/d/g/V__V   1, 9, 10, 16, 17, 24
2. *t > s/__i (before 1)   3, 23
3. *s > h (before 2)   4, 7, 11, 13, 15, 18

Lg. C
1. *p/t/k/ > b/d/g/V__V   1, 9, 10, 16, 17, 24
2. *h > ?   2, 4, 6, 7, 11, 13, 15, 18, 22, 24
3. *r > l   2, 9, 12, 14, 17, 19
4. *t > s/__i (before 1)   3, 23
5. *s > h (before 2, 4)   4, 7, 11, 13, 15, 18

Lg. D.
1. *p/t/k/ > b/d/g/V__V (before 2)   1, 9, 10, 16, 17, 24
2. *b/d > v/r   1, 9, 12, 17, 24
3. *h > ?   2, 4, 6, 7, 11, 13, 15, 18, 22, 24
4. *t > s/__i (before 1)   3, 23
5. *s > h (before 3, 4)   4, 7, 11, 13, 15, 18
6. *l > r   8–10, 12, 15, 19

2. Lgs. B, C and D appear to form a subgroup.

Discussion. There is fairly clear evidence for a subgroup that includes Lgs. B, C and D, but not A, defined by the following exclusively shared innovations:

1. voicing of *p, *t and *k intervocalically
2. *t > s/__i (before 1)
3. *s > h (before 2)

In addition two innovations further distinguish Lgs. C and D from Lg. B. These are:

4. *h > ?
5. merger of *l and *r

It is useful to keep in mind that both *h and *ʔ have limited change path options, since it is unlikely that a supraglottal articulation will develop from either of these consonants. The sound correspondence Ø : h : ʔ : ʔ can therefore only plausibly go back to *h or *ʔ. Since the correspondence Ø : ʔ : ʔ : ʔ is most convincingly attributed to *ʔ, this leaves *h as the source of Ø : h : ʔ : ʔ. Strengthening this association is the correspondence s : h : ʔ : ʔ, which must go back to *s, and in which *s > ʔ is very unlikely as a single change, implying the intermediate step *s > h.

SOLUTION TO SUBGROUPING PROBLEM 5

No.	Proto-ABCD	Lg. A	Lg. B	Lg. C	Lg. D	
01.	*bati	basi	pati	fet	vat	rat
02.	*koŋas	koŋas	koɲah	koŋ	koɲas	snake
03.	*tanor	tanor	tanol	tan	tanor	dog
04.	*pusaŋ	pusaŋ	puhaŋ	fu	fusaŋ	pig
05.	*lehip	lehip	lehip	he	lehif	liver
06.	*rupe	rupe	lupe	huf	ruf	blood
07.	*haluki	haluki	haluki	ohuk	haluk	skin
08.	*pahani	pahani	pahani	faen	fahan	hair
09.	*abutun	abutun	aputun	ofut	avutun	eat
10.	*sahil	sahil	hahil	e	sahil	sleep
11.	*tiapu	siapu	tiapu	tiof	tiaf	drink
12.	*kuhama	kuhama	kuhama	kuam	kuham	walk
13.	*apit	apit	apit	ef	afit	hit
14.	*orudu	orudu	oludu	ohud	orud	fall

1. Recurrent changes in Lgs. A, B, C and D in the order they are encountered are:

Change	Examples
Lg. A	
1. *t > s/__i	1, 11
Lg. B	
1. *b > p	1, 9
2. *s > h	2, 4, 10
3. *r > l	3, 6, 14
Lg. C	
1. *b > p (before 5)	1, 9
2. *a > e,o/__(C)i,u (before 3)	1, 7–11, 13
3. V > Ø/__#	1–14
4. C > Ø/__# (before 3)	2–5, 9, 10, 13
5. *p > f	1, 4, 6, 8, 9, 11, 13

6. *s > h (before 8)	4, 10
7. *l > h	5, 6, 7, 14
8. *h > Ø (before 7)	4, 5, 7, 8, 10, 12
9. *r > l (before 7)	6, 14

Lg. D

1. *b > v	1, 9
2. V > Ø/__#	1, 6–8, 11, 12, 14
3. *p > f	4–6, 8, 11, 13

2. Languages B and C form a subgroup apart from the other two languages. The evidence for a BC group is as follows:

1. merger of *b and *p
2. merger of *s and *h
3. merger of *r and *l.

Discussion. The sound correspondences in this set of data can be explained most simply by assuming that in addition to Proto-ABCD there was an intermediate proto-language Proto-BC in which Proto-ABCD *b and *p merged as PBC *p (and then lenited to *f* in Lg. C), Proto-ABCD *s and *h merged as PBC *h (and then disappeared in Lg. C), and Proto-ABCD *r and *l merged as PBC *l (which then lenited to *h* in Lg. C).

An exclusively shared innovation that cross-cuts these is the loss of final vowels in Lgs. C and D. However, there are two reasons for not using this as subgrouping evidence. First, it is a natural development that could have happened independently in these languages. Second, and perhaps more importantly, Lg. C lost both -V and -VC, while Lg. D lost only -V. Since the loss of -VC is most simply explained by ordering loss of final consonants before loss of final vowels, the loss of final vowels in these two languages is best attributed to independent historical changes. Another innovation that Lgs. C and D share exclusively is *p > *f*, but again there are two reasons for not using this as subgrouping evidence. First, it is one of the commonest types of lenition, and so has little diagnostic value in itself. Second, Lg. C shows both *p > *f* and *b > *f* (hence merger of *b/p), while Lg. D shows *p > *f* but *b > *v* (hence a shift of each proto-phoneme). The change *p > *f* thus had different *structural results* in the two languages, and for this reason it is best considered an independent innovation. Looked at another way, the change *b > ƒ in Lg. C is most likely to have gone through an intermediate step *b > p, followed by the change *p > ƒ, while Lg. D shows no evidence of such a development.

SOLUTION TO SUBGROUPING PROBLEM 6

No.	Proto-ADKF	Ayon	Dunas	Kwosi	Fafak	
01.	*cuyu	suu	cuy	cuyu	cuyu	water
02.	*ʔusa	ʔusa	ʔus	usa	uha	rain
03.	*mʷapa	mʷapa	ŋin	mʷafa	mafa	wind
04.	*kuti	kuti	kud	xuti	huti	earth
05.	*lisa	yisa	top	lisa	liha	stone
06.	*panua	panua	panu	sano	hano	grass
07.	*soka	soka	sok	soxa	hoha	mud
08.	*paya	paa	pay	faya	faya	lake
09.	*xuma	xuma	xum	xuma	huma	island
10.	*ʔulo	ʔuyo	ʔul	ulo	ulo	river
11.	*kiana	yaya	kian	xiana	hala	fish
12.	*muta	muta	mud	lua	lua	bird
13.	*patu	patu	pad	fatu	fatu	tree
14.	*tuya	tua	tuy	tuya	tuya	leaf
15.	*pixi	pixi	pix	fixi	fihi	branch
16.	*koulu	kouyu	koul	suli	houlu	fruit
17.	*paci	pasi	pac	faci	faci	seed
18.	*kumʷi	hoya	kum	xumʷi	humi	field
19.	*mano	mano	man	mano	nafi	rock
20.	*xalu	xayu	xal	xalu	halu	cliff

1. Recurrent changes in these languages in the order they are encountered are:

Change	Examples
Ayon	
1. *c > s	1, 17
2. *y > Ø (before 3)	1, 8, 14
3. *l > y	5, 10, 16, 20
Dunas	
1. V > Ø/__#	1, 2, 4, 6–20
2. *t > d/V__V (before 1)	4, 12, 13

3. *mʷ > m   18

Kwosi
1. *ʔ > Ø   2, 10
2. *p > f   3, 8, 13, 15, 17
3. *k > x   4, 7, 11, 18

Fafak
1. *ʔ > Ø   2, 10
2. *s > h   2, 5, 7
3. *mʷ > m   3, 18
4. *p > f   3, 8, 13, 15, 17
5. *k > x (before 6)   4, 7, 16, 18
6. *x > h   4, 7, 9, 15, 16, 18, 20

2. Kwosi and Fafak appear to form a subgroup.
3. The Kwosi-Fafak group is justified by three exclusively shared phonological innovations: (1) *ʔ > Ø, (2) *p > f, and (3) *k > x (with subsequent *x > h in Fafak).
4. Lexical innovations that support the same subgroup are reflexes of *sano 'grass' (6), and *lua 'bird' (12).

Discussion. Kwosi and Fafak share the innovations *ʔ > Ø, *p > f and *k > x apart from the other two languages. The first of these is technically a merger (with zero), the second is a shift and the third is a merger of *k and *x. None of these is especially strong evidence in itself, but the combination of the three provides a measure of confidence that the subgroup is real, since otherwise it would be necessary to assume three convergent innovations, an inference that decreases in likelihood as exclusively shared innovations increase in number.

Dunas and Fafak share a single innovation, *mʷ > m, but without other evidence this is best attributed to convergent change. Since there is no convincing evidence that Ayon and Dunas form a subgroup, cognate terms shared by them must be attributed to the proto language of the entire group. It follows that the original terms for 'grass' and 'bird' were *panua and *muta, and that Proto-Kwosi-Fafak must have innovated *sano and *lua for these meanings.

SOLUTION TO SUBGROUPING PROBLEM 7

No.	Proto-ABCD	Lg. A	Lg.B	Lg. C	Lg. D	
01.	*pomu	pomu	fomu	fomu	fomu	stone
02.	*lahuk	lahuk	hau	hou?	auk	fish
03.	*ritas	litas	rita	ritah	litas	water
04.	*ayun	ayut	au	ouŋ	ayun	wave
05.	*hesam	hesap	eha	ehaŋ	esam	sky
06.	*irup	ilup	iru	iruf	iluf	wind
07.	*tula	tula	tuha	tuha	tua	earth
08.	*wasiŋ	wasik	vahi	vehiŋ	vasiŋ	grass
09.	*maru	malu	maru	moru	malu	wake
10.	*uyas	uyas	ua	uah	uyas	wash
11.	*haŋati	haŋati	anahi	aŋehi	muli	walk
12.	*solet	solet	hohe	hohe?	soet	speak
13.	*rahim	lahip	rai	reiŋ	laim	fire
14.	*tiap	tiap	hia	hiaf	tiaf	smoke
15.	*kayili	kayili	haihi	mutuh	kayii	burn
16.	*nitaŋ	nitak	lita	nitaŋ	nitaŋ	house
17.	*oyaka	pukap	oaha	oaha	oyaka	roof
18.	*tikuŋ	tikuk	hihu	hihuŋ	tikuŋ	work
19.	*ŋatik	ŋatik	nahi	ŋehi?	sihaf	sleep
20.	*unan	unat	ula	unaŋ	unan	dream
21.	*sapep	sapep	hafe	hafef	safef	eat
22.	*lirahu	lilahu	hirau	hirou	ilau	drink
23.	*kiwis	kiwis	hivi	hivih	kivis	run

1. Recurrent changes in Lgs. A, B, C and D in the order they are encountered are:

Change	Examples
Lg. A	
1. *r > l	3, 6, 9, 13, 22
2. *m,n,ŋ > p,t,k/__#	4, 5, 8, 13, 16, 18, 20

Lg. B

1. *p > f	1, 21
2. *l > h (before 11)	2, 7, 12, 15, 22
3. *h > Ø (before 2, 6)	2, 5, 11, 13, 22
4. -C > Ø	2–6, 8, 10, 12–14, 16, 18–21, 23
5. *y > Ø	4, 10, 15, 17
6. *s > h	5, 8, 11, 12, 14, 18, 19, 21
7. *w > v	8, 23
8. *ŋ > n	11, 19
9. *t > s/__i (before 6)	11, 14, 18, 19
10. *k > h	15, 17, 18, 23
11. *n > l (before 8)	16, 20

Lg. C

1. *p > f (before 5)	1, 6, 14, 21
2. *l > h	2, 7, 12, 22
3. *a > e,o/__(C)i,u	2, 4, 8, 9, 11, 13, 19, 22
4. *h > Ø (before 2, 6)	2, 5, 11, 13, 22
5. *t,k > ʔ/__#	2, 12, 19
6. *s > h	3, 5, 8, 10–12, 14, 18, 19, 21, 23
7. *y > Ø	4, 10, 17
8. *m,n > ŋ/__#	4, 5, 13, 20
9. *w > v	8, 23
10. *t > s/__i (before 6)	11, 14, 18, 19
11. *k > h/__V	17, 18, 23

Lg. D

1. *p > f	1, 6, 14, 21
2. *l > h (before 3, 4)	2, 7, 12, 15, 22
3. *h > Ø	2, 5, 7, 12, 13, 15, 22
4. *r > l	3, 6, 9, 13, 22
5. *w > v	8, 23

2. Lgs. B, C and D can be grouped together on the basis of four shared innovations in phonology, and Lgs. B and C can be further subgrouped based on four other phonological innovations.

Discussion. There is evidence for a BCD subgroup based on: (1) the shift of *p to *f*, (2) the merger of *h with zero, (3) the shift of *l to *h*, and (4) the shift of *w to *v*, where change 2 must be ordered before change 3, and *h* from *l underwent further merger with zero in Lg. D. It is simplest to assume that each of these changes had already taken place in Proto-BCD. In addition, lgs. B and C form a rather clear subgroup based on: (1) the merger of *y and zero, (2) the merger of *s and *t before a high front vowel followed by (3) *s > h, and (4) *k > *h*, which merged with *s in all positions, and with *t before a high front vowel. The support for this group is strong enough that it probably would be accepted as a likely phylogenetic unit by virtually any historical linguist.

Lgs. A and D share the change *r > *l*. However, in Lg. D this change followed *h > Ø, and since *h was not lost in Lg. A the change of *r to *l* must have been independent in the two languages.

SOLUTION TO SUBGROUPING PROBLEM 8

No.	Proto-Hamuan	Hamu	Fiak	Tolno	Luk	Gloss
01.	*fortis	hottis	furdis	fortis	foltis	bear
02.	*azuli	alli	azuri	azli	azuw	fish
03.	*rukod	ruhod	rugut	ruod	lukot	fox
04.	*sunek	suneh	sunik	sune	sunek	storm
05.	*dimaku	dikku	dimagu	dimo	rimak	sky
06.	*patina	hanna	padina	fatna	patin	wind
07.	*mayaw	mayaw	mayaw	mayo	mazaf	cloud
08.	*luka	luha	ruga	lua	wuk	rain
09.	*tomay	tomay	tumay	tome	tomas	earth
10.	*biwa	biwa	bia	viva	bif	stone
11.	*vasola	valla	vazura	vasla	vasow	grass
12.	*bazu	bazu	bazu	vazu	bas	eat
13.	*kelop	heloh	kirup	elof	kewop	drink
14.	*wirma	wimma	irma	virma	vilm	walk
15.	*uyak	uyah	uyak	uya	uzak	talk
16.	*tilpani	tiffani	tirbani	tilfani	tiwpan	sleep
17.	*karni	hanni	karni	arni	kaln	black
18.	*falay	halay	faray	fale	fawas	white
19.	*kalub	halub	karup	aluv	kawup	red
20.	*dayap	dayah	dayap	dayaf	razap	yellow
21.	*rilno	rinno	rirnu	rilno	liwn	green
22.	*pulkan	hukkan	purgan	fulan	puwkan	not yet
23.	*zufuri	zurri	zuvuri	zufri	zuful	still
24.	*lenis	lenis	rinis	lenis	wenis	worm
25.	*pulug	hulug	puruk	fulug	puwuk	snake
26.	*taki	tahi	tagi	te	tak	lizard
27.	*arpik	ahhih	arbik	arfi	alpik	hill
28.	*lasigo	laggo	razigu	lasgo	wasik	river

1. Recurrent changes in Hamu, Fiak, Tolno and Luk in the order they are encountered are:

Change	Examples
Hamu	
1. *f > h (geminates excluded)	1, 6, 13, 16, 18, 20, 22, 25, 27
2. $C_1C_2 > C_2C_2$ (before 1, 4)	1, 2, 5 ,6, 11, 14, 16, 17, 21, 22, 23, 27, 28
3. V > Ø /VC__CV (before 2)	2, 5, 6, 11, 23, 28
4. *k > h (geminates excluded)	3, 4, 8, 13, 15, 17, 19, 26, 27
5. *p > f (before 1, 2)	6, 13, 16, 20, 22, 25, 27
Fiak	
1. *e,o > i, u	1, 3, 4, 9, 11, 13, 21, 24, 28
2. *p,t,k,f,s > b,d,g,v,z/vd__vd	1, 3, 5, 6, 8, 11, 16, 22, 23, 26, 27
3. *l > r	2, 8, 11, 13, 16, 18, 19, 21, 22, 24, 25, 28
4. *b,d,g > p,t,k/__#	3, 19, 25
5. *w > Ø/__V	10, 14
Tolno	
1. V > Ø/VC__CV	2, 6, 11, 23, 28
2. *k > Ø (before 1, 4)	3–5, 8, 13, 15, 17, 19, 22, 26, 27
3. *p > f	6, 13, 16, 20, 22, 25, 27
4. *i,u > y,w/V__ (before 5)	5, 26
5. *ay, aw > e,o (before 7)	5, 7, 9, 18, 26
6. *b > w (before 7)	10, 12, 19
7. *w > v	10, 12, 14, 19
Luk	
1. *r > l (before 5)	1, 3, 14, 17, 21, 23, 27
2. *l > w (before 1)	2, 8, 11, 13, 16, 18, 19, 21, 22, 24, 25, 28
3. V > Ø/__# (before 4)	2, 5, 6, 8, 10–12, 14, 16, 17, 21, 23, 26, 28
4. *b,d,g,v,z > p,t,k,f,s/__# (before 5)	3, 7, 9, 12, 18, 19, 25
5. *d > r	5, 20
6. *w,y > v,z (before 2, 4)	7, 9, 10, 14, 15, 18, 20

2. Hamu and Tolno form a subgroup based on medial vowel syncope in original trisyllables, lenition of *k, and merger of *p and *f.

Discussion. In the immediate ancestor of Hamu and Tolno a vowel synco-
pated in the environment VC__CV, producing heterorganic clusters, as seen in
examples 2, 5, 6, 11 and 23, where the second vowels of Fiak and Luk are otherwise unpredictable. After the separation of these languages medial clusters
underwent complete assimilation to produce geminates in the subsequent
history of Hamu, and these resisted further lenition, as geminates commonly do.

A second innovation defining this group is the lenition of *k to *h*, with
subsequent loss of *h* in the separate history of Tolno.

Third, both of these languages show a merger of *p and *f, with further
lenition to *h* in the separate history of Hamu.

Although both Fiak and Luk show final devoicing this change must have
been independent in the two languages, since it followed the loss of final
vowels in Luk, and this change did not occur in Fiak.

Perhaps the main obstacle to seeing the evidence for this subgroup is that
innovations in Proto-Hamu-Tolno invariably underwent further change in
various daughter languages, including medial cluster assimilation, *f > *h* in
Hamu, and *k > *h > Ø in Tolno.

SOLUTION TO SUBGROUPING PROBLEM 9

No.	Proto-ABC	Lg. A	Lg. B	Lg. C	
01.	*pasul	fasul	pahun	pau	fence
02.	*terap	tiraf	tenap	tera	garden
03.	*dambot	dambut	dambot	davo	water
04.	*tilam	silam	tinam	tira	rain
05.	*kumar	kumar	kuman	kuma	cloud
06.	*poŋga	fuŋga	poŋga	poɣa	flood
07.	*lampak	lampak	nambak	rava	drown
08.	*sipe	sifi	hipe	ipe	mud
09.	*araŋ	araŋ	anaŋ	ara	swim
10.	*hora	hura	hona	ora	fish
11.	*sondu	sundu	hondu	oru	frog
12.	*kimos	cimus	kimoh	kimo	hill
13.	*untin	unsin	undin	uri	grass
14.	*raŋki	ranci	naŋgi	raɣi	sun
15.	*panop	fanuf	panop	pano	day
16.	*lohik	luhik	nohik	roi	wind

1. Recurrent changes in Lgs. A, B and C in the order they are encountered are:

Change	Examples
Lg. A	
1. *p > f / [-nas]__	1, 2, 6, 8, 15
2. *e,o > i,u	2, 3, 6, 8, 10–12, 15, 16
3. *t > s / __i (before 2)	4, 13
4. *k > c / __i	12, 14
5. nasal place assimilation	14
Lg. B	
1. *s > h	1, 8, 11, 12
2. *l > n	1, 2, 4, 5, 7, 9, 10, 14, 16
3. *r > l (before 2)	2, 5, 9, 10, 14
4. *p,t,k > b,d,g / N__	7, 13, 14

Lg. C

1. *s > h (before 7)	1, 8, 11, 12
2. *h > Ø	1, 8, 10, 11, 12, 16
3. C > Ø/__$ (before 3)	1–7, 9, 11–16
4. *b,d,g > v,r,ɣ/V__V	3, 6, 7, 11, 13, 14
5. *l > r	4, 7, 16
6. *p,t,k > b,d,g/N__ (before 2)	7, 13, 14

2. There is evidence for a BC subgroup.

Discussion. Lgs. B and C form a subgroup based on three shared innovations:

1. merger of *s and *h (with further change *h > Ø in Lg. C)
2. merger of *l and *r, most likely as *l*, (further merging with *n in Lg. B)
3. postnasal voicing (with further reduction of medial clusters and spirantisation of intervocalic voiced stops in Lg. C)

The primary point of this problem is to show that mergers need not have the same phonetic outcome in the languages that undergo them. Although phonetic considerations dictate a likely directionality in many cases, especially if one of the corresponding phonemes is *h* or glottal stop, which have limited change options, the merger of two phonemes A and B can result in A, in B, or in C. Hence *l and *r could merge as *l*, as *r*, or as something else (*n*, *y*, *h*, zero, etc.). Where one language shows one of these options and another language shows another, the merger tends to be less apparent on the surface.

SOLUTION TO SUBGROUPING PROBLEM 10

No.	Proto-ABCD	Lg. A	Lg. B	Lg. C	Lg. D	
01.	*pəka	fəko	hoka	hiha	paxa	fire
02.	*hiso	hiho	hiso	hiho	hiso	ashes
03.	*kupis	kufih	kuhis	huhih	xupis	hearth
04.	*tanili	tanidi	tanili	təniri	tanini	pot
05.	*dirap	dilaf	dirah	rirah	rirap	stone
06.	*uturi	utuli	uturi	duri	ururi	ember
07.	*senuba	henubo	šenuba	hənuba	senuva	smoke
08.	*susin	huhin	sušin	huhin	susin	burn
09.	*batən	batən	baton	badin	varan	cook
10.	*lidik	didik	lidik	ririh	nirix	boil
11.	*rata	lato	rata	rada	rara	roast
12.	*mosio	mohio	mošio	məhio	mosio	fry
13.	*rihe	lihe	rihe	rihe	rihe	stand
14.	*folus	foluh	holus	holuh	fonus	sit
15.	*əpət	əfət	ohot	ihit	apat	walk
16.	*datəf	datəf	datoh	radih	raraf	bird
17.	*matis	matih	masis	madih	maris	wing
18.	*hulap	hulaf	hulah	hulah	hunap	feather
19.	*tilin	tidin	silin	tirin	tinin	beak
20.	*ikada	ikado	ikada	hara	ixara	claw
21.	*luti	luti	lusi	ludi	nuri	stick
22.	*linu	dinu	linu	rinu	ninu	stone

1. Recurrent changes in Lgs. A, B, C and D in the order they are encountered are:

Change	Examples
Lg. A	
1. *p > f	1, 3, 5, 15, 18
2. *a > o/__#	1, 7, 11, 20
3. *s > h	2, 3, 7, 8, 12, 14, 17
4. *l > d/__i (before 6)	4, 10, 19, 22
5. *r > l	5, 6, 11, 13

Lg. B
1. *p > f (before 2)   1, 3, 5, 15, 18
2. *f > h   1, 3, 5, 14–16, 18
3. *ə > o   1, 9, 15, 16
4. *s > š/__i,e (before 5)   7, 8, 12
5. *t > s/__i   17, 19, 21

Lg. C
1. *p > f (before 2)   1, 3, 5, 15, 18
2. *f > h   1, 3, 5, 14–16, 18
3. *ə > i   1, 9, 15, 16
4. *k > h   1, 3, 10, 20
5. *s > h   2, 3, 7, 8, 12, 14, 17
6. V > ə/#_CV(C)V(C) (before 10)   4, 6, 7, 12, 20
7. *l > d/__i (before 8)   4, 10, 19, 22
8. *d > r (before 9)   5, 10, 16, 20
9. *t > d/V__V   6, 9, 11, 16, 17, 21
10. *ə > Ø/#_CV(C)V(C) (before 9)   6, 20

Lg. D
1. *ə > a   1, 9, 15, 16
2. *k > x   1, 3, 10, 20
3. *l > n   4, 10, 14, 18, 19, 21, 22
4. *d > r   5, 10, 16, 20
5. *t > d/V__V (before 4)   6, 9, 11, 16, 17, 21

2. Lgs. A and C form an apparent subgroup apart from B and D, although the evidence for this is limited.

Discussion. Lgs. A and C exclusively share two innovations:

1. the merger of *s and *h
2. *l > d/__i (with further lenition to r in Lg. C)

Although *s > h carries little weight in itself, the merger of *l and *d just before *i is a much more distinctive change that marks off these two languages from the others.

In addition, Lgs. A and C share the merger of *p and *f with Lg. B. In Lg. A the outcome is f, and in Lgs. B and C it is h. We can assume that *f > h was an independent change in Lgs. B and C, since Lg. B has undergone neither of the changes shared exclusively by Lgs. A and C. Finally, Lgs. C and D share the changes (1) *d > r, and (2) *t > d/V__V, but in Lg. C these changes must be ordered (1), (2), since *t and *d did not merge, whereas in Lg. D they must be ordered (2), (1), since merger occurred.

Tentatively, then, we can posit an ABC subgroup based only on the merger of *p and *f as f, and a smaller AC subgroup based on the merger of *s and *h, and of *l and *d before a high front vowel.

SOLUTION TO SUBGROUPING PROBLEM 11

No.	Proto-ABC	Lg. A	Lg. B	Lg. C	
01.	*tifɛŋ	hifɛŋ	tihen	tihe	pine tree
02.	*ɔsup	ɔhup	osup	osu	canyon
03.	*alati	alah	alati	alati	suspension bridge
04.	*hokəl	okal	ukin	hokə	cliff
05.	*ŋufa	ŋuf	nuha	nuha	eagle
06.	*hiŋe	iŋ	ini	hine	rattlesnake
07.	*fɔsi	fɔh	hosi	hosi	squirrel
08.	*netim	nehim	litim	neti	fish
09.	*səfon	hafon	sihun	səho	bird
10.	*fɛtiŋi	fɛhiŋ	hetini	hetini	river
11.	*kɔhəti	kɔah	koiti	kohəti	riverbank
12.	*peŋia	peŋi	pinia	penia	canoe
13.	*sɔnəs	hɔnah	solis	sonə	person
14.	*oŋe	oŋ	uni	one	man
15.	*fusəhɛ	fuha	husie	husəhe	woman
16.	*nuɛf	nuɛf	lueh	nue	child
17.	*tasɔ	tah	taso	taso	eat
18.	*motufa	motuf	mutuha	motuha	drink
19.	*amal	amal	aman	ama	talk

1. Recurrent changes in Lgs. A, B and C in the order they are encountered are:

Change	Examples
Lg. A	
1. *t > s/__i (before 2)	1, 3, 8, 10, 11
2. *s > h	1–3, 7–11, 13, 15, 17
3. –V > Ø	3, 5–7, 10–12, 14, 15, 17, 18
4. *h > Ø (before 2)	4, 6, 11, 15
5. *ə > a	4, 9, 11, 13, 15
Lg. B	
1. *f > h	1, 5, 7, 9, 10, 15, 16, 18

2. *ɛ,ɔ > e,o   1, 2, 7, 10, 11, 13, 15–17
3. *ŋ > n   1, 5, 6, 10, 12, 14
4. *h > Ø (before 1)   4, 6, 11, 15
5. *e,o > i,u (before 2)   4, 6, 8, 9, 12, 14, 18
6. *ə > i   4, 9, 11, 13, 15
7. *l > n/__#   4, 19
8. *n > l/__V (before 3)   8, 13, 16

Lg. C
1. *f > h   1, 5, 7, 9, 10, 15, 16, 18
2. *ɛ,ɔ > e,o   1, 2, 7, 10, 11, 13, 15–17
3. C > Ø/__#   1, 2, 4, 8, 9, 13, 16, 19
4. *ŋ > n   5, 6, 10, 12, 14

2. The evidence is insufficient to support a subgrouping.

Discussion. Lgs. B and C share the following innovations:

1. *f > h
2. *ɛ/ɔ > e/o
3. *ŋ > n

At first sight this is impressive, and appears to support a BC subgroup. However, closer inspection shows that in Lg. B *f > *h* occurred after *h > Ø, since the two did not merge, while in Lg. C *h was never lost.

Similarly, the raising/tensing of the lax vowels *ɛ/ɔ in Lg. B could only have taken place after the raising of *e and *o, and since Lg. C did not undergo this change the raising/tensing of *ɛ and ɔ must have been an independent change in Lgs. B and C.

Finally, Lgs. B and C both show the change *ŋ > *n*, but in Lg. C this led to merger, while in Lg. B it did not, since *n > l occurred first. Based on the evidence given here, then, there are no grounds for grouping any two of these languages together as against the third. Rather, Lgs. A, B and C appear to form three primary branches of this hypothetical language family.

The lesson that this problem teaches is the need to find *structural* innovations (primarily splits and mergers) rather than simple shifts, since these may be due to convergent change. Finally, Lgs. A and B share the change *h > Ø, but this could easily have happened independently.

SOLUTION TO SUBGROUPING PROBLEM 12

No.	Proto-Arucan	Aruca	Atoyot	Tassap	Urabus	
01.	*cara	sara	al	saha	caa	man
02.	*totu	turu	tot	totu	tuu	woman
03.	*mata	mara	mat	mata	maa	child
04.	*pasu	pahu	pa	pahu	fasu	house
05.	*kila	sila	il	kila	cila	stone
06.	*kurap	hura	ulap	kuhap	kua?	village
07.	*metik	miri	meti	metik	mii?	water
08.	*kanip	hani	anip	kanip	kani?	black
09.	*kinap	sani	inap	kinap	cani?	white
10.	*ucin	usi	uin	usin	uciŋ	tree
11.	*aŋit	aŋi	aŋit	aŋit	aŋi?	cloud
12.	*takar	taha	taal	takah	taka	rain
13.	*katik	hari	ati	katik	kai?	storm
14.	*seraŋ	hira	elaŋ	hehaŋ	siaŋ	earth
15.	*aki	asi	a	aki	aci	sun
16.	*raŋal	raŋa	laŋal	haŋal	aŋaŋ	moon
17.	*pukin	pusi	puin	pukin	fuciŋ	day
18.	*cokat	suha	oat	sokat	cuka?	night
19.	*losum	luhu	loum	lohum	lusuŋ	wind
20.	*paraka	paraha	pala	pahaka	faaka	spirit
21.	*kutil	huri	util	kutil	kuiŋ	ghost

1. Recurrent changes in Aruca, Atoyot, Tassap and Urabus in the order encountered are:

Change   **Examples**

Aruca

1. *c > s   1, 5, 9, 10, 15, 17, 18
2. *e,o > i,u   2, 7, 14, 18, 19
3. *t > r/V__V   2, 3, 7, 13, 21
4. *s > h (before 1)   4, 14, 19
5. *k > c/__i (before 1, 6)   5, 9, 15, 17
6. *k > h   6, 8, 12, 13, 18, 20, 21

7. -C > Ø   6–14, 16-19, 21
8. vowel metathesis   9

Atoyot
1. *c > s (before 2)   1, 10, 18
2. *s > Ø   1, 4, 10, 14, 18, 19
3. *r > l   1, 6, 12, 14, 16, 20
4. V > Ø/__# (before 5)   1–5, 15, 20
5. *k > Ø   5–9, 12, 13, 15, 17, 18, 20, 21

Tassap
1. *c > s   1, 10, 18
2. *r > h   1, 6, 12, 14, 16, 20
3. *s > h (before 1)   4, 14, 19

Urabus
1. *r > O   1, 6, 12, 14, 16, 20
2. *t > r/V__V (before 1)   2, 3, 7, 13, 21
3. *e,o > i,u   2, 7, 14, 18, 19
4. *p > f   4, 17, 20
5. *k > c/__i (before 7)   5, 9, 15, 17
6. *p,t,k > ʔ/__# (before 4)   6–9, 11, 13, 18
7. vowel metathesis   9
8. *m,n > ŋ/__#   10, 16, 17, 19, 21
9. *l > n/__# (before 8)   16, 21

2. Aruca and Urabus form one branch of the family.

Discussion. The evidence for an Aruca-Urabus subgroup is quite strong, including:

1. the unconditioned merger of mid vowels with high vowels
2. a split-merger of *t with *r intervocalically
3. a split-merger of *k with *c before *i
4. a sporadic metathesis of the vowels in number 9 which must have occurred after *k > c/__i

While the subgrouping value of regular changes correlates with how unusual they are in languages generally, it is very unlikely that the same sporadic change would happen independently unless it was due to an inherited structural pressure. If this were natural language data the evidence for this subgroup would therefore be considered as close to conclusive as one can expect in doing science (which is based on inductive logic and so concerned with inferences that are always probabilistic to some degree).

Both Atoyot and Tassap have undergone the following changes:

1. *c > s
2. *s > h (followed by *h > Ø in Atoyot)

However, in Atoyot 1 preceded 2, thus leading to merger, while in Tassap 2 preceded 1, producing a shift, and eliminating any possibility of considering this a shared innovation.

It is noteworthy that Aruca and Tassap share the changes *s > h, followed by *c > s. However, if we were to consider this an innovation in a proto-language ancestral only to Aruca and Tassap it would clash with the far stronger evidence that Aruca and Urabus shared an immediate common ancestor, and for this reason it must be considered a convergent development.

In addition, *c and *k merged before a high front vowel in Aruca and Atoyot, but in Aruca this was a conditioned change, while in Atoyot it was part of the broader unconditioned change *k (> h) > Ø.

In conclusion, then, there is no firm evidence for any subgroup other than Aruca-Urabus, which is robustly supported by three exclusively shared innovations in phonology, and one in lexicon (the sporadic metatheis of the vowels in the word for 'white').

The ordering requirements for sound changes in these languages are more complex than in most problems in this workbook. For Aruca *s > h had to precede *c > s, since *c and *s did not merge. It is also likely that *k > s/__i passed through an intermediate stage *k > c/__i which preceded the change *c > s, and palatalisation of *k before *i must have antedated the more general change *k > h. Changes 1, 4, 5 and 6 in Aruca could thus have formed any of four chronological sequences:

(1)	(2)	(3)	(4)
4. *s > h	4. *s > h	5. *k > c/__i	5. *k > c/__i
5. *k > c/__i	5. *k > c/__i	4. *s > h	4. *s > h
1. *c > s	6. *k > h	1. *c > s	6. *k > h
6. *k > h	1. *c > s	6. *k > h	1. *c > s

In Atoyot *c > *s* probably preceded *s > *h*, since otherwise we would need to assume that *s > *h* happened twice (*s > *h*, then *c (> s) > *h*). Although *k also merged with *c and *s it has no required ordering relationship to the preceding changes, since there is little likelihood that it would have passed through an intermediate stage in which it became either *c or *s as an unconditioned change.

SOLUTION TO SUBGROUPING PROBLEM 13

No.	Proto-ABC	Lg. A	Lg. B	Lg. C	
01.	*lubaw	lubaw	rubo	lubaw	water
02.	*ələg	ilik	ərəg	ili?	grass
03.	*udud	udut	ulur	udu?	stone
04.	*alisət	lisit	arisət	əlisi?	butterfly
05.	*lərak	lirak	lərak	lira?	bird
06.	*rilap	rilap	lirap	rila?	wing
07.	*tasil	tasil	tasir	tasi	feather
08.	*karur	karur	kalur	karu	river
09.	*turab	turap	turab	tura?	fish
10.	*watiŋ	watiŋ	watiŋ	watiŋ	mountain
11.	*ulilit	lilit	ulirit	əlili?	wind
12.	*adul	adul	alur	adu	sky
13.	*ilik	ilik	irik	ili?	sun
14.	*rarana	rərana	larana	rərana	moon
15.	*diti	diti	riti	diti	star
16.	*pasay	pasay	pase	pasay	house
17.	*siti	siti	siti	siti	woman
18.	*tisud	tisut	tisur	tisu?	man
19.	*əpun	ipun	əpun	ipuŋ	child
20.	*putər	putir	putər	puti	grandmother
21.	*lulub	lulup	lurub	lulu?	grandfather
22.	*duri	duri	luri	duri	fire
23.	*dimam	dimam	rimam	dimaŋ	hearth
24.	*tinulid	tənulit	tinulir	tənuli?	charcoal

1. Correspondences that include at least one liquid are:

1. l : r : l (1, 2, 4, 6, 11, 13, 21)
2. d : l : d (3, 12, 22)
3. l : l : l (5, 11, 21, 24)
4. r : r : r (5, 9, 14, 22)
5. r : l : r (6, 8, 14)

6. l : r : Ø (7, 12)
7. r : r : Ø (8, 20)
8. d : r : d (15, 23)
9. t : r : ? (3, 18, 24)

2 Recurrent changes in Lgs. A, B and C in the order they are encountered are:

Change	Examples
Lg. A	
1. *ə > i (before 4)	2, 4, 5, 19, 20
2. *b,d,g > p,t,k/__#	2, 3, 9, 18, 21, 24
3. *ə > Ø/__(C)V(C)V(C)	4, 11
4. V > ə/__(C)V(C)V(C) (before 3)	4, 11, 14, 24
Lg. B	
1. *l > r (before 4)	1, 2, 4–7, 11–13, 21, 24
2. *-ay,aw > -e,o	1, 16
3. *d > r (before 4)	3, 12, 15, 18, 22–24
4. *rVr > lVr	3, 5, 6, 8, 11, 12, 14, 21, 22, 24
Lg. C	
1. *ə > i (before 4)	2, 4, 5, 19, 20
2. *b,d,g > p,t,k__# (before 3)	2, 3, 9, 18, 21, 24
3. *p,t,k > ʔ/__#	2–6, 9, 11, 13, 18, 21, 24
4. V > ə/__(C)V(C)V(C)	4, 11, 14, 24
5. *l,r > Ø/__#	7, 8, 12, 20
6. *m,n > ŋ/__#	19, 23

3. AC is the most likely subgroup.

Discussion. The strongest indications are for an AC group, based on the following shared innovations:

1. merger of schwa and *i
2. devoicing of final stops in Proto-AC, followed by shift of all final stops to glottal stop in the separate history of Lg. C
3. merger of prepenultimate vowels as schwa

Since both final devoicing and the centralisation of unstressed vowels are fairly common, these changes taken individually have only weak subgrouping value. However, when considered together their value is increased to a level that requires serious consideration. Finally, the merger of schwa and *i is sufficiently distinctive to place the argument for an AC subgroup beyond reasonable doubt.

Probably the most difficult feature of this problem is the reconstruction of the liquids *l and *r, since the sequence *rVr, whether original or resulting from *d > r and *l > r dissimilated to lVr in Lg. B, producing nine different sound correspondences with at least one liquid phoneme, as shown in discussion point 1 above.

SOLUTION TO SUBGROUPING PROBLEM 14

No.	Proto-ABCD	Lg. A	Lg. B	Lg. C	Lg. D	
01.	*waŋi	weŋi	wani	wani	waŋi	wind
02.	*hana	hana	hana	ana	ana	rain
03.	*kume	ʔume	kume	hume	kumi	cloud
04.	*pehu	fehu	pehi	pei	piu	star
05.	*bulat	bulat	vula	bulat	bulat	moon
06.	*sahup	sohuf	dahi	taip	haup	sun
07.	*dalim	delim	lali	ralim	dalim	earth
08.	*koruk	ʔoruʔ	koli	horik	kuruk	water
09.	*talipa	telifa	dalipa	talipa	talipa	stone
10.	*lubun	lubun	luvi	lubin	lubun	grass
11.	*pasu	fosu	padi	pasi	pahu	person
12.	*naŋip	neŋif	nani	nanip	naŋip	man
13.	*tilak	tilaʔ	dila	silak	tilak	woman
14.	*idu	idu	ili	iri	idu	child
15.	*simumu	simumu	dimumi	simumi	himumu	dog
16.	*kiruŋ	ʔiruŋ	kili	hirin	kiruŋ	house
17.	*sinati	sineti	dinadi	sinasi	hinati	village
18.	*putim	futim	pudi	pusim	putim	eat
19.	*mesiŋ	mesiŋ	medi	mesin	mihiŋ	sleep
20.	*saŋo	saŋo	dano	tano	haŋu	go
21.	*riŋus	riŋus	lini	rinit	riŋuh	stand

1. Recurrent changes in Lgs. A, B, C and D in the order they are encountered are:

Change	Examples
Lg. A	
1. *a > e,o/__(C)i,u	1, 6, 7, 9, 11, 12, 17
2. *k > ʔ	3, 8, 13, 16
3. *p > f	4, 6, 9, 11, 12, 18
Lg. B	
1. *ŋ > n	1, 12, 20, 21

2. *u > i/__(C)#   4, 6, 8, 10, 11, 14–16, 21
3. *b > v   5, 10
4. C > O/__#   5–8, 10, 12, 13, 16, 18, 19, 21
5. *s > t (before 6)   6, 11, 15, 17, 19, 20
6. *t > d/__V   6, 9, 11, 13, 15, 17–20
7. *d > r (before 6, 8)   7, 14
8. *r > l   7, 8, 14, 16, 21

Lg. C
1. *ŋ > n   1, 12, 20, 21
2. *h > Ø (before 3)   2, 4, 6
3. *k > h/__V   3, 8, 16
4. *u > i/__(C)# (before 7)   4, 6, 8, 10, 11, 14–16, 21
5. *s > t (before 7)   6, 11, 15, 17, 19–21
6. *d > r   7, 14
7. *t > s/__i   11, 13, 17, 18

Lg. D
1. *h > Ø (before 3)   2, 4, 6
2. *e,o > i,u   3, 4, 8, 19, 20
3. *s > h   6, 11, 15, 17, 19–21

---

2. There is a BC subgroup.

Discussion. This is a problem of only moderate difficulty, and one which has a very clear solution. Lgs. B and C form a subgroup, distinguished by the following exclusively shared innovations:

1. *ŋ/n > Proto-BC *n
2. *s/t > Proto-BC *t, then *t > d/__V in Lg. B and *t > s/_i in Lg. C
3. *u > Proto-BC *i/__(C)#
4. *d/r > Proto-BC *r, then *r > l in Lg. B

There is no evidence for joining Lgs. A or D with BC or with one another. Proto-ABCD thus split into three primary branches, A, BC and D, with a subsequent split of BC into Lgs. B and C.

SOLUTION TO SUBGROUPING PROBLEM 15

No.	Proto-ABCD	Lg. A	Lg. B	Lg. C	Lg. D	
01.	*likat	lihata	riat	lika?	likat	wind
02.	*safu?	sahu	hou	safu?	hafu?	cloud
03.	*mawan	mawana	mawan	mag^{w}aŋ	maan	sky
04.	*turap	tulapa	turap	tula?	turap	rain
05.	*kampi	habi	appi	kampi	kapi	earth
06.	*risuk	lisuhu	rihu	lisu?	rihuk	water
07.	*suripa	sulipa	huripa	sulipa	huripa	stone
08.	*nuhar	nuhala	nuar	nuhan	nuhar	grass
09.	*fiaŋ	hiana	ian	fijaŋ	fiaŋ	tree
10.	*takuŋu	tahunu	tounu	takuŋu	takuŋu	wood
11.	*amala	amala	amara	amala	amala	fire
12.	*hikati	hihasi	iehi	hikasi	hikati	hearth
13.	*uyu?	uyu	uyu	uju?	uu?	smoke
14.	*aŋkuŋ	agunu	akkun	aŋkuŋ	akuŋ	cook
15.	*ma?ul	maulu	mour	ma?un	ma?ul	eat
16.	*tisuma	sisuma	hihuma	sisuma	tihuma	walk
17.	*rakis	lahisi	reih	lakis	rakih	sit
18.	*uhatik	uhasihi	uehi	uhasi?	uhatik	stand
19.	*rintanu	lidanu	rittonu	lintanu	ritanu	reach
20.	*sukum	suhumu	suum	sukuŋ	hukun	push
21.	*wawas	wawasa	wawah	g^{w}ag^{w}as	aah	carry

1. Recurrent changes in Lgs. A, B, C and D in the order they are encountered are:

Change	Examples
Lg. A	
1. *k > h	1, 5, 6, 10, 12, 17, 18, 20
2. -V$_1$C > V$_1$CV$_1$	1, 3, 4, 6, 8, 9, 14, 15, 17, 18, 20, 21
3. *f > h	2, 9
4. *? > O (before 2)	2, 13, 15
5. *r > l	4, 6–8, 17, 19

6. N > O/__C   5, 14, 19
7. *p/t/k > b/d/g/N__ (before 1, 6)   5, 14, 19
8. *ŋ > n   9, 10, 14
9. *t > s/__i   12, 16, 18

Lg. B
1. *l > r   1, 11, 15
2. *k > h/[-nas]__ (before 3)   1, 5, 6, 10, 12, 17, 18, 20
3. *h > O (before 4)   1, 2, 5, 6, 8–10, 12, 17, 18, 20
4. *s > h   2, 6, 7, 12, 16–18, 20, 21
5. *a > e,o/__Ci,u   2, 10, 12, 15, 17–19
6. *f > h (before 3)   2, 9
7. *ʔ > O   2, 13, 15
5. $C_1C_2 > C_2C_2$ 5, 14, 19
9. *ŋ > n   9, 10, 14
10. *t > s/__i (before 4)   12, 16, 18

Lg. C
1. *p,t,k > ʔ/__#   1, 4, 6, 18
2. *w,y > gʷ,j   3, 9, 13, 21
3. *m,n > ŋ/__# (before 5)   3, 20
4. *r > l (before 5)   4, 6–8, 17, 19
5. *l > n/__#   8, 15
6. *t > s/__i   12, 16, 18

Lg. D
1. *s > h   2, 6, 7, 16, 17, 20, 21
2. *w,y > Ø   3, 13, 21
3. *p/t/k > b/d/g/N__   5, 14, 19

2 There is evidence for an ABC group, which contains a small AB group within it.

Discussion. The evidence for an ABC subgroup consists of two mergers:

1. *l and *r merged as *l*
2. *t > s/__i (followed by *s > h in Lg. B)

The evidence for an AB subgroup consists of two further mergers:

3. *ŋ and *n merged as n
4. *ʔ merged with zero

The last change provides rather weak subgrouping evidence, but the two changes together are sufficient to support AB as a unit, although not with a high level of confidence.

SOLUTION TO SUBGROUPING PROBLEM 16

No.	Proto-ABCD	Lg. A	Lg. B	Lg. C	Lg. D	
01.	*pites	piteta	fireh	pite	pitit	head
02.	*tasi	tati	tahi	tasi	tasi	hair
03.	*uriŋ	urina	uriŋ	uriə	uriŋ	eye
04.	*kadun	kaduna	karun	kadu	karun	nose
05.	*opay	ope	ofay	opa	upi	mouth
06.	*pohak	pohaka	fohak	poa	puak	tooth
07.	*sutiŋ	tutina	huriŋ	sutiə	tusiŋ	ear
08.	*ŋomin	nomina	ŋomin	ŋomi	ŋumin	neck
09.	*tedok	tedoka	terok	tedo	tiruk	hand
10.	*lanu	nanu	lanu	ranu	nanu	blood
11.	*sikuk	tikuka	hikuk	sikuə	sikuk	liver
12.	*sibo	tibo	hibo	sibo	sibu	skin
13.	*atip	atipa	arip	ati	asip	sky
14.	*titay	tite	tiray	tita	siti	rain
15.	*numit	numita	numit	numi	numit	wind
16.	*huŋa	huna	huŋa	uŋa	uŋa	water
17.	*ile	ine	ile	ire	ini	tree
18.	*duyuŋ	duyuna	duyuŋ	duyuə	ruyuŋ	climb
19.	*bataw	bato	baraw	bata	batu	stone
20.	*sahik	tahika	hahik	sayə	taik	fish
21.	*saŋaw	tano	hanaw	saŋa	taŋu	bird
22.	*daban	dabana	daban	daba	raban	eat
23.	*satuŋ	tatuna	haruŋ	satuə	tatuŋ	sleep
24.	*leraŋ	nerana	leraŋ	nera	niraŋ	walk
25.	*kalim	kanima	kalim	kari	kanim	speak

1. Recurrent changes in Lgs. A, B, C and D in the order they are encountered are:

Change   **Examples**

Lg. A

1. *s > t   1, 2, 7, 11, 12, 20, 21, 23

2. Ø > -a/C__#   1, 3, 4, 6–9, 11, 13, 15, 18, 20, 22–25

3. *ŋ > n   3, 7, 8, 16, 18, 21, 23, 24
4. *–ay,aw > e,o (before 2)   5, 14, 19, 21
5. *l > n   10, 17, 24, 25

Lg. B
1. *p > f/__V   1, 5, 6
2. *t > r/V__V   1, 7, 13, 14, 19, 23
3. *s > h   1, 2, 7, 11, 12, 20, 21, 23
4. *d > r/V__V   4, 9

Lg. C
1. C > Ø/__#   1, 3–9, 11, 13–15, 18–25
2. *i,u > iə,uə/__k,ŋ (before 1) 3, 7, 11, 18, 20, 23
3. *h > Ø (before 5)   6, 16, 20
4. *l > r   10, 17, 24, 25
5. *ai > ay/__V   20

Lg. D
1. *s > t (before 3)   1, 2, 7, 11, 12, 20, 21, 23
2. *e,o > i,u   1, 5, 6, 8, 9, 12, 14, 17, 19, 21, 24
3. *t > s/__i (before 2)   7, 13, 14
4. *d > r   4, 9, 18, 22
5. *-ay/aw > e/o (before 2)   5, 14, 19, 21
6. *h > Ø   6, 16, 20
7. *l > n   10, 17, 24, 25

---

2. AD form a subgroup.

Discussion. There is a clear AD group, defined by the following innovations:

1. *s and *t merged as *t (with further *t > $s/\_\_i$ in Lg. D)
2. *-ay/aw merged with *-e/o (with further *e/o > i/u in Lg. D)
3. *l and *n merged as *n (with further merger of *-ŋ with *-n in Lg. A)

The merger of *h with zero is shared by Lgs. C and D, but this could easily be a product of convergence, and is heavily outweighed by the evidence for the AD group.

SOLUTION TO SUBGROUPING PROBLEM 17

No.	Proto-ABCD	Lg. A	Lg. B	Lg. C	Lg. D	
01.	*sasak	haha	utap	haha	aaʔ	wind
02.	*pusaka	puhka	pusak	puha	pukka	dust
03.	*pusak	puha	pusak	puha	puaʔ	forest
04.	*uluna	ulna	kasi	uluna	unna	trail
05.	*utuk	utu	utuk	utu	utuʔ	pond
06.	*pakit	paki	pakit	pait	pekiʔ	eagle
07.	*tikup	tiku	sehap	siup	tikuʔ	hawk
08.	*kukan	kuka	kukã	wan	kukaŋ	crow
09.	*hokat	hoka	okat	wat	temiŋ	day
10.	*katine	katne	katin	asini	kanne	night
11.	*semak	hema	semak	hima	emaʔ	moon
12.	*lupuka	lupka	lupuk	lupua	lukka	black
13.	*akiti	akti	akit	aisi	atti	white
14.	*opor	opo	opor	upur	opo	red
15.	*sapuna	hapna	sapun	hapuna	anna	yellow
16.	*tosaka	tohka	tosak	tuha	tokka	big
17.	*rakami	rakmi	rakam	rami	rammi	long
18.	*tetim	teti	tetĩ	tisim	tetiŋ	small
19.	*hatika	hatka	atik	asia	akka	short
20.	*akun	aku	akũ	aun	okuŋ	heavy
21.	*motis	mosi	motis	musi	moi	round
22.	*tasik	tahi	tasik	tahi	teiʔ	hand
23.	*pahul	pahu	paul	paul	pou	foot
24.	*oten	ote	otẽ	utin	pasu	walk

1. Recurrent changes in Lgs. A, B, C and D in the order they are encountered are:

Change   **Examples**

Lg. A
1. *s > h   1–3, 11, 15, 16, 21, 22
2. C > Ø/__#   1, 3, 5–9, 11, 14, 18, 20–24
3. V > Ø/VC__CV   2, 4, 10, 12, 13, 15–17, 19

Lg. B
1. V > Ø/__# (before 3)   2, 10, 12, 13, 15–17, 19
2. V > Ṽ/__m,n# (before 3)   8, 18, 20, 24
3. *m,n > Ø/__#   8, 18, 20, 24
4. *h > Ø   9, 19, 23

Lg. C
1. *s > h (before 4)   1–3, 11, 15, 16, 21, 22
2. *k > Ø (before 3, 5)   1–3, 5–13, 16, 17, 19, 20, 22
3. V$_i$V$_i$ > V$_i$ 2, 16, 17
4. *t > s/__i (before 7)   7, 10, 13, 18, 19, 21
5. *u > w/__V   8, 9
6. *h > Ø (before 1, 5)   9, 19, 23
7. *e,o > i,u (before 5)   9–11, 14, 16, 18, 21, 24

Lg. D
1. *s > h (before 2)   1–3, 11, 15, 16, 21, 22
2. *h > O   1–3, 11, 15, 16, 19, 21–23
3. *p,t,k > ?/__#   1, 3, 5–7, 11, 22
4. V > O/VC__CV (before 6)   2, 4, 10, 12, 13, 15–17, 19
5. C$_{21}$C$_2$ > C$_2$C$_2$ 2, 4, 10, 12, 13, 15–17, 19
6. *a > e,o/__(C)i,u   6, 20, 22, 23
7. *m,n > ŋ/__#   8, 18, 20
8. *l,r > O/__#   14, 23

2. There is an AD subgroup.
3. The sporadic change is found in item 21, where *t > s/__i.

Discussion. The one clear subgroup to emerge from this data contains Lgs. A and D, which share the following innovations:

1. weakening of final stops in Lg. D, followed by complete loss in Lg. A
2. V > Ø /VC__CV
3. merger of *s and *h (with subsequent *h > Ø in Lg. D)
4. the sporadic assibilation of *t > s/__i in #21 before *s (> h) > Ø in Lg. D

Lgs. B, C and D all show *h > Ø. However, in Lg. D it is simplest to assume that *s > *h* preceded *h > Ø since these phonemes merged, as seen in e.g. items 22 and 23. Since *s did not change in Lg. B the loss of *h in this language must have been independent of that in Proto-AD, and since *s > *h* followed *h > Ø in Lg. C, the loss of *h in the latter language must also have been independent of that in Proto-AD.

SOLUTION TO SUBGROUPING PROBLEM 18

No.	Proto-ABCD	Lg. A	Lg. B	Lg. C	Lg. D	
01.	*bayat	bayat	bayata	wat	baya?	river
02.	*hiŋu	in	hiŋu	hit	hinu	water
03.	*usan	usan	usana	usat	uhal	rain
04.	*tafahi	tafa	tawahi	tahah	tafahi	cloud
05.	*ŋusu	nus	ŋusu	nus	nuhu	earth
06.	*afal	afa	awala	ahal	afal	sand
07.	*kumin	kumin	kumini	kumit	kumil	grass
08.	*falaŋ	faan	walaŋa	halat	falaŋ	tree
09.	*niar	nia	nera	nial	liar	leaf
10.	*limot	imot	limoto	limut	limo?	root
11.	*moraŋa	moan	moraŋa	mulat	morana	house
12.	*siba	sib	siba	siw	hiba	roof
13.	*fuŋu	fun	wuŋu	hut	funu	person
14.	*durepa	duef	durepa	rulip	durepa	woman
15.	*itam	itam	itama	itap	itaŋ	man
16.	*yupiti	yufit	yupiti	upit	yupiti	child
17.	*feka	fek	weka	hik	feka	dog
18.	*habe	ab	habe	haw	habe	bird
19.	*duap	duaf	dopa	ruap	dua?	snake
20.	*raus	aus	rosu	laus	rauh	fish
21.	*kolam	koam	kolama	kulap	kolaŋ	black
22.	*urak	uak	uraka	ulak	ura?	white

1. Recurrent changes in Lgs. A, B, C and D in the order they are encountered are:

Change   Examples

Lg. A
1. *h > Ø   2, 4, 18
2. *ŋ > n   2, 5, 8, 11, 13
3. V > Ø/__#   2, 4, 5, 11–14, 16–18
4. *l > Ø   6, 8, 10, 21
5. *r > Ø   9, 11, 14, 20, 22
6. *p > f   14, 16, 19

Lg. B

1. -ViC > -ViCVi (before 3)	1, 3, 6–10, 15, 19–22
2. *f > w	4, 6, 8, 13, 17
3. *ia > e	
*ua,au > o	9, 19, 20

Lg. C

1. *b > w	1, 12, 18
2. *y > Ø	1, 16
3. Vi Vi > Vi	1
4. *ŋ > n (before 6)	2, 5, 8, 11, 13
5. V > Ø/__# (before 6)	2, 4, 5, 11–14, 16–18
6. *m,n > p,t/__#	2, 3, 7, 8, 11, 13, 15, 21
7. *f > h	4, 6, 8, 13, 17
8. *r > l (before 10)	9, 11, 14, 20, 22
9. *e,o > i,u	10, 11, 14, 17, 18, 21
10. *d > r	14, 19

Lg. D

1. *p,t,k > ʔ/__#	1, 10, 19, 22
2. *ŋ > n	2, 5, 8, 11, 13
3. *s > h	3, 5, 12, 20
4. *n > l (before 2, 5)	3, 7, 9
5. *m > ŋ/__#	15, 21

2. There is evidence for an AC subgroup.

Discussion. Lgs. A and C share three innovations exclusively of the other languages. These are:

1. V > Ø/__#
2. merger of *n and *ŋ
3. merger of *l and *r (with subsequent *l > Ø in Lg. A)

Lg. D also shows the change *ŋ > n, but *n > l had to precede this change. Since *n > l did not occur in A or C the conclusion must be that *ŋ > n reflects a single change in Proto-AC, but an independent change in Lg. D.

Even though there is no direct evidence for it, the change *n > *l* in Lg. D is ordered before *m > ŋ/__# since to do otherwise would imply an implausible sequence of events, namely that *m had become a velar nasal word-finally while *n was unchanged in this position until it was converted to a lateral. Attested mergers of word-final nasals, however, show that *-m and *-n are most likely to merge as *-n before further change leads to merger with -*ŋ.

The most difficult feature of this problem arises from the fact that fairly drastic changes affected phonemes after merger, giving rise to very different phonetic outcomes in the languages that share the innovation. For example, *ŋ and *n merge as *n* in all positions in Lg. A, but in Lg. C the merger appears as *n* only in non-final position (5 and 9) and otherwise as -*t* (2, 3, 7, 8, 11, 13), and *l and *r merge as zero in Lg. A but as *l* in Lg. C. One of the purposes of this problem is to show that exclusively shared innovations may sometimes be apparent on the surface, while in other cases they are concealed beneath additional changes and require a more dedicated effort to uncover.

SOLUTION TO SUBGROUPING PROBLEM 19

No.	Proto-ABCD	Lg. A	Lg. B	Lg. C	Lg. D	
01.	*wahir	were	waro	ahi	gʷel	water
02.	*tapi	dafi	tewi	tapi	tafi	lake
03.	*kakip	efe	kekiwo	kaɣi	ef	river
04.	*ikəb	yəva	ikopo	iɣi	iəb	forest
05.	*anut	anudu	onuto	anu	anut	snake
06.	*ahis	ehe	aso	ahi	es	fish
07.	*pasim	fahimi	wesimo	pasi	fasim	lizard
08.	*suak	ho	suako	sua	so	bird
09.	*domu	romu	domu	domu	lomu	bee
10.	*kubal	uvara	kupalo	kuba	ubal	wasp
11.	*pakur	foro	wokuro	paɣu	fol	cricket
12.	*dawi	rawi	dewi	dai	lagʷi	ant
13.	*ukar	wara	ukaro	uɣa	ol	cook
14.	*nahup	nofo	nawo	nahu	nof	eat
15.	*sakima	hema	sekima	saɣima	sema	drink
16.	*bəran	vərana	porano	bira	bəlan	walk
17.	*ohor	oro	oro	oho	ol	run
18.	*pəkət	fəda	wokoto	piɣi	fət	fall
19.	*kawap	awafa	kawawo	kaa	agʷaf	give
20.	*rahat	rada	rato	raha	lat	heavy
21.	*lukup	rufu	lukuo	luɣu	luf	light
22.	*mitək	mida	mitoko	miti	mitə	big
23.	*ikid	iri	ikido	iɣi	il	small
24.	*bakis	vehe	pekiso	baɣi	bes	wet
25.	*akup	ofo	okuo	aɣu	of	dry
26.	*ihus	yuhu	yuso	ihu	üs	hot
27.	*təruka	dəro	toruka	tiruɣa	təlo	sun
28.	*supit	hufidi	suito	supi	sufit	moon
29.	*udul	ururu	udulo	udu	ulul	star
30.	*pihak	fe	piako	piha	fe	meteor
31.	*ukin	wini	ukino	uɣi	ün	rain

1. Recurrent changes in Lgs. A, B, C and D in the order they are encountered are:

Change   **Examples**

Lg. A
1. *h > Ø (before 2, 9, 10, 12)   1, 6, 14, 17, 20, 26, 30
2. *ai,ia > e, *au,ua > o (before 3)   1, 3, 6, 8, 11, 14, 15, 24, 25, 27, 30
3. -V$_i$C > -V$_i$CV$_i$ (before 9)   1, 3–8, 10, 11, 13, 14, 16–26, 28–31
4. *t > d   2, 5, 18, 20, 22, 27, 28
5. *p > f   2, 3, 7, 11, 14, 18, 19, 21, 25, 28, 30
6. *k > h (before 1, 7)   3, 4, 8, 10, 11, 13, 15, 18, 19, 21–25,
                                              27, 30, 31
7. *i,u > y,w/__V (before 2)   4, 13, 26, 31
8. *b,d > v,r (before 4)   4, 9, 10, 12, 16, 23, 24, 29
9. *ə > a/__#   4, 18, 22
10. *s > h   6–8, 15, 24, 26, 28
11. *l > r   10, 21, 29
12. V$_i$V$_i$ > V$_i$ 17, 18, 20, 21, 23, 30

Lg. B
1. *h > O (before 2, 10)   1, 6, 14, 17, 20, 26, 30
2. *aV > a (before 5)   1, 6, 14, 20
3. O > ə/C__# (before 4)   1, 3–8, 10, 11, 13, 14, 16–26, 28–31
4. *ə > o   1, 3–8, 10, 11, 13, 14, 16–31
5. *a > e,o/__Ci,u   2, 3, 5, 7, 11, 12, 15, 24, 25
6. *p > w (before 7)   2, 3, 7, 11, 14, 18, 19, 21, 25, 28, 30
7. *b > p   4, 10, 16, 24
8. ViVi > Vi   17, 20
9. w > O/u__V   21, 25, 28
10. *i > y/#__V   26

Lg. C
1. *w > Ø   1, 12, 19
2. C > Ø/__#   1, 3–8, 10, 11, 13, 14, 16–26, 28–31
3. *k > γ   3, 4, 8, 10, 11, 13, 15, 18, 19, 21–25,
                                              27, 30, 31
4. *ə > i   4, 16, 18, 22, 27

Lg. D

1. *w > gʷ	1, 12, 19
2. *h > Ø (before 3, 8)	1, 6, 14, 17, 20, 26, 30
3. *ai,ia > e, *au,ua > o	1, 3, 6, 8, 11, 13–15, 24, 25, 27, 30
4. *r > l	1, 11, 13, 16, 17, 20, 27
5. *p > f	2, 3, 7, 11, 14, 18, 19, 21, 25, 28, 30
6. *k > h (before 2)	3, 4, 8, 10, 11, 13, 15, 18, 19, 21–25, 27, 30, 31
7. *d > r (before 4)	9, 12, 23, 29
8. $V_iV_i > V_i$	17, 18, 20, 21, 23
9. *iu,ui > ü	26, 31

2. There is strong evidence for an AD group.

Discussion. This is clearly an advanced-level problem. Lgs. A and D form a subgroup based on the following exclusively shared innovations:

1. merger of *l, *r, *d
2. *p > f
3. merger of *h and *k
4. monophthongisation of the derived sequences *ai,ia to *e* and *au/ua to *o*

Although this result is clear, achieving it requires an adequate set of reconstructions, which is difficult, given the complexity of the sound correspondences. Comparisons such as *efe* : *kekiwo* : *kaɣi* : *ef* 'river' do not appear initially to involve a single cognate set, and one would be tempted to dismiss the items in Lgs. A and D as unrelated to those in Lgs. B and C were it not that the correspondences do, in fact, prove to be recurrent once they are treated with sufficient care and patience.

SOLUTION TO SUBGROUPING PROBLEM 20

No.	Proto-ABCD	Lg. A	Lg. B	Lg. C	Lg. D	Gloss
01.	*ŋatin	lehil	ʔarit	aŋele	nasina	ant
02.	*kusa	xuha	ʔuza	ko	kuso	bee
03.	*rupek	rufex	rupiʔ	lupeke	hupeka	worm
04.	*iap	izaf	iap	epe	yapa	fly
05.	*tiluŋ	hizul	tiluʔ	tihuŋu	siluna	wasp
06.	*siŋi	hili	siʔi	iŋi	sini	dog
07.	*wasir	vehir	wazir	wele	wasiha	bird
08.	*puhak	fuvax	puhaʔ	poko	puaka	pig
09.	*uala	uvaza	uala	oha	walo	one
10.	*paŋat	falat	paʔat	paŋata	panata	two
11.	*lutum	zutum	lurup	hutumu	lutuma	three
12.	*sial	hizaz	lira	ehe	siala	eye
13.	*nasu	lohu	nazu	no	nasu	nose
14.	*taŋus	toluh	taʔus	taŋu	tanusa	ear
15.	*hisan	ihal	hizat	ene	isana	mouth
16.	*kasil	xehiz	ʔazil	kehe	kasila	tooth
17.	*tonar	tolar	tunar	tonala	tonaha	sky
18.	*heŋa	ela	hiʔa	eŋa	eno	sun
19.	*rekit	rexit	riʔit	lekiti	hekita	star
20.	*ilas	izah	ilas	iha	ilasa	moon
21.	*manor	miaxa	manur	manolo	manoha	walk
22.	*tiŋan	hilal	tiʔat	tiŋana	sinana	eat
23.	*kawin	xevil	ʔawit	kawini	kawina	drink

1. Recurrent changes in Lgs. A, B, C and D in the order they are encountered are:

Change	Examples
Lg. A	
1. *ŋ > n (before 2)	1, 5, 6, 10, 14, 18, 22
2. *n > l	1, 5, 6, 10, 13–15, 17, 18, 22, 23
3. *a > e,o/__Ci,u	1, 7, 13, 14, 16, 23
4. *t > s/__i (before 5)	1, 5, 22

5. *s > h	1, 2, 5–7, 12–16, 20, 22
6. *k > x	2, 3, 8, 16, 19, 23
7. *p > f	3, 4, 8, 10
8. O > y,w/i,u__V (before 9)	4, 8, 9, 12
9. *y,w > z,v	4, 5, 7, 8, 9, 11, 12, 16, 20, 23
10. *l > y (before 2, 9)	5, 9, 11, 12, 16, 20
11. *h > O (before 5, 8)	8, 15, 18

Lg. B

1. *ŋ > k (before 2)	1, 5, 6, 10, 14, 18, 22
2. *k > ʔ	1–3, 5, 6, 8, 10, 14, 16, 18, 19, 22, 23
3. *t > r/V__V	1, 11
3. *m,n > p,t/__#	1, 11, 15, 22, 23
5. *s > z/V__V	2, 7, 13, 15, 16
6. *e,o > i,u	3, 17–19, 21

Lg. C

1. *s > h (before 6)	2, 6, 7, 12–16, 20
2. *ua, au > o, *ia, ai > e (before 4)	2, 4, 7–9, 12, 13, 15, 16
3. *r > l	3, 7, 17, 19, 21
4. *V₁C > V₁CV₁/__#	3–5, 7, 8, 10–12, 14–17, 19–23
5. *l > h (before 3)	5, 9, 11, 12, 16, 20
6. *h > O (before 2, 4, 5)	2, 6–8, 12–16, 18, 20

Lg. D

1. *ŋ > n	1, 5, 6, 10, 14, 18, 22
2. *t > s/__i	1, 5, 22
3. O > a/C__#	1, 3–5, 7, 8, 10–12, 14–17, 19–23
4. *a > o/__# (before 3)	2, 9, 18
5. *r > h	3, 7, 17, 19, 21
6. *i,u > y,w/#__V	4, 9
7. *h > O (before 5)	8, 15, 18

2. Unrelated forms are *aŋele* 'ant' (Lg. C), *lira* 'eye' (Lg. B), *miaxa* 'walk' (Lg. A).

3. There is evidence for an AD group.

Discussion. This is a challenging problem because extreme sound change in all four languages makes cognate recognition difficult. Nonetheless, once a set of reconstructions has been achieved it becomes clear that Lgs. A and D share the following innovations:

1. merger of *ŋ and *n (with subsequent change *n > *l* in Lg. A)
2. merger of *t and *s before *i (with subsequent change *s > *h* in Lg. A)
3. merger of *h and zero

The last of these mergers provides weak subgrouping evidence, since it could easily be a product of independent change, but the first two are much stronger, and together provide a reasonable basis for proposing an AD subgroup within this collection of languages. Lg. C also shows *h > Ø, but this is part of a merger of *s and *h, whereas the loss of *h in Lgs. A and D did not lead to merger with *s, and so is best considered the product of a historically independent change.

APPENDIX:

A SURVEY OF WORKBOOKS AND TEXTBOOKS IN HISTORICAL LINGUISTICS WITH REFERENCE TO PROBLEM-SOLVING

The following survey is intended as an overview of where hands-on problems in historical linguistics can be found. As should be clear, there are relatively few publications which provide solutions, and in the few workbooks that have been written in the past many of the problems are either not challenging, or ask the reader to engage in only partial reconstruction. Moreover, nearly all problems which are presented to students concern sound change, phonological reconstruction, or, less commonly, internal reconstruction. Virtually no published source offers problems concerned with the establishment of genetic relationship or subgrouping, both of which are vital topics with much current debate in historical linguistics.

Anttila, Raimo ([1972, 1989] 2009), *Historical and comparative linguistics*. 3rd ed. New York: Macmillan.

All three editions of this text have included thorough discussions of principles and analyses of data in the body of the book, but only six exercises on comparative reconstruction are given (five with artificial language data, one with natural data), and none on any other topic.

Arlotto, Anthony (1972), *Introduction to historical linguistics*. Lanham, New York and London: University Press of America.

This short, clearly-written text, which covers some topics better than many longer texts, contains an appendix on writing rules but no problems for students to solve on their own.

Benware, W. A. (1998), *Workbook in historical phonology: sound change, internal reconstruction, comparative reconstruction*. Lanham, MD: University Press of America.

This book, which is one of the most complete workbooks in historical linguistics produced to date, presents twenty-one problems in sound change, twelve in internal reconstruction and fifteen in comparative reconstruction. However, it contains no problems which address the establishment of genetic relationship or subgrouping, both of which are issues of central importance in historical linguistics, nor does it discuss ordering relations among changes. Moreover, it provides no solutions, although the reader is told that these can be obtained by sending payment for what is in effect a separate component of the book. Finally, many of the problems in the earlier parts of the book can be solved in little more than a minute, and are therefore unchallenging to the better student.

Bhat, D. N. S. (2001), *Sound change*. Delhi: Motilal Banarsidass Publishers.

Although this small book provides useful discussions of particular sound changes in the languages of India, it contains no hands-on exercises.

Bynon, Theodora (1977), *Historical linguistics*. Cambridge Textbooks in Linguistics. Cambridge: Cambridge University Press.

Covers most basic areas of the field with scattered illustrations using natural language data, but there are no problems for students to solve independently.

Campbell, Lyle (2013), *Historical linguistics: an introduction*. 3rd ed. Cambridge, MA: The MIT Press.

Earlier editions of this textbook contained a number of interesting problems, some of which were marred by typographical irregularities introduced by the printer, or had no clear-cut solutions based on the data given. This would have been a less serious problem if solutions had been provided, but these were missing, leaving even the best students frustrated after struggling with data that were challenging, but sometimes unclear.

This shortcoming has now been largely corrected in the third edition, which includes a 148-page instructors' manual for problems that cover a wide range of topics, including: (1) sound change, (2) borrowing, (3) analogical change, (4) comparative method (= phonological reconstruction), (5) language classification, (6) internal reconstruction, (7) semantic and lexical change, (8) syntactic change, (9) distant genetic relationship, and (10) linguistic prehistory. This makes the third edition probably the most useful, hands-on textbook in historical linguistics that has been produced to date. Some of the problems, such as Exercise 5.3 'Polynesian', still contain errors, but there are fewer than in earlier editions. The only desideratum which has not been met from the standpoint of the present volume is that the solutions are part of an instructors' manual that is, by definition, not available to the students, and for this reason the problems cannot be used for independent study and self-testing.

Columbus, Frederick (1974), *Introductory workbook in historical phonology.* Cambridge, MA: Slavica Publishers, Inc.

This is a useful little book of forty pages which contains twelve problems on what it calls 'phonetic change' (much if not all of it is actually phonemic change), another twelve on comparative reconstruction and six on internal reconstruction. Columbus uses only natural language data, and the selection of languages is diverse, representing at least fifteen distinct families. The principal shortcoming is that solutions are not given for any of the problems, and like virtually all other workbooks in historical linguistics that have been produced so far, there are no problems concerned with the establishment of genetic relationship, or with subgrouping. Moreover, some of the statements about the internal structure of language families could have been written a century earlier, as where the note to the Rade problem holds that 'The Malayo-Polynesian languages are divided into the Indonesian and the Polynesian groups.'

Cowan, William (1971), *Workbook in comparative reconstruction.* New York: Holt, Rinehart & Winston.

Although Boyd-Bowman (1954) contains exercises on cognate identification, this appears to be the first workbook ever produced in historical linguistics. It contains seventeen problems on comparative reconstruction, seven problems on internal reconstruction and twelve problems on sound change, together with solutions followed by brief comments. In many ways it remains the best source in print, despite some problems that are unchallenging and others that seem almost painfully tedious. A general shortcoming is that nearly all problems in comparative reconstruction focus only on individual segments, leaving the reconstruction of whole morphemes almost untouched. In addition, like solutions to most other problems in historical linguistics, whether these are presented in textbooks or in workbooks, there is no discussion of ordering.

Cowan, William and Jakomira Rakušan (1987), *Source book for linguistics*. 2nd rev. ed. Philadelphia/Amsterdam: Benjamins.

This book is designed as a practical manual for both synchronic and diachronic language analysis. The historical sections include thirty-six problems on sound change and twenty-seven on comparative reconstruction that represent an updated version of Cowan (1971). Most of these are extremely elementary, and the student is asked to reconstruct only some fragmentary part of the words compared (consonants, vowels, or even just the first vowel, the initial consonant or the initial vowel). A key to the exercises is provided, but the information given is minimal, with no discussion of why the solution chosen should be preferred. Several comparative reconstruction problems are given using Austronesian data, and the solutions suggested contain multiple errors.

Crowley, Terry (1997), *An introduction to historical linguistics*. 3rd ed. Oxford: Oxford University Press.

Problems are generally useful. However, many of these are extremely simple and contain large numbers of forms that require no analysis. An example is the Aroma-Hula-Sinaugoro problem on pp. 114–116, which includes eighty-two partly or fully represented cognate sets, of which twenty-four contain forms that are identical in both or all languages represented. Like virtually all other texts, solutions are not given. In addition, the Austronesian sets contain a number of erroneous reconstructions.

Crowley, Terry and Claire Bowern (2010), *An introduction to historical linguistics*. 4th ed. Oxford: Oxford University Press.

This is a carefully crafted revision of Crowley (1997), following his untimely death in January 2005, at the age of fifty-one. As Bowern says in her preface, the changes she has made consist mostly of additions rather than alterations to the text, although she has clearly updated the content in line with newer developments in historical linguistics and general linguistic theory. The twelve data sets of the third edition – which represented the following genetic groupings: Austronesian (five sets), Australian (three sets), Papuan (three sets), and Indo-European (Québec French) – have been expanded to sixteen by inclusion of Tiene (Niger-Congo), Cypriot Arabic (Semitic), Nyulnyulan (Australian), and Proto-Gazelle Peninsula and its daughters (Austronesian). The original Australasian emphasis of the problem sets has thus been retained, but broadened to include two languages from other parts of the world.

Fox, Anthony (1995), *Linguistic reconstruction: an introduction to theory and method.* Oxford Textbooks in Linguistics. Oxford: Oxford University Press.

As its title states, this textbook is a discussion of method and theory. However, it gives no problems to relate theory to data, and in addition contains serious errors in discussing the work of other scholars, as in claiming (1995: 290) that Blust (1980b) used the Swadesh-Lees glottochronological formula to estimate the time-depth of etymologies in the Austronesian languages, a statement that has no foundation in fact.

Haas, Mary R. (1969), *The prehistory of languages.* The Hague/Paris: Mouton.

This slender volume is a classic in American Indian historical linguistics, and provides a valuable discussion of the comparative method in general, but contains no problems.

Hale, Mark (2007), *Historical linguistics: theory and method.* Oxford: Blackwell.

This is an ambitious attempt to marry historical linguistics with contemporary syntactic theory. In doing so it largely fails to address the more traditional framework of historical linguistics in a way that might be meaningful to beginning students trying to understand the basic principles of the field. As in most other texts, it contains no problems for the student to solve.

Hewson, John (1998), *Workbook for historical Romance linguistics.* LINCOM Studies in Romance Linguistics 03. München/Newcastle: LINCOM Europa.

While in many ways this is an excellent introduction to historical Romance linguistics, it consists largely of thumbnail sketches of the historical phonology of individual languages followed by exercises in which the student is asked to trace the derivation of given words, answer questions about isolated observations, and explain why paradigmatic irregularity exists in certain forms, etc.

There are no reconstruction problems (presumably because the starting point for nearly all exercises is classical Latin), no problems in establishing genetic relationship or subgrouping, and no solutions. In many ways it is thus closely parallel to Boyd-Bowman (1980), which surprisingly is missing from its references.

Hock, Hans Henrich (1986), *Principles of historical linguistics*. Berlin: Mouton de Gruyter.

This 700-page textbook covers a number of topics in historical linguistics in considerable detail, and is richly illustrated with examples from Indo-European languages, and occasionally from languages belonging to other families. However, it contains no exercises nor problems for the student to solve independently.

Hock, Hans Henrich and Brian D. Joseph ([1996] 2009), *Language history, language change, and language relationship: an introduction to historical and comparative linguistics*. 2nd rev. ed. Trends in Linguistics Studies and Monographs 218. Berlin: de Gruyter Mouton.

This co-authored text differs from the earlier single-authored text by Hock (1986) by including more 'cultural' information (history of writing, a much fuller treatment of sociolinguistic topics, a fuller treatment of 'linguistic paleontology', etc.). Unfortunately, it is flawed by misinformation about Austronesian languages (p. 432), and more to the point for present purposes, contains no exercises nor problems of any kind.

Jeffers, Robert J. and Ilse Lehiste (1979), *Principles and methods for historical linguistics*. Cambridge, MA: The MIT Press.

At fewer than 200 pages (without the index) this text is far shorter than most, and does not touch on all relevant topics. The centrally important topic of subgrouping, for example, is mentioned only in passing, rather than receiving unified treatment in a chapter of its own. It contains a useful glossary of fifteen pages, but no problems.

King, Robert D. (1969), *Historical linguistics and generative grammar*. Englewood Cliffs, NJ: Prentice-Hall, Inc.

This ambitious if somewhat programmatic text was the first to try to apply the then-new ideas of Generative Grammar to historical linguistics.

It is conceptually interesting, and in many ways unique, but contains no problems.

Lass, Roger (1997), *Historical linguistics and language change*. Cambridge: Cambridge University Press.

This book provides a detailed treatment of method in historical linguistics and extensive discussion of examples, but contains no practical exercises for the student.

Lehmann, Winfred P. (1962), *Exercises to accompany Historical linguistics: an introduction*. New York: Holt, Rinehart and Winston, Inc.

This ninety-four-page exercise book, which is intended as a hands-on companion piece to the first edition of Lehmann's introductory textbook, covers a wide range of topics, including genealogical classification, typological classification, use of written records, the comparative method, internal reconstruction, glottochronology, dialect geography, phonological change, morphological change, semantics and borrowing. The material is drawn almost exclusively from Indo-European languages.

Despite some virtues, this work has many shortcomings as a workbook. For example, the treatment of genealogical classification never touches on subgrouping, the treatment of the comparative method contains just two problems concerned with Proto-Germanic, neither of which asks the student to reconstruct entire morphemes, the treatment of lexicostatistics (called 'glottochronology') does not require the coding of cognate decisions followed by counts between language pairs that are then converted into percentages, the treatment of sound change is just six pages, and discusses only Germanic languages, and so on. In short, although it clearly contains much information that is useful as an introduction to Indo-European comparative linguistics, this book is a hodgepodge of topics, most of which are treated quite superficially, and by means of a very narrow language base.

Lehmann, Winfred P. (1992a), *Historical linguistics: an introduction*. 3rd ed. London and New York: Routledge.

This textbook, which has gone through several editions, covers basic issues in historical linguistics. It is strongest when covering Indo-European topics, but misrepresents the state of comparative-historical research in other language families (pp. 177–178), and offers no problems for the student to solve.

Lehmann, Winfred P. (1992b), *Workbook for historical linguistics*, 2nd ed. Dallas, TX: Summer Institute of Linguistics and the University of Texas at Arlington.

At 167 pages this is a considerably expanded revision of the *Exercises to accompany historical linguistics* that Lehmann published thirty years earlier, and was clearly designed to accompany the third edition of his widely-used textbook. However, it addresses none of the shortcomings of the earlier edition.

Luraghi, Sylvia and Vit Bubenik (eds) (2013), *The Bloomsbury companion to historical linguistics*. London/New York: Continuum.

This is an edited volume with chapters written by a number of historical linguists with different specialisations. While the treatment of topics is generally thorough (if patchy and uneven), the book contains no hands-on exercises of any kind.

McMahon, April M. S. (1994), *Understanding language change*. Cambridge: Cambridge University Press.

This text contains excellent discussions of theoretical issues, but contains no problems.

Meillet, Antoine ([1925] 1967), *The comparative method in historical linguistics*. Paris: Champion.

A classic general treatment of the comparative method which focuses on issues in reconstruction, but provides no hands-on exercises to ground theory in data.

Palmer, Leonard R. (1972), *Descriptive and comparative linguistics: a critical introduction*. London: Faber & Faber.

A general survey of concepts with no practical exercises of any kind.

Paul, Hermann ([1880] 1920), *Prinzipien der Sprachgeschichte*. 5th ed. Tübingen: Max Niemeyer.

This is the classic statement of the Neogrammarian position on sound change. Like most comprehensive treatments of topics in historical linguistics produced in Europe, it is exclusively concerned with the discussion of theory.

Pike, Kenneth L. ([1950] 1957), *Axioms and procedures for reconstruction in comparative linguistics: an experimental syllabus*. Glendale, CA: Summer Institute of Linguistics.

This slim, mimeographed volume is concerned mostly with a discussion of method in historical linguistics, but contains thirteen short problems (five to eight examples each) using artificial language data. Topics include: (1) determining which two of three dialects are more closely related, (2) making charts of consonant reflexes based on cognate sets (reconstructions must be supplied, but the reader is not asked to do this), (3) reconstruction of proto-segments, and a single very short problem asking for the reconstruction of whole forms. All problems in this experimental work are very sketchy, and no solutions are provided.

Schiffman, Hal (2009), *Asian linguistics workbook*, compiled and edited by Zev Handel. Online resource.

This online resource, which is indicated as a draft version not for distribution or citation, contains both synchronic and diachronic problems generally connected with languages of East Asia (plus some from South Asia). It is intended for use in an undergraduate course, and contains just seven problems in historical linguistics, all of them in phonological reconstruction.

Sihler, Andrew L. (2000), *Language history: an introduction*. Amsterdam/Philadelphia: John Benjamins.

This is a valuable text in many respects, with extensive discussion of data, but no problem sets to apply what has been learned.

Trask, R. L. (1996), *Historical linguistics*. London: Arnold.

This text provides a thorough treatment of many topics, as well as some exercises on dialect geography, comparative reconstruction, internal reconstruction and sound change in progress. While many of these are excellent in stimulating the student to think through issues, no solutions are given.

Prior to the 1960s few if any general textbooks on historical linguistics existed. Rather, the topic was treated as a chapter or two in more general introductions to linguistics, as in the classic text of Bloomfield (1933). In addition to the introductory texts cited here, useful problems on historical linguistics are found in a few general overviews of the entire field of linguistics. Two of the more noteworthy of these are *Language files*, published by the Department of Linguistics (2011) at The Ohio State University (now in its 11th edition), and O'Grady et al. (2016), *Contemporary linguistics*, now in its 6th American edition (8th Canadian edition). The first of these contains a small number of problems on sound change and reconstruction, together with solutions. The second contains seventeen practice exercises in historical linguistics, including six that deal with sound change, one with spelling pronunciations, one with morphological change, one with word order change, three with semantic change, one with borrowing, one with identifying the effects of Grimm's law, two dealing with reconstruction, and one dealing with a combination of topics. Solutions are provided in a separate Instructors' Guide available from the publisher.

REFERENCES

Anceaux, J. C. (1961), *The linguistic situation in the islands of Yapen, Kurudu, Nau and Miosnum, New Guinea*. Verhandelingen van het Koninklijk Instituut voor Taal-, Land- en Volkenkunde, 35. The Hague: Martinus Nijhoff.

Anttila, Raimo ([1972, 1989] 2009), *Historical and comparative linguistics*. 3rd ed. New York: Macmillan.

Arlotto, Anthony (1972), *Introduction to historical linguistics*. Lanham, New York and London: University Press of America.

Atkinson, Quentin D. and Russell D. Gray (2005), Curious parallels and curious connections – phylogenetic thinking in biology and historical linguistics. *Systematic Biololgy* 54.4: 513–526.

Bancel, Pierre J. and Alain Matthey de l'Etang (2002), Tracing the ancestral kinship system: the global etymon KAKA. *Mother Tongue* VII: 209–222.

Bender, Byron W. (1969), Vowel dissimilation in Marshallese. *Working Papers in Linguistics* 1.1: 88–96. Honolulu: Department of Linguistics, University of Hawai'i.

Bender, Byron W., Ward H. Goodenough, Frederick H. Jackson, Jeffrey C. Marck, Kenneth L. Rehg, Ho-min Sohn, Stephen Trussel and Judith W. Wang (2003a), Proto-Micronesian reconstructions – 1. *Oceanic Linguistics* 42: 1–110.

Bender, Byron W., Ward H. Goodenough, Frederick H. Jackson, Jeffrey C. Marck, Kenneth L. Rehg, Ho-min Sohn, Stephen Trussel and Judith W. Wang (2003b), Proto-Micronesian reconstructions – 2. *Oceanic Linguistics* 42: 271–358.

Benware, W. A. (1998), *Workbook in historical phonology: sound change, internal reconstruction, comparative reconstruction*. Lanham, MD: University Press of America.

Berg, René van den (1989), *A grammar of the Muna language*. Ph.D. dissertation, University of Leiden.

Berg, René van den (1991), Muna historical phonology. In J. N. Sneddon, ed., *Studies in Sulawesi linguistics*, Part 2. NUSA 33, pp. 1–28.

Berg, René van den (1996), *Muna-English dictionary*. Leiden: Koninklijk Instituut voor Taal-, Land- en Volkenkunde Press.

Bhat, D. N. S. (2001), *Sound change*. Delhi: Motilal Banarsidass Publishers.

Biggs, Bruce (1965), Direct and indirect inheritance in Rotuman. *Lingua* 14: 383–415.

Blevins, Juliette (2004), The mystery of Austronesian final consonant loss. *Oceanic Linguistics* 43: 179–184.

Blevins, Juliette and Daniel Kaufman (2012), Origins of Palauan intrusive velar nasals. *Oceanic Linguistics* 51: 18–32.

Bloomfield, Leonard (1933), *Language*. New York: Holt, Rinehart & Winston.

Blust, Robert (1971a), A Tagalog consonant cluster conspiracy. *The Philippine Journal of Linguistics* 2.2: 85–91.

Blust, Robert (1971b), Fieldnotes on 41 language communities of northern and central Sarawak.

Blust, Robert (1972), Proto-Oceanic addenda with cognates in non-Oceanic Austronesian languages: a preliminary list. *Working Papers in Linguistics* 4.1: 1–43. Honolulu: Department of Linguistics, University of Hawai'i.

Blust, Robert (1974), A Murik vocabulary, with a note on the linguistic position of Murik. *The Sarawak Museum Journal* 22.43 (new series): 153–189.

Blust, Robert (1975), Fieldnotes on 32 languages of the Admiralty Islands and adjacent regions, Papua New Guinea.

Blust, Robert (1980a), Fieldnotes on Rejang (southwest Sumatra).

Blust, Robert (1980b), Austronesian etymologies. *Oceanic Linguistics* 19: 1–181.

Blust, Robert (1984), On the history of the Rejang vowels and diphthongs. *Bijdragen tot de Taal-, Land- en Volkenkunde* 140: 422–450.

Blust, Robert (1988), Sketches of the morphology and phonology of Bornean languages, 2: Mukah Melanau. In H. Steinhauer, ed., *Papers in Western Austronesian linguistics*, no. 3, pp. 151–216. Canberra: Pacific Linguistics.

Blust, Robert (1990), Three recurrent changes in Oceanic languages. In J. H. C. S. Davidson, ed., *Pacific Island languages: essays in honour of G. B. Milner*, pp. 7–28. London: School of Oriental and African Studies.

Blust, Robert (1992), On speech strata in Tiruray. In Malcolm D. Ross, ed., *Papers in Austronesian linguistics*, no. 2, pp. 1–52. Canberra: Pacific Linguistics.

Blust, Robert (1995), Sibilant assimilation in Formosan languages and the Proto-Austronesian word for 'nine': a discourse on method. *Oceanic Linguistics* 34: 443–453.

Blust, Robert (1996), Low vowel dissimilation in Ere. *Oceanic Linguistics* 35: 95–112.

Blust, Robert (1997), Nasals and nasalization in Borneo. *Oceanic Linguistics* 36: 149–179.

Blust, Robert (1998), Seimat vowel nasality: a typological anomaly. *Oceanic Linguistics* 37: 298–322.

Blust, Robert (1999), A note on covert structure: Ca- reduplication in Amis. *Oceanic Linguistics* 38: 168–174.

Blust, Robert (2000a), Chamorro historical phonology. *Oceanic Linguistics* 39: 83–122.

Blust, Robert (2000b), Low vowel fronting in northern Sarawak. *Oceanic Linguistics* 39: 285–319.

Blust, Robert (2001a), Reduplicated colour terms in Oceanic languages. In Andrew Pawley, Malcolm Ross and Darrell Tryon, eds, *The boy from Bundaberg: studies in Melanesian linguistics in honour of Tom Dutton*, pp. 23–49. Canberra: Pacific Linguistics.

Blust, Robert (2001b), Language, dialect and riotous sound change: the case of Sa'ban. In Graham W. Thurgood, ed., *Papers from the Ninth Annual Meeting of the Southeast Asian Linguistics Society*, pp. 249–359. Arizona State University Program for Southeast Asian Studies Monograph Series. Tempe: Arizona State University.

Blust, Robert (2002a), Formalism or phoneyism? The history of Kayan final glottal stop. In K. Alexander Adelaar and Robert Blust, eds, *Between worlds: linguistic papers in memory of David John Prentice*, pp. 29–37. Canberra: Pacific Linguistics.

Blust, Robert (2002b), Kiput historical phonology. *Oceanic Linguistics* 41: 384–438.

Blust, Robert (2003), *Thao dictionary*. Language and Linguistics Monograph Series A5. Institute of Linguistics (Preparatory Office), Academia Sinica. Taipei: Academia Sinica.

Blust, Robert (2005), Must sound change be linguistically motivated? *Diachronica* 22: 219–269.

Blust, Robert (2006), The origin of the Kelabit voiced aspirates: a historical hypothesis revisited. *Oceanic Linguistics* 45: 311–338.

Blust, Robert (2007), The prenasalised trills of Manus. In Jeff Siegel, John Lynch and Diana Eades, eds, *Language description, history and development: linguistic indulgence in memory of Terry Crowley*, pp. 297–311. Amsterdam/Philadelphia: John Benjamins.

Blust, Robert (2009), Palauan historical phonology: whence the intrusive velar nasal? *Oceanic Linguistics* 48: 307–336.

Blust, Robert (2012a), The Proto-Malayo-Polynesian multiplicative ligature *ŋa: a reply to Reid. *Oceanic Linguistics* 51: 538–566.

Blust, Robert (2012b), Hawu vowel metathesis. *Oceanic Linguistics* 51: 207–233.

Blust, Robert (2016a), Kelabit-Lun Dayeh phonology, with special reference to the voiced aspirates. *Oceanic Linguistics* 55: 247–278.

Blust, Robert (2016b), Austronesian vs. the world: where the P-map ends. Talk presented *in absentia* at the 42nd Annual Meeting of the Berkeley Linguistics Society (BLS 42), 5 February 2016.

Blust, Robert (2017), Odd conditions: context-sensitive sound change in unexpected contexts. *Journal of Historical Linguistics* 7.3:321–370.

Bopp, Franz (1841), *Über die Verwandtschaft der malaisch-polynesischen Sprachen mit den indo-europäischen. Gelesen in der Akademie der Wissenschaften am 10. Aug. und 10. Dec. 1840*. Berlin: Dümmler.

Boyd-Bowman, Peter (1954), *From Latin to Romance in sound charts*. Washington, DC: Georgetown University Press.

Brugmann, Karl (1884), Zur Frage nach den Verwandtschaftsverhälltnissen der indogermanischen Sprachen. *Internationale Zeitschrift für allgemeine Sprachwissenschaft* 1: 226–256.

Bynon, Theodora (1977), *Historical linguistics*. Cambridge Textbooks in Linguistics. Cambridge: Cambridge University Press.

Campbell, Lyle (2003), How to show languages are related. In Brian D. Joseph and Richard D. Janda, eds, *The handbook of historical linguistics*, pp. 262–282. Oxford: Blackwell.

Campbell, Lyle (2013), *Historical linguistics: an introduction*. 3rd ed. Cambridge, MA: The MIT Press.

Campbell, Lyle and William J. Poser (2008), *Language classification: history and method*. Cambridge: Cambridge University Press.

Chen, Matthew and William S.-Y. Wang (1975), Sound change: actuation and implementation. *Language* 51: 255–281.

Churchward, C. M. (1940), *Rotuman grammar and dictionary*. Sydney: The Australasian Medical Publishing Co.

CIA – The world factbook (2016, February) <www.cia.gov/library/publications/the-world-factbook/index.html>.

Columbus, Frederick (1974), *Introductory workbook in historical phonology*. Cambridge, MA: Slavica Publishers, Inc.

Coolsma, S. ([1884] 1930), *Soendaneesch-Hollandsch woordenboek*. 3rd ed. Leiden: A. W. Sijthoff.

Cowan, William (1971), *Workbook in comparative reconstruction*. New York: Holt, Rinehart & Winston.

Cowan, William and Jakomira Rakušan (1987), *Source book for linguistics*. 2nd rev. ed. Philadelphia/Amsterdam: Benjamins.

Crowley, Terry (1997), *An introduction to historical linguistics*. 3rd ed. Oxford: Oxford University Press.

Crowley, Terry and Claire Bowern (2010), *An introduction to historical linguistics*. 4th ed. Oxford: Oxford University Press.

Deonna, Waldemar (1965), *Le symbolisme de l'oeil*. Societe Suisse des Science Morales, Publication 5. Berne: Francke.

Department of Linguistics (2011), *Language files: materials for an introduction to language and linguistics*. 11th ed. Columbus, OH: Ohio State University.

Donegan, Patricia and David L. Stampe (1983), Rhythm and the holistic organization of language structure. In John F. Richardson, Mitchell Marks and Amy Chukerman, eds, *The Interplay of phonology, morphology and syntax*, pp. 337–353. Chicago: Chicago Linguistic Society.

Dyen, Isidore (1949), On the history of the Trukese vowels. *Language* 25: 420–436.

Dyen, Isidore (1956), The Ngaju-Dayak 'Old speech stratum'. *Language* 32: 83–87.

Fox, Anthony (1995), *Linguistic reconstruction: an introduction to theory and method*. Oxford Textbooks in Linguistics. Oxford: Oxford University Press.

Fox, C. E. (1970), *Arosi-English dictionary*. Canberra: Pacific Linguistics (PL C-11).

Garrett, Andrew (1998), Adjarian's law, the glottalic theory, and the position of Armenian. In Benjamin K. Bergen, Madelaine C. Plauche and Ashlee C. Bailey, eds, *Proceedings of the twenty-fourth annual meeting of the Berkeley Linguistics Society, Special session on Indo-European subgrouping and internal relations*, pp. 12–23. Berkeley, CA: Berkeley Linguistics Society.

Gibson, Eleanor J. (1969), *Principles of perceptual learning and development*. New York: Meredith Corporation.

Goddard, Ives (2007), Phonetically unmotivated sound change. In Alan J. Nussbaum, ed., *Verba docenti: studies in historical and Indo-European linguistics presented to Jay H. Jasanoff by students, colleagues and friends*, pp. 115–130. Ann Arbor, MI: Beech Stave Press.

Goodenough, Ward H. and Hiroshi Sugita (1980), *Trukese-English dictionary*. Memoirs of the American Philosophical Society, vol. 141. Philadelphia, PA: American Philosophical Society.

Gray, R. D., A. J. Drummond and S. J. Greenhill (2009), Language phylogenies reveal expansion pulses and pauses in Pacific settlement. *Science*, 323, 23 January 2009: 479–483.

Greenberg, Joseph H. (1957), Genetic relationship among languages. In Joseph H. Greenberg, ed., *Essays in linguistics*, pp. 35–45. Chicago: The University of Chicago Press.

Greenberg, Joseph H. (1966), Some universals of grammar with particular reference to the order of meaningful elements. In Joseph H. Greenberg, ed., *Universals of Language*, 2nd ed., pp. 73–113. Boston, MA: The MIT Press.

Greenhill, Simon J., Robert Blust and Russell D. Gray (2008), The Austronesian basic vocabulary database: from bioinformatics to lexomics. *Evolutionary Bioinformatics* 4, 2008: 1–13.

Haas, Mary R. (1969), *The prehistory of languages*. The Hague/Paris: Mouton.

Hale, Horatio (1846), Notes on the language of Rotuma; Rotuman vocabulary. *United States exploring expedition under the command of Charles Wilkes*, vol. 6, pp. 469–478. Philadelphia, PA: C. Sherman.

Hale, Kenneth (1968), Review of Hohepa (1967). *Journal of the Polynesian Society* 77: 83–99.

Hale, Mark (2007). *Historical linguistics: theory and method*. Oxford: Blackwell.

Hasselt, J. L van and F. J. F. van Hasselt (1947), *Noemfoorsch woordenboek*. Amsterdam: J. H. de Bussy.

Hennig, Willi (1950), *Grundzüge einer Theorie der phylogenetischen Systematik*. Berlin: Deutscher Zentralverlag.

Hewson, John (1998), *Workbook for historical Romance linguistics*. LINCOM Studies in Romance Linguistics 03. München/Newcastle: LINCOM Europa.

Hock, Hans Henrich (1986), *Principles of historical linguistics*. Berlin: Mouton de Gruyter.

Hock, Hans Henrich and Brian D. Joseph ([1996] 2009), *Language history, language change, and language relationship: an introduction to historical and comparative linguistics*. 2nd rev. ed. Trends in Linguistics Studies and Monographs 218. Berlin: Mouton de Gruyter.

Hohepa, Patrick (1967), *A profile Generative Grammar of Maori*. Indiana University Publications in Anthropology and Linguistics, Memoir 20.

Horne, Elinor C. (1974), *Javanese-English dictionary*. New Haven, CT: Yale University Press.

Jackson, Frederick H. (1983), *The internal and external relationships of the Trukic languages of Micronesia*. Ph.D. dissertation, Honolulu: Department of Linguistics, University of Hawai'i.

Jakobson, Roman (1960), Why mama and papa? In Bernard Kaplan and Seymour Wapner, eds, *Perspectives in psychological theory; essays in honor of Heinz Werner*, pp. 124–134. New York: International Universities Press, Inc.

Jeffers, Robert J. and Ilse Lehiste (1979), *Principles and methods for historical linguistics*. Cambridge, MA: The MIT Press.

King, Robert D. (1969), *Historical linguistics and generative grammar*. Englewood Cliffs, NJ: Prentice Hall, Inc.

Kiparsky, Paul (1968), Linguistic universals and linguistic change. In Emmon Bach and Robert T. Harms, eds, *Universals in linguistic theory*, pp. 170–202. New York: Holt, Rinehart & Winston.

Ladefoged, Peter (1971), *Preliminaries to linguistic phonetics*. Chicago: The University of Chicago Press.

Lass, Roger (1997), *Historical linguistics and language change*. Cambridge: Cambridge University Press.

Lehmann, Winfred P. (1962), *Exercises to accompany historical linguistics: an introduction*. New York: Holt, Rinehart and Winston, Inc.

Lehmann, Winfred P. (1992a), *Historical linguistics: an introduction*. 3rd ed. London and New York: Routledge.

Lehmann, Winfred P. (1992b), *Workbook for historical linguistics*. 2nd ed. Dallas, TX: Summer Institute of Linguistics and the University of Texas at Arlington.

Lewis, M. Paul, Gary F. Simons and Charles D. Fennig (eds) (2015), *Ethnologue: languages of the world*. 18th ed. Dallas, TX: Summer Institute of Linguistics, International. <http://www.ethnologue.com>

Lichtenberk, Frantisek (1988), The Cristobal-Malaitan subgroup of Southeast Solomonic. *Oceanic Linguistics* 27: 24–62.

Luraghi, Sylvia and Vit Bubenik (eds) (2013), *The Bloomsbury companion to historical linguistics*. London/New York: Continuum.

Lynch, John (2002), The Proto-Oceanic labiovelars: some new observations. *Oceanic Linguistics* 41: 310–362.

Lynch, John (2003), Low vowel dissimilation in Vanuatu languages. *Oceanic Linguistics* 42: 359–406.

Maan, G. (1951), *Proeve van een Bulische spraakkunst*. Verhandelingen van het Koninklijk Instituut voor Taal-, Land- en Volkenkunde 10. The Hague: Nijhoff.

Maddieson, Ian (1984), *Patterns of sounds*. Cambridge Studies in Speech Science and Communication. Cambridge: Cambridge University Press.

Maddieson, Ian (1989a), Aerodynamic constraints on sound change: the case of bilabial trills. *UCLA Working Papers in Phonetics* 72: 91–115.

Maddieson, Ian (1989b), Linguo-labials. In Ray Harlow and Robin Hooper, eds, *VICAL 1, Oceanic languages: papers from the Fifth International Conference on Austronesian Linguistics, Part 2*, pp. 349–375. Auckland: Linguistic Society of New Zealand.

Matisoff, James A. (1975), Rhinoglottophilia: the mysterious connection between nasality and glottality. In Charles A. Ferguson, Larry M. Hyman and John J. Ohala, eds, *Nasálfest: papers from a symposium on nasals and nasalization*, pp. 265–287. Stanford, CA: Language Universals Project, Department of Linguistics, Stanford University.

McGinn, Richard (1997), Some irregular reflexes of Proto-Malayo-Polynesian vowels in the Rejang language of Sumatra. *Diachronica* 14: 67–107.

McGinn, Richard (2005), What the Rawas dialect reveals about the linguistic history of Rejang. *Oceanic Linguistics* 44: 12–64.

McMahon, April M. S. (1994), *Understanding language change*. Cambridge: Cambridge University Press.

McManus, Edwin G. and Lewis S. Josephs (1977), *Palauan-English dictionary*. PALI language texts: Micronesia. Honolulu: The University Press of Hawai'i.

Meillet, Antoine ([1925] 1967), *The comparative method in historical linguistics*. Paris: Champion.

Nichols, Johanna (1992), *Linguistic diversity in space and time*. Chicago: The University of Chicago Press.

Nothofer, Bernd (1975), *The reconstruction of Proto-Malayo-Javanic*. Verhandelingen van het Koninklijk Instituut voor Taal-, Land- en Volkenkunde 73. The Hague: Nijhoff.

Nothofer, Bernd (1988), A discussion of two Austronesian subgroups: Proto-Malay and Proto-Malayic. In Mohd. Thani Ahmad and Zaini Mohamed Zain, eds, *Rekonstruksi dan cabang-cabang Bahasa Melayu Induk* [Reconstruction and ramification of Proto-Malayic], pp. 34–58. Siri Monograf Sejarah Bahasa Melayu. Kuala Lumpur: Dewan Bahasa dan Pustaka.

O'Grady, William, John Archibald, Mark Aronoff and Janie Rees-Miller (2016), *Contemporary linguistics: an introduction*. 6th ed. Boston and New York: Bedford/St. Martin's.

Palmer, Leonard R. (1972), *Descriptive and comparative linguistics: a critical introduction*. London: Faber & Faber.

Paul, Hermann ([1880] 1920), *Prinzipien der Sprachgeschichte*. 5th ed. Tübingen: Max Niemeyer.

Pigeaud, Th. (1938), *Javaans-Nederlands handwoordenboek*. Groningen and Batavia: J. B. Wolters.

Pike, Kenneth L. ([1950] 1957), *Axioms and procedures for reconstruction in comparative linguistics: an experimental syllabus*. Glendale, CA: Summer Institute of Linguistics.

Pukui, Mary Kawena and Samuel H. Elbert ([1957] 1971), *Hawaiian dictionary*. Honolulu: The University of Hawai'i Press.

Reid, Lawrence A. (2010), Palauan velar nasals and the diachronic development of PMP noun phrases. *Oceanic Linguistics* 49: 436–477.

Richards, Anthony (1981), *An Iban-English dictionary*. Oxford: Clarendon Press.

Ross, M. D. (1988), *Proto Oceanic and the Austronesian languages of western Melanesia*. Canberra: Pacific Linguistics.

Ruhlen, Merritt (1987), *A guide to the world's languages, vol. 1: classification*. Stanford, CA: Stanford University Press.

Ruhlen, Merritt (1994), *On the origin of languages: studies in linguistic taxonomy*. Stanford, CA: Stanford University Press.

Sapir, Edward (1921), *Language: an introduction to the study of speech*. New York: Harcourt, Brace & World, Inc.

Schiffman, Hal (2009), *Asian linguistics workbook*, compiled and edited by Zev Handel. Online resource. <http://courses.washington.edu/asian401/Asian401_Linguistics_Workbook.pdf>

Schmidt, Johannes (1872), *Die Verwandtschaftsverhälltnisse der indogermanischen Sprachen*. Weimar: Hermann Böhlau.

Sihler, Andrew L. (2000), *Language history: an introduction*. Amsterdam/Philadelphia: John Benjamins.

Suzuki, Keiichiro (1998), *A typological investigation of dissimilation*. Ph.D. dissertation, Tucson: Department of Linguistics, University of Arizona.

Thomason, Sarah Grey and Terrence Kaufman (1988), *Language contact, creolization, and genetic linguistics*. Berkeley: University of California Press.

Topping, Donald M., Pedro M. Ogo and Bernadita C. Dungca (1975), *Chamorro-English dictionary*. PALI Language Texts: Micronesia. Honolulu: The University Press of Hawai'i.

Trask, R. L. (1996), *Historical linguistics*. London: Arnold.

Tryon, Darrell T. (1976), *New Hebrides languages: an internal classification*. Canberra: Pacific Linguistics.

Uhlenbeck, E. M. (1964), *A critical survey of studies on the languages of Java and Madura*. Koninklijk Instituut voor taal-, land- en volkenkunde Bibliographical Series 7. The Hague: Martinus Nijhoff.

Vaux, Bert (1992), Adjarian's law and consonantal ATR in Armenian. In John A. C. Greppin, ed., *Proceedings of the Fourth International Conference on Armenian Linguistics*, pp. 271–293. Delmar, NY: Caravan Books.

Vaux, Bert (1998), *The phonology of Armenian*. Oxford: Oxford University Press.

Verner, Karl (1875), Eine Ausnahme der ersten Lautverschiebung. *Zeitschrift für vergleichende Sprachforschung auf dem Gebiete der Indogermanischen Sprachen* 23.2: 97–130.

Walsh, D. S. and Bruce Biggs (1966), *Proto-Polynesian word list I*. Te Reo Monographs. Auckland: Linguistic Society of New Zealand.

Wang, William S. Y. (1969), Competing changes as a cause of residue. *Language* 45: 9–25.

Wijngaarden, J. K. (1896), *Sawuneesche woordenlijst*. The Hague: Nijhoff.